D0758941

Verstehen and Humane Understanding

ROYAL INSTITUTE OF PHILOSOPHY SUPPLEMENT: 41

EDITED BY

Anthony O'Hear

CAMBRIDGE
UNIVERSITY PRESS

PUBLISHED BY THE PRESS SYNDICATE OF THE UNIVERSITY OF CAMBRIDGE
The Pitt Building, Trumpington Street, Cambridge, CB2 1RP, United
Kingdom

CAMBRIDGE UNIVERSITY PRESS
The Edinburgh Building, Cambridge CB2 2RU, United Kingdom
40 West 20th Street, New York, NY 10011–4211, USA
10 Stamford Road, Oakleigh, Melbourne 3166, Austr lia

Printed in the United Kingdom at the University Press, Cambridge
Typeset by Michael Heath Ltd, Reigate, Surrey

*A catalogue record for this book is available
from the British Library*

Library of Congress Cataloguing in Publication Data

Vestehen and humane understanding/edited by Anthony O'Hear
p. cm.—(Royal Institute of Philosophy supplement: 41)
Includes index
ISBN 0 521 58742 5
1. Hermeneutics. 2. Comprehension. 3. Knowledge, Theory of.
I. O'Hear, Anthony. II. Series.
BD241.V283 1997
121—dc2D   96–35175
                                                        CIP

ISBN 0 521 58742 5 paperback
ISSN 1358–2461

Contents

iii

Contents

Notes on Contributors

Anthony O'Hear—Professor of Philosophy, University of Bradford.

John Haldane—Professor of Philosophy, University of St. Andrews.

Leon Pompa—Professor of Philosophy, University of Birmingham.

Roger Hausheer—Lecturer in German, University of Bradford.

Friedel Weinert—Lecturer in Philosophy, University of Bradford.

David Cooper—Professor of Philosophy, University of Durham.

Patrick Gardiner—Fellow of Magdalen College, Oxford.

Andrew Bowie—Professor of Philosophy, Anglia Polytechnic University.

İlham Dilman—Professor of Philosophy, University of Swansea.

T. S. Champlin—Senior Lecturer in Philosophy, University of Hull.

Stephen Mulhall—Reader in Philosophy, University of Essex.

Barrie Falk—Lecturer in Philosophy, University of Birmingham.

Cyril Barrett—Formerly Reader in Philosophy, University of Warwick; Tutor in Philosophy, Campion Hall, Oxford

Ronald Hepburn—Professor of Philosophy, University of Edinburgh.

Robert Grant—Reader in English, University of Glasgow.

Roger Scruton—Formerly Professor of Aesthetics, University of London and University Professor at Boston University.

Preface

The essays which follow are an attempt to explore the questions as to whether reason might take different forms depending on subject matter. More specifically, the contributors to the series—which formed the Royal Institute of Philosophy's annual lecture series for 1995–6—were interested in examining whether in the human world forms of thought and knowledge exist which, while not conforming to the patterns of the natural sciences, can nevertheless be thought of as expressing and adumbrating canons of rationality.

The first two essays, in contrasting ways, map out the territory. There then follow six essays, mainly devoted to examining the thought of various thinkers who since the eighteenth century have maintained that history and human action require forms of discourse and analysis not assimilable to the scientific. The remaining seven essays explore in more depth the requirements of realms such as the psychological, the theological, and the aesthetic, and the collection concludes with the latest of the recently unearthed Xanthippic dialogues.

'Two Cultures' Revisited

ANTHONY O'HEAR

Vanity of Science Knowledge of physical science will not console me for ignorance of morality in time of affliction, but knowledge of morality will always console me for ignorance of physical science.
(Pascal, Pensées, No. 23)

Pascal's pensée is calculated to irritate leader-writers, politicians and curriculum theorists, among whom there is almost universal agreement that knowledge of physical science is a key component of any suitably modern education. This consensus is routinely signalled by a reference to 'the two cultures', a phrase that has by now become the inevitable cliché whenever anyone wants to deplore ignorance of physical science either among humanists or among the population at large, or, more rarely, whenever someone wants to point to philistinism among scientists.

A first reaction to the second of these matters might be to observe that philistinism is not confined to scientists; if the experience of no-doubt jaundiced academics can be trusted, it is alive and well among young people. Even more striking, one might, in looking at university literature departments and the fine art world, point to rampant philistinism within the professional heart of the humanities. In any case, while Matthew Arnold might have raised discussion of some topics related to our theme in terms of philistinism, philistinism was certainly not a category used by Pascal to interpret the world. Nor, I think, would it have commended itself to Dr Leavis in his now infamous, but today largely misunderstood wrangle with C. P. Snow over the 'two cultures'. How, though, can a controversy be both infamous, cliché-generating and largely misunderstood? Easily, one surmises, given that even at the time few seemed to understand clearly what was at stake, and given that this obfuscation of issues extended to the principals themselves, as well as to contemporaneous by-standers and commentators.

Even today, at a distance of more than a quarter of a century, one can read Snow's original lecture[1] and Leavis's impassioned battery of response[2] and still fail to see the wood for the trees.

[1] 'The Two Cultures and the Scientific Revolution' Rede Lecture (1959).

[2] Collected in *Nor Shall My Sword* (London: Chatto and Windus, 1972).

1

There can be little doubt that at one level, Leavis was outrageous. Snow's lecture was certainly irritating, even at times silly, in ways we will come to. Nevertheless, what he was actually proposing was largely inoffensive, largely platitudinous in fact—which is probably why it has been so warmly embraced by leader-writers, politicians and curriculum theorists, as well as sixth-form masters preparing their pupils for Cambridge entrance exams (something which particularly got under Leavis's skin). What we have in *Nor Shall My Sword*, splendid invective though it is, is very much a case of the full weight of the Leavisian artillery being unleashed on a small and slender, but, as it has turned out, remarkably resilient blade of common grass. What Snow said in his original lecture was that while it was a pity that so few scientists read literature, it was also equally to be deplored that so few humanists knew any science. He urged that education should remedy the divide between what he called the 'two cultures', and begin to produce what would nowadays be called scientifically literate humanists and (I suppose) plain literate scientists. Actually, in his initial reply ('Two Cultures'), Leavis concurs with Snow over the need for improvements in scientific education, and also in regretting the existence of 'two' cultures, dividing, so it seems, the educated sections of the country into two mutually uncomprehending classes. Although Leavis is particularly scathing about Snow's talk of *two* cultures, it is not as if Snow thought cultural duality a good thing: he actually saw himself as advocating its eradication. But, from Leavis's point of view, while Snow's professed concern here is justified, his concern—or at least the way in which he conceives his concern—is not enough, 'disastrously not enough'.

In fact, despite an ostensible even-handedness about science and the arts, and their role in education, Snow in his sub-text is far from being even-handed. He does not confine himself to pointing out the material advances made by science and technology over the past two centuries or so, or to advocating better or more specialist technical education; If he had, there could have been little cause for complaint, even from Leavis. But as Nöel Annan put it,[3] Snow was determined to 'strike a blow for science and put the narrow humanists in their place'. Whereas scientists and technologists are hard at work improving material conditions, representatives of what Snow calls 'traditional culture' are 'natural Luddites'. Whereas our natural human condition is one of horror and individual tragedy, we do have social hope, hope largely, it seems, in the matter of providing for the masses more jam tomorrow:

[3] *Our Age* (London: Fontana, 1991), p. 383.

> common men can show extraordinary fortitude in chasing jam
> tomorrow. Jam today, and men aren't at their most exciting; jam
> tomorrow, and one often sees them at their noblest.

—a nobility made possible only by the transformations wrought by
'the' scientific culture. If we don't take these scientific and technological transformations in our stride, it makes us 'look silly'—a
dig, doubtless, at the literateurs who are unable to recite the second law of thermodynamics or who fail to recognize that
Rutherford is what Snow styled the Shakespeare of science. But,
in Snow's book, literary culture is not just silly and/or irrelevant.
Whereas 'statistically' slightly more scientists are religious unbelievers compared with the rest of the intellectual world, 'nine out
of ten of those who dominated literary sensibility (like Yeats or
Pound) were not only politically silly but politically wicked'.

The tone of Snow's lecture, the crassness of his judgments and
his button-holing man-of-the-world insensitivity all enraged
Leavis. For Leavis, Snow is not just ignorant, he is portentously
ignorant; that is, 'he is a portent in that, being in himself negligible, he has become for a vast public on both sides of the Atlantic a
master-mind and a sage'. Leaving aside this and other invective
(non-entity, intellectual nullity, banality, ineffable blankness,
embarrassing vulgarity, as undistinguished as it is possible to be),
what Leavis thinks is that Snow is simply a reflection of the
received wisdom of his time ('he has been created as authoritative
intellect by the cultural conditions manifested in his acceptance').
This impression time has done little to dispel. Yet, if there is anything in the debate beyond invective (on both sides, it must be
said, for Leavis's own entry into the area had been provoked by
Snow's initial over-statements and answered in intemperate terms
by at least some of Snow's defenders), we must be clear what it is.
Once again, an initial glance may produce bafflement, not least
because of the many striking similarities between the two protago-
nists, both provincial grammar-school boys, both eventually anti-
modernist on art, both élitists on education, both anti-religious,
and both broadly on the left in open politics.

However, despite everything so far said, there is a point of real
significance which underlies the Two Cultures Debate, and which
continues to be missed by most of those who consider the matter
or refer to it. To bring this out, we could do far worse that point to
one of Leavis's apparently more surprising remarks:

> I don't believe in any 'literary values', and you won't find me
> talking about them: the judgments the literary critic is con-
> cerned with are judgments about life. What the critical

discipline is concerned with is relevance and precision in making and developing them.[4]

Leavis was, as has often been pointed out, a moralist and not an aesthete about literature (which is why his attack on Snow would be ill-represented by calling it an attack on philistinism). And, whatever we think about the efficacy of the average literary critic in developing judgments about life, an education in science will fail to address the relevant issues. The reason for this is in no way a criticism of science *per se*; indeed, it stems from science's very strength, what is sometimes, but perhaps unhelpfully described as science's value-freedom.

It is important, though, to be clear about what might sensibly be meant by speaking of science as value-free. What is meant is not (or should not be) a denial of the fact that science is a matter of human interest, or that values of various sorts are involved in taking part in scientific work and in choosing the focus of that work. These include what might be seen as values external to the scientific enterprise itself, such as the particular desires which motivate individual scientists and the ends chosen by those directing and funding research, but we should not forget the internal values generated by scientific work of any description. These will include the need to solve a particular problem thrown up in the course of research, or the need to produce results replicable by fellow-scientists, or the need to produce theories which survive empirical testing. What is right about thinking of science as value-free derives from the subject matter and the methods of science. The subject matter of science is the description, analysis and explanation of natural processes, as they are caused and brought about by other natural processes according to natural laws and regularities. The methods of science involve the observation and measurement of phenomena by any competent, suitably placed observers, whatever their beliefs, motives or cultural backgrounds, and the rigorous testing of theories against such observations and measurements, again by any scientist or scientists, regardless of ideology or background. The widely canvassed notion of science as presenting an absolute view of the world, or, alternatively, as a view from nowhere, represents an ideal unattainable by human observers, limited as we are by our concepts and sensory apparatus. Nevertheless, there is something right about it in so far as in science the attempt is made to chart the course of nature (or of various facets of nature) as it goes on independently of human interest, however close to our interests the investigation of some facet of

[4] *Nor Shall My Sword*, p. 97.

nature might be. Thus, for example, things very important to us, including colour, sound and taste, are relegated by science to the status of secondary quality, causally and scientifically irrelevant to the fundamental processes of nature. The picture modern science presents of the world is of a humanly unrecognizable world, one in which not only secondary qualities are removed, but in which the familiar objects of everyday use and appearance become lattices of particles, fuzzy at the edges and occupied largely by empty space. We are familiar with this effect from Eddington's famous discussion of the two tables, but the start of a similar process of scientific kenosis of human meaning is well described by Proust:

> the town that I saw before me had ceased to be Venice. Its personality, its name, seemed to be lying fictions which I no longer had the courage to impress upon its stones. I saw the palaces reduced to their constituent parts, lifeless heaps of marble with nothing to chose between them, and the water as a combination of hydrogen and oxygen, external, blind, anterior and exterior to Venice, unconscious of Doges or of Turner.[5]

Proust is writing of the sense of depersonalization which came over him as part of his remorse for allowing a piece of selfish cruelty to his mother. But a dispassionate scientific account of Venice would know no more of its human meaning than did Proust in his neurasthenic state. In a scientific account, water does indeed become hydrogen and oxygen, palaces complexes of molecules, the very name 'Venice' a fiction, and Doges and Turner and their works but insignificant moments in the natural history of but one short-lived species, of no more interest or value than any other moment or moments.

To put all this another way, science aims at an observer-independent account of the world, transcending human meaning, culture and ideology. Its success derives from its success in approximating to this aim, for it is in so far as we go beyond looking at the natural world in terms of its first meanings for us that we are able to penetrate further its causally essential core, and so become rather more adept at manipulating and directing it than those who remain at the level of first impassions. The lesson of post-Galilean science is that there is no reason to suppose that the effects and processes we identify in our first transactions with nature will turn out to be those which are fundamental from a causal point of view.

What all this amounts to is that science has come to abstract from many of the properties which are of importance to us in our

[5] Marcel Proust, *Remembrance of Things Past*, vol. XI, trans. C. K. Scott Moncrieff (London: Chatto and Windus, 1969), p. 320.

everyday lives. Even more, it teaches us to look at the world in a way which prescinds from its value for us. We look at it as it is in itself, according to its causal determination and structure, and not at how it affects us or how we might like it to be. Even where, as in medicine, say, or in some technological application, we are dealing with matters of direct value to us, and precisely because of their value to us, in science and in technology we take a detached view in order to establish just what the processes of nature are. In science, we decentre from the meaning and value the world has for us; it is in that sense that science is value-free, and it is precisely for that reason that science cannot constitute a culture, or even half a culture. In the explanations and descriptions given by science, the terms in which discussions of value are framed are rigorously excluded, as well as many of the predicates signalling the manner in which we feel attraction or repulsion to the world, and in terms of which our normal human concerns and interests are expressed and conceived.

If 'culture' refers to the context in which parts of the world are singled out as having meaning and value for us and the background of evaluative agreement against which particular judgments of value are made, then it becomes clear that there certainly can be human cultures which contain no science in our modern sense. There have been many cultures in which there has been no systematic attempt to get behind empirical appearance and to remove oneself, if only for a time, from considerations of value. It would be wrong to think that in such cultures it has been impossible to lead a fully human life, and it would certainly need argument to show that modern western culture represents progress in domains outside the scientific and technological, or indeed to show that even within our culture scientific and technological as it is, a perfectly good life could not be lived in more or less blissful ignorance of the details of modern science, which, I take it, is Pascal's point. Moreover, even though in our history and culture science plays an important role, and we certainly need some people well up in science, science itself cannot make judgments of value (what Leavis used to call 'judgments about life'); further, many of the explanations and concepts of science occlude or simply by-pass the considerations which are relevant to life as lived.

It is of course, true that an exclusive concentration on scientific modes of thought can affect the way in which judgments of value are made. In particular, it can lead to an importation of quantitative considerations, and a tendency to see social and moral problems in terms of hygiene and environmental manipulation. Leavis's hostility to Snow was partly due to the fact that he discovered such tendencies in Snow. But to treat the Two Cultures Debate as being mainly about an old-fashioned moralism objecting to what Leavis called technologico-Benthamism (and for which he himself was in his term dubbed Luddite) is to miss the fundamental point. This point is that culture is concerned with the living of life as a whole, and that science, quite properly, prescinds from the terms in which concerns relevant to that can be discussed or even raised. If, as Leavis implies, a non-literary education may fail to advance relevance and precision in this area, this is not so much because scientists have the wrong values as because science in itself does not address questions of value at all. (It is striking that Leavis, just as much as Snow, is unprepared to look to religion as a source of the required relevance and precision. We could in a way see the whole dispute as one in which each party turns to his own favoured discipline to supply the gap left by the passing of religion, another point at which the two are rather closer than either would have wanted to admit.)

What, though, is culture? Whence are what I am calling cultural judgments derived, and how are they to be justified? A striking feature of what I am calling culture is that, historically, cultures have been embedded in specific and local traditions. Unlike modern science, which just because it aims at universally acceptable, observer-independent theories, transcends particular religions, ideologies, and races, culture by contrast is particular, and has been recognized to be so since the time of Vico (1668–1744).

It is here, of course, that we encounter theories of *Verstehen*, that is the idea that when we study a culture, part of what we should be asking is what it feels like to be a member of that culture and what it is to share in its traditions, history and commonality. The implied contrast here is once more a contrast with natural science. In speaking about the behaviour of atoms or genes, say, we are not asking what it is like to be an atom or a gene, if only because it is not like anything to be an atom or a gene, nor do we have to enquire into the tradition or culture of particular groups of atoms or genes, for groups of atoms or genes do not have traditions or cultures marking them off from other atoms or genes. And for most philosophers of science a complete account of atomic or genetic behaviour will have been given when we are able objectively to predict the behaviour in question, given initial conditions and the relevant laws. Understanding human behaviour demands both more and less. It involves less because it does not require more than very general predictability or general laws. Indeed, and this is a key point of difference, locating an agent's motives and self-understanding within a specific tradition or culture tells us the terms in which he will conceive his actions, but not what actions he will do. Understanding human behaviour, on the other hand, requires more than predictions of behaviour because understanding an action will always involve reference to an agent's reasons, and, implicitly, given the value-ladenness of the notion of reason, reference to values, those of both agent and observer. But, it will be said, we can know nothing of an agent's reasons without some grasp of his cultural background, and of what it might feel like to be an agent in that sort of society. And so we return to the particularity of culture, and of cultural understanding. In contrast, scientific understanding is general and impervious to the changes and contingencies of human history (that is, the behaviour of atoms and even genes follows laws which, if valid, are true for the whole of space and time).

The idea that human conduct and the norms underlying it are intimately affected by history and by the development of culture runs counter to the tenets of the European enlightenment. The enlightenment, strongly influenced be it noted by scientific modes of thinking and by a progressivist attitude to human history, took human nature to be as invariant and unchanging as a carbon atom or a molecule of water. It also believed that there was one rational standard—that, roughly, of the eighteenth century liberal-cum-sceptical intellectual—to which all mankind could and should aspire. Informed by a rationalistic, scientific picture of the world, and by a similarly enlightened reading of human history, the prejudices and rivalries which caused hatred, fanaticism and factionalism could be eliminated. As Diderot put it, the ideal is a

> philosopher who, trampling underfoot prejudice, tradition, venerability, universal assent, authority—in a word, everything that overawes the crowd—dares to think for himself, to ascend to the clearest general principles, to examine them, to discuss them, to admit nothing save on the testimony of his own reason and experience.[6]

The assumption is that having done all this, genuinely independent thinkers will converge on a universal rationality. In matters of conduct, enlightenment thinking tended to stress the goals of self-preservation and pleasure-seeking which the new moral sciences were allegedly revealing as the mainsprings of human action. Once we were freed from the obfuscations and repressions of religion and the old order, and allowed innocently to seek pleasure and self-preservation, we would also be able to act with rational benevolence to our fellow-men. Rationality regarding our own nature

[6] In his article on Eclecticism in the *Encyclopaedia*, quoted in Arthur M. Wilson, *Diderot* (Oxford University Press, 1972), p. 237.

and desires would reveal a harmony between our own ends and those of others. And, accustomed by science to the disengaged scrutiny of nature, we would similarly be induced to transcend egoism in our own behaviour.

In a sense some of these ideals were put to the test in the French Revolution: at least some of the revolutionaries conceived themselves as attempting to harmonize interests by means of universal rationality unfettered by old prejudice and authority, which, it was held, militated against such painless harmonization. The Russian Revolution, too, is a classic case of an attempt to reform men by remoulding society on rational principles. Both these instances, and others one can think of, certainly highlight the pitfalls of rationalism in politics. But a more telling, because more fundamental, objection to the enlightenment view of human nature is given by those who, like Vico, stressed the effect on human beings of their cultural and historical background. With characteristic force and hyperbole the basic point is put by de Maistre:

> In the course of my life, I have seen Frenchmen, Italians, Russians. ... I know, too, thanks to Montesquieu, that one can be a Persian. But as for man, I declare that I have never met him in my life; if he exists, he is unknown to me.[7]

Being rooted is not simply the condition of man's existence and identity, it is also the basis of a calm and fulfilled human life:

> All known nations have been happy or powerful to the degree they have faithfully obeyed (the) national mind, which is nothing other than the destruction of individual dogmas and the absolute and general rule of national dogmas, that is to say, useful prejudices.[8]

Prejudice is a good because it binds communities and nations together and gives otherwise rudderless human beings a sense of purpose and direction. This is more than Burke's notion of prejudice as the deposit of long experience and wisdom, or than Hume's test of time, or even than Chesterton's plea that in our search for instant solutions to our problems we do not disenfranchise the dead, though de Maistre would certainly not have dissented from any of these sentiments. It is rather the idea that a community, or anything approaching a community, must be firmly embedded in a cocoon of all-embracing and unquestioned thought and feeling, a thought expressed around the same time by Herder:

[7] J. de Maistre, *Oeuvres Complètes*, 14 vols. (Lyons: Vitte, 1884–1887), vol. I, p. 74.

[8] Ibid. p. 376.

Prejudice is good in its time and place, because it makes people happy. It takes them back to their centre, attaches them firmly to their roots, lets them flourish in their own way, makes them more impassioned, and, as a result, happier in their inclinations and purposes. The most ignorant nation, the one with the most prejudices, is often superior in this respect. When people dream of emigrating to foreign lands to seek hope and salvation, they reveal the first symptoms of sickness and flatulence, of approaching death.[9]

Herder's motivation may seem entirely praiseworthy: a desire to defend the primitive and the rural and the communal against the hubris of the urban sophisticate. It is hard not to see his words as an anticipation of Nietzsche's ideas about the centrality of myth to a strong people, and of the impact of Socratic rationality as a type of sickly internal emigration loosening the bonds of allegiance to common values and myths which hold a community together. And it is hard not to see his whole stance through the prism of rather darker nineteenth and particularly twentieth century interpretations of culture and nation.

Our recent reflections on culture have begun to take us into deep, if not murky, waters. We began by looking at the differences between scientific theories and the terms in which discussions of value are framed. In particular, in scientific theories, abstraction is made from ethical and evaluative considerations, and often even from the properties and predicates on which such evaluations focus. If by 'culture' is meant the context in which what Leavis calls judgments about life can be made, then science can be at most one specific element of culture as a whole. Science will in various ways inform discussions of value, by, for example, outlining what it is possible to do, or by explaining some of the causal background to specific human capacities or tendencies. But it cannot in itself provide justifications for evaluations or decisions, even including the decision to engage in science itself. The fact, if it is a fact, that the reductive and quantitative approaches characteristic of modern science have entered so much of our political and moral thinking does not show that science itself is forcing our mind-sets in that way, or that being a faithful scientist implies that one is bound to do this. What it shows is that a particular culture has begun to move in a Benthamite direction, and critics would say, has begun

[9] J. G. Herder, 'Yet Another Philosophy of History Concerning the Development of Mankind', quoted in *J. G. Herder on Social and Political Culture*, ed. F. M. Barnard (Cambridge University Press, 1969) pp. 186–187.

to look at moral and political questions in terms and conditions which are inappropriate. But scientific investigations, properly conceived, neither encourage nor licence such a shift of mind or emphasis. Leavis, in his criticisms of Snow fails clearly to distinguish the thesis that science cannot be a culture from the thought that our culture (or Snow's) encourages inappropriate incursions of quasi-scientific modes of thinking (what might be called 'scientism'). Leavis clearly hopes that a literary education will help to alert sensitive people to the dangers of scientism, and in this he may well be right. Important as this is, it remains subsidiary to the main argument, and also vulnerable to Snow's *ad hominem* about the reactionary tendencies of writers other than Ibsen (to the extent, anyway, that it is (a) true and (b) if true, undesirable).

However, when we begin to look at the notion of culture, as it has been developed and been analysed in practice, we notice that it is not a matter of there being just one context in which values have developed. Culture is not centred on mankind as a whole, but rather on specific groups. There appears to be something facile about the assumption of a single human culture, and something dangerously hubristic about the assumption that all cultures are converging on a single point, or converging on a single set of values. In Herder's case, indeed, it was dismay at the hubris involved in enlightenment rationalism which led him to stress the plurality of culture and the incommensurability of value—and one doesn't have to be objectionably Spenglerian to question whether the superiority of twentieth-century liberal democratic culture over, say, fifth century BC Athens or thirteenth century France is simply self-evident.

However sympathetic some of the sources of his thought may be, there are obvious disadvantages in Herder's position. If he himself refused to rank cultures, or even to compare them, his view that human cultures are incommensurable gives him no redress against the position of one who, like Fichte, simply declares the German people the *Favoritvolk*, the favoured nation. A Herderian position would in any case, seem to argue for a form of apartheid, multi-cultural if not supremacist; that is to say, if each human being's identity rests on his or her assimilation to his or her national culture, should the aim of social policy not be to preserve groups (and hence individuals) in their purity, rather than encourage or even allow cultural assimilation?

Against the holism of Vico, Herder and their followers, the enlightenment stressed the individual. While enlightenment thinkers like Diderot and Condorcet certainly underestimated the rootedness of individuals in particular traditions and cultures, nothing so far said shows that they were wrong to stress the autonomy of the individual. The remarks I have quoted from de Maistre and Herder suggest that happiness comes from sinking one's individuality in the nation. Far from suggesting that this is inevitable, they are quite conscious of the possibility, the danger as they would see it, of doing the opposite. So, even while recognizing the importance and significance of cultural roots, it remains an open question as to just what one should take to follow from this. The situation here, indeed, is analogous to that regarding science: just because science is an important aspect of culture, it does not follow that ethical or political issues should be discussed as if they were scientific questions; just because my culture is a significant aspect of my identity, it does not follow that I should envisage my activities in exclusively nationalistic terms, or seek to subordinate my personality in that of the nation.

In his book *La Défaite de la Pensée*[10] Alain Finkielkraut has drawn an interesting contrast between Herder's attitude to national culture—and by extension those of Fichte, Nietzsche, Spengler and many of our contemporary multi-culturalists—and that of Goethe. In his essay on German architecture of 1772,[11] shortly after he had met Herder and had been impressed by him, Goethe had praised the Gothic at the expense of the classical, which was, we may suppose, the *international* style of the eighteenth century. In the form of an address to Magister Ervinus, (Erwin von Steinbach) the architect of Strasbourg Cathedral, Goethe comments how the Italian would describe the Minister as in niggling taste, with the Frenchmen childishly babbling 'Puerilities' while 'triumphantly snapping open his snuffbox, à la Greque'. Moreover,

the first time I went to the Minister my head was full of the common notions of good taste. From hearsay I respected the harmony of mass, the purity of forms, and I was the sworn enemy of the confused caprices of Gothic ornament ... no less foolish than the people who call the whole of the foreign world barbaric, for me everything was Gothic that did not fit in my system ... (pp. 106–7)

And yet, on actually seeing it, 'how surprised I was when I was confronted by it', and, as a result of the magical and above all natural impression given by all its ornament and detail, he quickly came

[10] Translated as *The Undoing of Thought* by D. O'Keefe (London: Claridge Press, 1988).
[11] 'On German Architecture (1772)', in *Goethe on Art*, ed. John Gage (London: Scolar Press, 1980), pp. 103–112.

to thank God that he can proclaim that this is German architecture, our architecture. For the Italian has none he can call his own, still less the Frenchman. (p. 108)

The German Gothic is a characteristic art. As such it is the only true art

unadorned by, indeed unaware of, all foreign elements, (and) whether it be born of savagery or of a cultivated sensibility, it is a living whole. (p. 109)

Hence among different nations you will see countless different degrees of characteristic art, and in the case of Strasbourg, what we have is an example of the

deepest feeling for truth and beauty of proportion, brought about by the strong, rugged German soul on the narrow, gloomy, priest-ridden stage of the *medii aevi*. (p. 109)

Even as late as 1823, Goethe endorsed the favourable impression the Minister had made on him in 1772, but by then his attitude to national culture had been somewhat transformed.

Finkielkraut in his book focuses on a conversation Goethe had with Eckerman on 21 January 1827.[12] Goethe had been reading a Chinese novel, expecting to be struck by its strangeness and difference, but he had been struck instead by its closeness in theme and treatment to his own *Hermann and Dorothea* of 1797, and also to the English novels of Richardson. Of course men were rooted in particular places, and up to a point creatures of their traditions, histories and geographies, but these divisions and fragmentations could be transcended, particularly through art:

I am more convinced that poetry is the universal possession of mankind, revealing itself everywhere and at all times in hundreds and hundreds of men. One makes it a little better than another, and swims on the surface a little longer than another— that is all ... we Germans are very likely (not) to look beyond the narrow circle that surrounds us. I therefore like to look about me in foreign nations. ... The term 'national literature' does not really mean much today. We are moving towards an era of universal literature, and everyone should do his best to hasten its development ... While we value what is foreign, we must not bind ourselves to some particular thing, and regard it as a model.

And he says that if we want a model we must look to the ancient Greeks, where the beauty of mankind is universally and constantly

[12] See J. P. Eckermann, *Conversations with Goethe* (London: Everyman's Library, 1970).

13

represented. The rest we must look at historically, taking for ourselves what is good, as far as it goes. On 14 March 1832, shortly before his death; Goethe appeals even more forcefully to universal standards:

> as a man, as a citizen, the poet is bound to love his native land ... but the native land of his poetic powers and poetic action is the Good, the Noble, the Beautiful, which have no particular province or country, and which the poet seizes on and forms wherever he finds it.

The poet, for Goethe, is like an eagle, hovering and gazing over the whole countries, it being of no consequence to him whether the hare he pounces on is running in Prussia or Saxony. What then could be meant by love of one's country, other than setting aside the narrow views of his countrymen and so ennobling their feelings and thoughts?

The Herderian position on culture will deny this, and insist that each individual becomes even more rooted in his or her own particular culture, though whether this is intended as an epistemological or a moral-cum-political claim, or a mixture of the two, is not always entirely clear. As an epistemological claim, it is, of course, refuted by the experience of Goethe with the Chinese novel, by the experience of anyone today who reads Homer with some understanding, and at a significant but lower level, by the universal popularity of originally American pop music. It is this last phenomenon, indeed, that might lead many to see something attractive in Herder's position from a moral or aesthetic point of view. Doesn't universalism lead to a destruction of much that is worthwhile, and to an abrogation of value-judgments, leading in the end to a universal mediocrity? Here, I think, one has to beware of a sentimental form of primitivism. Vulgarity and worse do not occur only in Disneyland, but *may* be evident in village culture. And, as the example of Goethe himself shows, transcultural borrowing and assimilation can be conducted on the highest level.

In fact, on analysis, it turns out, perhaps paradoxically, that a Goethean position is far more conducive to the making of value judgments and to the preservation of the worthwhile than Herder's. For it was Herder who denied the possibility of making value judgments across cultures and who thus in effect deprived the admirer of a peasant culture of any firm ground on which to criticize the incursions of satellite television or Coca-Cola. In a Herderian dispensation, he will appear simply to be defending the picturesque against the popular, having been deprived of any notion of any objective value on which to argue his case.

Goethe, by contrast does appeal to a universal sense of value, which is manifested in but transcends particular cultures. He is neither committed to the defence of everything in a culture he admires overall, nor need his defence of ancient cultures against modernization be simply a lament for the passing of the old: he can point to universal values its passing will offend. To return to Leavis, his complaints against the effects of industrialization need not be sheerly Luddite, mere obstinacy in the face of universal progress. Paradoxically, then, it is Herder, with all his affection for the particularity of primitive cultures who reduces their defender to the position of the Luddites castigated by the likes of Snow. Goethe, with his references to the Good, the Noble and the Beautiful, and with his extolling of the man who stands *above* nations opens up the logical space needed to rank and assess cultures and their elements. There is, then, no contradiction between an appeal to universal values and a defence of particular aspects of particular cultures. Quite the contrary: what would be contradictory would be to attempt such a defence while denying any transcultural standards of assessment.

If such denial is what is meant by pluralism, then Leavis's strictures on pluralism are well taken:

> 'Pluralism' denotes a sitting-easy to questions of responsibility, intellectual standard, and even superficial consistency, the aplomb, or suppleness being conditioned by a coterie-confident sense of one's own unquestioned sufficiency—or superiority.[13]

Leavis's target here is Nöel Annan; whether his sally is justified in that case, it could certainly be said that the sort of non-judgmental pluralism he criticizes here received an early exposition in Herder, and after various incarnations on the political right and on the political left, is with us today as those forms of multi-culturalism which would refuse to allow one to judge the worth of other cultures or their customs. In most, if not all of its incarnations, there has also been the sense from proponents of pluralism that they consider themselves somehow superior, intellectually and morally, to those benighted folk *within* particular cultures, who insist on the unique correctness of their views.

But one does not have to subscribe to the enlightenment view of human progress or deny the fact of our own situatedness in particular traditions or cultures to think of values as universal. Indeed, a proper account of judgment would be that it is both individual in expression and formulation, and, in intention, universal: while judgments may indeed depend on backgrounds of communal

[13] *Nor Shall My Sword*, p. 32.

15

agreement, they cannot in the first instance be communal. Any judgment is made by an individual who then takes some responsibility for it. As Leavis himself puts it, speaking of judgment about poems,

a judgment is personal or it is nothing; you cannot take over someone else's.

And in describing the process by which critical judgments are then discussed, amended and ratified, he goes on to speak of

the collaborative-creative process in which the poem comes to be established as something 'out there', of common access in what is in some sense a public world.[14]

Leavis goes some way here to capturing both the individual and the universal poles of judgments of all sorts—that they are made by individuals, while seeking general or universal agreement. He then goes on to make the important point that a culture can exist only in so far as it provokes renewed responses from the individuals in it, 'who collaboratively renew and perpetuate what they participate in—a cultural community or consciousness'. In other words, a culture, if alive, is always changing in response to the judgments and reactions of those who live in it.

What all this amounts to is that while individual stem from their cultures, as rooted in them, if you like, they are never completely determined by them. They are individuals, and in making their judgments, they appeal implicitly at last, to standards of correctness which stand above the particular, and by which the particular is judged, whether the particular is the individual person or his or her society. And there are some types of judgment no human being can avoid having to make. The point about the 'two' cultures is that necessarily we all make judgments about what Leavis calls 'life'; in this sense—to return to Pascal's initially quoted pensée—we all have knowledge about morality, knowledge which is vital to us all in a way in which knowledge about science is not. While there is a clear sense, as we have seen, in which scientific judgments are cross-cultural, it is not the case that even in a scientifically dominated culture, each individual will have to engage with science. On the other hand, we do all have to make judgments of value; and while our value judgments are initially in the presuppositions common to our culture, in making them we take a personal responsibility for them, which gives us the chance at least of loosening the bonds of cultures as given, and of moving into a more universal environment.

[14] Ibid. p. 62.

16

Rational and Other Animals

JOHN HALDANE

The soul has two cognitive powers. One is the act of a corporeal organ, which naturally knows things existing in individual matter; hence sense knows only the singular. But there is another kind of power called the intellect. Though natures only exist in individual matter, the intellectual power knows them not as individualised, but as they are abstracted from matter by the intellect's attention and reflection. Thus, through the intellect we can understand natures in a universal manner; and this is beyond the power of sense. (St Thomas Aquinas, *Summa Theologiae*, Ia, q. 12, a. 4; *responsio*.)[1]

Introduction

I shall approach the theme of understanding and *verstehen* by way of considering the purported (and I believe, real) difference between human and other animals in respect of the intellectual rationality of the former.

English-language philosophy in the broadly analytical tradition is currently in a humanistic phase. I mean by this that there is now a widely-shared inclination to reassert the existence and the validity of interpretative and evaluative styles of description and explanation. Sometimes (indeed, for the most part) this gives rise to forms of conceptual dualism, as in some of the uses made of the contrast between *scientific* and *manifest* images, *objective* and *subjective* views and *causal* and *rational* explanations.

Of course, to observe a duality is not necessarily to accord parity of esteem to both parties. Quine famously conceded the irreducibility of intentional idiom in everyday discourse, but concluded that it must therefore be dispensed with when it comes to describing reality. Since then, and under the influence of Davidson, he has softened his attitude, recognizing the ineliminability of psychological and semantic categories for any comprehensive account that *we* humans might ever wish to construct. Even so, the

---

[1] Quotations from Aquinas are taken (and in some cases adapted) from *The Summa Theologica* Literally Translated by the Fathers of the English Dominican Province (London: R. & T. Washbourne, 1912).

acceptance is reluctant, the acknowledgment a concession to human weakness.

In contrast there is a growing reaction against the disposition to give priority to the scientific, the objective and the causal. Some humanist 'reactionaries', like Thomas Nagel, look to a future synthesis; to forms of description and explanation that transcend existing dualities while acknowledging the validity of the perspectives they embody. Others are resigned to, reconciled with, or rejoice at an ineliminable dualism within epistemology and metaphysics. On this account there are two ways of knowing, and two kinds of fact—the personal and the scientific. One important source of inspiration for this pluralist attitude is Dilthey's observation 'nature we explain; man we understand'.[2]

Dilthey was himself influenced by Kant and Hegel in thinking that there is an important difference between the experimental, quantitative and inductive methods of natural science and the meaning-discerning practices of the humanities. For Dilthey, it is of the nature of human beings to seek for meanings and purposes and to express these in their behaviour, thus constituting the 'life-world' (lebenswelt). Accordingly, any study of distinctly human phenomena must be interpretative. By contrast the domain of the natural sciences is one in which cause and quantity are all, and the comprehension of events is arrived at by discerning the structural properties of things and observing (or inferring) external relations between them.

This line of thought and its subsequent development within the hermeneutic tradition are familiar enough, and it is quite evident how a clear and ineliminable duality of cause and meaning might serve the interests of those who wish to resist various tendencies to scientistic reductionism. However, while I share the belief that there is real and distinctive domain of meaning and value, I have doubts about the ways in which the line between this and the area proper to natural science has been drawn. Later I shall consider a contemporary instance of this delineation and show why it is problematic and is itself surprisingly scientistic (given its source).

A further and general point which I wish to emphasize is that an adequate theory of knowledge requires an interlocking account of the nature of knowers. Cast in Kantian form, this amounts to the claim that a philosophy of cognition needs a philosophy of mind to specify the (subjective) metaphysical preconditions of the possibility of knowledge. In the telegraphic idiom of late twentieth-century philosophy: *no epistemology without ontology*. One half of this requirement involves demonstrating what follows about the

---

[2] For relevant texts of Dilthey see H. P. Rickman (ed.), *Dilthey, Selected Writings* (Cambridge University Press, 1976).

objects of knowledge from the fact that they are knowable (and known), the other half involves showing what must be true about the bearers of cognitive powers as such. As the earlier mention of 'subjective' conditions indicates, here I am more concerned with the second task.[3]

A pre-modern humanism

There is an old Aristotelian principle according to which acts are distinguished by their respective objects, powers are known by their acts, and substances are defined by their powers. This principle is deployed in Book II, chapter IV of the *De Anima* to distinguish different kinds of souls and is picked up and developed by Aquinas in his commentary on the text (in *Aristotelis Librum de Anima Commentarium, lectio* 6, § 304–308).[4] It is also at work in the passage from the *Summa Theologiae* with which I began this essay. Recalling the rubric *'no epistemology without ontology'* we can see that Aquinas is telling us that intellect differs from the senses in as much as the objects of each are of different kinds. With his eye a man can see a dog but he cannot see the abstract nature dogness. With his mind a man may think of dogs as such, but not of this dog in its singularity (*pace* neo-Russellians, there are no singular concepts or individual *de re* senses).

What can a dog do? Following Aquinas we should have no difficulty with the idea that one dog may see another (i.e. be aware of it visually); but if we are to say that a dog can think of dogness then we must be willing to attribute *intellectual* abilities to it, and these are, according to Aquinas, immaterial powers. The propriety of intellectual attributions to animals is a recurrent subject of philosophical discussion; the issue of immateriality turns on Aquinas's identification of the intellectual with the abstract and *seems* to rest on a generally discarded dualist conception of thought. In both

[3] Elsewhere I have addressed the issue of the objective metaphysical preconditions of cognition arguing that the objects of knowledge must instantiate intelligible structures. Knowledge is of form. See John Haldane, 'Mind–World Identity Theory and the Anti-Realist Challenge', in J. Haldane and C. Wright (eds), *Reality, Representation and Projection* (New York: Oxford University Press, 1993), and 'The Forms of Thought', in L. Hahn (ed.), *The Philosophy of Roderick Chisholm* (La Salle, Illinois: Open Court, forthcoming).

[4] For an English translation see Kenelm Foster O.P. and Silvester Humphries O.P., *Aristotle's De Anima in the Version of William of Moerbeke and the Commentary of St. Thomas Aquinas* (London: Routledge and Kegan Paul, 1951).

cases, however, St Thomas's reasoning is clear and plausible (in fact, I believe that, given suitable development, it is compelling).

First animal perception. Recall the specification principle: *substances by powers; powers by acts; acts by objects*. Perceptual acts of the same sense-modality are distinguishable (in part) by their material objects. Acts of different modalities are distinguished (in part) by their formal objects—colour and sound, say. Powers are specified as capacities exercised in performances of certain kinds: sight in seeing, taste in tasting, touch in touching, and so on. Thus, an action that takes as its object the visible features of a thing is of necessity an exercise of sight.

This is something that we have overwhelmingly good evidence that animals possess. They modify their behaviour in response to visible features of their circumstances. Indeed, our principal ground for concluding that a part of an animal is an eye, say, is precisely that when this region of the animal is irradiated with various intensities and wavelengths of light there are changes in the subject's behaviour. If we want to arrive at a more definite account of the content of the animal's experience then we vary its environment and study the behavioural consequences. What is of prime importance in determining if an individual is sensate is not the question of what it is *like* to be it, or even whether that Nagelian question arises; but rather the issue of how the individual is related to its environment. We do not need telepathy in order to attribute sensory awareness, for perception shows itself in the eye of the perceiver—*vultus est index animi*. On this basis there can be no serious doubt that dogs see other dogs.

Why then suppose that they do not *think* about them also? Once again, acts are specified by their formal objects. The correlates of thought are intelligible structures, whatever can be comprehended and analysed in articulated propositions. Imagistic thought applies the categories through which these structures are comprehended to the content of sense experience. It is therefore something of a mixed medium. Pure intellection, however, is directed towards nature as such. The reason for saying that this is not something of which animals are capable, is that we have no evidence that they do it. On the contrary, our best interpretations of their behaviour find no place for the attribution of abstract reflection. In identifying and making sense of animals' dealings with the world we do not find occasion to attribute to them cognitive acts whose extensions may be empirically equivalent but whose intensions are conceptually distinct—let alone to attribute acts of 'second intention', i.e. ones directed upon the relevant conceptual content. Certainly, 'there is no evidence that p' is not by itself equivalent to 'there is evidence that not p', nor, *a fortiori*, to 'there is evidence that not possibly p'. But the price of holding on to the idea that for all we know animals may engage in abstract thought is a weakening of the link between mental powers and their behavioural expression, which then introduces an (uncontainable) 'other minds' problem. That problem is excluded, however, once we recognize that performance is a non-contingent criterion of capability.

For Aquinas the immateriality of thought is implied by the fact that its objects (or, *equivalently*, its contents) are abstract. In perception the sensible form is 'received' into the sense without the original matter of its source, but nonetheless under material conditions, principally those of the sense organ. I feel vibrations in my ears deriving from the beating of a distant drum. Although they are separated from the substance of the drum itself the vibrations are nevertheless spatio-temporally located and their character reflects the material medium of the sense-organ. By contrast, when I *think* about the ideas of vibration, or of distance, or of matter, these various features are entertained as purely abstract, and the content of my thinking does not reflect the medium of a thought-organ. Alpha-Centaurans and human beings may hear a sound differently but to the extent that they can both think correctly about the nature of sound as such, then what they think will be the same in content. There may be many ways of sensing a dog but (nominalism excluded) there is only one way of correctly conceiving the nature dogness.[5]

A post-modern humanism

So much for Aquinas. My title 'Rational and Other Animals' is taken from the last of John McDowell's Locke Lectures delivered in Oxford in 1991 and subsequently published under the title *Mind and World*.[6] This book was long awaited and it deserves the attention which it has already attracted. McDowell is an important and influential advocate of humanism in philosophy and his work has a laudable purpose: to liberate thinkers from the snares of scientism. If I am right, however, McDowell grants too much to reductive naturalism.

[5] For nominalistic worries about this see Hilary Putnam, 'Aristotle after Wittgenstein', in *Words and Life* (Cambridge, MA: Harvard University Press, 1994). A reply is presented in John Haldane, 'On Coming Home to (Metaphysical) Realism', *Philosophy*, **71** (1996).

[6] John McDowell, *Mind and World* (Cambridge, MA: Harvard University Press, 1994).

John Haldane

The central issues of *Mind and World* are the nature of thought and the role of concepts in structuring human perceptual experience. McDowell is concerned to present a form of direct realism in opposition to views that embody one or another form of epistemological dualism. If we suppose that there are two domains: that of the world and that of the mind, each with its own internal structure and principals of operation, then the idea of commerce between them will seem to involve some kind of causal exchange with attendant 'interactionist' difficulties. More importantly, for epistemology, there will be the problem of how anything received in this way could count as, or contribute to, a reason or justification for belief. Being caused to think that p is not a form of rational warrant.

McDowell's suggestion is that there can be no general gap or barrier between thought and world; what we think and what is the case must be one reality 'thinking does not stop short of facts. The world is embraceable in thought.'[7] Moreover such influence as the world exerts on thought is already in the order of reason rather than that of material causes. Aristotelians, especially Thomists, may find these claims reminiscent of the principle of the formal identity of the knower and the known, and of the scholastic formula *intelligible in actu est intellectus in actu*. However, McDowell's way of viewing the issues is Wittgensteinian in inspiration, and unlike the medievals with their accounts of intentional existence (*esse intentionale*) he has little to say about the metaphysical nature of the relation between thought and its objects.

He does insist, however, that 'reality is not located outside a boundary that encloses the conceptual'.[8] This is aimed at forestalling the possibility of general scepticism deriving from a two-realm understanding of thought and world; critics, however, have been apt to read it as a latent version of idealism. To some extent McDowell's prose invites this interpretation; and although he explicitly disavows idealism the lack of an account of the metaphysics of intentionality leaves the charge partly unanswered. Even so, as the realism of Aristotle and Aquinas demonstrates, so long as one holds fast to the priority of the world over our thoughts of it (even though they be 'world-involving') it is possible to construct a position akin to McDowell's that is without any taint of idealism.

The main problems with McDowell's views, I believe, lie elsewhere and arise from his use of a correlate of the Dilthey/Weber explanation vs. understanding distinction. According to *Mind and*

[7] *Mind and World*, p. 33.
[8] *Mind and World*, p. 44.

22

World we are to identify two domains: *the realm of law* and *the space of reasons*. The first is nature conceived as the order of physical objects and events held together by law-like causal relations. The second is the intentional-*cum*-rational-*cum*-normative sphere of perception, thought and action.

> Modern science understands its subject matter in a way that threatens, at least, to leave it disenchanted, as Weber put the point in an image that has become a commonplace. The image marks a contrast between two kinds of intelligibility: the kind that is sought by (as we call it) natural science, and the kind we find in something when we place it in relation to other occupants of 'the logical space of reasons' ... It was an achievement of modern thought when this second kind of intelligibility was clearly marked off from the first. In a common medieval outlook, what we now see as the subject matter of natural science was conceived as filled with meaning, as if all of nature were a book of lessons for us; and it is a mark of intellectual progress that educated people cannot now take that idea seriously, except perhaps in some symbolic role.[9]

'Bald naturalism' is the view that seeks to explain everything human in terms of the realm of law; while 'rampant platonism' is the position that both denies this possibility and regards responsiveness to meaning, reason and value as wholly autonomous of the natural order. The first view fails inasmuch as it cannot account for the normativity of reason and the subjectivity of thought. The second preserves these but at the unacceptable cost of severing human subjectivity and occupancy in the space of reasons from any foundation in nature.

Thus the stage is set for the discovery of a *via media* which, in McDowell's lexicon, bears the description 'naturalised platonism'. In effect, we are to find a way of having our heads in the clouds while keeping our feet on the ground. For present purposes a brief characterisation of McDowell's positive view will suffice. We are animals and as such are part of nature. However, we are also thinkers and doers; and in virtue of their being conceptually—and rationally—structured, our thoughts and deeds both have meaning and are liable to normative assessment. Below the space of reasons lies the realm of the law; here the patterns of things are geometric and causal. Thus, while there may be correlations between these two sets of structures, there is no way in which the causal explains the rational order. At best, we might regard it as a material

[9] *Mind and World*, p. 71.

23

precondition or medium of embodiment and effect, rather as is the pigment of a painting in relation to the scene depicted within it. But just as there is no principle of inference from pigment to picture, so there is no method of projection from the causal to the rational. Equivalently, given McDowell's insistence on the ineliminably conceptual aspect of experience, there is no principle of inference from the irradiation of a sense organ to the perception of the world.

These ideas are very interesting and provocative. Were I disposed to 'bald naturalism', I might regard McDowell's characterisation of that position as tendentious, and insist that his claim that it cannot account for the intentional domain is question-begging. As it is, however, I am already of the view that normativity is not reducible to frequency, nor intentionality to causal dependence.[10] What troubles me, therefore, is not the rejection of bald naturalism but the concession that it is the right account of the whole of the sub-personal realm. Put in terms of the Diltheyan categories, I am questioning whether the explanation/understanding distinction is as sharp and simple as is generally assumed by those who like to invoke it on behalf of humanism.

Experience and emergence

It would be crazy to regret the idea that natural science reveals a special kind of intelligibility, to be distinguished from the kind that is proper to meaning. To discard that part of our intellectual inheritance would be to return to medieval superstition. It is right to set a high value on the kind of intelligibility we disclose in something when we place it in the realm of law, and to separate it sharply from the intelligibility we disclose in something when we place it in the space of reasons.[11]

McDowell's strict dualism of law and reason gives rise to two important questions. First, what is to be said about (non-human) animal experience if it is assumed that the beasts of air, land and sea are not concept-users? Second, how is our ascent to rational intentionality to be explained if it is also assumed that we originate in and remain attached to the realm of nature as that is conceived of by modern science? McDowell addresses these questions, but

---

[10] See John Haldane, 'Folk Psychology and the Explanation of Human Behaviour', *Proceedings of the Aristotelian Society, Supplementary Volume*, **62** (1988); and 'Naturalism and the Problem of Intentionality', *Inquiry*, **32** (1989).

[11] *Mind and World*, p. 109.

24

the answers he provides appear unsatisfactory, for they are either highly contentious or regressive. Beyond observing this, I want to suggest that his difficulties arise from not having developed a more complex view of nature and its levels of organisation.

The first problem is to make sense of the idea of animal experience without crediting animals with perception. Following Kant, McDowell wishes to maintain that 'the objective world is present only to a self-conscious subject, a subject who can ascribe experiences to herself; *it is only in the context of a subject's ability to ascribe experiences to herself that experiences can constitute awareness of the world'*[12] (my emphasis). This seems unwarrantedly intellectualist. Earlier I gave an argument for attributing perceptual awareness to animals; in brief, their behaviour is responsive to features of the environment in ways that license the attribution of discriminatory powers: *perceiver is as perceiver does*. I then noted that the question of abstract conceptualisation does not arise as one contemplates the actions of animals. However, there is space for further organisational principles between, on the one hand, patterns of sensation, and on the other, conceptual relations between abstracted universals. In this space may lie percepts: individuating perceptual sortals constituted out of the sensible and behavioural features of things. The case for positing these is simply that they are implied by familiar styles of experience–attribution. We describe and explain animal behaviour by reference to what they are looking at and how things of that sort feature in their lives.

In terminology borrowed from Gadamer, McDowell speaks of animals as inhabiting an 'environment' but not a 'world'—as do humans. These are both terms of art designed to mark a contrast; but to concede a significant difference between human and animal perception is not to yield to the inevitability of this way of defining it. On the contrary, the evident difference between human and other animals emerges at the point where humans proceed to intellection by abstracting from the content of perception. For that to be possible there must be a (logically) prior perceptual content, and the conditions and behaviour which warrant the attribution of acts with that content are very much the same as those noted in relation to animals. As Aquinas observes:

> The life of a higher animal (*animalis perfecti*) requires that it apprehend a thing not only when it is present to the senses but also when it is absent. Otherwise, since animal movement and activity depend upon cognition, an animal would not be moved by anything absent, the contrary of which may be observed

[12] *Mind and World*, p. 114.

25

especially among higher animals ... Consider also that an animal has to seek and avoid certain things, not only because they are pleasing or otherwise to the sense but because they are also useful or harmful; just as the sheep runs away when it sees a wolf, not as something the colour and shape of which it does not like but as its natural enemy ... The principle of memory in animals is found in some such category [*intentione*] as that something is harmful or otherwise.[13]

McDowell's second problem is how to explain the emergence of the distinctly human form of existence, in such a way as not to lose touch with nature conceived of as the realm of law. He asks: 'How has it come about that there are animals that possess the spontaneity of understanding? That is a perfectly good question. There was a time when there were no rational animals'.[14] However, what follows this is, in effect, a refusal to let the question be asked in the form presented here. Instead we are to regard 'the culture a human being is initiated into as a going concern ... Human infants are mere animals, distinctive only in their potential, and nothing occult happens to a human being in ordinary upbringing (*Bildung*)'.[15]

This response is triply flawed. First, the original question remains to be answered. To continue to press the point is not to urge the cause of reductionism. On the contrary, the force with which it arises stems from the manner and strength of McDowell's own division between the natural and the personal realms. Second, to trace the emergence of understanding to the educational influence of the surrounding human culture is evidently regressive. From whence in turn comes its *Bildung,* and so on? Third, to say, as McDowell does, that 'human infants are mere animals distinctive only in their potential' fails to address the point of how it can be that such a potential is possessed. How can that the proper mode of comprehension of which is causal–explanatory, be intrinsically such as to give rise to that whose required method of comprehension is *Verstehen?* Thus are left unexplained the actual rationality of the culture and the potential rationality of the infant; *no epistemology without ontology.*

Naturalisms modern and pre-modern

Perhaps the emergence of rational animals is an ultimate mystery. McDowell encourages us away from recourse to 'supernaturalism'

[13] *Summa Theologiae*, Ia. q. 78. a. 4.
[14] *Mind and World*, p. 123.
[15] Ibid.

in the explanation of it. More precisely I take it he means to eschew *praeternaturalism*—appeal to forces beyond those of nature itself—for the supernatural is strictly a theological category (pertaining to the order of Divine grace). Of course, one might combine *praeter* and *supernaturalism* in explanation of the origin of rational, value-seeking agents, as in the Judaeo-Christian *imago dei* doctrine. My own view is that this indeed is the direction in which the argument leads.[16] In conclusion, however, I want to return to McDowell's account of sub-personal or primary nature to raise a doubt as to whether we are obliged to accept this and to register some surprise that he should ever have advanced it.

Earlier we read him commending the achievement of modern thought in arriving at an understanding of nature as the realm of causal regularity, and then go on to insist that this be separated sharply from the kind of intelligibility disclosed when something is placed in the space of reasons. Furthermore, opposition to the modern conception of natural science is said to represent a 'return to medieval superstition'. Certainly, if someone were to insist that nature is mind- or text-like they would need to produce some very interesting arguments to sustain that position. However it is tendentious to set up the opposition between advocates and opponents of a 'modern scientific' view in this way.

McDowell's descriptions of natural science appear reductionist. At any rate we are entitled to ask whether, on the account he favours, a properly scientific view has any place for (non-rational) natural teleologies, or whether he believes that talk of biological functions and purposes is merely a convenient *façon de parler*. Certainly it is far from obvious that purposive descriptions and explanations are out of place in science. Not only are many teleological concepts irreducible, but a commitment to the reality of objective natures, functions and associated values is presupposed by actual scientific enquiry and speculation. Functional intelligibility—not just invariable succession—is a common presupposition in the life sciences and it brings with it certain orders of value. An animal, organ or vital process admits of objective evaluation by reference to its proper operation or development as a thing of that natural sort. Far from excluding such ideas real sciences are built around them, and the picture of the world that emerges is one of living things developing in accord with intrinsic teleologies. I doubt, in fact that McDowell would want to deny this; but the tenor of his discussion of natural science suggests a preoccupation

[16] See John Haldane, 'The Mystery of Emergence', *Proceedings of the Aristotelian Society*, **96** (1996), and J. J. C. Smart and J. J. Haldane, *Atheism and Theism* (Oxford: Blackwell, 1996).

with the physico-chemical that is inappropriate in a context in which the goal is to achieve or defend a non-reductionist understanding of rational animals. What may be called for, then, is a return to the scheme and way of thinking displayed in Aristotle's *De Anima* and in Aquinas's commentary upon it. There the ultimate gap is between intellection and every other activity of animals—human and otherwise. In terms of that tradition, to comprehend the nature and activity of any living system calls for a form of *understanding* that is not reducible to explanation by reference to laws of efficient causation. Though the latter may well be apt for describing the behaviour of the matter of which living things are made. The distinctive point about abstract thought is that it calls for a unique form of understanding, the contemplation of natures, which is the preserve of *nous*, the active intellect. Suffice it to say that neither Aquinas *nor* Aristotle supposed that this could be the work of a bodily organ: *immaterial objects*; *immaterial acts*; *immaterial power*.

Vico and Metaphysical Hermeneutics

LEON POMPA

My aim in this paper is to outline and discuss Vico's conception of the nature and importance of hermeneutics. Vico never used the word 'hermeneutics' but since we would now recognize one aspect of what he was offering in his *New Science* as a theory for the interpretation and understanding of past cultures, I shall occasionally talk in terms of a theory of hermeneutics. My procedure will be to indicate first the context which led Vico to think that it was important to have a theory of hermeneutics and why he thought that such a theory ought to have a certain form. I shall then try to show that there are two forms of the theory. The first, in which hermeneutics is dependent upon metaphysics, involves certain unacceptable features which arise from the context in which he originally formulated it. The second, in which metaphysics is dependent upon hermeneutics, requires that the theory be freed from an important aspect of this context. Finally, I shall ask whether, in this second form, the theory has something to commend it to contemporary thinkers.

I

On the question of the context in which Vico came to develop a theory of hermeneutics, I shall make two brief initial points. The first is that, from a very early period in his thought, Vico was convinced that philosophy ought to include among its concerns theories which would enable us to know how to regulate societies in such a way as to be of benefit to their members.[1] He was particularly anxious to see how it could enable us to avoid the potentially catastrophic effects of certain vices to which, as individuals, he believed we were all prone. This aim clearly presupposed a view of man as vulnerable to the consequences of original sin and in making the presupposition Vico was certainly accepting a primary feature of most forms of Christian thought.[2] But it is not necessary to

[1] *On Method in Contemporary Fields of Study*, in *Vico: Selected Writings*, trans. Leon Pompa (Cambridge University Press, 1982), pp. 44–45.

[2] In his early works Vico is explicit about the theological origins of this doctrine. See *Oration VI*, in *On Humanistic Education* (*Six Inaugural Orations*), trans. Giorgio A. Pinton and Arthur W. Shippe (Ithaca: Cornell University Press, 1993), pp. 128ff.

29

be a Christian to hold that, if left to their own devices, and without the constraints which life in a structured society imposes, individuals are likely to act in such ways as to bring about their own mutual destruction.

The desire to produce a philosophy which would support and enhance the conditions of humane living lay behind Vico's relatively early rejection of Cartesianism, which, he felt, not merely offered no help in this respect but advocated a method of study which was positively inimical to it.[3] What he did find helpful was a theory which he found in Grotius's *Law of War and Peace*.[4] In this work Grotius had tried to establish the legitimacy of international law by showing that it was an extension of a rationality which evinced itself in the private law of all nations, and which was accessible to all men at all times because of their common rational nature. What Vico found attractive in this view was the notion that the apparently different legal systems of different nations could be expressions of some single set of universal principles. For this suggested that if one could gain access to them one would be in possession of a set of principles governing at least the legal framework of human conduct, from which we might be able to see how to avoid the potentially disastrous consequences of our 'fallen' natures. In fact, Vico saw this conception as a possible adaptation of Plato's theory of ideas.[5] But, impressed though he was by this aspect of Grotius's theory, Vico also had some serious criticisms of it. The most important of these, for my present purposes, was its ahistorical character. For, according to Grotius, human nature had the same rational character at all times and places, i.e., the same ability to cognize rational truths. But to Vico, who was steeped in the tradition of topics and the multitudinous classical references which this involved, this seemed wholly implausible. His readings of the great literary remnants of antiquity, particularly the writings of Lucretius and Homer, had convinced him that one could make little coherent sense of them unless one accepted that humanity had originated historically in a barbaric and largely non-rational nature, a nature which was responsible not only for any legal system which might then have obtained but also for the content and character of the whole set of cultural beliefs and the social structure of the peoples concerned. So although he was attracted to the

[3] This is one of the main points in *On Method in Contemporary Fields of Study*, Pompa, *Vico*, pp. 41–44.

[4] *The Autobiography of Giambattista Vico*, trans. Max Harold Fisch and Thomas Goddard Bergin (Cornell University Press, Great Seal Books, 1963), pp. 154–155.

[5] Ibid. p. 155.

idea that something like a Platonic pattern determined the development of the law of nations, he came to two further conclusions. First, since the nature of law could not be understood in isolation from all other aspects of a nation's life, any underlying pattern could not be confined to the legal structure but must be much more fundamental, and capable of explaining all the major aspects of public life. Secondly, any such pattern, if it were to apply to human societies, could not be a static pattern, as Plato would have conceived of it, i.e., one which assumed that human nature was everywhere the same. It must, on the contrary, be one which expressed a course of the *development* of human cultural and social practices, one based upon the conception that human nature changed through time.

II

The key points in these conceptions come together in two 'arts' which Vico proclaimed in his *First New Science* (1725). The first is what he called an art of criticism, which is basically his theory of hermeneutics.[6] The second is an art of diagnosis, i.e., an art whereby we shall be able to know where we are in the universal pattern.[7] Together, therefore, the two arts constitute the aim and the method of his science, the one establishing its practical aim, the other showing how we are to come to that knowledge which we require, if the aim is to be accomplished. Now it seems clear that a critical or hermeneutical art ought to be independent of any diagnostic art, in the sense that we ought to be able to know how to interpret and understand past cultures without *necessarily* gaining any knowledge of some underlying universal pattern. In other words, it ought to be an open question whether, as a result of our interpretations of the cultures and careers of past societies, we discover that they exhibit a universal pattern of development in relation to which we can place ourselves. It might therefore seem that the main features of Vico's hermeneutical theory can be discussed without attending to the diagnostic context in which it occurred. But this is not so, because Vico was so intent on showing that philosophy could fulfil its diagnostic function that he allowed his belief that it could do so to colour certain aspects of his hermeneutical theory. So, in order to gain a clearer idea of these aspects, and to ask whether or not they are necessary, I shall touch briefly on his diagnostic art.

[6] Paragraphs 91–93. Pompa, *Vico*, pp. 127–128.
[7] Paragraphs 90 and 391. Ibid. pp. 127 and 154–155.

There is evidence that Vico rather lost confidence in his diagnostic art, without ever quite bringing himself entirely to abandon it, as he developed the later versions of the *New Science*.[8] And, although he made considerable improvements in his art of criticism, i.e., his hermeneutical theory, in these later works, he never fully managed to free it from assumptions which derived from his original conception of a diagnostic art. So, to see what these elements were, I shall outline his diagnostic art as he stated it in the *First New Science* (1725).

In the Second Chapter of the First Book, entitled 'Meditation of a new science', he writes as follows:

All the sciences, disciplines and arts have been directed towards the perfection and regulation of man's faculties. Yet none of them has so far contained a meditation upon certain origins of the humanity of nations from which, beyond doubt, all the sciences, disciplines and arts have issued; nor, through these origins, established a certain *acme*, or state of perfection, which would enable them to judge the stages through which the humanity of nations must pass and the limits within which, like everything mortal, it must terminate. From this they might have gained a scientific grasp of the customs by which the humanity of a nation, as it develops, attains this perfect state, and those by which, as thence it wanes, it is reduced to its former condition.[9]

From here Vico goes on to discuss the content of this state of perfection or *acme*, but the point of importance for my present concern is not its content but the claim that the *acme* is part of a sequence of stages through which the humanity of a nations must pass and limits within which it must terminate *just like everything mortal*. In other words, there appears to be an *a priori* assumption that the diagnostic art can be helpful only if there is a single pattern of *birth, perfection and decay*, the features of which can be established and analysed, in the hope, as Vico later makes clear, of averting the final period of decay. Although this suggestion is first made explicit in the *First New Science*, it is not confined to this work, but reappears in the later versions, much elaborated in Vico's account of the three ages through which all nations must pass and, in particular, in his claim that, after their termination, the nations will go through the same sequence again, i.e., in his

---

[8] In the *New Science* of 1744, there is no explicit reference to the 'art of diagnosis' and the few paragraphs which Vico wrote which bear upon this conception were excluded from publication.

[9] *The New Science* (1725), paragraph 11. Pompa, op. cit., p. 23.

well-known theory of historical recurrence.[10] Many explanations, both historical and philosophical, have been offered as to why Vico thought that the pattern must have this terminal and, ultimately, cyclical form. But I shall ignore them here. The most important fact about it with regard to its influence on his theory of interpretation is that he seems to have thought that unless history had this cyclical character, the diagnostic art would serve little or no purpose. For unless the pattern were recurrent any knowledge we might have of it would be of little avail in deciding how to avoid our disastrous decline. If it were, for example, simply unilinear, our knowledge of where we now were historically would offer no guidance as to what we ought next to do, even if we believed that we were in such a state of decadence that we ought to take remedial measures. But, having come to this conclusion, Vico then built this cyclical presupposition into his theory of interpretation. Now it is clear that this was a mistake. For no *a priori* assumptions about the cyclical character of history can be treated as essential to a theory of interpretation if the sole reason for their presence lies in a desire to show that, through a diagnostic art, philosophy can have a *practical* and not merely theoretical value. To put this otherwise, we cannot assume *a priori* that history *must* have a cyclical character simply because unless it has we cannot make a successful diagnosis of our present condition. Nevertheless, this is the assumption which Vico made and which, as I shall explain, coloured aspects of his critical theory.

III

I wish now to turn to the art of criticism. Vico gives this various names but I shall start by drawing attention to his frequent description of it as a 'metaphysical' or 'philosophical' art.[11] His reason for doing so is that it involves the basic notion of a 'metaphysics of the human mind'. To understand this notion we must note Vico's constructivist ontological theory, i.e., the theory that we are collectively responsible for the creation of the whole world of human customs, practices and artefacts, i.e., the constituents of culture, as well as the structure and content of the forms of society and of the states which depend on them. Vico describes his art of criticism as 'metaphysical' in order to emphasize that, if we want

[10] *The New Science* (1744), paragraphs 1046–1096. See *The New Science of Giambattista Vico*, trans. Thomas Goddard Bergin and Max Harold Fisch (Ithaca: Cornell University Press, 1968), pp. 387–415.

[11] *The New Science* (1977), paragraph 348. Bergin and Fisch, p. 104.

33

to understand the nature of this world, we need to understand the most basic characteristics of the minds of those who have created it. This is brought out clearly in the following passage in the *First New Science*. Here, having complained about the lamentable anachronisms which abounded in scholarly interpretations of the most obscure periods of past thought and culture, Vico asks himself what assumptions we can make if we want to avoid such anachronisms and understand past thought and culture for what they were. In answer to this question, he writes:

> Hence, we must reduce ourselves to a state of extreme ignorance of all learning, human and divine, as if, for the purposes of this enquiry, there had been neither philosophers nor philologists to help us. And whoever wishes to profit from this Science must reduce himself to such a state, in order that, in the course of his meditations, he should be neither distracted nor influenced by preconceptions for long held in common. For all these doubts combined can cast no doubt whatsoever upon this one truth, which must be the first in such a science ... that the world of the gentile nations has certainly been made by men. Hence in this vast ocean of doubt, one small island appears, upon which we may stand firm: that the principles of this Science must be rediscovered within the nature of our human mind and in the power of our understanding, by elevating the metaphysics of the human mind ... to contemplate the common sense of mankind as a certain human mind of nations. ... In this way, without a single hypothesis, (for metaphysics disowns hypotheses) this Science must in fact seek its principles among the modifications of our human mind in the descendants of Cain, before the flood, and in those of Ham and Japhet, after it.[12]

I shall single out five claims here. First, it is a necessary condition of understanding past cultures that we free ourselves from (long-standing) presuppositions which give rise to anachronistic interpretations. Secondly, if we ask ourselves what presuppositions would be legitimate in such an enquiry, we must start from the fact that the world of the nations has been made by men. Thirdly, if we wish to understand this world, we must seek its principles within the human mind. Fourthly, however, this mind, as the later part of the passage shows, is not the mind of individual man. It is what Vico calls 'the common sense of mankind', which he also refers to as 'a certain human mind of nations'. But, fifthly and finally, this is, in some sense a *metaphysical* enquiry requiring knowledge of the modifications of the human mind. And, being

[12] Paragraph 40. Pompa, *Vico*, p. 99.

'metaphysical', it involves no hypotheses, for 'metaphysics disowns hypotheses'.

There is a clear, if not wholly uncontentious, line of reasoning here. A difficulty arises, however, when, towards the end of the passage, having announced that we need a theory about the nature of our communal mind—what he calls 'the common sense of mankind'—Vico announces that this is, in some sense a 'metaphysical' enquiry and that, because it is metaphysical, it is also unhypothetical, since, as he says, 'metaphysics disowns hypotheses'. I say that this gives rise to a difficulty because one might think that in an enquiry in which the key to a correct understanding of the past will lie in the discovery of the modifications of our human mind, the process of discovery ought to be empirical and to involve the use of hypotheses. But I shall leave this point without further comment for, although it is important to note that Vico never abandoned the claim that a 'metaphysics of the human mind' was essential to his science, he came to have a different view about the role of hypotheses. So, I wish now to turn to some more specific conceptions involved in Vico's theory of interpretation, particularly as it was developed in the *Third New Science*.

IV

In the *Third New Science* Vico distinguishes a number of principal aspects of his science, upon which I shall comment in a moment. But first I want to mention what I believe to be the central methodological concept underlying his whole project: that of a mutual collaboration of philosophy and philology. Philosophy, Vico maintains, should be concerned with the true, which is always universal and necessary; philology, on the other hand, is concerned with the particular or 'certain'. So the proposal for a collaboration between philosophy and philology entails a relationship between the universal and the particular. The idea, as he envisages it, is that philosophy should be responsible for a theory of the development of cultures and societies which claims to be universal and necessary and historians should proceed to interpret past evidence in the light of this, thus bestowing over-all coherence on their specific historical accounts and freeing them from the arbitrariness and anachronisms of which Vico accused them. On this conception, therefore, metaphysical theory provides the key to hermeneutical enquiry. And in the light of this it is not difficult to see why one aspect of Vico's thought seems to involve the notion that the fundamental underlying factors in the world of empirical history lie in certain features, the developing structure of mind, which have the character of a developmental Platonic form.

Now while such a conception may have seemed attractive to an early eighteenth-century thinker, it is clear that modern philosophers are unlikely to be attracted to the suggestion that, if no use is to be made of hypotheses, philosophy must produce some *a priori* theory of mind from which to derive the principles for the interpretation of past human activities. The problems here are obvious. One, of course, is where, or how, the philosopher is to get this theory of mind, particularly if it requires access to something like a Platonic form. Another is that it makes it difficult to see the point of the historian's activity, for whatever he comes up with will only be a detailed specification of what the *a priori* theory spells out more generally. Moreover, if the practical point of all this is to enable us gain the knowledge required to diagnose our present condition, we could get that simply on the strength of the philosophical theory. Nevertheless, although I accept these criticisms, many of Vico's remarks only make sense on the assumption that this was his theory. So I wish, for the moment, to disregard them and to explain more fully how the theory was supposed to work.

The first point to mention is Vico's conception of what he calls the 'ideal eternal history'. This, as it turns out, is a sort of ideal narrative which outlines the principal features of the development of the culture and society of a nation, *if this were dependent solely upon its internal nature*. Vico describes it in various degrees of detail. At the most basic level, there are three forms of mind. The first is the poetic or imaginative form, through which primitive man created the first fantastic world of human belief and the world of social practices and class structure which follow from those beliefs. For the sake of my later argument, I need here to make brief reference to certain features of this world. As Vico describes it, poetic man has enormous powers of imagination and relatively poor powers of reasoning. His mind works largely by spreading his view of himself over everything around him. Thus he imagines the physical universe to be a huge living body, and natural phenomena, such as thunder and lightning, to be the language of this being. And since poetic man has a cruel, retributive nature, this God—the Jove who, Vico claims, will naturally arise in the consciousness of all the gentile nations at their originating stages—will be equally cruel and vengeful. Given this belief, the need will arise for a class of priests who can read the auspices and explain what this God demands of people as sacrifice to placate his anger and to make amends for their sins, once, in accordance with conditions which Vico specifies, a humanizing sense of sin begins to arise.

Moreover, this class division will take on a political character because the priestly classes, as intermediaries between Jove and man, will develop a position of power *vis-à-vis* those who are dependent upon their mediation. The world of poetic man is followed, in the 'ideal eternal history', by the world of heroic man, the world exemplified, in Homer, by Achilles, Hector and so on. This is a world in which, although there is great cruelty, there is a punctilious regard for adherence to certain customary codes of honour and for conformity to the letter, rather than the spirit, of the law. Moreover, the political structure, in which the heroes will dominate, derives from the belief that they are descended from unions of gods with priestesses and goddesses with priests, i.e., unions of the divine and the sacerdotal.

The third stage in the 'ideal eternal history' is the world of 'fully developed human reason',[13] the world of, or just before, Vico's own day, a world in which human nature is 'intelligent and hence modest, benign, and reasonable, recognizing for laws, conscience, reason and duty'.[14]

Thereafter, however, there is a rapid deterioration in the conditions of humane life, because of the inherent viciousness in individual man, which becomes dominant when there is only reason rather than customary belief to constrain it, leading either to the end of the life of the nation in civil war and a recurrence of the whole cycle or to its conquest by other healthier nations.

Vico outlines this sequence in different ways, both diachronically and synchronically. I have mentioned only the development of the class structure of the poetic age, which follows from his theory of the poetic mind, but he argues for an ascending series of dependencies at each diachronic stage, which run from the customs of a nation, through its natural law to its kind of government. Parallel to, and interwoven with this, there is an appropriate kind of language and of characters; and, again, one of jurisprudence, authority and legal judgment. At each stage in the diachronic sequence, therefore, there is a harmony among its institutions, a harmony which Vico traces to the main characteristics of the dominant mode of mind.[15]

To complete this picture, I wish to note two points. If we consider first the diachronic sequence, what seems to govern its character is the development of mind from being almost wholly imaginative to being almost wholly rational. Indeed, it is to the

[13] *The New Science* (1744), paragraph 924. Bergin and Fisch, p. 338.
[14] Ibid. paragraph 918. Bergin and Fisch, p. 336.
[15] Ibid. paragraph 915. Bergin and Fisch, p. 336.

37

vices of the over-abstract intellect that Vico turns to explain the rather rapid termination of the sequence. But we can see how this notion of an increasing rationality works by considering just one transition, that from the world of heroic man to the fully human world. The political superiority of the heroes lay, Vico believed, in their claims to semi-divine lineage. And via the synchronic dependencies, this belief is enshrined in the law, giving rise to vast inequalities of status under the law. What explains its collapse is just the development of a capacity for critical reasoning on the part of the general public sufficient to see that this claim is false. But as soon as the claim that the nobility is of semi-divine birth is seen to be false, all the political and legal inequalities which depend upon it become challengeable, leading, more or less inexorably, to the need for a different class structure, different laws and a different kind of state and of government. Now all of this, in various degrees of specification, and dependent to some extent on Vico's own interests and knowledge, is included in the story which constitutes the 'ideal eternal history'. So if the 'ideal eternal history' is a Platonic pattern, as the words 'ideal' and 'eternal' suggest, it is a vast and complex pattern, comprehending almost all of the main constitutive features of the development of a nation.

The second point, however, is that there are some aspects of it which suggest that it cannot be a Platonic pattern in quite the sense in which Plato thought of the forms. This can best be seen by noting, if we attend just to the first stage, that Vico could not work out the account which he offers without making certain assumptions which can hardly have any necessity at all. He needs, for example, to make the assumption that there was thunder and lightning. Now he is quite explicit about this assumption and defends it by some very sketchy appeals to science.[16] But it does not matter whether we believe that he has adequately supported it. The important point is that references to the physical world are included in his 'ideal eternal history'. For this means, of course, that the 'ideal eternal history' cannot be a Platonic idea in the traditional sense, i.e., something to which we can gain access by reason alone.

Setting this aside for the moment, however, we can now see how this conception of a metaphysical hermeneutics is supposed to work. The actual history of all nations is assumed to be an instance of a developmental metaphysical pattern, with a sequence of kinds of mentality at its base. It is not claimed, of course, that everything about the life of a nation will depend upon conditions involved in this pattern. One of Vico's own examples of an exception to this is

[16] Ibid. paragraph 377. Bergin and Fisch, p. 117.

the different sounds and words involved in the different languages, for the explanation of which he turns to the different physical and climatic circumstances in which actual nations find themselves. Nor is it claimed that the careers of nations will be identical in all other respects. Actual nations exist in the real world, the world of contingency. Hence the degree to which their histories will differ will depend upon the degree to which these contingencies impede the development of the pattern which springs from their internal nature. Famines, floods, conquests, etc., can all divert the actual course which the career of a nation takes from that which is spelled out in the 'ideal eternal history'. Nevertheless, the first thing the interpreter should do, in the attempt to recover the meanings of past languages, systems of belief and, thence, to reconstruct the character of past practices and deeds, is to assume that the 'ideal eternal history' holds and to interpret the historical evidence in accordance with it. It may be, of course, that it will just not work out with regard to the range of things with which the 'ideal eternal history' is concerned but then, and only then, the task becomes that of establishing the contingent reasons why this is so.

It is useful to make two points in connection with this conception. First, although it is a purely contingent matter that different nations should have different forms of words, there ought, if there is a common pattern of mental development, to be a common pattern to the development of the concepts, beliefs and, in general, the wisdom involved in common sense. This implies at least the possibility of a 'common mental language', shared by all, or nearly all, nations at the appropriate stages in their development. And Vico explicitly asserted that there must be such a language and engaged on beginning a 'dictionary' specifying its contents.[17] These would consist in the key conceptions which arise in and through the general development of the life of the nation. Similarly, one might expect that there would be a shared popular wisdom and, again, Vico claimed, in the light of this assumption, that one could construe the proverbs of the different nations to be making the same points.

All this points to a certain conception of metaphysical hermeneutics. The basic idea is simple. It is that philosophy can construct a metaphysics of the human mind and, thence, an 'ideal eternal history'. This will give us the framework for the interpretation of past beliefs and societies, including some for periods very remote from our own, leading ultimately to the construction of continuous and coherent accounts of the careers of actual nations.

[17] *The New Science* (1725), paragraphs 387–388, Pompa, *Vico*, pp. 151–153. *The New Science* (1744), paragraph 143, Bergin and Fisch, p. 64.

V

But, as mentioned earlier, this conception of the relation of metaphysics to hermeneutics must now seem very implausible. So I wish to turn to the other conception of this relation to be found in Vico, which gives us a different view of metaphysical hermeneutics and one which is, I believe, much more plausible. A crucial point in the above conception is the idea, stated in the *First New Science*, that 'metaphysics disowns hypotheses'. This suggests a conception in which metaphysical knowledge determines *a priori* the outcome of empirical, historical interpretation. In the *Third New Science*, however, Vico appears, at least partially, to modify this view. Most of the conceptions mentioned above are still retained, including the suggestions that the art of criticism is 'metaphysical' and that it involves the idea of a 'metaphysics of the human mind', the concept of an 'ideal eternal history' outlining a necessary sequence of forms of consciousness and society, and the idea of a dictionary of a common mental language. Nevertheless, there is a change in the way in which Vico talks about the relation between philosophy and philology. For whereas he had earlier claimed that 'metaphysics disowns hypotheses', he now describes the relationship between philosophy and philology as involving a process of 'thinking and seeing'.[18] Whether this really points to a different conception of metaphysics depends, of course, upon the character of the thinking and seeing. But when we turn to some of his concrete interpretative proposals, it becomes apparent that there is a genuine difference because *hypotheses* now have a role in the procedure.

We might begin by noting that Vico is prepared to present two of his most famous interpretative claims—that the Laws of the Twelve Tables were not, as previously believed, imported into Rome from Greece but represented the customs of the peoples of Latium which derived from a much earlier period than that in which the Romans recorded them; and that the Homeric poems were civil histories of ancient Greek customs—as fruitful hypotheses, later to be shown to be true in fact, for understanding the ancient law of the gentes of Latium and of the peoples of ancient Greece.[19] To see how this is to be done, however, a helpful example occurs at a point where he is discussing a suggestion about the meaning of key concepts involved in the Publilian Law. He writes:

> If we read further into the history of Rome in the light of this hypothesis we shall find by a thousand tests that it gives support

[18] *The New Science* (1744), paragraph 163, Bergin and Fisch, p. 67.
[19] Ibid. paragraphs 154–157, Bergin and Fisch, p. 65.

and consistency to all the things narrated therein that have hitherto lacked a common foundation and a proper and particular connection among themselves ... whereof this hypothesis should be accepted as true. However, if we consider well, this is not so much a hypothesis as a truth meditated in idea which later will be shown with the aid of authority [i.e., with the aid of philology] to be the fact. ... This hypothesis gives us also the history of all the other cities of the world in times we have so far despaired of knowing. This, then, is an instance of an ideal eternal history traversed in time by the histories of all nations.[20]

The suggestion here is that the proposal is initially a hypothesis which should be accepted because it satisfies the demands of coherence and continuity demanded in understanding part of the constitutional history of a particular nation. Then, upon reflection, it will be seen to be more than a hypothesis; it will be seen to be a truth meditated in idea and, with the aid of philological support, to be true in fact. Next, but presumably with the aid of a much wider range of comparative philological support, the hypothesis provides a truth about all other cities (at a similar stage of development). This, then, makes it is an instance of an 'ideal eternal history'.

This sequence of claims suggests a different relationship between philosophy and philology. An interpretative proposal now starts life as a specific hypothesis about a specific historical event, in this case a city, at a certain point in its career. It then turns out to be true both in idea and in fact. Remembering that philosophy deals with the true, this means that, having by dint of its first measure of success, gained the right to philosophical consideration, the latter shows it to be wholly intelligible in itself while philology shows it, as such, to illuminate the evidence. Then, by a repetition of these procedures, i.e., by hypothesizing it as a principle applying to all other cities at a similar point in their careers, and finding that it is confirmed philologically, it becomes a truth about them all. Finally, that which is true of all cities, is an item in an 'ideal eternal history', i.e., in the most universal pattern which our understanding of the past can reach.

This is, admittedly, a broad reading of the passage, but it is supported by Vico's method of argument in many other passages. His general procedure is not to move from the metaphysical to the empirical but from the empirical to the metaphysical. The sources of his 'hypotheses' vary enormously, dependent upon the subject matter with which he is concerned. In some cases, he often either simply alights on some general or empirical claim made by, or

[20] Ibid. paragraph 114, Bergin and Fisch, p. 57.

attributed to, a respectable ancient or modern author, or, as in the above case, provides an alternative of his own, which coheres better with other interpretative claims. Where he is concerned with the developmental structure of mind, as in the case of the story of poetic man, he draws upon relatively familiar points about the mental development of children. Where he is concerned with the principles of the development of language, he adduces a theory about the natural development of the poetic tropes. But no matter what the source of his suggestion, his procedure is to attempt to incorporate it first as an element in the particular history into which he is enquiring, then, suitably modified, as an element in all histories and finally as an element in the 'ideal eternal history'. This procedure is basic, for example, to the whole of his mythological interpretations, according to which every nation had its own Jove, its own Solon, its own Romulus and so on, each of whom is seen as a poetic character standing for the same sets of things—God, civic wisdom, the laws of social classes—in the different nations.[21] His point here is that if we treat these ancient figures as poetic characters, corresponding to a type of thinking appropriate to a certain stage of the development of mind, rather than as real historical characters, we shall be in a better position to produce a consistent and coherent theory for the interpretation of the various myths in which they appear.

On this view, then, a proposition may well, indeed probably must, have metaphysical status, to play its full role in interpretation. But we cannot establish this status by *a priori* reasoning. What we can establish by such reasoning is its internal conceptual coherence and the way in which, given the theory of human nature it presupposes, certain effects must follow. But beyond this, its metaphysical status can be established only by demonstrating its indispensable role in a universal theory of interpretation.

Finally, however, it must be noted that, in proceeding in this way, Vico draws upon elements of our own modes of imagining, feeling and thinking which, although they now occupy a very different place in the general structure of our understanding, are familiar enough to give us access to principles from which we can work out and understand how they can function to provide quite different modes of understanding. Poetic thinking, for example, as we currently understand it, is largely a peripheral mode of thought. But it involves the use of tropes and metaphors and, through our familiarity with these, we can come to understand a mode of thought, that of poetic man, in which these were central and dominant. So the understanding which Vico's theory of

[21] Ibid. paragraphs 412–423, Bergin and Fisch, pp. 132–136.

hermeneutics will provide will have the methodology of a science but the content of more humane forms of thought proper to our understanding of ourselves.

All this, of course, is an enormous undertaking. Vico himself saw it as requiring that he should produce a universal history and, although he never claimed to have produced such a history, he thought that it could be achieved by using the principles of his hermeneutical art. Hence, he listed it as one of the seven principal aspects of his science.[22]

VI

It is time now to consider the merits of this second conception of a metaphysical hermeneutics. At first sight they may not appear to be strong, given that it still seems to involve the notions of a Platonic form, albeit knowable only as the terminus of enquiry and, en route to that, a universal history, neither of which are likely to be particularly popular today. So I would like to conclude by some more positive remarks on its behalf.

The main point for which I want to argue on this second conception is that if there is to be a science of anything, including interpretation, some systematic or universal principles must be invoked to eradicate the possibility of idiosyncratic or arbitrary claims being passed off as truths. In the case of the natural sciences this is hardly in dispute, since such principles are already in use. In the case of theories of interpretation, however, this is far from being so. Many have argued that the whole notion of a theory of interpretation for past cultures is misguided and that one can get little further than accepting the deliverences of a general capacity for empathetic insight. Suggestions along these lines have, indeed, been imputed to Vico by a number of commentators, albeit mistakenly, in my view. But it seems clear that interpretations cannot be left on this individual and subjective basis if they are to warrant any claims to truth. And the only way in which we can give them such warrant is by involving them in an attempt to apply a set of principles with something like the universality of those of the natural sciences. They do not, of course, need to hold without exception. But they do need to aspire to a broad basis of application and, should they prove inapplicable in some cases, as Vico himself allowed, for this fact to be susceptible of explanation. This, I suggest, is what Vico was trying to do in the later theory which I have attributed to him.

But, the objection might be raised, if there is anything in this

[22] Ibid. paragraph 399, Bergin and Fisch, p. 126.

idea, why is it that nobody has so far come up with anything which even remotely looks like a universal history, let alone an 'ideal eternal history'? My first suggestion to meet this difficulty is that it is not necessary on this conception that we should assume that it must ever ultimately be successful. I would prefer to think of it more as a method of reaching an ideal but possibly unattainable limit. Rather like a Kantian ideal of pure reason, it indicates a direction in which research should proceed, rather than establishing a feature of the world. Unlike a Kantian ideal, however, the direction involves the attempt to formulate *substantive* universal principles of interpretation. And if it is wondered what is the point of trying to establish substantive accounts of universal features of human development which may never be successful, I can only reply that I cannot see how, in this respect, it differs from the natural sciences, the point of which does not seem to be in question. The effort will at least take us to the limits of what we can achieve. It is not clear, however, that this line of argument adequately meets the point in question. But it will be easier to see whether or not it does after considering another objection. This concerns our warrant for assuming that there is a common developmental essence to different societies. Why, it may be asked, when attempting to understand our own past, do we need to make this assumption? To meet this objection it is necessary to distinguish between the assumption that there *must* be such an essence and the assumption that there *may* be such an essence. The former, I believe, cannot be justified. It must always be possible that we shall run up against aspects of the past, forms of culture or society, which simply defy comprehension. But in these cases, if the reason is that nothing that enables us to understand what we understand about ourselves is of any help, we must simply accept that we have reached the limits of our powers of understanding, the limits of what Vico himself described as 'the series of possibilities which we are allowed to understand'.[23] But it does not follow that, because the assumption that there *must* be such a common nature cannot be justified, the assumption that there *may* be one is equally unjustified. For this is tantamount to the assumption that there *cannot* be such a nature, and if we are to assume that there cannot be such a nature, which may be either wholly or partially captured in the substantive hermeneutical principles we employ, it is difficult to see why we should ever expect to avoid arbitrary and anachronistic interpretations, the plausibility of which will rest solely on the familiarity of the mode of thought which we purport to find in

[23] Ibid. Paragraph 345, Bergin and Fisch, p. 103.

them. I do not, of course, wish to deny that, on Vico's second theory, some degree of familiarity will be found. That is something upon which his theory depends. But familiarity is not sufficient for truth and if it is treated as such it cannot fail to generate arbitrary and unreconcilable interpretations. The method which I am attributing to Vico has the merit of recognizing this defect and seeking to remedy it.

But even if this is granted, it may still seem problematic why, if Vico is right, we have not reached even reached universal histories, let alone some Platonic form in the shape of an 'ideal eternal history'. One possible reply to the objection would be to claim, surely truly, that nobody has yet tried seriously to apply the second Vichian theory to the whole of the human past, or to the whole of past evidence. But this reply would supply the grounds for its own rejection, since the reason why nobody has yet tried to apply Vichian principles to 'the whole of the past' or to 'the whole of past evidence' is that these expressions lack any specifiable reference.

Rather than try to meet the objection by some such argument, it is more important, I believe, to concede that it is in principle correct but to show that, despite Vico's talk of a universal history, his theory does not imply the possibility of a reference for such conceptions as 'the whole of the human past' or 'the whole of past evidence'. This, in fact, is not difficult to do. For it does not follow from the conception which I have outlined that there needs to be a finite terminus to the procedure advocated. All that is required is that we proceed as if there may be. Doing this, of course, involves making some assumptions of the sort which Vico made. But these assumptions can be modified or indeed, abandoned, for a number of reasons. One obvious reason, of course, would be if they failed to reach the degree of universal applicability attainable by other sets of assumptions. Another, however, would be that our general theories about the nature of nations or of the causes of developments of consciousness might change as a result of ongoing intellectual changes in our own period, leading to different substantive hypotheses. The assumption which Vico initially made, for example, that human nature *must* have a finite essence, upon which his circular view of history may have depended, would now seem highly contentious. But that assumption depended, at least partly, upon his unwillingness to accept that his results might fail to provide the basis for a successful diagnosis of, and programme of recovery from, the ills of our present condition. But, as I have pointed out, it is simply a mistake to assume that a hermeneutical enquiry must be organized in such a way as to presuppose diagnostic success and that there therefore must be a finite developmental essence to human nature. So that particular assumption can certainly be abandoned without damage to this conception of hermeneutical theory. Indeed, it would need to be, if the conception is to provide a fruitful basis for our understanding of past cultures.

Ultimately, therefore, the thesis of metaphysical hermeneutics does not require that there must be such an essence. It requires only that we be prepared to admit that there may be one, that we have an acceptable way of devising hypotheses and theories, drawing upon aspects of our self-understanding, as to what it may be like, and that we conduct our hermeneutical enquiries on the sort of universal and comparative basis adequate to the pursuit of such a possibility.

Three Major Originators of the Concept of *Verstehen*: Vico, Herder, Schleiermacher

ROGER HAUSHEER

I

It is generally agreed by historians of modern thought that, at the end of the nineteenth century and the beginning of the twentieth, philosophers in the German-speaking world identified and defined a type or species of knowledge whose peculiar independent status had hitherto been largely overlooked. It was developed, clarified, and, with a sharpened awareness of its unique possibilities, made to work in practice above all by Dilthey, Windelband, Rickert and their numerous followers; and, to a degree, also by Max Weber. The general name by which it was, and is, most often referred to is '*Verstehen*'—understanding. It has to be admitted that it was from the first, and remains to this day, a highly problematic and hotly disputed concept. Positivists, materialists, behaviourists and monists of all kinds—all those whose ideal is a single structure of organized systematic knowledge—have tended to view it with deep suspicion, and even to deny its existence altogether, claiming that it is wholly illusory and doomed to disappear before the inevitable advance of positive scientific method. However that may be, it will not be my purpose in this paper to enter into these difficult controversies. It may indeed be that no watertight definition of it is possible; that its putative boundaries with other forms or types of knowledge are vague and shifting; and even that there is no ultimate discontinuity in principle between it and the knowledge we gain from other spheres of research and investigation. Nevertheless, although the task I set myself here will be largely historical, aiming at uncovering the roots of this idea in three seminal thinkers of an earlier period—Vico, Herder, and Schleiermacher (who are still, and especially the last, too little regarded in the English-speaking world)—I hope that in the course of what I say it will become plain that, whatever its correct philosophical analysis, some such distinction does exist; that it deserves to be considered with the serious sympathetic understanding of which it is the true originator and proponent; and, moreover, that it may be rich in implications for some aspects of our peculiar modern predicament. The burning contemporary relevance of the issues raised by any discussion of this subject will, I think, emerge very plainly.

At this point someone might well ask: What is the value of investigating the remote harbingers and precursors of this peculiar conception of understanding when it is available in its full-blown version in the thinkers I have already mentioned, especially since it is these that have been advanced, attacked, and defended with such sophistication, learning, and vigour, at any rate in the German world, in the first decades of this century. To this objection there are three possible answers.

The first will be very familiar to all historians of ideas, and indeed to students of individual philosophical problems generally. Put simply, it is that when a new concept, insight, or outlook emerges for the first time, it is in response to some urgently felt intellectual or spiritual need, and what it attacks and what it defends is of vital importance. The main lines of what is so vividly seen and felt tend to be starker and more simple and as yet uncluttered by the vast subsequent proliferation of sophisticated analysis, controversy, and debate. We can best recapture them in their freshness and simplicity by returning to their source.

My second answer will be at first sight rather less familiar, and I can only hope that by the end of this paper it will have become perhaps a little clearer and more plausible. For if the philosophers and intellectual and cultural historians most closely associated with *Verstehen* are right, one of the major defining features of their doctrine of knowledge is that it cannot be assimilated to any body or structure of systematic timeless truth, but that the sole avenue to it is necessarily historical. It is not just that we are dealing with the unique and the particular at specific times and places, which we must enter and with which we must empathize, but rather that new visions and conceptions of life, or of aspects of life, and the entire complex web of concepts and categories in which they are embodied, can only be fully understood genetically. They are part of a continuous and ceaselessly evolving historical pattern. To grasp any notion like *Verstehen,* therefore, it is not enough to settle for a ready-made definition of it, the late product of much refinement and purification; rather, we must view it in its growth and development and its scope for potential change.

My third justification, which is closely related to the second point, is that any genuine revolution of the spirit of the kind I believe we are dealing with will not yield all at once its myriad implications. It will prove an inexhaustible quarry of new and illuminating insights, aperçus, and intuitions about all or many aspects of human life. This is a point I shall return to in the final section of this paper.

II

The earliest sustained attack on universal, rationalist schemas came from the eighteenth-century Neapolitan thinker, Giambattista Vico, who in the course of it was the first to uncover the special properties of empathetic understanding. His principal enemy was the antihistorical Descartes, for whom history was a farrago of gossip, superstition, and travellers' tales. Vico, a tortured genius born before his time, struggled all his life to express a handful of revolutionary ideas about man, history, and society. The significance of his doctrines has become apparent only in the centuries since his death, and some of the most important among them are coming into their own for the first time in the present day. He was probably the first thinker ever to formulate explicitly the thesis that there is no universal, immutable human nature; he revived the ancient doctrine that men truly understand only what they themselves have made, and gave it a revolutionary twist by applying it to history: we understand historical processes, which everywhere bear the stamp of human will, ideals, and purposes, as it were from 'inside', by a species of sympathetic insight, in a way in which we cannot understand the 'senseless', 'external' operations of nature, which we did not ourselves make. Building perhaps on the embryonic insights of French jurists and universal historians, he virtually created the concept of a culture, all the activities of which bear a distinctive mark and evince a common pattern; he developed the closely connected notion that a culture progresses through an intelligible succession of phases of development which are not connected with each other by mechanical causality, but are interrelated as expressions of the continuously evolving purposive activities of men; he saw human activities as being in the first place forms of self-expression, conveying a total vision of the world; and, perhaps most exciting of all—and certainly what is most relevant here—he created the notion of a new type of knowledge, the reconstructive imagination, or *fantasia*, the knowledge we acquire of other men at other times and places through entering into their general outlooks, their ways of seeing themselves and their goals—a form of knowledge which is neither wholly contingent nor deducible *a priori*. The feeling of a kind of inner, almost aesthetic necessity, which accompanies this knowledge will

49

be of especial importance when we come to look at Schleiermacher.

For Vico, the outlook, activities, and goals of men are necessarily those of a particular stage of social and cultural development. Each stage in what he calls the *storia ideale eterna*[1] is linked to those before and after in an unaltering cyclical pattern. Since the earlier stages of the creative historical process are an essential part of our own origins, we are able to recreate and understand the past by discovering its potentialities in our own minds. But unlike idealist metaphysicians such as Hegel, who believe that nothing of value gets lost in the transition from one cultural phase to another, and unlike rationalist thinkers who believe that all values must by definition fit neatly into the completed jigsaw of the final perfect solution to all human problems, Vico takes a less optimistic view. Social development and cultural change bring absolute losses as well as gains. Some forms of valuable experience may disappear forever, a unique, integral part of the vanished world that gave them birth, not to be replaced by similar forms of equal value. Hence the paramount importance of empathetic understanding if we are to grasp the full potentialities of the human spirit. Inspired singers, of whom Homer is for Vico the most memorable example, in all their primitive vigour and concrete imaginative force, cannot—conceptually cannot—spring from the same stage of culture as the critical philosophers, with their pared down prose and bloodless abstractions. Thus for Vico the idea of perfection, of an order in which all true values will be fully realized, is excluded not for purely empirical reasons—ignorance, human weakness, lack of technical means—but because it is conceptually incoherent *a priori*.

It is in this connection that it is very fruitful to consider Vico's seminal distinction between two very different types of human knowledge,[2] which start from radically different presuppositions, and lead to profoundly divergent results. In Vico's view, the entire realm of 'external', non-human, physical nature is not continuous with the 'internal' human world of morality, art, language, forms of expression, thought, and feeling. Corresponding to these two distinct provinces, there are two independent methods of inquiry: there is what Vico terms *scienza* or knowledge per *caussas*, the only perfect knowledge of which we are capable, that, namely, of the products of human creation—mathematics, music, poetry, law—which are intelligible through and through precisely because they

---

[1] *The New Science of Giambattista Vico,* trans. Thomas Goddard Bergin and Max Harold Frisch, revised ed. (New York, 1968), paragraph 349.

[2] *De antiquissima italorum sapientia,* Chapter 3. *Opere,* ed. Roberto Parenti (Naples, 1972), Vol. I, p. 203.

are artefacts of the human mind; and there is *coscienza*, the knowledge of the external world acquired by the observer from 'outside', in terms of causal uniformities and compresences, which, because it can only tell us how things are or happen, but never why or for what intelligible reason or in pursuit of what purpose, must forever contain an area of impenetrable opaqueness. Vico's great originality consisted in applying the category of *scienza*—that which we know perfectly because we make it—to human history which men themselves 'make', and in instituting an 'anthropological historicism'[3] which required a systematic science of mind which would be identical with the history of its development and growth. This could be traced only through investigation of the changing symbols—words, monuments, works of art, laws and customs, and the like—in which mind expressed itself. This is essentially an historical and genetic approach. Memory and imagination, and the potential dispositions of one's own mind—most of which lie unactivated—provide the basic tools of understanding, upon which all humane studies ultimately rest: we know at first hand what it is to feel fear, love, hate, to belong to a family or a nation, to understand a facial expression or a human situation or a joke, to appreciate a work of art, to form and live by ideals, and to have an inexhaustible (and developing) variety of other kinds of immediate 'inner' experience besides.

This type of 'direct' knowledge is neither inductive nor deductive nor hypothetico-deductive. It is *sui generis* and can be described and analysed only in terms of itself. It cannot be yielded by nor translated into a Cartesian or a Newtonian or any similar system which correlates things and events from 'outside' in terms of causal regularities. This we know from our own first-hand experience: a familiar activity or an intimate aspect of our lives, which we have hitherto seen from inside in terms of freely chosen human goals and aspirations, can be alienated from us by being, as it were, 'objectified': it is suddenly seen as alien and external to ourselves, a causal product of forces beyond our control—sociological, biological, physical. And the converse of this: an activity or a work of art or a person, a code of rules or an institution, can become an intimate part of ourselves because, by a process of imaginative penetration, we see it from 'inside' in the light of autonomous human ends and values. This is the ill-defined and shifting boundary where rational explanation in terms of human ideals and intentions come into contact (and conflict) with causal explanation in terms of the 'senseless' non-human regularities of

---

[3] The term is Isaiah Berlin's, 'Vico's Concept of Knowledge', *Against the Current* (London: Hogarth Press, 1979), p. 116.

51

physical nature. It has been the scene of battles in the past; and it is likely to be the scene of even greater battles in the future.

The species of knowing uncovered by Vico was the seed of the doctrines of *Einfühlung* and *Verstehen* later developed by Herder, and after him by the great German historicists, Dilthey, Troeltsch, Windelband, Meinecke, and also Max Weber, and it had implications for epistemology and the philosophy of mind which were the major preoccupations of a great deal of nineteenth-century thought.

III

These Vichian themes, though there is no evidence of direct (or even indirect) transmission, were taken up by Johann Gottfried Herder, who was born in 1744 in Mohrungen in East Prussia, one of the most backward provinces of Germany. It was also the home of Kant and the irrationalist antinomian Hamann, both of whom had a great influence on him. Like them, he came from a strictly Pietist home, and the cultivation of inwardness and the inner life was strong from the start. Indeed, Dilthey goes out of his way to stress the importance of Pietism as one of the major sources of the German backlash against the European—above all the French— Enlightenment. Herder's environment early filled him with an almost unbearable sense of constriction and confinement, and a reactive longing for life, movement, colour. His two favourite slogans, repeated throughout his life, were 'Heart! Warmth! Blood! Humanity! Life!'[4] and 'I feel! I am!'.[5] His gravestone bears the simple inscription 'Licht, Liebe, Leben'[6]—'Light, Love, Life'. These were the central values he consciously and untiringly pursued throughout his life against the dominant tendencies of his age. In all this he is a representative of the *Sturm und Drang* movement, of which he was an inspirer and an integral part.

His attitude to the French Enlightenment and its German counterpart was ambivalent. He possessed a deep and detailed knowledge of recent scientific developments, especially in biology and physiology and his equivocation between a naturalistic and a religious interpretation of the world, with the former always predominating, marked a genuine clash within him between two incompatible traditions. And it is perhaps out of this unresolved

---

[4] J, G. Herder, *Sämtliche Werke*, ed. B. Supham (Berlin, 1877–1913), Vol, V, p. 538.

[5] Ibid. Vol. VIII, p. 96.

[6] Rudolf Haym, *Herder* (Berlin: Akademieverlag, 1954), Vol. II, p. 876.

tension that there sprang one of his deepest and most fruitful insights into what marks man off from the rest of the natural order and the consequent awareness of a unique type of knowledge—a mode of empathy and understanding—which is necessary if we are to make sense of human history, of man and his works in the largest sense. But even this and related insights never, despite what some critics have claimed, altered his espousal of the basic universal humanitarianism of Enlightenment—one of the words most often used in his writings is 'Humanität'. What he rebelled against were the scientistic sociological assumptions of the philosophers and Encyclopédistes of Paris. He believed that if we are to understand human beings, their activities and productions, then we must understand them in their individuality and development. For this a capacity is required which he was the first to call 'Einfühlung': one must 'feel oneself into everything.'[7] This meant 'entering' or 'feeling your way into' the subject before you, a total outlook, the individual character of a person or an artistic movement, a literature, a social organization or institution, a people or nation, a culture or a period of history. To seek to reduce these in their ineffable uniqueness to functional abstract elements in a causal theory was criminal folly. Equally odious to him were the absolute criteria of progress prevalent in the Paris of Voltaire, Diderot, Helveticus, Holbach, and Condorcet, for whom there can only be one universal civilization, of which now Athens, now Rome, now Florence, now Paris, realize the fullest flowering. Measured against these, all other places and peoples were at best approximations to the timeless universal standard, at worst grotesque botched specimens. In one of the most characteristic works of his early most 'relativistic' phase—*Auch eine Philosophie der Geschichte* ('Yet another Philosophy of History')—he enunciated what was to be his most fundamental and revolutionary principle: 'Every nation has its own inner centre of happiness, as every sphere its own centre of gravity'.[8] It is this that the historian and philosopher must grasp, enter into, appreciate. If you wish to understand the Bible, he says, which is the national poem of the Jews, a people of shepherds and tillers of the soil, then 'be a shepherd among shepherds ... an oriental among the primitive dwellers of the East'.[9] To understand the Icelandic sagas embark on a voyage in the Northern seas. The essential thing is to see all men's works as a form of action expressive of the total world of which they form a part. Above all, to grade peoples, cultures, civilizations,

[7] Ibid. Vol. V, p. 503.
[8] Ibid. Vol. V, p. 509.
[9] Ibid. Vol. X, p. 14.

to award marks for progress, testifies to a hopeless spiritual blindness. Hence Herder's intense concern to preserve primitive cultures which afford a unique window on the world, his love of all genuine expressions of the free creative human spirit, of all works of the imagination for what they are in themselves, and not for their ability to meet alien criteria outside themselves. This is what Sir Isaiah Berlin has identified as one of Herder's most original contributions to modern thought, the doctrine of expressionism. Art, morality, custom, religion, national life grow out of immemorial tradition, are created by entire societies living an integrated communal life. The frontiers and divisions drawn between and within such unitary expressions of collective imaginative response to common experience are nothing but artificial and distorting categorisations of a later, more rationalistic age. Such lines do not exist in the real world of lived experience.

If you ask: Who are the authors of the songs, the epics, the myths, the laws and mores of a people, their costumes, their language? The answer will be, the people itself, the entire soul of which is poured out in all they are and do and say. Herder is the originator of the terms 'Volksgeist', 'Volksseele', 'Nationalgeist',[10] which through Hegel and those who came after him had such a fateful career. But though this contributed to later forms of nationalism, it is not genuine nationalism in Herder. It is more a kind of patriotism and cultural integralism. It does not imply superiority of one's own people and culture over others, and contains absolutely no aggressive implications. On the contrary, Herder hated the Romans precisely for crushing a multitude of native cultures in the name of a supposedly superior civilization. German Lutheran clergymen forcibly converting Balts and the British in India were equally abhorrent to him. All peoples and cultures great and small can and must flourish side by side in the great garden of mankind.

This notion of expressionism is important here because the idea of *Verstehen*, understanding, is deeply embedded in it. Indeed, the two virtually entail each other. Let me quote *in extenso* Berlin's admirable summing up of the essence of this major insight of Herder's, since it leads naturally to a second original and revolutionary doctrine of Herder's, that of populism or the idea of belonging:

> For Herder, to be a member of a group is to think and act in a certain way, in the light of particular goals, values, pictures of the world: and to think and act is to belong to a group. The

---

[10] These terms abound throughout his writings.

notions are literally identical. To be a German is to be part of a unique stream of which language is the dominant element, but still only one element among others. Herder conveys the notion that the way in which a people—say the Germans—speak or move, eat or drink, their hand-writing, their laws, their music, their social outlook, their dance forms, their theology, have patterns and qualities in common which they do not share, or share to a notably lesser degree, with the similar activities of some other group—the French, the Icelanders, the Arabs, the ancient Greeks. Each of these activities belong to a cluster which must be grasped as a whole: they illuminate each other. Anyone who studies the speech rhythms, or the history, or the architecture, or the physical characteristics of the Germans, will thereby achieve a deeper understanding of German legislation, music, dress. There is a property, not capable of being abstracted and articulated—that which is German in the Germans—which all these diverse activities uniquely evince. Activities like hunting, painting, worship, common to many groups in widely differing times and places, will resemble each other because they belong to the same genus. But the specific quality which each type of activity will show forth will have more in common with generically different activities of the same culture than with specifically similar activities of another culture. Or, at the very least, that which the various activities of the same culture will have in common—the common pervasive pattern in virtue of which they are seen to be elements in one and the same culture—is more important, since it accounts for the characteristics of these activities at a deeper level, than their more superficial resemblances to the corresponding activities of other cultures and other human groups.[11]

This is absolutely critical. It is in virtue of this indefinable quality that I am more than just a human being—which for Herder would be anyway inconceivable—but *this* particular human being with *this* particular identity, surrounded by *my* relatives, friends, and people, involved together in *our* group or nation. It is in terms of these central patterns that each genuine culture—and the human beings who constitute it—can, and indeed must, be identified. At this point populism, the idea of having an identity and of belonging, and expressionism, the notion that all men's works and deeds express the total life of their group, can be seen to be two faces of the same coin. And Verstehen, empathy, understanding, is the only faculty by which they can be apprehended.

[11] Isaiah Berlin, *Vico and Herder* (London and New York: Hogarth Press, 1976), pp. 195–196.

Herder has much of interest and importance to say about the consequences that flow from this, his deepest discovery. One is that the individual can only be truly happy, creative, and fulfilled if he is not forcibly uprooted from his human habitat. His works are full of such examples. Germans only remain truly creative among Germans, he says. Icelanders who go to Denmark perish. Europeans in America lose their creative energy. And so on. Another is that just as any man expresses the collective life of his group or nation, so the artist, the poet, the musician does so in the fullest way possible, and for Herder an artist without roots is inconceivable. Finally, it is precisely humiliation of this quality of my being me and of *our* being us, failure of due recognition in the deepest sense, or still worse, conquest, oppression and exploitation, that does provoke a pathological condition of collective self-awareness and lead to aggressive self-assertion and nationalism. The need to belong to a recognized group and to express oneself in and through it is for Herder an inalienable part of being human.

IV

An especially sharp light is thrown on this notion of *Verstehen* by Friederich Daniel Schleiermacher,[12] who was born in Breslau in 1768 and died in Berlin in 1834. No doubt his greatest impact has been in the sphere of modern theology. In the wake of Kant's critical philosophy he forms an integral part of that great wave of speculative reflection in Germany which sought to rescue every manifestation of humanity from the shackles of blind tradition, superstition, and the heteronomy of brute nature; and to exemplify them as autonomous, reason-informed, and reason-driven realms of the human spirit. But Schleiermacher does not belong to the theologians alone, nor have they been allowed to monopolize him, though it is true that theologians have paid much more sympathetic attention to his ethics and dialectics than have philosophers, and

---

[12] In presenting Schleiermacher's views on this topic to an English audience, I have drawn heavily on Dilthey and the work of later German scholars, but quite especially on a most illuminating article by Wilhelm Gräb, 'Die unendliche Aufgabe des Verstehens', in *Friedrich Schleiermacher*, ed. D. Lange (Göttingen, 1985) pp. 47–71, to which I am deeply indebted because it opened my eyes to the importance of Schleiermacher. My own contribution is little more than a paraphrase and an extended gloss on this fine essay.

I wish to thank the author for his kind permission to make use of his work in this way.

perhaps rightly so. There is, however, an area of Schleiermacher's thought which, at any rate in the German-speaking world, and those countries which are wholly or in large part its cultural dependencies, has made an epoch in intellectual history, and that is his hermeneutics—his profoundly meditated, richly developed, and exceedingly sophisticated doctrine of *Verstehen*.

There is something of a paradox about this situation since neither Schleiermacher himself, nor his mainly theological interpreters, appear to have considered his 'Kunstlehre des Verstehen' or 'art of understanding' to occupy a central place in his philosophical production as a whole. Yet his claims to be taken seriously as a philosopher by philosophers, even to be regarded as a great philosopher albeit in a minor mode, do not derive from his philosophical ethics, or his dialectics, but from his special, and indeed unique and extraordinary, contribution to our understanding. And this paradox is if anything further compounded when we consider the external literary form taken by his major innovations in this field. For they are nowhere to be found in systematic exposition, bound together in finished form into a single book or treatise or course of published lectures, but rather in sporadic, repetitive, ever-renewed exploratory and tentative fragments, sketches, drafts, schemes for lectures, and notes taken from his lectures by students. Yet taken together it is hardly an exaggeration to say that they mark a revolution in human self-understanding, in our awareness of our peculiarly human status and capacities, and the interrelationships that hold between these capacities; and hence in the lines we draw in demarcating the value-laden human realm from the natural world of brute data, thus altering the map of human knowledge.

The true begetter of Schleiermacher's reputation as a philosopher and as the father of hermeneutics was, of course, Wilhelm Dilthey, who wrote the remarkable *Life of Schleiermacher*. It was Dilthey who was the first to write a history of hermeneutics, tracing its rise as a serious systematic discipline as opposed to a mere collection of scattered rules of thumb, and placing Schleiermacher firmly at its source.[13] This a view which, refined, developed, and in some minor respects critically revised by Gadamer and his school in our own century has remained in all essentials unchanged.

In his first semester as Professor in Halle in the winter of 1804/5, Schleiermacher conceived the plan for a course of lectures on hermeneutics. His duties requiring him to lecture on New Testament exegesis, he felt the need to make clear to himself the

[13] Wilhelm Dilthey, 'Die Enstehung der Hermeneutik', *Gesammelte Schriften*, Vol. V (Leipzig and Berlin, 1921), pp. 317–338.

principles which were to underlie his procedure, in order to be secure and consistent in his own interpretation as well as in the judgments he passed on that of others. There was, he tells us, no dearth of useful instructions for correct interpretation. And in particular Ernesti's *Institutio Interpretis* enjoyed high regard as the product of a sound philological school, offering useful rules of thumb. But, he goes on, such manuals themselves 'lacked an adequate foundation because the general principles had nowhere been established, and I then had to strike out on my own path'.[14] We see from this quite clearly that it is an immediate practical need that drives Schleiermacher to grapple with the problem of understanding in the deepest and most general sense, namely to interpret the Bible correctly as a responsible critical exegete. More importantly still, it demonstrates that Schleiermacher was aware that he himself was embarking on a new and radical venture, penetrating into hitherto unexplored territory.

In his correspondence with his friend Gass, he says that he will not begin with a general hermeneutics in the Enlightenment manner of a writer like Georg Friederich Meier, whose *Versuch einer allgemeinen Auslegungskunst* (1757)—*Essays in Universal Hermeneutics*—was widely acclaimed, but immediately with a *hermeneutica sacra*, and asks him specifically for bibliographical references. Gass in reply puts him on to Ernesti and Semler, two early eighteenth-century authorities, beyond whom the subject has made no advance. But Schleiermacher soon realizes that he must begin at a much deeper level, with the very foundations themselves: 'For if it is to be a sound and solid piece of work, then all the principles of the higher criticism, the entire art of understanding, of analytical reconstruction, must be worked into it.'[15]

Preoccupied with New Testament exegesis, and wishing to give renewed currency to theological hermeneutics, Schleiermacher recognized that the 'Kunst des Verstehens'—the 'art of understanding'—must itself first be clarified. But isolating the *object* of understanding is no help in this. On the contrary, this approach itself presupposes an act of understanding and an unexamined presupposition cannot be used to explain itself. As Schleiermacher himself pithily puts it, 'that Holy Scripture is holy we only know from the fact that we have understood it'.[16] We cannot as it were detach the holiness of scripture from our understanding of it *as*

[14] Friedrich Schleiermacher, *Hermeneutik*, nach den Handschriften neu herausgegeben von H. Kimmerle (Heidelberg, 1959), p. 123, note 4.

[15] Friedrich Schleiermacher's *Briefwechsel mit J. Chr. Gass*, ed. W. Gass (Berlin, 1852), p. 6.

[16] *Hermeneutik*, p. 55.

holy. And it is in this way that he turns our attention away from any putative object of investigation and any particular type of text—in this case the New Testament writings—to the subject of understanding himself, 'der Verstehende selbst', as Schleiermacher puts it. It is this that is the proper object of investigation for hermeneutics. The understanding subject; his activity; the process whereby he achieves understanding; this it is which must be clarified and explained. In this way Schleiermacher's programme of investigation takes on a universal sweep possessed by none of his predecessors.

First of all, he does follow in the footsteps of some of his Enlightenment precursors in ceasing to confine hermeneutics to the biblical canon. What they had done was to extend the practice of hermeneutics to any and every type of text. But going beyond them, Schleiermacher takes the much larger step of making all understanding problematic *as such*. And this step took him not only beyond Ernesti's New Testament hermeneutics, which was devoted to the study of individual difficult passages, but beyond all forms of hermeneutics as it had existed hitherto. Every specialized form of hermeneutics presupposes that, in the normal course of things, I understand quite unproblematically until I run up against a specific difficulty of some kind or other. As Schleiermacher puts this, 'I suppose myself to understand until I run up against a contradiction or a piece of nonsense.'[17] In response to this—and here he both confirms and goes far beyond the Enlightenment programme—he announces a far-reaching and immensely challenging programme: in words which are dark and pregnant with meaning, but whose general purport is not in doubt he says: 'I understand nothing which I cannot apprehend as necessary and which I cannot construct myself. Understanding in the light of the ultimate maxim is an infinite task.'[18] This remains his motto to the end. Understanding is an infinite and inexhaustible task.

In his early aphorisms on hermeneutics, he turns his new-found insight directly against the specialized hermeneutics of Ernesti, but at the same time indirectly contradicts the entire Enlightenment rationalist concept of historical philological interpretation. For the latter, the activity of understanding was in principle limited. The historical biblical criticism of the eighteenth century shows this quite clearly. And even as early as the seventeenth century, in Spinoza's theologico-political tractatus, one of the earliest and most influential exegetical documents, we see how a procedure of historical understanding is able skilfully to explain and interpret what is counter to natural reason in such a way that

[17] *Hermeneutik*, p. 31
[18] Ibid. p. 31.

it is made assimilable to it. All the wild, fantastic, supernatural events of which the Bible is so full can still be understood in rational terms if the proper methods are adopted. And even the most outlandish happenings are in this way brought before the court of reason, and explained or explained away. But it must be noted that the machinery of rational understanding devised and introduced here by Spinoza is only wheeled into action in those cases where claims and statements passed on by the tradition are in conflict with natural reason. Most of the time, we understand and give our rational assent to what we read, effortlessly and unproblematically. In Spinoza's case, and that of his successors, the transhistorical principle of interpretation remains timeless natural reason. This was an approach which to Schleiermacher seemed hopelessly narrow and doctrinaire.

Of course, he was not alone in such rejection. Hamann and Herder, Schlegel, Ast, and Wolf had either preceded him or were pursuing lines in some respects similar to his own. But nobody before Schleiermacher insisted with the same degree of emphasis and insight, of theoretical acumen and all-embracingness, on the fact that understanding entails an infinite task. That an ever-renewed, unique, and special hermeneutic effort had to be made whenever we sought to read out of texts the sense and meaning which had gone into them. Indeed, generally that the task of understanding must be repeated ever anew wherever we encounter the world of others, wherever we run up against what is new and unfamiliar to us, wherever we seek for understanding, insight, assimilation of what is alien and strange to us.

The task of understanding cannot be limited. It is literally boundless. This marks Schleiermacher's new point of departure and his revolutionary contribution in this sphere. Confined neither to specific unintelligible events, whether miracles or revelations, nor to the manner in which they present themselves, whether this is orally or in writing, whether in a foreign or one's own language, whether from our own or another time. We must always reckon with the fact that, contrary to the optimistic assumption of the Enlightenment exegetes, not understanding but 'failure of understanding or misunderstanding will be the natural and automatic outcome of our endeavours'. And so it is quite consciously understanding that is 'striven and sought after at every point'.[19]

Hitherto the desire, and the imperative need, to understand had always been contrasted with that which could be understood as a matter of course by way of universal rational insight. Schleiermacher was the first to annihilate this distinction and

[19] *Hermeneutik*, p. 86.

thereby to universalize the programme of hermeneutic reflection. Henceforth for Schleiermacher the explicit self-conscious process of understanding does not arise only when our own conceptions of rationality seem to collide with an instance of alien speech or writing, rather my own conception of rational insight, and the categories of interpretation by which I am guided in my encounters with the speech and writing of others, can no longer be taken for granted automatically as something unproblematic. I, my own speech, my own capacity for understanding, and all the concepts and categories by which it is organized and shot through, are seen in a perspective which calls its validity into question. All this becomes in some sense relativized. To make it explicit and secure I must embark on a most thorough-going analysis of understanding. And the long roundabout route Schleiermacher took in his life-long search for understanding proved peculiarly rewarding. For Schleiermacher came to what was at that time a relatively startling conclusion. The need for a self-conscious analysis of hermeneutics and understanding arises from the fact that there are conflicting notions of truth and of reality. But the end of his researches is to show that we are divided just as much by a vast variety of authentic perspectives on the world and on human experience as by our distance from some putative objective structure of timeless truth, as many Enlightenment thinkers seem to have believed. This notion of the possible plurality of equally valid total outlooks and views was to prove very fruitful indeed. The history of humanity was thereby presented literally in a new light. The perennial battle between conflicting views of the truth, between competing value and belief systems, does not, on this new view, show that necessarily and always we are mistaken, but rather bears witness to the literally inexhaustible variety and uniqueness of human beings and human groups, which cannot be reduced in principle to a single standard or criterion of judgment. A new and exciting and liberating prospect is thereby opened up for the human studies.

Schleiermacher's early notes on hermeneutics, where he first evolved his doctrine of the infinite task of understanding, were written when he was very much under the spell of, and was a major element in, the movement of early Romanticism in Germany. And it is with this experience in mind, and above all with thought of his friend Friederich Schlegel, whom he worshipped and admired, that he writes in a remarkable passage of the *Monologen*, published in 1800,

> For a long while I too was satisfied to have found Reason. And, worshipping the uniformity of the supreme and single Being, I

believed that there was one right thing for every specific case; that action must be the same in all human beings, and that only because each one had been given his appointed situation and place did one human being differ from another ... that each man, each individual, was not a peculiarly constituted creature, but merely an identical element that was everywhere the same ... But now it dawned upon me, and this has become my supreme vantage-point, ... that every man should manifestly express in his own unique fashion the humanity within him, in his own specific mixture of its elements, so that human nature should be revealed in every possible way, and that in the fullness of infinite time and space everything should become realized which can emerge from humanity's womb.[20]

It is against this background that we must read his celebrated words 'Jeder Mensch ist ein Künstler' (every human being is an artist).

It is this perception that the universal—human nature—will always express itself through the individual—and not timelessly in some once-and-for-all embodiment of absolute perfection—and the consequent irreducible variety of equally valid perspectives in which the human essence reveals itself in and through history, which both emerges from Schleiermacher's grappling with the problem of *Verstehen* and also gives it its validity. Its discovery is organically connected with the new Romantic doctrine of individuality and the new awareness of history, and had an immense impact on later developments in nineteenth-century German historiography, not least on the search for a rationally grounded hermeneutics and a soundly based 'Geisteswissenschaften', associated with men like Dilthey, Windelband, Rickert, and others. The consequence of the irreducible singularity of each and every human individual, of the fact that he cannot be dissolved without remainder into the universal and the general, is that understanding, and *only* understanding, can afford us a mode of ingress into the innermost being and particularity, the concrete meaning and truth, of another human being or group of human beings, And when we encounter another person we must not automatically assimilate his words, expressions, gestures, his whole range of expressive symbols which are the very embodiment of his entire world of thought, feeling, and aspiration to the familiar and well-worn concepts and categories of our own world. Just as every man must express his humanity in his own way and in his own peculiar combination of its potentialities, in such a way that his own indi-

---

[20] *Monologen* (Berlin, 1800), pp. 38ff.

viduality is a practical task on which he is ceaselessly engaged until death supervenes, and not something to be discovered by an objective science or a gift that falls inexplicably into his lap, so understanding must always set itself the task of discerning, grasping, 'entering into', that which is unique and particular in each and every person's solution to the perennial problem of human existence. In every encounter with others it is our task to explore and appreciate their unique, authentic singularity and to see the validity and universal significance of his being 'thus not otherwise'.

This task of understanding, which is incapable of completion, is bound upon us by the very fact of our own fallibility and finitude, by the inescapable fact that we too can only ever know the world from our own singular perspective. We are what we are, and there is no universal perspective open to us from which every single perspective could be as it were bound together into one unified vision. Understanding is indissolubly bound up with the activity of an individual subject which is bounded by its own finite horizon of understanding. It cannot outleap its own shadow. Each individual horizon can be extended by the sensitive exploration of other expressions of human existence, but never in such a way that one's own peculiar horizon is transcended. And it is this insight that inspired Schleiermacher to his celebrated image of an infinity of intersecting spheres. Along the path of hermeneutic communication he envisaged a condition which

> would place the sphere of each individual in a situation where it would be intersected by the sphere of others in as manifold a manner as possible; and at each point of his own boundaries, he would be granted a prospect onto another and alien world, so that by and by all the phenomenon of mankind should become familiar to him, and even the most alien outlooks and conditions should become, as it were, his friends and neighbours.[21]

In the early aphorisms on hermeneutics, Schleiermacher declares that understanding is an infinite task. But how, then, we may ask, does he combine this with the remarkable assertion, already quoted, that I understand nothing 'which I do not apprehend as necessary and which I cannot myself construct'? For this might suggest some infinite, timeless, standpoint-free faculty of direct rational intuition—the Reason of Descartes or Spinoza—but at all events it does not conjure up immediately the concrete, time-bound, history-imbued activity that Schleiermacher clearly has in mind. It is most certainly *not* timeless reason. What he means here must be seen in connection with his vision of history as consisting of a

[21] *Versuch einer Theorie des geselligen Betragens* (Berlin, 1799), p. 3.

potentially infinite and ever-changing variety of individuals, peoples, nations, cultures, civilizations, each with its own unique perspective, which cannot be reduced to that of another, and the associated notion of irreducible individuality. It is a question, first of all, of tracing and grasping the unique, specific, concrete sense and meaning of a particular human life or collection of human lives, in all the rich detail of a given historical context. Then, in the second place, it is an act of construction in the sense that I must use my own human capacities actively to re-create within my own breast the inner life, the hopes and fears, the ideals and aspirations, the acts of will, and so forth, of the relevant historical persons. In the third place, this must be of such a kind that I can recognize— indeed cannot escape—the *inner* necessity for it, given the circumstances, given the aims and goals, given the values and ideals, in this particular time and this particular place, of this or that individual or group of individuals. It is this special, quasi-aesthetic, quasi-psychological, sense of the word necessity, which is different from, though for those who have grasped its full significance as compelling as, logical necessity, which Schleiermacher was among the very first—after Vico—to identify and elucidate. Schleiermacher's 'art of understanding' aims at a kind of artistic act of creative production or reproduction, in some sense a new creation, where the interpreter resurrects the sense of a text, using his own creative substance and from his own sense of perspective, thereby giving the work a new life and a new voice to express, once again, its irreducible originality and uniqueness.

Certainly, gestures, bodily posture, facial expressions, dress, self-adornment, domestic decorations, and a thousand and one other human manifestations convey sense and meaning. But the locus par excellence of understanding and meaning is language. Here the problem of understanding is seen in its fullest and most sophisticated form. Language at once makes possible and also demands understanding. It is an objectively given web of general terms which makes understanding possible, yet every manifestation of it is indissolubly tied to an identifiable individual, which makes understanding a necessity. The much wider conception of understanding first introduced by Schleiermacher becomes both universally necessary and possible wherever we engage with linguistic expressions, whether in speech or in writing. Language is in the first place a common stock of identical signs and symbols which is shared to a greater or lesser degree by all those who participate in it. It opens up a vast realm of understanding. It is its vehicle. Schleiermacher says, 'every act of understanding is the conversion of an act of speaking; in this way must enter into consciousness that thinking that underlay the act of speaking'.[22] Here then understanding is an understanding *of* language and *through* language, an understanding of what it is that spoken or written language would have us understand. But language does not write and speak itself. And while all thought is only given its perfected form in speech, it is not words and speech themselves that do the thinking. Rather, language is thought of as a capacity and as a potentiality, not as something fixed and final and fully realized. Language is a system of signs and symbols which only generates sense and meaning when it is put into operation. Language speaks to us only to the degree to which it is used by men speaking, or has been used by men speaking, whether in oral or written form. For Schleiermacher then language possesses an element of generality and objectivity and at the same time of individuality and subjectivity. For this reason understanding is not only possible but absolutely necessary, and hence a sophisticated practical hermeneutics is indispensable. Language and language-users are the two vital ingredients in all this.

Now it is clear from this that hermeneutics is not a merely subjective activity, devoted to interpreting signs and expressions in any way it pleases. For understanding is concerned not only with the speaker but with what he says.

One of the consequences of Schleiermacher's position is that a final system of knowledge of all things and all people will never be achieved and should not be sought after. We will never be able to obviate the element of unique individual interpretation in any given situation. All things cannot be assimilated to a single system. In this respect Schleiermacher stands in stark contrast with the great idealist philosophers who were his contemporaries, and above all of course Hegel. Indeed, he is as sharply anti-Hegelian as Kierkegaard. Human beings are caught up unavoidably and eternally in a process of inter-subjective communication and understanding, to which there can be in principle no end.

Understanding, then, is perennial and unavoidable. But just as language does not itself speak, and just as a text does not itself directly communicate, so too understanding is not such that it falls automatically into our laps. To understand speech in any form, to avoid as far as possible misunderstanding, the basic talent and judgment required for understanding must be consciously developed and trained in accordance with a set of rules and systematic procedures. This sophisticated discipline of the art of understanding will rest on the insight that 'every instance of human speech will have a dual relationship: on the one hand with the totality of

[22] *Hermeneutik*, p. 80.

the language, and, on the other, with the total system of thought of its author'.[23] And that therefore every act of understanding will have to distinguish 'two moments, namely to understand speech as consisting of materials drawn from the language, and to understand it as a fact in the mind of the thinker'.[24] In the light of this— and all understanding turns upon speech and the thought that underlies it, upon language and its speakers and writers—the hermeneutic procedure must be so constituted that it naturally divides into two main branches, a grammatical interpretation and a psychological-technical interpretation. Grammatical interpretation confines itself to the language of a text. It treats the text as a finished artefact, as something given, as an object in the world. It seeks to understand the text simply as a text, as a structure, as an objectively given web of words. It is concerned with ascertaining and clarifying the meanings and nuances of words, with analysing and describing grammatical and syntactic structures, and, applying these methods, it is concerned with establishing the meaning of the text. And in this sense Schleiermacher's conception of the term grammatical is extremely wide and all-embracing. The totality of a language in all its aspects documents the totality of a world-view. In this way, to understand a piece of speech or a piece of writing in language and through language takes us into the social and historical roots of the society from which it sprang. But all this for Schleiermacher only gives half the story. So far what Schleiermacher offers us in his grammatical interpretation is in fact nothing more than a highly refined and developed form of what hermeneutics had hitherto traditionally consisted in, and in no way marks a break or a new departure. It is when we turn to the second aspect, the psychological-technical that we will see what is original about Schleiermacher's contribution. For the entire grammatical approach still remains in some sense 'external', objective, viewing the poem, the play, the philosophical treatise, whatever it may be, from the outside. It does not succeed, nor indeed does it even try, in penetrating to the productive act itself that underlies the example of speech or writing that lies before us. It may understand the content of a text, literally, the things it says, but it remains completely silent about how it came about. That is to say, it does not seek to penetrate or enter into the creative act of the original author. Texts do not just spring into existence of their own accord, but they presuppose the existence of a unique, individual, concrete, productive and creative talent. Somewhere we must be able to discover an author, a

[23] Ibid.
[24] Ibid.

living, breathing, historical individual who makes his own unrepeatable use of the language for his own specific purpose in his own special circumstances. This further reflexive step demanded by Schleiermacher of the interpreter is something utterly new.

In order to make the ubiquitous nature of the hermeneutic faculty clear, and to demonstrate the requirement of a certain degree of critical self-awareness in its use, Schleiermacher says the following:

> In the midst of an intimate conversation I very often catch myself engaged in hermeneutical operations when I am not satisfied with the normal degree of understanding but seek to discover how it is that the transition from one thought to another has been established in the mind of my friend; or when I go in search of the views, judgments, and aims which are bound up with his expressing himself with regard to the subject under discussion in precisely this way rather than some other.[25]

And this alert and intense capacity for self-observation leads him to the conclusion that hermeneutic theory 'is by no means confined to that form of speech which is fixed firmly before the eye, but that it will be ubiquitously present wherever we have to understand thoughts, or series of thoughts, by means of words'.[26] And what is true of *viva voce* conversation is also true of any literary work. It can only be understood in its uniqueness, in its 'grade so und nicht anders Sein', in the irreducible individuality of its meaning and through its peculiar genesis. Schleiermacher insists therefore,

> 'quite especially I should like to urge the interpreter of written words to exercise assiduously the interpretation of his more significant conversations. For the immediate presence of the speaker, the living expression which conveys the immediate participation of his entire mental and spiritual being, the manner in which in this situation the thoughts are developed out of the common human situation—all this stimulates one much more than the lonely contemplation of an utterly isolated text to understand a series of thoughts as something that burgeons into life in the living moment, and as an act or deed which is organically connected with many others of both a similar and of a different kind.'[27]

Schleiermacher is above all concerned with seeing a text, or an example of human speech, as a form of action, of doing, which is

[25] Ibid. It is altogether too fanciful to detect here, in Schleiermacher's vigilant attention to the connective links in even the most causal everyday processes of human thought, a remote anticipation of a tendency which later came to full flower in Freud?

[26] Ibid. p. 131.

[27] Ibid.

expressive of a total personality. For him the essential task is to isolate and grasp its starting-point, the 'Grundgedanken' or 'basic idea', the 'Keimentschluss' or the 'inner germination of creative decision', from which a piece or writing, or a series of writings, has sprung in just this particular form rather than any other. The philologico-grammatical approach alone is not enough. To examine vocabulary, grammar, syntax, style, literary genre, etc., is at best half the story. Above all one must go back to what he calls the 'Lebensmoment eines bestimmten Menschen'—the living moment of a specified human being, his vital centre of gravity. It is here, in the total context of the individual human life that the first germ of the work originates. It is this original conception which binds together and coordinates all the separate aspects of the author's speech and writing, and all the traditional elements that enter into his work and thought. It is this above all that we must seek and find. And in order to do this, the first and most important thing of all is to cleave closely to the author's own words and his own literary works. And this comes out in a technical sense. More especially, the critic examines the way in which an author manages and manipulates the particular literary form or genre that he has chosen as the vehicle for his ideas. The degree to which he entrusts it with the full burden of his fundamental conception, or to which again he modifies or adapts it, or enlarges and extends it, in order to make it accommodate his message. On this basis, Schleiermacher evolves a set of procedures which he calls the comparative–historical method. This is intended to help the interpreter to understand a text, a specific text, within the context of the general circumstances, the linguistic tradition, the particular literary genre, the historical conditions of the time. It elucidates what is peculiar about a text by an examination of its contents and of its author, and by contrasting these with other similar authors and texts. All the resources of scholarship are required, and a scrupulous regard is had to the establishing of facts. But there is about Schleiermacher's approach, as he himself was aware, a serious weak point. This is the notorious problem of the so-called hermeneutic circle, of which he is the true originator.

In understanding a text, I must begin somewhere, in order to gain a foothold to move from that which I understand to the whole of which it forms a part, and in order to move back from this whole to the part that it is a vital element in it. Schleiermacher solves this problem, at any rate to his own satisfaction, by simply cutting the Gordian knot.

The active, productive, meaning-creating, meaning-clarifying

[28] Ibid. p. 140.

generative powers of the individual subject are powerfully stressed. The fact that I must already be in possession of some form of understanding in order then to understand demonstrates, as Schleiermacher sees quite clearly, that the process of understanding is incapable of grounding and accounting for itself. The device he adopts for getting out of this difficulty is what he calls 'the act of divination'. In all understanding, he insists, there is an element of direct intuitive insight, of 'divination'. As he presents it this does not seem to be some kind of supernormal, non-empirical gift, but a faculty we all possess to some degree merely by dint of being human beings—though some possess a greater, while others possess a lesser measure of it. And, of course, it can be developed and trained. He describes the divinatory act that takes place in the interpreter as 'an inner spur motivating one's own creative activity, but whose original direction is aimed at assimilating what has been furnished by another'.[28] This divinatory element can never be excluded from understanding, least of all in those cases where it is a question of understanding what is absolutely novel and incomparable about a piece of speech or a text. Wherever there is a new irruption of creativity in the medium of language, the power of divination is absolutely indispensable. This inner agility making for one's own productive activity in the interpreter goes in search of what is new and incapable of formulation in terms of pre-existent rules, and cannot itself be reduced to rules. Not even the most perfect and extensive knowledge in the comparative–historical or the comparative–critical field, nor exhaustive information about the author and his life, can possibly replace this radical act of divining which Schleiermacher sometimes terms 'Errathen'[29]—a kind of inspired guess-work. This original act of free creation on the part of the interpreter is indispensable. The text, and the tradition and the language in which it stands, of course motivates and demands such interpretation, yet the text itself cannot as it were take this work in hand on its own account nor prescribe rules for its performance. Yet here too in the case of the divinatory act, Schleiermacher clings to the notion of the interpreter's rootedness in a specific time and place. It is not therefore a question of some timeless flight of imaginative empathy, of entering some quasi-Platonic heaven of immutable meanings, where I can contemplate face-to-face the author's unchanged and unchanging message, rather it is a process whereby the interpreter sketches forth anew the original meaning of the text and, coming to the task with his own particular perspective, both re-creates the original message and at the same time enriched its meaning. By such tiny accretions is our sense of what

[29] Ibid. p. 132.

the author meant extended. This is an essential part of what Schleiermacher meant with his maxim that it is a question of understanding an author better than he understood himself.

By thus emphasizing the autonomous activity of the interpreter, as he performs his act of understanding, Schleiermacher tacitly opposes all those attempts to break out of the bounds of the specific, concrete, self-unfolding subject with its unique perspective on things, in favour of some ineluctable, impersonal, objective historical structure, which in some sense precedes and determines all meaning. But on the other hand, he offers no succour to all those who, like the post-modernist critics of our own time in particular, seem unwilling to allow any objective checks on their interpretative bacchanals. On the contrary, his infinitely sensitive, imaginative, scrupulous, self-conscious, cautious and delicately respectful probings—amounting to a kind of supreme spiritual courtesy—of the objective human artefacts of the cultural–historical realm, backed up by the immense historical and philological learning of a lifetime, afford a sobering lesson for all of us today.

V

I suggested at the beginning of this paper that the three thinkers I've talked about touch upon a cluster of notions that lie at the heart of our humanity, and lay bare for the first time some of the basic categories which organize, permeate and enter into what is most distinctive about us as human beings, both as individuals and groups. They raised to consciousness, and made analytically explicit for the first time, what hitherto had been at best unconscious and implicit. It is one of the tasks of the historian of ideas to identify and describe such moments of growth in our collective self-awareness.

But it also seems reasonable to conjecture that if the truths that are thus uncovered about ourselves are deep and genuine, then each successive age will discover in them new and important implications. And so I would like to end with a few tentative indications as to what some of these may be against the contemporary scene.

It is, for example, irresistible to ask what Herder would have made of the multi-cultural societies of our day. For him, my identity must first be firmly formed un-self-consciously in my own group, speaking my own language, sharing common memories, traditions, ways of life with my fellows, unconcerned by invidious comparisons with others. Whether viewing my own language, culture, religion and values from an early age at school from the standpoint of comparative anthropology as just one belief-system among others, would generate the intimate bonds of mutual love, affection, and recognition required in his view by full human flourishing, may perhaps still be an open question. 'One man's religion is another man's anthropology' becomes almost inevitably 'all religion is just anthropology'. In any event, the reverse process is inconceivable, i.e. that every religion should become equally a binding religion to every man. And is it so with values generally? This is far from saying that attempts at multi-culturalism are to be viewed with anything but deep sympathy, admiration, and respect as the noble experiments they certainly are; but, if Herder's analysis and understanding of our condition is correct, it is simply to guard against the possibility of bitter disappointment.

Again Herder (and Schleiermacher also) would have been appalled, but scarcely at all surprised, by the growing tide of nationalism in the modern world. Aggressive nationalism was something Herder detested and polemicized against all his life. And he was one of the first and profoundest critics of European imperialism. But he was all too well aware that a long history of conquest, oppression, exploitation and humiliation took its toll in a violent backlash of burning resentment and insane self-glorification. The world of happy, flourishing, self-centred (but not selfish) nations, who admired, loved, esteemed and helped one another as individuals do at their best, which he envisaged as the best and perhaps, in the end, the only possible solution to the problems of the mass global organization of mankind, would require the healing of wounds over generations. And connectedly, he would not be in the least surprised by the virtual breakdown in a country such as America of the melting-pot theory, and the re-coagulating out of a vast variety of ethnic groups.

And again, our increasingly scientistic, technological, quantified world, with its sinister creeping regimentation of human individuals and systematic.suffocation of originality, spontaneity and verve, denying our human essence as these thinkers understood it, would have depressed them as much as many of the most widely applauded (but also deplored) responses to it. That the starvation of a hunger for expressiveness as deep and imperious as bodily hunger itself would lead to contorted, exhibitionistic, nihilistic, violent, and finally self-defeating manifestations of thwarted self-expression, would be no source of wonderment to men who were familiar with—and in the case of Herder influenced and participated in—the German *Sturm und Drang* of the 1770s. And though the specific examples would no doubt have filled them with horror and distaste, the general tendency exemplified by bissected pickled sheep or nappies befouled with excrement, is a phenomenon to which they would in turn have applied their diagnostic scalpels with unerring accuracy. A great deficit of expressiveness in a society will have its own special pathology, and may finally rend it asunder.

Relatedly, that the right to individual self-expression should have become a corner-stone of contemporary Western societies would have seemed to these thinkers axiomatic. And the relevance of Schleiermacher's conception of self-creation and self-revelation—of every man being his own artist and his own work of art—to modern existentialism and other related contemporary trends is very plain.

Finally, a test of the depth and permanence of the central categories these thinkers exposed will be afforded by the ultimate fate of some of the most influential, and apparently glamorous theories of literature and of literary criticism that seem to hold sway today wherever we turn. If there is anything at all in the views of Herder and Schleiermacher, the fate of so-called post-modernism as anything other than an exceedingly odd chapter in the pathology of modern criticism may reasonably be questioned. Severance of the work from the author—his values and his intentions—indeed, denial of his existence altogether; the granting of total autonomy to language as some kind of self-propelling non-human subject; the throwing open of the field of literary works to the wildest, most irresponsible, and most arbitrary interpretations—the more bizarre and improbable the better; all this could not run more counter to the central expressivist categories of our three thinkers—and quite especially to Schleiermacher's profound and scrupulous exposition of hermeneutic principles of interpretation and textual exegesis. And though they move on an entirely different plane altogether, all types of formalism and neo-formalism, which view the work of art as an artefact detached from its creator, as an object or structure in the world, and not as a human voice seeking to communicate a total vision, are equally alien to them.

Our three thinkers may of course prove wrong. The categories that seem (to them) so permanent and central, so evidently constitutive of ourselves as human beings, could turn out to be time- and culture-bound, and so doomed to pass away and be replaced by others. This may be so. But with what consequences for human sanity and humane culture as we know, and have known, and deeply prize these, is anybody's guess. Indeed, their passing would be tantamount to a mutation of the species.

Weber's Ideal Types as Models in the Social Sciences

FRIEDEL WEINERT

There has recently been a great interest in models in the natural sciences. Models are used mainly for their representational functions: they help to concretize certain relationships between parameters in studying physical systems. For instance, we might be interested in representing how the planets orbit around the sun—a scale model of the solar system is an ideal tool for achieving this end. We are free to leave out one or two planets or ignore the moons which many of the planets have. Alternatively, we might be interested in studying the relationship between two particular parameters—how one may be dependent on the other. Then we construct a functional model and determine the functional relationship between them. For instance, the orbital period of a planet is functionally dependent on the average distance of the planet from the sun.[1] Models are rather widespread in the social sciences, especially in economics where functional models are used to study relationships between, say, supply and demand. Economics, however, also uses a different kind of model which is also used in the natural sciences: the hypothetical or *as if* model. Economists employ *as if* constructions when they assume economic agents to be perfectly rational beings who always seek to maximize their utilities. It is common knowledge that economic agents are not perfectly rational and that the assumptions of perfect rationality and optimal information are at best idealizations which do not, strictly speaking, correspond to the economic reality of how economic agents behave in the market-place.

Still, *as if* models serve important functions. If it is assumed that certain events happen as presented in the model, then it is often possible to work out patterns of regularity which accurately describe or even explain the data at hand. Niels Bohr, the Danish physicist, used a planetary model of the atom—which it strictly speaking false—to work out some equations (the ground level

---

[1] According to Kepler's third law $P^2 = A^3$ where P is the orbital period in years and A is the average distance of the planet measured in astronomical units, i.e. in multiples of the distance of the earth from the sun. For instance, if a planet is 4 times the earth–sun distance away from the sun, then its orbital period is 8 years.

energy of the hydrogen atom and the derivation of the Ritz and Balmer series) which are still regarded as perfectly valid today. Equally, economic theory uses the utility theory to make predictions about household consumption choices.

It is in this connection that Weber's ideal types enter the picture. Ideal types, too, are hypothetical constructions of a socio-economic, political or historical nature which seek to delineate pure cases, abstracted from the empirical data but with complete disregard for their diversity. Weber was concerned with logically precise conceptions and not with their exact correspondence to empirical cases. His pure types of legitimate authority—which are subdivided into charismatic, traditional and rational forms—were not expected to be *descriptions* of historico-empirical realities. Rather, they were understood as ideal limits against which empirical cases could be gauged. Once such pure types were constructed, empirical occurrences of social action could be regarded as 'factors of deviation' from the ideal type.[2] Paradoxically, Weber claimed that the reality of the social or economic life in a given society could be understood by comparison to the ideal cases which nevertheless claimed no correspondence to reality. Empirical reality was always an overlapping mixture of several ideal types with additional accidental features into the bargain.

It should not be taken for granted that ideal types can simply be understood as models in the social sciences. An ideal type for Weber is no more than a means to an end with no correspondence to reality; but most models in the natural sciences have more than just heuristic functions. They are used to represent aspects of the real world. In addition, hypothetical models seem to be more complicated than Weber's ideal types: although economic agents are not strictly and exclusively rational, they largely do act according to rational principles, although these are intermingled with other elements. The hypothetical model states what the agent would do under certain conditions. Finally, there is one important aspect of models in the natural sciences which is not accounted for in Weber's ideal types; models in the natural sciences may be improved with the emergence of more sophisticated data and can thus achieve a better approximation to reality. This happened with Bohr's planetary model of the hydrogen atom. Are Weber's ideal types amenable to this treatment? And is there a way in which we can speak of them as hypothetical models in the social sciences?

[2] M. Weber, *Economy and Society*, ed. Guenther Roth and Claus Wittich, (New York: Bedminster Press, 1968), p. 6.

I. Weber's Concept of Ideal Types

At least one commentator has distinguished three phases of Weber's methodological thinking about ideal types: In the early phase he regarded ideal types simply as heuristic devices in an endeavour to comprehend social and historical phenomena. They were means rather than ends and hence involved no claim to represent empirical reality. In a brief middle phase the formulation of ideal types seems to have become the aim of the social sciences.[3] In the final phase, marked by the publication of *Economy and Society* (1921), Weber systematized ideal types into broad categories permitting analyses of universal history: Types of authority, types of economic organizations and types of religious communities. Other commentators have pointed out that Weber implicitly uses two different kinds of ideal types: the individualizing and the generalizing type.[4] Nevertheless, there is an overall tendency in Weber to treat ideal types as heuristic means rather than ends of sociological research. This is stressed both in the early essay on 'Objectivity in Social Science' and in *Economy and Society*.[5]

The answer to the question why ideal types are predominantly not seen as the objective of social research but rather as heuristic means is to be sought in Weber's characterization of ideal types. Weber is wont to stress that ideal types are *mental constructions*[6] or alternatively that they are *limiting concepts*[7] against which reality is to be measured. He also uses the term 'pure types' when discussing forms of legitimate authority.[8] These ideal types are

[3] See for instance M. Weber, 'Über einige Kategorien der verstehenden Soziologie', *Logos IV* (1913), pp. 253–294. Reprinted in M. Weber, *Soziologie, Universalgeschichtliche Analysen, Politik*, ed. J. Winckelmann (Stuttgart: Kröner, 1973), p. 99. For this distinction see W. Mommsen, *Max Weber*, Gesellschaft, Politik und Geschichte (Frankfurt: Suhrkamp, 1974), pp. 229–232.

[4] See W. J. Goode, 'A Note on the Ideal Type', *American Sociological Review* **XII** (1947), 473 and J. W. W. Watkins, 'Ideal Types and Historical Explanation', *Readings in the Philosophy of Science*, ed. H. Feigl and M. Brodbeck (New York: Appleton-Century-Crofts, 1953), pp. 23–28.

[5] '"Objectivity" in Social Science and Social Policy' (1904), reprinted in *Max Weber on The Methodology of the Social Sciences*, (trans and ed. E. A. Shils and H. A. Finch) (Glencoe Ill.: The Free Press, 1949), p. 92 and *Economy and Society*, p. 7.

[6] 'Über einige Kategorien der verstehenden Soziologie', p. 525 fn. 99; 'Objectivity in Social Science', pp. 90, 91, 100.

[7] 'Objectivity in Social Science', p. 93.

[8] *Economy and Society*, p. 215.

characterized by logical consistency and conceptual precision. They are sharply defined. In the spirit of the Kantian philosophy, Weber valued a clear conceptualization more than a murky description. For instance,

'Charismatic authority' shall refer to a rule over men, whether predominantly external or predominantly internal, to which the governed submit because of their belief in the extraordinary quality of the specific *person*. The magical sorcerer, the prophet, the leader of hunting and booty expeditions, the warrior chieftain, the so-called 'Caesartist' ruler, and, under certain conditions, the personal head of a party are such types of rulers for their disciples, followings, enlisted troops, parties et cetera. The legitimacy of their rule rests on the belief in and the devotion to the extraordinary, which is valued because it goes beyond the normal human qualities, and which was originally valued as supernatural. The legitimacy of charismatic rule thus rests upon the belief in magical powers, revelations and hero worship. The source of these beliefs is the 'proving' of the charismatic quality through miracles, through victories and other successes, that is, through the welfare of the governed.[9]

Sociology is a generalizing science. Sociological concepts must therefore be relatively devoid of content (*inhaltsleer*) with respect to the concrete reality of things. The gain lies in the determinacy of its concepts. The sharper the concepts the more removed they are from empirical reality.[10] But such purity comes with a price. Given the stipulated vacuity of these concepts, what is the purpose of ideal types for an empirical social science? 'The goal of ideal-typical concept-construction is always to make clearly explicit not the class or average character but rather the unique individual character of cultural phenomena.'[11] Hence, the ideal type, in Weber's conception, does not generalize over empirical phenomena but idealizes these phenomena to bring out the peculiarities

[9] 'The Social Psychology of the World Religions' (1915), reprinted in *From Max Weber, Essays in Sociology*, ed. H. H. Gerth and C. Wright Mills (London: Routledge & Kegan Paul, 1948), pp. 295–296; italics in original.

[10] *Economy and Society*, p. 21.

[11] 'Objectivity in Social Science', pp. 101. ' ... Zweck der idealtypischen Begriffsbildung ist es überall, *nicht* das Gattungsmäßige, sondern die Eigenart von Kulturescheinungen scharf zum Bewußtsein zu bringen.' M. Weber, 'Die Objektivität sozialwissenschaftlicher Erkenntnis', *Archiv für Sozialwissenschaft und Sozialpolitik*, IX, 24-87, reprinted in M. Weber, *Soziologie, Universalgeschichtliche Analysen, Politik*, (Kröner, Stuttgart: J. Winckelmann 1973), p. 248.

of a historical or societal situation. It is immaterial whether the historical or societal reality actually corresponds to the types. The ideal type is a

conceptual construct (*Gedankenbild*) which is neither historical reality nor even the 'true' reality. It is even less fitted to serve as a schema under which a real situation or action is to be subsumed as one *instance*. It has the significance of a purely ideal *limiting* concept with which the real situation or action is *compared* and surveyed for the explication of certain of its significant components.[12]

The social or historical reality will then appear as a departure or deviation from the ideal type construction, just as the behaviour of real economic agents comprises deviations from how the ideal-typical economic agent *would* behave. The deviations are brought about by 'irrational factors.'[13]

Given this function of ideal types, Weber distinguishes several tasks which might be accomplished with their help: *First*, the ideal type allows the social scientist to conceptualize certain historical phenomena or movements to a maximum of conceptual clarity— examples are 'imperialism', 'feudalism', 'mercantilism'.[14] The ideal type highlights the essential components of, say, feudalism, even though no such pure form of feudalism may ever have existed. *Second*, the ideal type serves as a limiting concept (*Grenzbegriff*), whereby historical individuals, like 'church' and 'sect' can be sharply distinguished by reference to ideal type constructions. But Weber warns against a characterization of the ideal type as a representation of the essence of reality or of some underlying structure.[15] *Third*, ideal types may be used to reconstruct the 'developmental sequences' in history where this reconstruction is, however, not to be identified with the actual course of history.[16] Weber cites Marx as an example for this use of ideal types:

[12] 'Objectivity in Social Science', p. 93. ' ... ein Gedankenbild, welches nicht die historische Wirklichkeit oder gar die "eigentliche" Wirklichkeit *ist*, welches noch viel weniger dazu da ist, als ein Schema zu dienen, *in* welchem die Wirklichkeit als *Exemplar* eingeordnet werden sollte, sondern welches die Bedeutung eines rein idealen *Grenzbegriffes* hat, an welchem die Wirklichkeit zur Verdeutlichung bestimmter bedeutsamer Bestandteile ihres empirisches Gehaltes *gemessen*, mit dem sie *verglichen* wird.' 'Objektivität der Erkenntnis', pp. 238–239; italics in original.

[13] *Economy and Society*, pp. 4–6.

[14] 'Objectivity in Social Science', p. 92.

[15] Ibid. p. 94.

[16] Ibid. p. 101.

All specifically Marxian 'laws' and developmental constructs, in so far as they are theoretically sound, are ideal types. The eminent, indeed *heuristic* significance of these ideal-types when they are used for the *assessment* of reality is known to everyone who has ever employed Marxian concepts and hypotheses. Similarly their perniciousness, as soon as they are thought of as empirically valid or real (i.e. truly metaphysical) 'effective forces', 'tendencies', etc., is likewise known to those who have used them.[17]

Fourth, ideal types are the 'cornerstone of the theory of objective possibility and adequate causation'.[18] As we shall see, the determination of ideal types as models in the social sciences centres on an appropriate understanding and reinterpretation of the concept of objective possibility. The notion of adequate causation is Weber's attempt to introduce causal relationships into historical studies. Counterfactual questions, he asserts, are not idle in the study of history. By considering what *would* have happened *if* certain conditions had either been absent or modified, Weber hopes to throw light on the 'historical significance' of the actual determinant factors in the emergence of some historical event. While there is an infinity of determining factors, the 'attribution of effects to causes take(s) place through a series of *abstractions*',[19] guided by the interest the historian has in the event. Thus through abstractions, isolations and generalizations, the historian is to construct a complex of possible causal relations which 'should culminate in a synthesis of the "real" causal complex'.[20] Weber speaks of 'adequate causation', when there is a high probability that the historian's reconstruction of conceptually isolatable conditions is such that they are the likely cause of an actual historical event or events of that type.[21]

[17] Ibid. p. 103. 'Daher sei hier nur konstatiert, daß natürlich *alle* spezifisch-marxistischen "Gesetze" und Entwicklungsconstrucktionen— soweit sie *theoretisch* fehlerfrei sind—idealtypischen Charakter haben. Die eminente, ja einzigartige *heuristische* Bedeutung dieser Idealtypen, wenn man sie zur *Vergleichung* der Wirklichkeit mit ihnen benutzt, und ebenso ihre Gefährlichkeit, sobald sie als empirisch geltend oder gar als reale (d.h. in Wahrheit: metaphysische) "wirkende *Kräfte*", "Tendenzen" usw. vorgestellt werden, kennt jeder, der je mit marxistischen Begriffen gearbeitet hat.' 'Objektivität der Erkenntnis', pp. 250–251; italics in original.

[18] J. Freund, *The Sociology of Max Weber* (London: Allen Lane, The Penguin Press, 1968) pp. 71–79. (Translation of *Sociologie de Max Weber* Paris: Presses Universitaires de France, 1966).

[19] M. Weber, 'Objective Possibility and Adequate Causation in Historical Explanation' (1905), reprinted in: *Max Weber on The Methodology of the Social Sciences*, p. 171; italics in original.

[20] Ibid. p. 173.

The rather substantial role which Weber assigns to ideal types in the methodology of the social sciences, makes him a proponent of a 'primacy of theory' view in the social sciences—a theme which both Einstein and Popper were to express a little later for the natural sciences. For Einstein, scientific theories are free constructions of the human mind; for Popper they are bold conjectures. With the emphasis on the primacy of theory and the theory-ladenness of empirical data comes a serious doubt concerning inductivism. Weber pronounces for the social sciences, what others pronounced for the natural sciences. He argues against an inductive view of the methods of the social sciences, according to which

> it is the end and goal of every science to order its data into a system of concepts, the content of which is to be acquired and slowly perfected through the observation of empirical regularities, the construction of hypotheses, and their verification ... [22]

Rather, Weber explicitly appeals to the basic Kantian idea that 'concepts are primarily analytical instruments for the intellectual mastery of empirical data'.[23] But unlike Kant, Weber insists on the inevitability of ever new ideal-typical constructions, depending on the changing perception of the problems which in turn depend on different cultural contexts. Because of the changeability of the contents of historical concepts, their sharp definition is essential.[24]

Thus, Weber's own delineation of ideal types seems to possess all the clarity which he requires of ideal types; they are theoretical constructions whose function is to bring out the specific and typical characteristics of historical movements, individuals or developmental sequences and to determine adequate causes without, however, claiming that these specific characteristics correspond to the actual reality of these events. Weber declares that

[22] 'Objectivity in Social Science', p. 106. ' ... es sei das Endziel, der Zweck, jeder Wissenschaft, ihren Stoff in einem System von Begriffen zu ordnen, deren Inhalt durch Beobachtung empirischer Regelmäßigkeiten, Hypothesenbildung und Verifikation derselben zu gewinnen sei ... ' 'Objektivität der Erkenntnis', p. 254.

[23] 'Objectivity in Social Science', p. 106. ' ... daß die Begriffe vielmehr gedankliche Mittel zum Zweck der geistigen Beherrschung des empirisch Gegebenen sind und allein sein können'. 'Objektivität der Erkenntnis', p. 255.

[24] See 'Objectivity in Social Science', pp. 104–110, where Weber points out (pp. 110–111) that the dangers which lie in the lack of sharp definitions is illustrated in expressions like 'the interest of agriculture' or 'the class interest of the worker'.

the coming of age of science in fact always implies the transcendence of the ideal-type, insofar as it was thought of as possessing empirical validity or as a class *concept (Gattungsbegriff)*[25]

—again explicitly disavowing any claim to the empirical validity of ideal types.

However, the clarity in Weber's conception of ideal types, suggested earlier, must be contrasted with the emphasis on the usefulness of ideal types for an empirical social science. For Weber their utility lies in the determination of the unique individual character of cultural phenomena.[26]

But if they are to serve as models in the social sciences, their applicability to empirical reality must be probed further. What is the origin of ideal types? Are they free inventions of the human mind or theoretical constructions suggested by some familiarity of the social scientist with empirical reality? The latter hypothesis is probably the correct one:

An ideal type is formed by the one-sided *accentuation* of one or more points of view and by the synthesis of a great many diffuse, discrete, more or less present and occasionally absent *concrete individual* phenomena, which are arranged according to those one-sidedly emphasized viewpoints into a unified *analytical* construct *(Gedankenbild)*.[27]

All ruling powers, profane and religious, political and apolitical, may be considered as variations of, or approximations to, certain pure types. These types are constructed by searching for the basis of *legitimacy*, which the ruling power claims.[28]

Only through ideal-typical concept-construction do the viewpoints with which we are concerned in individual cases become

---

[25] 'Objectivity in Social Science', pp. 104, 92. ' ... die reif werdende Wissenschaft bedeutet in der Tat immer *Überwindung* des Idealtypus, sofern er als empirisch *geltend* oder als *Gattungsbegriff* gedacht wird'. 'Objektivität der Erkenntnis', pp. 252, 237–238; italics in original.

[26] See 'Objectivity in Social Science', p. 106.

[27] Ibid. 90. 'Er wird gewonnen durch einseitige *Steigerung eines* oder *einiger* Gesichtspunkte und durch Zusammenschluß einer Fülle von diffus und diskret, hier mehr, dort weniger, stellenweise gar nicht, vorhandenen *Einzel*erscheinungen, die sich jenen einseitig herausgehobenen Gesichtspunkten fügen, zu einem in sich einheitlichen *Gedanken*bilde.' 'Objektivität der Erkenntnis', p. 235; italics in original.

[28] 'The Social Psychology of the World Religions', p. 294; italics in original.

explicit. Their peculiar character is brought out by the *confrontation* of empirical reality with the ideal type.[29]

... nothing should be more sharply emphasized than the proposition that the knowledge of the *cultural significance of concrete historical events and patterns* is exclusively and solely the final end which, among other means, concept construction and the criticism of constructs also seek to serve.[30]

These quotes, I hope, make clear that the validity of the ideal types must be grounded in empirical reality. They are—at least potentially—not such pure constructs that a concern for their relevance to the empirical evidence is misplaced. They cannot be as devoid of content (*inhaltsleer*), as Weber describes them in *Wirtschaft und Gesellschaft*. On the contrary, Weber not only stresses the empirical significance of ideal types but also the degree to which they may approximate empirical reality:

They enable us to see if, in particular traits or in their total character, the phenomena approximate one of our constructions: to determine the degree of approximation of the historical phenomenon to the theoretically constructed type.[31]

Thus, despite appearances to the contrary, there is a certain tension in Weber's conception of ideal types: They need to be abstractions from, rather than descriptions of, empirical reality to determine the typical and possibly repeatable aspects of this reality but they cannot be so removed from the concrete world that they lose their empirical validity. If the ideal types do not, in some sense, *fit* the realm of empirical data to which they supposedly refer, then any comparison and any attempt at determining their deviation from or approximation to the historical or social phenomena would be out of question. This tension in Weber's

[29] 'Objectivity in Social Science', p. 110. 'Nur durch idealtypische Begriffsformeln werden die Gesichtspunkte, die im Einzelfall in Betracht kommen, in ihrer Eigenart im Wege der *Konfrontation* des Empirischen mit dem Idealtypus wirklich deutlich.' 'Objektivität der Erkenntnis', p. 259; italics in original.

[30] 'Objectivity in Social Science', p. 111. ' ... nichts sollte hier schärfer betont werden als der Satz, daß der Dienst an der Erkenntnis der *Kulturbedeutung konkreter historischer Zusammenhänge* ausschließlich und allein das letzte Ziel ist, dem, nach anderen Mitteln, *auch* die begriffsbildende und begriffskritische Arbeit dienen will.' 'Objektivität der Erkenntnis', p. 261; italics in original.

[31] 'Religious Rejections of the World and their Directions', in H. H. Gerth and C. Wright Mills (eds.), *From Max Weber*, Essays in Sociology (London: Routledge & Kegan Paul, 1970), p. 324.

conception of ideal types can be described in terms of the difference between objective possibilities and objective probabilities.

II. Wavering between objective possibility and objective probability

Ideal types have been characterized as *theoretical constructions* to which no empirical reality strictly corresponds. Still, Weber places heavy emphasis on their comparative functions so that it is a reasonable requirement on ideal types that they should refer to and make a statement about this reality. They do not have to be faithful replicas of the socio-historical world in order to serve the function of stating important aspects of this world. Casting them as pure types, Weber is tempted to construct ideal types as objective possibilities only; but if their confrontation with reality is to be fruitful, a better approach may be to cast them as objective probabilities. Indeed, Weber wavers between objective possibility and objective probability. This becomes clear, for instance, in his determination of collection action (*Gemeinschaftshandeln*) as

> either 1. a *historically* observed or 2. *theoretically* construed behaviour—as objectively 'possible' or 'probable'—of individuals compared to the actual or imagined potential behaviour of other individuals.[32]

The only piece of writing in which the major emphasis is on the objective possibility of ideal types is to be found in *Objective Possibility and Adequate causation in Historical Explanation* (1905). A historical event is objectively possible when it is made to differ from the actual event by a modification or exclusion of certain conditions which brought about the actual event. By such exercises in abstraction the historian tries to determine the significance of the 'real' causes of the event. 'Like the ideal type, objective possibility constructs an "imaginary picture", a Utopia, except that, instead of accentuating characteristic traits, it abstracts one or several elements of the actual situation in order to discover what might have happened.'[33] But even in the determination of historical cases, Weber finds an analogy between the causality to be attributed to a chain of events in history and the objective probability to be found

---

[32] ' ... ein entweder 1. *historisch* beobachtetes oder 2. ein *theoretisch*, als objektiv "möglich" oder "wahrscheinlich" konstruiertes Sichverhalten von *Einzelnen* zum aktuellen oder zum vorgestellten potentiellen Sichverhalten anderer Einzelner.' 'Über einige Kategorien der verstehenden Soziologie', p. 114; italics in original; translated by the author.

[33] Freund, *Weber*, p. 74.

in, say, the throwing of dice. There is of course 'no numerical measure of chance' by which an historical event may occur, given certain antecedent conditions. Still it is possible to determine, even in the field of history, with a certain degree of certainty which conditions are more likely to bring about an effect than others.[34]

In a characteristic passage of *Wirtschaft und Gesellschaft*, Weber points to the *as if* construction of ideal types:

> The ideal types of social action which for instance are used in economic theory are thus unrealistic or abstract in that they always ask what course of action would take place if it were purely rational and oriented to economic ends alone.[35]

This characterization does not necessarily conflict with the emphasis on the heuristic functions of ideal types noted earlier, especially if we are ready to accept a purely instrumentalist interpretation of ideal types. But given Weber's wavering between objective possibility and objective probability, and his concern for the empirical relevance of ideal types, the alternative would be to understand ideal types not as heuristic devices but as hypothetical models. It is typical of models in the natural and social sciences to make abstractions from certain real factors to such an extent that the consequent behaviour is only true *ceteris paribus*, i.e., under the assumption that the other factors do not interfere or have no real influence on the parameters under consideration. This does not prevent these models from claiming empirical relevance and hence from having significance as statements about the real world. How is this achieved?

Whilst Weber failed to move ideal types clearly towards objective probabilities, Howard Becker and J. C. McKinney have attempted to develop Weber's ideal types into a tool of empirical science. Rather than speaking of *ideal* types, they call their constructions *constructed* types which McKinney defines as

> a purposive, planned selection, abstraction, combination, and (sometimes) accentuation of a set of criteria with *empirical* referents that serves as a basis for the comparison of empirical cases.[36]

[34] 'Objective Possibility and Adequate Causation', p. 183.

[35] *Economy and Society*, p. 21. 'Jene idealtypischen Konstruktionen sozialen Handelns, welche z.B. die Wirtschaftstheorie vornimmt, sind also in dem Sinn "wirklichkeitsfremd", als sie—in diesem Fall—durchweg fragen: wie würde im Falle idealer und dabei rein wirtschaftlich orientierter Zweckrationalitat gehandelt werden ... ' M. Weber, *Wirtschaft und Gesellschaft*, ed. J. Winckelmann, (Fifth edition, J. C. B. Mohr, Tubingen, 1972), p. 10.

[36] J. C. McKinney, *Constructive Typology and Social Theory* (New York: Appleton-Century-Crofts, 1966), p. 25; italics added.

The Becker-McKinney model moves away from the mere logical possibility expressed by the ideal type, which according to Weber's preferred understanding contains no more than a mere fiction bereft of empirical reference, to an emphasis on the objective probability of the empirical occurrence of the type.

> The Becker-McKinney model of constructed type is an ideal type shorn of any purely fictional qualities, firmly grounded in the particularities of actual situations, and constituted by attributes that are empirically discoverable.[37]

> The constructed type is a theoretically plausible course of action or structure which has been *constructed* on the basis of observed empirical occurrences ... It is the concept of probability that puts an empirical interpretation upon the constructed type and bridges the gap between the heuristic device and the empirical occurrence.[38]

Such a procedure could, for instance, be used to study the role of intellectuals in dictatorial societies. As we have seen, there is little in Weber's writing which would resist this reorientation of the ideal type towards the constructed type. Indeed, McKinney asserts that Weber's ideal type is merely a special case of the more general category of constructive types.[39] These should be conceived as *systems* wherein the relations between the characteristics are held constant. 'As a system, the type has the character of a theoretical model that is susceptible of empirical interpretation.'[40]

The ability of the type to idealize or abstract from the particularities of the historical manifold had already arrested our attention. But now it appears that constructed types and by implication ideal types must be understood as *systems* or ordered sets of elements between which certain relations hold. 'The constructed type organizes experience in a somewhat different fashion than does the ordinary concept in that it forms a series of attributes into a configuration that is not necessarily directly experienced and accentuates one or more of the attributes for theoretical purposes.'[41] Thus it is required of types that they do not only idealize and abstract from concrete experience but also that they systematize experience. Experience comes in sets of elements with many relations between them so that any viable type must be able to express some of these relations. It is characteristic of models in the natural

[37] Ibid. p. 26.
[38] Ibid. p. 51.
[39] Ibid. p. 2.
[40] Ibid. p. 7.
[41] Ibid. p. 11; cf. Goode, 'A Note on the Ideal Type', pp. 473–474.

sciences that they also perform these three functions: *Abstraction, Idealisation* and *Systematisation*. Before we can justify the interpretation of ideal types as hypothetical models in the social sciences, it is convenient to briefly review the different types of models in the natural sciences.

III. Models in the Natural Sciences

It is important to distinguish *roles* of models from *types* of models. Their role is to idealize, abstract and systematize. The attraction of models in science resides in their *tractability*,[42] i.e. the fact that models allow the study of selected relationships between selected parameters. In a general sense, all models represent structures: in Roman's terminology 'topologic structures' in which the emphasis is on the spatial ordering of the elements or 'algebraic structures' in which the emphasis is on various mathematical relationships between elements of the model.[43] Sophisticated models may combine both structures. There are different types of models to play these roles. Fürth distinguishes **functional** models, **structural** models, **analogue** models and **scale** models.[44] *Scale* models or mechanical models are imitations of real-life objects which may either be reduced in size (like cars, planetary models) or enlarged in size (like the double helix of the DNA molecule or the Aids virus). *Analogue* models represent the unfamiliar or unobservable in terms of the familiar or observable and suggest that material or formal analogies exist between the two systems. A parallel electric circuit may be represented by a system of water tubes to illustrate such notions as electric current and potential difference. It is based on the material analogy of flow.

Typical *functional* models are the Carnot cycle for an ideal gas, relating volume and pressure, or the supply and demand curves in economics, determining the price equilibrium at their intersection (Figure 1). These models display a fair degree of abstraction, and are not representational in a naive sense, in which, for instance, a scale model is representational. But the loss of pictorial representation is made good by the functional information gained, either in terms of the information about the net work done by the gas

[42] M. Redhead, 'Models in Physics', *Brit. J. Phil. Sc.*, **31** (1980), 147.

[43] P. Roman, 'Symmetry in Physics', *Boston Studies in the Philosophy of Science*, Volume V, ed. R. S. Cohen and M. W. Wartofsky (Dordrecht: D. Reidel, 1969), p. 364.

[44] R. Fürth, 'The Role of Models in Theoretical Physics', *Boston Studies in the Philosophy of Science* Volume V, pp. 327–340.

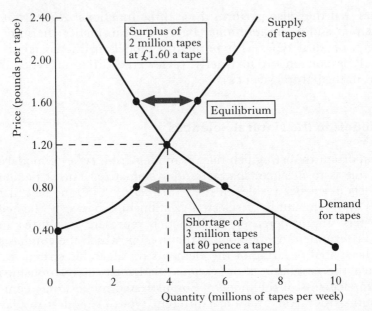

Figure 1. Equilibrium (from M. Parkin and D. King, *Economics* (Addison Wesley, 1992). p. 73).

during one cycle or in terms of the price determination. Thus these models represent the functional dependence of parameters.

Structural models do not give functional information by relating several parameters but place a number of parameters in some order to represent, again in an abstract way, the structure, usually of microsystems. Often these models combine topologic and algebraic features. In the case of quantum mechanics, these structural models often grew out of analogue models. For instance the Rutherford-Bohr model of the hydrogen atom was inspired by an analogy with planetary systems in which one planet orbits a central massive gravitational body. But as quantum mechanics progressed, these early models gave way to more precise structural models which become more abstract—less representational in a pictorial sense—but again accompanied by a considerable gain in structural information. This can be illustrated by reference to the model of the normal Zeeman effect (Figure 2), i.e. the splitting of energy levels of an atom when placed in an external magnetic field. This model illustrates the function of tractability: First, it gives the energy levels under the abstracting condition that there is no orbit-spin interaction; but it still contains precise mathematical information about the interaction of the orbital angular momentum of the electron and the influence of a uniform magnetic field.

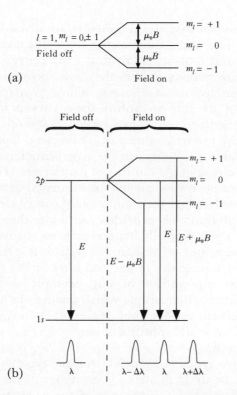

Figure 2. (a) The Zeeman splitting of an $l=1$ level in an external magnetic field. (The effects of the electron's spin angular momentum are ignored.) The energy in a magnetic field is different for different values of m_l. (b) The normal Zeeman effect. When the field is turned on, the single wavelength λ becomes three separate wavelengths. (From K. Krane, *Modern Physics* (Chichester: John Wiley, 1983), p. 194.)

In this sense it represents an algebraic structure. Second, it illustrates the *relative* nature of idealizations and abstractions.[45] When the spin-orbit interaction of the electron is considered, the model becomes more complicated, since more spectral lines appear.

[45] The fact that idealizations and abstractions are subject to modifications such that the parameters in the model can be brought into closer agreement with the actual parameters in the physical systems is stressed by Ronald Laymon in several publications: 'Idealizations and the Testing of Theories by Experimentation', *Observation, Experiment, and Hypothesis in Modern Physical Science*, ed. P. Achinstein and O. Hannaway (Cambridge: MIT Press, 1985), pp. 147–174; 'Cartwright and the Lying Laws of Physics', *Journal of Philosophy*, **86/7** (1989), 353–372; 'The Computational and Confirmational Differences Between the Social and the Physical Sciences', *Philosophia*, **22** (1993), 241–273.

Better experimental data also required relativistic corrections to the Bohr model. The approximation or fit of the model to the real physical system it represents can thus be improved. These corrections to the abstractions and idealizations incorporated in models are a significant feature of research. Third, revised models of the hydrogen atom are able to capture these various interactions and hence satisfy the third role, noted earlier, that models must be able to represent the interrelatedness of parameters. Computer models offer innumerable advantages in the representation of interrelatedness and an increase in the number of parameters. This is especially important when observational and experimental data are limited, as in climate modelling and the simulation of galaxy formations.

Thus structural models provide much more than just functional information. They typically represent a mechanism of how the observable behaviour of a natural system is generated—as for instance in the appearance of spectral lines or the normal Zeeman effect. Because the model in our example is related to the quantum-mechanical equations which govern the normal and the anomalous Zeeman effects, they represent the algebraic structure of what is known as the splitting of energy levels, or at least part of this phenomenon.

To the above types of models a further type should be added: **hypothetical** or *as if* models. These types of models emphasize what would happen if a given natural or socio-economic system would only consist of a limited number of parameters. The perfectly rational economic agent is such a hypothetical model. Inclined *frictionless* planes are examples from Newtonian physics (Figure 3).

As far as ideal types are concerned, an interpretation either as analogue models or hypothetical models may seem to be the most appropriate. As indicated above, Weber alternatively emphasizes both the heuristic nature of ideal types and their approximation to empirical reality. Weber's insistence on the empirical nature of sociology provides a reason why an understanding of ideal types in terms of hypothetical models may be the most adequate interpretation. Additionally, there are also features of analogue models which render them inappropriate for an identification with ideal types.

IV. Ideal Types as Hypothetical Models in the Social Sciences

Several writers have identified ideal types with *as if* models. According to Alan Ryan, 'Max Weber coined the term "ideal type" to describe the process of reasoning about a kind of "entity" which we quite clearly know could never have existed. (...) The

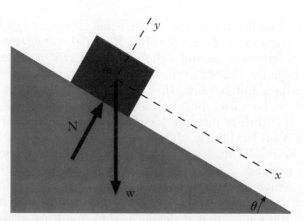

Figure 3. Forces acting on a block of mass m on a frictionless incline. It is convenient to choose the x axis parallel to the incline (from P. A. Tipler, *Physics*, second edition (Worth Publishers, 1982), p. 95).

Newtonian concept of the "point mass" is an ideal type in just the same sense in its context as is economic man in his.'[46] We recall that Weber tends to treat ideal types as uninstantiated constructs. Yet non-instantiation happens both in the case of analogue models and *as if* models. Water currents serve as analogue models to aid our understanding of electric currents. Equally, planetary models of atoms may serve as analogue models in our understanding of atoms. But it is known in these cases that the analogy is *false*. Electric currents are not water currents and atoms are not planetary systems. It is misleading to identify ideal type concepts simply with analogue models of which it is known that the analogy is false. Analogue models do not involve idealizations from factors we expect to find in the system modelled. In fact, it seems to be a characteristic of analogue models that they do not refer, even partially, to any of the components which make up the natural system which is to be modelled. Despite Weber's insistence to the contrary, this cannot be true of ideal types. Ideal types comprise idealizations and abstractions from the real socio-historical world. They must be models in the *hypothetical* sense: '*If* this were a true model, then people would be likely to behave in certain ways.'[47] In this sense a rational economic agent is an idealization and abstraction from economic reality. By idealizing and abstracting from

[46] A. Ryan, *The Philosophy of the Social Sciences* (London: Macmillan, 1970), p. 92. See also J. Lewis, *Max Weber and Value-Free Sociology. A Marxist Critique* (London: Lawrence and Wishart, 1975), p. 51.

[47] Lewis, *Max Weber*, p. 51. McKinney, *Constructive Typology and Social Theory*, pp. 9–19, 46, 66.

Friedel Weinert

empirical reality the model of the *homo economicus* expresses some salient features of economic life. Rational considerations are not alien to economic agents although they hardly ever exist in pure form. Equally, Weber's types of authority refer to existing types of domination, not because they are heuristic analogues which are known to be false, but because they are idealized *hypothetical* forms of authority just like Newton's point masses: 'If this were x, then it would exhibit y.' The point is that in its very hypothetical form the model makes a statement about the empirical reality to which it refers. There is a structure embedded in the empirical reality which the model at least approximates. In principle this is true of the point mass *and* Weber's ideal types. It is not an objection to the model that it deviates from empirical reality; it has to deviate by virtue of being a model with its three essential functions. But the structure which the model expresses must contain at least an approximation to the empirical cases it refers to; otherwise any hope of comparison, on which Weber insisted, is thwarted. Thus it must be the case in actual examples of traditional authority that in one way or another 'legitimacy is claimed for it and believed in it by virtue of the sanctity of age-old rules and powers';[48] it must be the case if the ideal type is properly constructed, because these features express the essential structure of traditional authority. Hypothetical models involve idealizations and abstractions from factors we expect to be part of the actual physical or socio-economic system which is modelled but no such idealizations and abstractions are involved in analogue models. Analogue models are simply heuristic devices with no referential claims.

Yet there is a serious objection to this attempt to interpret ideal types as empirically meaningful models in the social sciences. It is due to David Papineau and states that ideal types are unfalsifiable because they are cast in non-instantiated terms.[49] They are neither to be identified with *as if* models nor with *ceteris paribus* laws. Furthermore, the utility of ideal types cannot be rescued, as Weber so confidently assumes, by pointing out that real situations approximate to the ideal type. The problem is that the degree of approximation is not in general specified. Papineau's conclusion can be stated in Weber's own words: the ideal type 'is no "hypothesis" but it offers guidance to the construction of hypotheses.'[50]

At least the first part of Papineau's criticism can be deflected. There are other passages in Weber's work, apart from the above-

[48] *Economy and Society*, p. 226.
[49] D. Papineau, 'Ideal Types and Empirical Theories', *Brit. J. Phil. Sc.*, **27** (1976), 137–146.
[50] 'Objectivity in Social Science', p. 90.

quoted statement from *Economy and Society*, in which Weber explicitly interprets ideal types as hypothetical models.[51] More importantly, the non-instantiation is no obstacle to the referential function of hypothetical models. If it is 'a distinguishing characteristic of ideal type concepts (...) that they have no instances',[52] then this is also true of *as if* models (ideal gases) and *ceteris paribus* laws (Newton's First law). For it is the characteristic achievement of models that they idealize, systematize and abstract from parameters in the particular systems they are intended to model. Many models, with the exception of analogue models, are referential; their task is to represent the algebraic or topologic structure of the systems which they model. This representation is rarely pictorial. For the sake of representation many factors must be left out. Physical situations are often vector products of various forces which the model ignores. If it is a good model, the factors ignored are known to have negligible effects on the relationships represented. But it would be a mistake to think that because a concept, law or model is not instantiated, it has no significance for the empirical world. The often-repeated statement that Newton's First Law is vacuous—it applies only to systems on which no other forces are exerted—is misleading. The fact that there are no physical systems in the known universe in which no other forces interfere with Newton's First Law, does not mean that in actual physical situations Newton's law does not apply. On the contrary, Newton's First Law applies on conjunction with other forces, producing a physical situation which is the resultant of the various forces. Newton's First Law is only vacuous in the sense that it cannot be found acting exclusively in a particular physical situation. Physical situations like orbits are not possible without Newton's First Law. Whatever the resultant of various forces, the physical world remains subject to each one of the component forces.

The second part of Papineau's criticism, however, poses a serious challenge: the degrees of approximation of ideal types are often either left unspecified or cannot be specified for empirical reasons. It is characteristic of the natural sciences, however, that degrees to approximation can often be specified and that interfering factors can be shown to be negligible. Although Weber leaves us in no doubt that the point of the construction of ideal types is their *comparison* with empirical reality:

Whatever the content of the ideal type ... it has only one function (*Zweck*) in an empirical investigation. Its function is the

[51] M. Weber, 'The Meaning of Ethical Neutrality', reprinted in *Max Weber on The Methodology of the Social Sciences*, pp. 42–44.

[52] Papineau, 'Ideal Types', p. 137.

comparison with empirical reality in order to establish its divergences or similarities, to describe them with the *most unambiguously intelligible concepts*, and to understand and explain them causally,[53]

he fails to meet Papineau's charge—the degree of approximation is nowhere specified. It is a well-known problem in the social sciences—more so than in the physical sciences—that it is well-nigh impossible to specify in the models all the determinant factors which enter into real social situations and hence to achieve closure.[54] However, the purpose of ideal types is to specify the salient features of social or economic situations, stripping away, in the process, accidental features which account for differences between various situations which fall under the ideal type.[55] While this is Weber's statement of the purpose of ideal types, it is far more difficult to draw the line between the essential and accidental features. Weber's ideal types are not quantitative scientific concepts and hence any degree of approximation which can be specified will tend to be qualitative. The real situations, which fall within the range of the ideal type, will be combinations of many different factors and it may be difficult to determine precisely how they deviate from the ideal type. Different social scientists, even if

[53] M. Weber, 'The Meaning of Ethical Neutrality', p. 43, cf. 44; italics in original. 'Denn welchen Inhalt immer der rationale Idealtypus hat (...) stets hat seine Konstruktion innerhalb empirischer Untersuchungen nur *den* Zweck: die empirische Wirklichkeit mit ihm zu "vergleichen", ihren Kontrast oder ihren Abstand von ihm oder ihre relative Annäherung an ihn festzustellen, um sie so mit möglichst eindeutig *verständlichen Begriffen* beschreiben und kausal zurechnend verstehen und erklären zu können.' M. Weber, 'Der Sinn der Wertfreiheit', reprinted in Weber, *Soziologie*, p. 304, cf. S. 306; italics in original.

[54] Cf. N. Cartwright, '*Ceteris Paribus* Laws and Socio-Economic Machines', *The Monist*, **78/3** (1995), 276–294. P. Pietroski and G. Rey, 'When Other Things Aren't Equal: Saving *Ceteris Paribus* Laws from Vacuity', *Brit. J. Phil. Sc.*, **46** (1995), 81–110. Laymon, 'The Computational and Confirmational Differences'. McKinney, *Constructive Typology and Social Theory*, p. 214. F. Weinert, 'On the Status of Social Laws', forthcoming.

[55] Popper recommended a very similar procedure for the social sciences, which he called 'zero method': 'the method of constructing a model on the assumption of the possession of complete rationality (and perhaps the assumption of the possession of complete information) on the part of all the individuals concerned, and of estimating the deviation of the actual behaviour of people from the model behaviour, using the latter as a kind of zero co-ordinate'. K. Popper, *The Poverty of Historicism*, (London: Routledge & Kegan Paul 1961), p. 141.

they agree on the usefulness of the ideal type, may disagree about the deviation and the factors which can be safely regarded as accidental and those which are essential. This may have an effect on any attempt to establish the approximation of the ideal type to its corresponding empirical reality. This is probably the most serious difference between the natural and the social sciences in their respective employment of hypothetical models.[56] There are numerous examples in the physical sciences where an improvement in the approximation of the parameters in the hypothetical model to the parameters in the real physical system has led to a better correspondence between the equations in the model and the physical system: examples are the transition from the simple pendulum to the physical pendulum and from the ideal gas laws to the van der Waals' equation. If ideal types are to function as hypothetical or *as if* models in the social sciences on a par with similar models in the natural sciences, a serious obstacle presents itself: Deviations from or empirical exceptions to the models must be explicable in terms of independent factors or even lawlike regularities. In other words, it must be known whether the exception is only apparent and can be accounted for by appeal to some additional boundary conditions or whether the exception is genuine and constitutes a 'refutation' of the model.[57] Furthermore, the model should be sensitive to improvements by bringing some of its parameters into closer approximation with parameters in the real system which is being modelled. In other words there must be an increase in output sensitivity to variations in input error.[58] These obstacles present themselves under the interpretation of ideal types as hypothetical models and their concomitant representational nature. If the approximation of the ideal-typical situation to the real cannot be handled in an appropriate way and if exceptions cannot be properly classified as genuine or apparent, the danger for ideal types is that they are reduced to the purely logical constructs or heuristic devices in which at least one strand of Weber's thinking cast them. But then they are threatened by vacuity, creating a source of tension for Weber's conception of sociology as an empirical science.

[56] Laymon, 'The Computational and Confirmational Differences'.

[57] Pietroski and Rey, 'When Other Things Aren't Equal'. Weinert, 'On the Status of Social Laws'.

[58] Laymon, 'The Computational and Confirmational Differences', p. 250. A. Rosenberg, *Philosophy of Social Science*, second edition (Boulder: Westview Press 1995), pp. 159–161.

Verstehen, Holism and Fascism

DAVID E. COOPER

A subtitle for this paper might have been 'The ugly face of *Verstehen*', for it asks whether the theory of *Verstehen* has, to switch metaphors, 'dirty hands'. By the theory of *Verstehen*, I mean the constellation of concepts—life, experience, expression, interpretative understanding—which, according to Wilhelm Dilthey, are essential for the study of human affairs, thereby showing that 'the methodology of the human studies [*Geisteswissenschaften*] is ... different from that of the physical sciences' (SW 177):[1] for in the latter, these concepts have no similar place. Even critics of Dilthey tend to agree that his heart, if not his head, was in the right place: that *Verstehen* was designed as an antidote to 'dehumanizing' attempts by positivists to reduce the categories used in explaining human behaviour (value, meaning, purpose etc.) to just those equally operative in the physical sciences (cause and effect, stimulus and response, etc.). As Dilthey himself put it, 'there is no real blood flowing in the veins' of human beings as examined by the positivists and their precursors: they do not treat of 'the whole man' (HS 73). The idea of *Verstehen*, it seems, is doubly humane: a humanizing approach to the humane studies.

A rather indirect reason for pausing before this favourable verdict is the reputation of an earlier thinker much admired by Dilthey—J. G. Herder. In Herder, we find several themes taken up by Dilthey: the critique of Enlightenment projects to encompass mental life within the boundaries of the natural sciences; the idea that we must 'enter the spirit of a nation ... before [we] can share even one of its thoughts or deeds';[2] and reference to a vital 'energizing principle' which is the source for action within a community. But if Herder—with his 'congenial empathy into the spirit of ages', as Dilthey put it (SW 256)—is a precursor of *Verstehen*,

---

[1] References in the text to Dilthey are to page numbers of *Dilthey: Selected Writings* (SW), ed. H. P. Rickman (Cambridge University Press, 1986); *Introduction to the Human Sciences* (HS), trans. R. Betanzos (London: Harvester, 1988); *Gesammelte Schriften* (GS), 19 volumes (Leipzig: Teuber, 1923–); and *The Essence of Philosophy* (EP), trans. S. and W. Emery (Chapel: University of North Carolina Press, 1954).

[2] *On Social and Political Culture*, trans. F. Barnard (Cambridge University Press, 1969), p. 181.

he is also now recognized as the wellspring of currents in twentieth-century fascism and, as one might call it, militant multi-culturalism.[3] It was Herder who invented the notion of the *Volksgeist*, that 'folk soul' without which there can be no genuine community, national identity or culture, and who came close to regarding each *Volksgeist* as being at once hermetically sealed off from any other and above rational criticism. A culture informed by such a *Geist* is no more to be adjudicated from the outside than its language is from the standpoint of an alien language, Dilthey, to be sure, is critical of the 'folk soul', but primarily because he thinks it insufficiently precise. For all its defects, the idea of a '*Volksgeist* creating unconsciously' and developing 'living expressions' of itself, such as a literary tradition, was a 'marvellous intuition' (HS 111).

But there is no need for this indirect strategy in order to suggest that *Verstehen* may have an ugly, specifically fascistic, face. For the charge that Dilthey—though himself a political liberal by nineteenth-century German criteria—was responsible for important ingredients in National Socialist philosophy has been levelled by Georg Lukács. In Chapter IV of his massive *The Destruction of Reason*, Lukács traces what he sees as an inexorable development from Dilthey's remarks on 'Life', *via* the 'vitalist' views of such fascistically inclined writers as Oswald Spengler and Ernst Jünger, to the full blown irrationalist *Lebensphilophien* of Nazi ideologues like Alfred Rosenberg and Alfred Baeumler. These latter, he writes, 'drew the ultimate conclusions of vitalism and completed that journey which began with Nietzsche and Dilthey', so that the 'barbaric cul-de-sac' they entered was the 'necessary climax' of the attack on scientific reason launched by those earlier writers.[4]

Lukács is right to emphasize the central role that 'Life' plays in Dilthey's philosophy. 'Life', wrote Dilthey, 'is the fundamental fact ... that behind which it is impossible to go' (GS VII 359). Understanding (*Verstehen*) is for him a matter, in the final analysis, of grasping the 'Life' which human actions and products 'express'. Lukács is right, too, to stress the role of 'Life' in the aetiology of fascist thought. Here, for instance, is Spengler in full flight in a book subtitled 'A contribution to a philosophy of life': Life is nothing that can be understood by science with its 'chemical',

[3] See Alain Finkielkraut, *The Undoing of Thought*, trans. D. O'Keeffe (London: Claridge, 1988) and Samuel Fleischacker, *The Ethics of Culture* (Ithaca: Cornell University Press, 1994) on Herder's influence on fascism and multi-culturalism.

[4] *The Destruction of Reason*, trans. P. Palmer (London: Merlin, 1980), pp. 536ff.

'static' methods, but is only revealed 'through unsophisticated living with it'. Since Life is thereby revealed as 'active, fighting, and charged', each person and nation which would swim with and not against it, must live as a 'beast of prey', a 'Viking of the blood'.[5]

For two reasons, however, the journey from Dilthey's conception of Life to the fascist vitalism of a Spengler cannot be the direct and inexorable one that Lukács maps. 'Life, has altered its sense on that journey. First, as Lukács concedes, Dilthey 'did not believe in an irreconcilable antithesis between reason and life'.[6] On the contrary, Dilthey refers to a 'deep coherence' between knowledge and Life; to the way, for example, 'increase of certainty' raises the level of our life-activity, which in turn promotes further 'well-grounded knowledge', and so on (EP 36). For the fascist vitalists, on the other hand, 'Life' was defined precisely by way of contrast with reason and intellect.' Thus the title of Ludwig Klages' best-selling work of the 1930s was *Der Geist* als *Widersacher der Seele*, in which he makes such pronouncements as 'mind (*Geist*) signifies a force which is directed *against* life'—a view parallelled by Spengler's opposition between 'Vikings of the blood' and 'Vikings of the mind', or D. H. Lawrence's vow to 'answer to my blood, direct, without the fribbling intervention of mind'.[7] Second, Dilthey restricts the term 'Life' to human cultural and mental life. It is not a biological concept, let alone a cosmic one applicable—as it was for Bergson, say—to the whole process of Nature. Yet these were precisely the ways in which 'Life' was understood by the fascist vitalists, as we saw in the case of Spengler. The main reason offered by a more authoritative spokesman for fascism, Adolf Hitler, for 'the subordination of ... the individual to the community', the *völkisch* nation, is that the division into such nations 'corresponds ... to the ultimate will of Nature': it is an 'expression of [Nature's] most vital urge'.[8]

If Dilthey is to blame, then, it is not because he spoke of Life in the blatantly irrationalist, biological and cosmic terms of later vitalists, but because 'Life' was hardly the most apt choice, perhaps, for conveying his point. When we have understood that

[5] *Man and Technics: a contribution to a philosophy of life*, trans. C. Atkinson (London: Allen & Unwin, 1932), pp. 10ff.

[6] *Destruction of Reason*, p. 430.

[7] Klages quoted in Herbert Schnädelbach, *Philosophy in Germany 1831–1933*, trans. E. Matthews (Cambridge University Press, 1984), p. 151; Lawrence quoted in George Lichtheim, *Europe in the Twentieth Century* (London: Cardinal, 1974), p. 184.

[8] *Mein Kampf*, trans. D. Watt (London: Hutchinson, 1974), pp. 271, 258.

point, we can then ask again whether his position has an 'elective affinity' with aspects of fascist thought. My argument so far is simply that any such affinity is not, as Lukács imagined, with vitalism as promulgated by Spengler, Klages, Hitler and other precursors or practitioners of Nazism.

Imprudent as the choice of the term 'Life' may have been, it registers a central ingredient in Dilthey's theory of *Verstehen*. I shall refer to this as Dilthey's 'deep holism'. By holism, with respect to some domain of investigation, I mean the view that items in that domain can only be understood by recognizing their place within the whole domain. To cite Dilthey's favourite illustration: the significance of a musical note is only grasped by appreciating its position in the whole melody. Of course, the melody is nothing in addition to its notes, hence it is a typical instance of the hermeneutic principle that 'the whole must be understood in terms of its individual parts, [these] in terms of the whole' (SW 262). Dilthey's holism operates at different levels, according to the size, as it were, of the domain investigated. Thus, since a person's life is 'not a sum ... of successive moments but a unity [of] relationships which link all the parts' (SW 185), the meaning of episodes in that life can only be understood through their contribution to the whole which is completed by death. But the whole of that life, in turn, can only be understood in relation to a larger whole. Thus 'Luther's life' has its 'historical meaning' through 'form[ing] part of a more comprehensive context of actual events' (SW 239), the Reformation, events which in their turn 'can only be understood completely in terms of [their] relation to [a larger] whole' (SW 196).

But where, if 'meaning means nothing except belonging to a whole' (SW 233), does the process of understanding end? What is that ultimate whole or 'total conception' to which, finally, full understanding of anything human—a person's life, the historical events in which it is embroiled, the institutions in which he participates—must eventually refer us? Dilthey's name for this ultimate whole is 'Life', the whole 'context of interactions between people' which therefore 'forms the basis for all its individual forms and systems, for our experience, understanding, expressions and comparative study of them' (SW 231–232). Life, as he put it earlier, is 'that behind which it is impossible to go', the final term in the process of understanding anything by referring it to ever more comprehensive wholes. It is this insistence on a total context to which all understanding is finally referred which I have in mind when I speak of Dilthey's 'deep holism'.

Since this 'total conception', this basis for all understanding, is not a biological one, and since it embraces things that are not living—buildings, town squares, pieces of music—'Life' is not an ideal epithet for it. It has much in common with what Heidegger called our 'thrown being-in-the-world' and Wittgenstein 'the background to our language-games': but in order to avoid commitment to any specific theses of theirs, let us blandly refer simply to 'The Context'. It is The Context 'behind which it is impossible to go', but against which everything human must be understood.

It is here, in the deeply holistic thesis of The Context where—if anywhere—affinity with aspects of fascist thinking is found. I shall argue this later: for the moment, I content myself with another indirect indication, parallel to Herder's dual reputation as a precursor of both *Verstehen* and fascism. This time the dual reputation is that of Martin Heidegger, who was both immensely indebted to Dilthey's deep holism (far more so than his scant acknowldgements would suggest) and, of course, a Nazi. In his case, certainly, the connection is not accidental: Heidegger saw a real link between the thesis of The Context and the attractions of fascist social and political theory. When in 1936 he explained to a former student that 'the concept of historicity was the basis for his political engagement', it was to a concept imbued with a deeply holistic attitude inherited from Dilthey that he referred.[9] But more of that later.

There is something else I first need to establish. If it is deep holism, the idea of The Context behind which one cannot go, which connects up with fascist thinking, it needs to be shown that holism of this ilk is essential to *Verstehen*. If it is a redundant addendum, easily excisable from the wider theory, then it would be wrong to accuse the theory itself of having 'dirty hands'. I want now to show that deep holism is indeed essential to the idea of *Verstehen*, and this is because it is essential to Dilthey's central claim that the human sciences are different in kind from the natural. No holism more shallow than *deep* holism, I suggest, could establish that humane understanding is different in principle from natural scientific explanation.

Dilthey's main targets were social scientists and psychologists, like Comte and Mill, who wanted to emulate the positivist, atomistic model of explanation prevalent in the natural sciences of the time. The trouble here is that, to today's ears, models of this kind for *any* type of scientific explanation sound badly dated. Consider the following, very familiar model for explaining human actions: an action is explained when we identify the constellation of beliefs and desires which caused it. Now it is happily conceded by those

[9] Quoted in Richard Wolin (ed.), *The Heidegger Controversy: a critical reader* (Cambridge, MA: MIT Press, 1993), p. 142.

who employ this model that it has various holistic dimensions. For one thing, beliefs and desires are not 'raw data' transparent to the theorist: for he is only entitled to ascribe a given belief or desire to an agent if this coheres with a much wider ascription of such mental states, not only to that agent, but to others in the agent's society or culture. The theorist is warranted in radically revising his first guesses for the sake of a smooth and systematic theory of the agent's behaviour—in reconstruing, say, what at first seemed a sincere religious belief as a desire to conform with traditional custom. For another thing, it is conceded that such a model does not operate in a vacuum, but presupposes a range of assumptions (about human rationality and interests, say) challenges to which would prompt revision of the model and the ascriptions of beliefs and desires in which it issues. In social science, then, there are interplays between, as it were, the smaller and the larger pictures, just as Dilthey said there must be.

The problem is that just these points about the holistic dimensions of explanation are also made, these days, by philosophers of natural science. Indeed, claims like the following have become virtual clichés: there are no 'raw data'; data are 'theory-laden' and hence require interpretation; 'the facts' can be radically reinterpreted for the sake of 'fit' with a well-grounded theory; scientific theories are not 'autonomous', but shaped by rich social contexts and 'prejudices' (in Gadamer's sense) from which they emerge. For many recent philosophers, once these ubiquitous holistic dimensions of scientific explanation are appreciated, any principled line between the human and natural sciences is erased.[10]

Surely, however, there is a difference. As Hubert Dreyfus puts it, 'the human sciences, unlike the natural sciences, must take account of those human activities which make possible their own discipline'—of that social context, those 'prejudices', from which their theories emerge and by which they are shaped.[11] It is not simply that, as Dilthey noted, the human sciences are less 'esoteric' than the natural; that in the former a strong 'connection between

[10] See, e.g., Richard Rorty, *Philosophy and the Mirror of Nature* (Princeton University Press, 1979), pp. 350ff.

[11] 'Holism and Hermeneutics', in R. Hollinger (ed.), *Hermeneutics and Practice* (Indiana: Notre Dame University Press, 1985), p. 240. I am much indebted to this perceptive essay, but take issue with its judgment that Heidegger was the first to articulate certain themes which, in fact, Dilthey had already announced. For an historically more judicious account, detailing the younger thinker's debt to the older, see Charles B. Guignon, *Heidegger and the Problem of Knowledge* (Indianapolis: Hackett, 1983), pp. 45ff.

life and science is retained', so that 'thought arising from daily life' serves as their 'foundation' (SW 182). The point, in addition, is that this 'foundation'—the context of everyday thought, behaviour, attitudes—is a proper object of investigation by the human scientist. Nuclear physics may well have its remote 'roots' in 'daily thought', but this context is one which the scientist legitimately ignores: if, perchance, he turns his attention to it, he does so, no longer as a nuclear physicist, but as a philosopher or sociologist.

But does this difference, interesting though it may be, exhibit an essential difference between human and natural scientific forms of understanding? It won't, it seems to me, if, as I shall put it, the everyday context can be 'surveyed' by those who at once work within it and upon it. If, that is, the social scientist can stand back from this context and submit it to the same treatment as he or the natural scientist can submit any other data to, then the mere fact that, ordinarily, his work is shaped and informed by that context is of no great moment. He won't, admittedly, be in the happy position of a visiting student from Mars, unencumbered by 'prejudices' that go with being a member of the culture he studies. But to the extent that, with effort, he can emulate the detached Martian observer, he can submit that culture to investigation and, in principle, come up with a systematic theory of its ways.

Now it is precisely this possibility that Dilthey, with his talk of 'Life',—The Context behind which it is impossible to go—rejects. 'Life gives the fundamental preconditions of knowledge, and thinking cannot reach behind them' (GS V 136). It is impossible for the human scientist studying his own culture to stand outside of it and achieve a survey of all its ways. Two reasons are given for this. First, the student is too interwoven with his culture to obtain a detached vantage-point. 'The individual always experiences [and] thinks ... *in* a common sphere and *only there* does he understand ... We live in this atmosphere ... immersed in it ... woven into this common sphere' (SW 191). Second, as those remarks also imply, it wouldn't help even if the human scientist *were* to achieve the vantage-point of the Martian: for truly to understand a culture's ways, one must be a participating member, not a detached observer and theorist, of it. The crucial point here, later elaborated by Heidegger, is that people's basic relation to their environing world is not one of having thoughts or beliefs about it, but of 'comportment', of practical engagement with it. As Dilthey puts it, I understand what is around me, not primarily through observation and rumination, but in relation to 'the goal of some striving or a restriction on my will' (SW 178). I understand the pen when I am able to put it to proper use; I understand what a policeman is when I run to him, not the butcher, to report a crime, and refrain from doing anything nefarious in his presence. Before a child can speak and form articulated beliefs, it is already possessed of massive understanding of its world—of 'the customs of the family', of 'gestures and facial expressions', and so on—and solely through 'encountering' and becoming 'oriented' towards it (SW 221–222).

Deep holism, with its postulate of The Context which one cannot go behind, is therefore crucial to the claim that *Verstehen* is different in kind from natural scientific explanation. Not only is it illegitimate for the human scientist to isolate his enquiries from this Context, since they encompass it, but he cannot isolate *himself* from it. He is too woven into it, his understanding too much a function of participation in it, to attain the detached standpoint of natural scientists which enables them, in principle, to construct a total theory of the natural world. It is for these reasons that we find Dilthey appealing to 'empathy', 'intuition' and other modes of understanding which have no analogues in natural scientific methodology.

Let me now return to what all this might have to do with fascist thinking. People will reasonably wonder how the seemingly abstract epistemological thesis of deep holism could connect with a particular political ideology—how, indeed, anyone could imagine that it might. Still, there are *clues* to the existence of such a connection. One I already mentioned: Heidegger's insistence that what he coyly called his 'political engagement' was based on a concept of 'historicity' profoundly owing to Dilthey's philosophy. Another is the rhetoric of fascism, for this betrays above all else what might be called a cultural or political holism. It is a rhetoric which expresses what Peter Gay, in his study of the Weimar Years, labels 'the hunger for wholeness'. One of the most acute witnesses of those years, Hugo von Hofmannsthal, captured the mood of many people who were flocking to the Nazi banner: they believed in 'wholeness of existence ... [and] seek, not freedom, but connection', perceiving that 'scattered worthless individuals' must be forged together into 'the core of the nation' and that 'all partitions into which mind has polarized life must be ... transformed into spiritual unity'.[12]

These were the years, recall, when the great clarion calls of the Right were *Kultur* and *Gemeinschaft*. Unlike *Zivilization* and *Gesellschaft*—the modern world of uprooted individualism, class conflict, and 'folkish splintering' (as Hitler called it)—'culture' and 'community' represented a lost, but retrievable, world of organic

[12] Quoted in Peter Gay, *Weimar Culture: the outsider as insider*. (London: Secker & Warburg, 1968), p. 85.

unity. The anti-individualistic, holistic rhetoric was ubiquitous: it is there in Mussolini's Minister of Education, Giovanni Gentile's, insistence that 'at the root of the "I" there is a "We". The community ... is the basis of [a person's] spiritual existence', and there in Hitler's pronouncement that a person's life only 'articulates' itself within a community, a life which is a 'dust particle' in the whole order that shapes it. It is there, finally, in these words of a leading Nazi socialist: what is required is a 'strong, structured unity that seizes and encompasses the individual completely ... a productive will ... a reawakening of shared constants of willing and believing' that will shake Germany 'out of fragmentation and clever materialism'.[13]

Such rhetoric is only a clue: maybe the connection between the deep, theoretical holism of Dilthey and Heidegger and the cultural/political holism of fascism is only verbal. Is there really an affinity between the contextual whole to which understanding of individual lives eventually refers us, and the political whole (the Nation, the *Volk*) which ought to 'seize and encompass' those lives? I certainly don't argue that there is anything approaching entailment here, that fascist holism is the inevitable destination of Dilthey's holism. Moreover, it would be unfair to Dilthey not to record aspects of his position which are thoroughly at odds with fascist ideology.[14] Nevertheless, I hold that there are a number of claims associated with theoretical holism—with the idea of The Context—which are (a) made by Dilthey himself and those he influenced (above all Heidegger), (b) not unnatural claims to make, and (c) have obvious resonance in fascist thought. I'll present those claims under the three headings of 'arationality and self-enclosure', 'historicality and heritage' and 'individuals as expressions'.

Life or The Context is, for Dilthey, *a*rational in at least two respects. 'All understanding', he writes, 'contains something irrational because life is irrational'. Although, as we saw, he does not portray Life as a primordial force inimical to reason, he speaks of

[13] Giovanni Gentile, *Genesis and Structure of Society*, trans. H. Harris (Urbana: University of Illinois Press, 1966), p. 82; Hitler, *Mein Kampf*, pp. 270–271; Hans Freyer, quoted in Jeffrey Herf, *Reactionary Modernism: Technology, Culture and Politics in Weimar and the Third Reich* (Cambridge University Press, 1984), p. 125.

[14] Dilthey never resolved a number of deep tensions in his position; those, for example, between relativism and rationalism, and between a reductive and non-reductive account of the individual. The aspects on which I focus are, therefore, only part of the story. For an emphasis on the opposing aspects, see Michael Emarth, *Wilhelm Dilthey: the critique of historical reason* (University of Chicago Press, 1978).

its 'dark instincts' and 'mystery', aspects which, together with its unsurveyability, mean that it 'cannot be represented by a logical formula' (SW 230). Considerations like this had great appeal to fascist theorists, not least because they encouraged the idea of the 'great man', the Leader, who short-circuits the anyway fruitless endeavour to understand the Age through rational scientific enquiry by exercising his special insight. Only a man so blessed, it might seem, could be capable of what Dilthey calls a 'total awareness ... based on empathy' into an age (SW 181).

Life or The Context is arational, second, in that it cannot be 'cited before the tribunal of reason' (GS VII 259). Since The Context is what generates prevailing criteria of rationality, it cannot itself be measured by them. This is part of Dilthey's wider claim that Life is, so to speak, self-enclosed. Thus one cannot look for the meaning of The Context outside of it: 'like notes in a melody, life expresses nothing but itself' (SW 237). As the source of meanings and purposes, The Context as a whole has none, for these are contained within it, like the notes within the melody. Moreover, each 'cultural system' is a systematic whole incorporating 'a conception of reality' and a way of 'valuation' (SW 197). It is hard to see, therefore, how it can be 'valuated', justified or criticized. Someone from outside that system who criticizes it merely reflects the values of the system to which he or she belongs: it is as if one were to criticize French or Urdu for not being English. Though he sometimes denies it, it is hard to see what this is but relativism, and in places, Dilthey is happy to concede that 'even when they think they are being objective, [people] are determined by their horizon' (SW 183) and that every *Weltanschauung* 'springs from the state of being-within-life' (GS VIII 99). The journey is not a long one to the cultural relativism of which fascists were enamoured: to Hitler's insistence that a State cannot be evaluated 'in the frame of the outside world', but only in terms of its 'virtue' relative to a particular 'nationality', or to Mussolini's boast of having 'applied relativism' to politics, relativism being 'contempt for ... external objective truth', a recognition that 'all ideologies are of equal value'.[15]

It is clear from Dilthey's references to all-embracing 'cultural systems'—to move to the second theme—that he does not think of Life as something singular and unchanging. There is no one Context, but different Contexts which succeed one another or co-exist in different parts of the globe. One implication of this is that,

[15] Hitler, *Mein Kampf*, p. 358; Mussolini, quoted in Franz Neumann, *Behemoth: the structure and practice of National Socialism* (London: Gollancz, 1942), p. 378.

while there may be a 'general human nature', it is also the case that 'the human type melts away in the process of history' (quoted in Lukács, *Destruction of Reason*, p. 433). There emerge different 'types' of human beings, therefore, corresponding to different historical Contexts. Human beings, put differently, are indelibly historical creatures: for it is only in relation to a 'historical whole ... of [an] Age' that any human action or thought has 'significance'. As a whole Context, therefore, an Age is self-enclosed: the mediaeval world, for example, has a 'closed horizon ... is centred on itself' (SW 198). On the other hand, a given Age is what it is only in virtue of being shaped by and developed from an earlier one. The earlier Age belongs to the *heritage* of the present one, and we fail to understand the latter if we lack all understanding of the former. After all, we are constantly surrounded by its products—institutions, laws, literature, buildings, and so on—and to the degree that we lack empathetic insight into the world which produced them, we do not properly fathom the one we are in.

Ideas like these were exploited in several ways by fascist writers. First, the notion of different, historical 'types' loomed large. Spengler liked to speak of the different 'morphological forms' of succeeding cultures and the human beings who were 'stamped' by them. For Ernst Jünger, too, history is a series of 'forms', each of whose 'stamps' is borne by everything and everyone under 'the compulsion of iron lawlikeness'.[16] For both men, the modern Western 'type' is the disciplined man of will—'Faustian man', 'the Worker'—harnessed to the 'total mobilization' of the earth through technology. It was the belief that fascism—with its 'steely romanticism', as Goebbels called it—recognized that here is the modern 'type' whose energies are to be tapped and commandeered which attracted these and other so-called 'reactionary modernists' to fascism, rather than to the nostalgic, insufficiently steely, romanticism of more conservative movements.

Other writers, notably Heidegger, emphasized less the current 'stamp' of a people than its 'heritage'. In virtue of what has been 'handed down', people's existence is 'fateful' and 'destined'. To know how we should act in the present, 'in the moment of vision for "[our] time"'—we must face up to our 'authentic historicality'. In particular, we must appreciate, through 'taking over' our heritage, the lessons of our history for the 'possibilities' of 'resolute' action in the present. We must 'choose hero[es]' from the past and hence look for one in the present who can at once imbibe their

[16] Spengler, *The Decline of the West*, 2 vols. (New York: Knopf, 1939), I, pp. 40ff; Jünger, *Der Arbeiter*, in *Essays II* (Stuttgart: Klett, 1964), p. 159.

lessons and emulate them.[17] By 1933, it became clear who NSDAP member Heidegger thought was the heroic paragon of 'authentic historicality'.

It is perfectly possible, of course, to emphasize the way people are shaped by their historical Context without concluding that their duty is to submit to the prevailing 'stamp' or tide of the times. But there is a further theme in Dilthey which eases the path to that conclusion—the theme of individual lives as 'expressions'. 'What is given', writes Dilthey—including beliefs and actions— 'always consists of expressions' (SW 218). This is intended, at first, as an epistemological principle: understanding a belief or action is akin to understanding a linguistic expression, and involves the same holistic reference to a wider system. But it easily tips over into a sociological principle: just as a linguistic expression has no identity outside the language to which it belongs, so says Dilthey 'every individual is ... a point where webs of relationships intersect' (SW 180). The idea that an individual is nothing but an expression of 'vital relationships' in a whole social Context, when linked with the emphasis on historicality, results in Dilthey's remarks on the notion of generations. The point of these remarks, according to one commentator, is that the generation 'is the basic unit of history since it provides the context ... in which individuals can first be identified ... the individual is only an abstraction from this wider context'.[18] It follows from this, it seems, that someone who fails to be thoroughly embedded in the 'vital relationships' of prevailing Life lacks identity, like a word without a language to belong to. This conclusion would be consonant with Dilthey's stress—ubiquitous in German writing earlier in this century—on the need for people to 'belong' in order to overcome a crippling sense of 'the strangeness of life', of the world as 'something other, alien' (SW 136).

It is consonant, too, of course with the cultural or political holism of fascist thought which I documented earlier—with, for example, Gentile's maxim that the 'We' is at the root of the 'I'. Nor is it an accident that Heidegger refers his readers to Dilthey when, in his account of 'authentic historicality', he speaks of a people's 'fateful destiny in and with its "generation"'.[19] Heidegger's authentic individual is not, as sometimes imagined, the existentialist loner who stalks the novels of Albert Camus, but someone who

[17] *Being and Time*, trans. J. Macquarrie and E. Robinson (Oxford: Blackwell, 1980), p. 437.

[18] Guignon, *Heidegger*, p. 141. The point I make in n. 14 above should be borne in mind here.

[19] *Being and Time*, p. 436.

seeks to escape from a sense of 'not-being-at-home' by 'resolute' identification with the 'fate' of a community, with something his life can express. To 'will that our *Volk* fulfil its historical mission' is to 'will *ourselves*'.[20] Finally, it is hard not to discern a link between Dilthey's emphasis on our lives as expressive and Walter Benjamin's insight that 'fascism sees its salvation in giving [the] masses ... a chance to express themselves'.[21] There is no reason to think Dilthey would have welcomed the fascists' 'aestheticization of politics', as Benjamin put it, its turning politics into a theatre for communal self-expression. But once even rational behaviour and enquiry were deemed to be forms of Life-expression, as they were by Dilthey, it was not going to be long before someone would regard these as inferior, 'inauthentic' forms, suited only perhaps to people in whose veins 'no real blood' flows.

One of the best-known characterizations of fascism is Ernst Nolte's: it is 'resistance to transcendence'.[22] A more recent author has retorted that, on the contrary, fascism is 'the result of succumbing to a perverted and peculiarly modern form' of transcendence, for it caters to 'the human need for *self*-transcendence' in the corrupt form of something like '*identification* with [a] suprapersonal entity' such as the *Volk*.[23] But there is shadow-boxing here, for the urge to identify with a larger whole, of which one can see one's own life as a partial expression, is perfectly compatible with rejection of values and purposes that transcend that whole, of any meaning—religious or otherwise—not embraced in that whole. And it is this rejection which Nolte had in mind when speaking of 'resistance to transcendence'. My argument has been that both tendencies—the urge for self-transcedence and yet for identification with something self-enclosed, the Life in which one is 'thrown'—can find intellectual succour, however unintended, in the view of human beings required by the idea of *Verstehen* as a distinctive form of understanding.

---

[20] In Wolin, *The Heidegger Controversy*, p. 39.

[21] Quoted in Herf, *Reactionary Modernism*, p. 34.

[22] *Three Faces of Fascism* (New York: Holt, Rhinehart & Winston, 1965).

[23] Roger Griffin, *The Nature of Fascism* (London: Pinter, 1991), p. 188.

Interpretation in History: Collingwood and Historical Understanding

PATRICK GARDINER

When considering a suitable topic for inclusion in this collection, it occurred to me that it might be worth discussing a writer whose interests were largely centred on themes directly related to those cited in the collection's title, and who throughout most of his philosophical career remained particularly insistent upon the need to define the boundaries separating humanistic modes of understanding from ones associated with the physical sciences. The writer in question was R. G. Collingwood. Although Collingwood has justly been credited with perceptive insights into the metaphysical origins and presuppositions of natural science, as well as with raising pointed questions concerning the nature of conceptual change in scientific thought, he had in fact little first-hand knowledge of the subject and it is not in this sphere that his chief claims to importance and originality lie. Rather, they are to be found in an area with which he was certainly intimately acquainted and in which as a practitioner he helped to make significant discoveries on the ground. That was history, a discipline requiring in his view a type of thinking that had either been ignored by his philosophical contemporaries or else misconceived and distorted by those who had troubled to consider it. Thus, as a result of making a serious effort on his own account to come to terms with what it involved, he became—in his own words at the time—'more and more conscious of being an outlaw'.

In propounding a conception of historical enquiry that stressed its autonomy and methodological independence of other studies, Collingwood was conscious of belonging to a tradition which stretched back to Vico and Herder in the eighteenth century and which included such later theorists as Rickert and Dilthey in Germany and Croce in Italy. It is difficult, indeed, not to see in Vico's particular application of the so-called *verum factum* principle, according to which we can only fully know what we ourselves have made, an anticipation of an idea that lay at the heart of many of Collingwood's contentions regarding the distinctive character of historical knowledge. For Vico employed this principle in a way that was designed to present in a wholly new light the relation between on the one hand the historical studies and on the other the physical sciences. The latter were concerned with the world of nature and that was something which, since God had created it, he alone could truly know. By contrast, the historical world had been made by human beings; there was therefore, according to Vico, a sense in which it did not confront us as something ultimately opaque and foreign to ourselves, and as such subject only to purely external types of investigation. On the contrary, it could be approached instead as embodying or giving expression to projects and states of mind which we, in our own capacity as purposive and intelligent agents, were uniquely qualified to grasp and comprehend from within. Historical knowledge, in other words, presupposed as an essential condition an imaginative ability to enter into the mentality of past societies and periods, the reconstruction of forms of life and outlook this involved representing a kind of understanding that had no counterpart in scientific modes of comprehending the workings of the natural world.

It was one thing to argue along such lines that the subject-matter of history was self-evidently fitted to be an object of human knowledge. It was another to go further and maintain—as Vico incontrovertibly did—that knowledge of the sort in question was intrinsically superior to any achievable within the domain of the natural sciences. The first rather than the second of the above claims is the one that finds a responsive echo in Collingwood's writings. It was the nature and grounds of the distinction Vico had drawn between the two spheres of enquiry, and not some supposed extra difference in comparative value, which he saw as anticipating the fundamental division between *Naturwissenschaft* and *Geisteswissenschaft* that was to acquire widespread recognition on the Continent towards the close of the nineteenth century. And it was the particular implications of this division, seen as impinging upon ideas of history which he believed to be pervasive in the British philosophy of his time, that he set out to explore and articulate in his own work. For in his opinion a 'false' notion of history had been 'so often and so authoritatively' taught that—as he put it —'the very meaning of the word has become debauched through the assimilation of historical process to natural process.'

The strong language in which Collingwood couched his complaint reflected a dissatisfaction that was not in fact confined to contemporary trends, the latter being regarded by him as continuous with earlier approaches of the kind endorsed by Hume when he spoke of the essential dependence of historical thought and understanding upon 'constant and universal principles of human nature' such principles were specifically connected by Hume and his empiricist successors with the conception of man as a subject for science, and from this it seemed to follow that no methodological gulf could be said to separate the spheres of historical and scientific enquiry. Admittedly, there were obvious differences of goal and direction of interest, the historian being centrally concerned with the description and detailed analysis of particular happenings in the past whereas the scientist was primarily, though not exclusively, engaged in framing universal laws or hypotheses which could be used for purposes of prediction or of future control. When, however, the question was one of explaining or rendering intelligible the behaviour of historical figures, proponents of what Collingwood labelled the 'positivist' view were prone to present this as a matter of bringing the events in question under some 'general formula or law' that was held to obtain irrespective of variations in time or place. According to him, such a model was wholly inappropriate in the context of human affairs; not only did it represent 'an endemic error in modern philosophical thought about history', it also posed a threat to historical thought itself. In the first place, it presupposed a fixed and static conception of human nature when in fact human beings were continually involved in revising, criticizing and transforming the ideas or attitudes handed down to them by previous generations; thus, insofar as it ignored such considerations, it could be said to rest on unacceptable empirical foundations. Secondly, and more crucially, it was beset by confusions in principle concerning categories fundamental to historical understanding. These comprised the notion of agency, together with the associated concepts of thought and mind.

Collingwood's contention that the historian's essential concern is with human actions, with things done rather than 'mere happenings', underlies his stress on the autonomy of history and his uncompromising insistence upon the irreducibility to other terms of the key ideas and methods it employs. To regard something as an action was to comprehend it as an expression of human thought, thereby endowing it with a dimension of significance which precluded treating it as no more than an observable occurrence or 'spectacle to be watched'. As Collingwood himself portrayed the situation, an action could be said to have an 'outside' and an 'inside', historical differing from scientific understanding in being a matter of 'penetrating' an event to uncover its interior meaning as opposed to 'analysing or classifying it from an external point of view'. Thus in underlining the contrast he had in mind, he wrote:

To the scientist, nature is always and merely a 'phenomenon', not in the sense of being defective in reality, but in the sense of being a spectacle presented to his intelligent observation; whereas the events of history are never mere phenomena, never mere spectacles for contemplation, but things which the historian looks, not at, but through, to discern the thought within them. (*The Idea of History*, Oxford University Press, p. 214)

From this Collingwood went on to draw the conclusion that history, considered as the history of thought, was 'free from the domination of natural science' (ibid. p. 318). But, as he himself recognized, what the latter claim amounted to could only be ascertained in the light of an account of the actual manner in which the historian might be held to 'discern' the thoughts of historical agents. If—as had been asserted—empirical laws or generalizations played no necessary part in the explanation of action, what was required instead? The answer given was that it demanded the 're-enactment' or 'rethinking' of past thought in the historian's own mind.

It is here, if anywhere, that Collingwood's particular contribution to the doctrine of *Verstehen* as applying to the historical studies is to be found. Even so, it must be allowed that what he wrote on this score was not always as clearly or unambiguously expressed as could have been wished; in consequence, it gave rise to a number of different interpretations, not least in connection with his use of the 'inner–outer' distinction to characterize the nature of human actions. Thus it seemed to some of his early critics that, in appearing to separate the bodily movements involved in what a person did from the unobservable thinking processes held to underlie or 'cause' them, he was committed to a radical and ultimately unacceptable form of psycho-physical dualism. And to this was sometimes added the objection that awareness of the thought-side of an action which the re-enactment theory postulated required an intuitive capacity to apprehend the mind of an historical agent that transcended ordinary modes of cognition. I admit that I was amongst those who then held such a view, allowing myself—as I now think and as I have indicated on various occasions since—to be unduly influenced by Collingwood's metaphorical terminology, as well as taking for methodological precepts what are more plausibly interpreted as conceptual claims regarding the implications of the notions of historical knowledge and understanding. Despite the tenor of some of his remarks, it seems to me that in general his description at one point of an action as a 'unity' of the outside and inside of an event is more consonant with a position according to which thinking processes can be held to inform or find readable expression in conduct in ways that render it intelligible without there being any occasion to presume the use of recondite cognitive powers. To describe an event as an action is certainly to portray it as more than a mere phenomenal occurrence; to do so is to bring into play reflective and intentional concepts that would be totally inapposite if it were treated as a bare 'fact of nature'. But in underlining this—defenders of Collingwood might argue—he need only be regarded as drawing attention to a type of understanding that is already familiar enough at the level of everyday experience and whose crucial relevance to history he was concerned above all to emphasize. If so, his conception of *Verstehen* as re-enactment could be seen to entail no untoward consequences from an epistemological standpoint. On the contrary, he might be credited instead with giving it a more down-to-earth meaning and edge than ones favoured by some of its earlier idealist exponents.

How, then, should his own version of the doctrine be construed? In what follows I shall set out in broad terms what I take to be its central features. It will be helpful to begin with a passage from the section of *The Idea of History* dealing specifically with history as re-enactment. Collingwood asks us to suppose that a historian is reading the Theodosian Code and that he has before him a certain edict of an emperor. He goes on:

> Merely reading the words and being able to translate them does not amount to knowing their historical significance. In order to do that he must envisage the situation with which the emperor was trying to deal, and he must envisage it as that emperor envisaged it. Then he must see for himself, just as if the emperor's situation were his own, how such a situation might be dealt with; he must see the possible alternatives, and the reason for choosing one rather than another; and thus he must go through the process which the emperor went through in deciding on this particular course. Thus he is re-enacting in his own mind the experience of the emperor; and only in so far as he does this has he any historical knowledge, as distinct from a merely philological knowledge, of the meaning of the edict. (ibid. p. 283)

In reading this, it may be tempting to imagine that re-enactment should primarily be understood as a method of discovering what was in the mind of historical figures; by putting himself in the place of the agent he may hope to arrive at an explanatory hypothesis as to the latter's motivation. But although Collingwood does on occasions use words that suggest this, I think it is a mistake to suppose that it represents what the passage quoted is primarily intended to illustrate, or indeed that it reflects in general the sort of point his re-enactment thesis is really concerned to make. The question at issue is not so much one of the techniques the historian uses in his search after knowledge and understanding as one of what *constitutes* such knowledge and understanding when he has it. Thus in the example given the historian is portrayed as envisaging through the emperor's eyes both the situation with which he was called upon to deal and the possible options open to him; only insofar as he inwardly grasps the weight of such considerations and sees, from the emperor's point of view, how they provided reasons justifying the issue of the edict can he be said to have re-enacted the thinking that lay behind it in the requisite fashion. For he will then have apprehended its significance in a context, not of theoretical enquiry, but of practical deliberation. In mentally following the steps of such deliberation in a manner that exhibits the emperor's decision to have been a well-founded or appropriate one, the historian is himself engaged in thinking himself into, and appreciating the force of, a practical argument. As upholders of Collingwood's position concerning the role of re-enactment sometimes put it, the historian so to speak works as an agent 'at one remove' from his subject, envisaging matters from the latter's standpoint and assuming the perspective of an active participant as opposed to that of a detached spectator. So construed, talk of his taking an 'internal' rather than an 'external' view of his material, of his striving to interpret the activities of historical figures 'from the inside', seems the reverse of being obscurantist or gratuitously paradoxical. It would appear instead to underline the relevance to history of an approach that is central to our everyday dealings with each other in the world. For there we often, and sometimes inescapably, find ourselves interpreting what people do in a way that would supposedly 'make sense' to them from their own position as active and purposive beings. Looked at in this light, the identificatory and participatory attitudes adopted towards past individuals in the context of historical thinking may appear to be essentially an extension—albeit one often involving great imaginative effort and skill—of familiar habits of thought and experience.

The above is a rough but (I hope) reasonably accurate summary of some of the cardinal ideas underlying the conception of history as involving re-enactment. As Professor William Dray has argued in a number of persuasive and illuminating studies of Collingwood's contribution to the philosophy of history, the type of understanding he had in mind may be held to differ 'in concept' from those he associated with the positivist model. The aim is one of recovering the rationale of what was done rather than of subsuming it under generalizations, such recovery involving what Dray has aptly called 'vicarious practical reasoning' on the part of the historian while at the same time remaining strictly answerable to the available evidence. Inasmuch as this is to construe *Verstehen* or empathetic understanding as an essentially rational activity, different from but no less reputable than the thinking encountered in other disciplines, it is easy to comprehend its appeal; nor was Collingwood himself averse to drawing attention to such aspects, sometimes indeed going to the length of suggesting that the historian's sole business was with the problems human beings had met with in the past and the solutions that had been found for them. Further, and notwithstanding reservations about his more unguarded claims, it is noteworthy that Collingwood's general approach to the subject has tended to receive a markedly more sympathetic response from working historians than have accounts of the kind he attacked. For these reasons amongst others his work has attracted a far greater amount of commentary, both favourable and critical, than that of any comparable twentieth-century philosopher of history in the English-speaking world. Much of the latter has focused on his re-enactment doctrine, with controversies arising concerning its alleged inadequacy as well as about its possible limitations. In the remainder of the lecture I propose to offer some remarks on each of these scores.

The first comprises a point that is sometimes raised about the extent to which the account of understanding Collingwood provides can be said to afford a complete or sufficient interpretation of a certain kind of explanatory claim. So far I have spoken of understanding rather than of explanation, since this largely accords with Collingwood's own practice. Nonetheless, he often writes readily enough as if what he said was meant to encompass explanation, the latter being a matter of specifying the particular reasons that accounted for the performance of a given action. But here—it has been contended—a difficulty presents itself for his theory whose significance he does not seem to have fully recognized.

According to the theory, re-enactment explanation consists in exhibiting an action to have been appropriate when seen in relation to such things as what the agent wanted or intended, his conception of his situation, his beliefs as to how to achieve certain ends, and perhaps his acceptance of certain normative principles; taken together, these factors may be appraised as representing compelling considerations from the agent's point of view, making what he did in that context seem acceptable or justifiable in rational terms. It is arguable, however, that to present a historical figure's behaviour as having been appropriate under such conditions is not by itself sufficient to count as explaining why he did what he did. Showing that an action fitted in with, or made good sense in the light of, a set of putative reasons is not equivalent to demonstrating that it was in fact done *because* of these; it is conceivable that the deed was in accord with them without its having been actually determined by them, something further being necessary to establish a connection of the requisite type. One proposal has taken the form of seeking to supplement the account with empirical generalizations or laws assumed to govern the propensities or behaviour of rational agents; another has been the suggestion that there is a conceptual rather than a merely contingent link between the possession of certain beliefs and intentions and their expression in appropriate conduct, what a person does being in certain circumstances logically entailed by the thoughts attributed to him. Collingwood, on grounds already mentioned, would almost certainly have turned down the first proposal, while on the fact of it the second one is not easy to reconcile with the standpoint of deliberation and practical decision implicitly assumed by his reenactment model. The general issue dividing him here from his critics may, indeed, be ultimately related to the distinction between the two contexts—the internal and the external—within which actions can be viewed. Considerations that can appear explanatorily incomplete and in need of supplementation when they are regarded from the standpoint of a detached investigator or observer may appear in a very different light when the outlook adopted is that of an agent confronted by a practical problem of choice and in whose eyes they play a deliberative rather than an interpretative role. Since it was with the latter perspective that Collingwood conceived the historian to be primarily concerned, the kind of point that some objectors to his position have raised might have seemed to him not to arise. He could well have been mistaken about this. Even so, the presumed challenge of satisfactorily accommodating the respective claims of each side within a unitary account that does justice to both has engaged the attention of a number of writers to whom the issue has looked far from clear-cut.

The second aspect of Collingwood's position which has drawn criticism concerns what have been alleged to be the inacceptably rationalistic implications inherent in his analysis of the nature of historical understanding itself. If understanding a past action requires a capacity on the part of the historian to re-enact or rethink within his own mind the reasons for which it was done, does this commit him to finding it rationally justified? To what extent, indeed, does understanding so conceived presuppose the rationality of human agency in general? Clearly distinctions are in order here. There is a sense, for instance, in which a historian might consider an action to be irrational on the grounds that, retrospectively regarded, it was based on such things as objectively incorrect beliefs about the situation, a misconception as to relevant means/end relations, and even the acceptance of an eccentric or objectionable scheme of values. Would he be thereby precluded from understanding the action in the requisite fashion? That certainly would seem tantamount to setting bizarre limits to the scope of historical intelligibility, and it appears equally certain that Collingwood's conception of re-enactive understanding was not intended to rule out cases of the sort in question. For—as has already been sufficiently stressed—what he had in mind when he spoke of such understanding was essentially related to how things looked from the agent's actual, and not the historian's subsequent, point of view: thus it may be argued that for an action to be intelligible in Collingwood's sense it need only appear rationally justifiable or appropriate when considered in the light of the agent's own beliefs and goals together with the temporal context in which they were entertained. Collingwood in fact showed, in both his theoretical writings and his historical practice, a noteworthy sensitivity to the dangers of adopting superficial or anachronistic attitudes towards the subject-matter of history. When confronted by instances of behaviour that seemed at first sight to fly in the face of reason, it was the proper task of the historian to exercise his imagination; only by entering into the outlooks of past agents in ways that might involve the hypothetical acceptance of ideas or principles sometimes far removed from those current in his own age and milieu was it possible to show how such *prima facie* problematic conduct was after all susceptible to construal in rationally rethinkable terms.

Nevertheless, and despite such disclaimers, it may still be objected that the re-enactment conception of understanding remains unrealistically restrictive in the amount it seems to exclude from the historian's proper scope. However scrupulous the care taken to judge an action from the agent's own standpoint, there can be no *a priori* guarantee that the reasoning ascribable to him will turn out to have been cogent or sound; as Francis Bacon once remarked, 'it is a great mistake to suppose men too rational'. It is always conceivable in principle, and it is surely often the case in practice, that there is a lack of coincidence between the conclusions people actually draw on the basis of their beliefs and purposes and the conclusions that rationally they should have drawn. Thus in history as elsewhere people may engage in faulty practical

thinking, whether because of such things as haste or unimagina-
tiveness or as a result of underlying emotional factors that sway or
distort their judgment. But when that happens—the objection may
continue—it does not follow that their behaviour is unintelligible
in terms of reasons, only that the reasons are liable to be poor or
inadequate ones. Faced with cases like these a historian might have
no option but to conclude that the judgment of the agents concerned was defective, and he might look for an explanation. That
is not the same, though, as treating what was done as beyond
understanding in the wider sense of its being possible to reconstruct, and see the appeal of, the processes of argument or reasoning that led to it. To the extent that Collingwood denied this, his
account remained implausibly narrow.

Much clearly depends here on how the crucial notion of 're-
thinking' is to be interpreted. If it is taken to be equivalent to
'rationally understanding' and the latter confined to recognizing
the validity or cogency of a practical argument, it follows that
there can be no such thing as re-thinking an agent's defective cal-
culation. This, indeed, has been maintained by Professor Dray
himself when, in the course of referring to theories of 'empathy' in
history, he said that 'one cannot re-think a practical argument one
knows to be invalid'.[1] And so far as I can tell he, along with a number of other commentators, interprets what Collingwood meant
along those lines. They may be right. On the other hand,
Collingwood would be less vulnerable to some of the criticisms
brought against him on the present score if his conception were
interpreted in a more flexible manner. So construed, it would also
cover empathetically appreciating how an agent could have been
tempted or misled into accepting a particular practical conclusion
without recognizing the faultiness of the reasoning involved;
slipping into errors of this kind is often comparatively easy to
comprehend, especially in cases where extraneous pressures or
preoccupations can allow apparently slight or even irrelevant factors to assume a deceptive significance and weight. The attraction
exercised upon a historical figure by certain considerations might
not have made them good or sound reasons for his doing what he
did, but this need not prevent a perceptive historian from being
able imaginatively to grasp or—on a wider construal of the term—
're-think' how they could have appealed to the agent and plausibly
influenced the decision he formed. I suggest that historical practice in general conforms to this interpretation of what historical
understanding may encompass.

[1] *Philosophy and History: A Symposium*, ed. Sidney Hook (New York,
1963), p. 113.

To conclude. It may be the case that, when faced by an action where what is done does not appear to accord with the requirements of rationality, a historian will not be prepared to leave things at that and will instead try to determine whether the action cannot after all be seen to have been guided by considerations of the requisite kind. Furthermore, an account that succeeds in showing this may well be more intellectually satisfying than one that does not. That is not, however, to say that such an account will always be available. The historian may have in the end to acquiesce in the conclusion that the person behaved irrationally, the reasons that led him to do what he did not being—even from his own point of view—good reasons. A true account and a satisfying one may not always be the same thing. But this is not to imply that there can be no restriction at all on what may legitimately count as an agent's reasons. There may, in other words, be a point at which we should want to say, not that the agent's reasons for an action were unsound but nonetheless in some acceptable sense intelligible, but rather that it seems incomprehensible or inconceivable how someone could have acted in such a way and on such grounds. Where such a point lies is another matter, and different people, different historians, can be expected to draw the line at different places depending upon variations in experience, imagination or temperament: but that the line always may be drawn, or at least implicitly presupposed, seems clear. And this is no doubt connected with a consideration that emerges from Collingwood's account of re-enactment when regarded as a whole; namely, that the historical understanding of actions is intimately and inextricably tied to the lived experience of what it is like to deliberate and think purposively in practical contexts. Such a consideration may appear evident enough, but in some philosophical treatments of history it has not, even so, been sufficiently appreciated.

The Meaning of the Hermeneutic Tradition in Contemporary Philosophy

ANDREW BOWIE

In his *Notes on Philosophy*, which he began writing in 1796, Friedrich Schlegel asserts that 'The fact that one person understands the other is philosophically incomprehensible, but it is certainly magical.'[1] In the interim a large amount of philosophical effort has been expended on trying to refute Schlegel's first claim. The fact is, though, that what Michael Dummett calls a 'full-blooded theory of meaning' is now looking less and less like a really feasible philosophical enterprise, so Schlegel may have actually been right. Dummett maintains that a 'full-blooded theory of meaning' 'must give an explicit account, not only of what anyone must know in order to know the meaning of any given expression, but of what constitutes having such knowledge'.[2] However, as I shall try to show via aspects of the hermeneutic tradition, it is precisely this way of talking about meaning and understanding that renders them incomprehensible. The differences between approaching the issue of understanding from the hermeneutic tradition and approaching it from the analytical tradition can, I want to suggest, tell us something important about the state of philosophy today. My aim is eventually to suggest that we need to understand the analytical version of the 'linguistic turn' in modern philosophy as a perhaps rather questionable aspect of a much more important 'hermeneutic turn', whose implications are now becoming apparent in more and more diverse areas of contemporary philosophy. The initial hermeneutic question in this context is to ask when and why the idea that a central aim of philosophy should be to establish a theory of meaning came about in the first place. Any answer to this question will of necessity involve telling a story. Once this is admitted, however, a major problem already becomes apparent, because the very choice of which story to tell will already affect the answers that one offers to the initial question.

[1] Friedrich Schlegel, *Kritische Schriften und Fragmente 1–6* (Paderborn: Ferdinand Schöningh, 1988), vol. 5, p. 71.

[2] Michael Dummett, *The Seas of Language* (Oxford University Press, 1993), p. 22.

The story I want to tell does, I hope, at least have the advantage of being anything but widely familiar in the form I wish to tell it, but I also want to make the stronger claim that the structure it reveals is the decisive structure in relation to the issues that concern me. Before telling the story, though, we need to get a somewhat clearer sense of what is at stake in wanting to tell it.

Richard Rorty has argued that a dominant concern of the analytical tradition is with the idea, derived in the main from a certain perception of the natural sciences, that 'metaphor is a distraction from [ahistorical] reality'. The story of the modern natural sciences is here regarded as a story of the elimination of myth, theology and bad metaphysics—which is continued in the elimination of metaphor—from truth-determinate scientific discourse. The continental tradition, on the other hand, is concerned, Rorty asserts, with the idea that metaphor is 'the way of escaping from the illusion that there is such a [ahistorical] reality'.[3] History tells us that there is always a way of redescribing in other terms what we hold as true and that what we hold as true is anyway fundamentally unstable.

Rorty considers the two enterprises to be inherently distinct and to be largely unable to communicate with each other. However, even for his schematic distinction between the enterprises to work, we already require some means of drawing a clear line between literal language and language as metaphor, and this is where the trouble starts, in a form which is germane to my argument. Is the language with which we draw the line itself literal or metaphorical, and what are the criteria for deciding this, without invalidly presupposing the distinction which one is supposed to be establishing? This decision cannot, as Rorty wishes to make it, always be made pragmatically, in terms of the problem-solving aspect of literal use based on established language games, which we rely on in 'argument', as against the 'meaningless' use of metaphorical language in expressive innovation. How do we know for sure which we are engaged in without making the kind of metaphysical distinction Rorty himself prohibits? Is it not possible to solve problems—even technical and scientific problems—via metaphors, when, for example, a new metaphor provides the solution to a cognitive dilemma? Such metaphors can become literalized and (metaphorically) 'die' as they are incorporated into an existing conception, but the moment of literalization will itself depend upon shifting boundaries between the literal and the metaphorical. Furthermore, there is nothing to say that what

[3] Richard Rorty, *Essays on Heidegger and Others. Philosophical Papers Volume Two* (Cambridge University Press, 1991), p. 23.

becomes literalized may not in a subsequent context be restored to metaphorical status by a new piece of literalization elsewhere in the language. Clearly the validity of these contentions depends upon one's conception of truth. However, if one thinks of truth as idealized consensus, the description of cognitive innovation in terms of moves between the metaphorical and the literal does avoid a series of long-standing objections to the notion of truth as correspondence. In the light of Kant, Schlegel already suggested of the idea of truth as the correspondence of object and representation that: 'the object would, as such, have to be compared with the representation; but that is not at all possible, because one only ever has a representation of the object, and thus can only ever compare one representation with another'.[4] He even formulates this in linguistic terms, which presage those of Saussure, maintaining that the idea of the correspondence of 'idea' (*Vorstellung*) and 'object' (*Gegenstand*): 'says no more ... than what a sign says of what is to be signified'.[5]

Rorty himself says much that comes close to anti-representationalist Romantic ideas of the kind developed by Schlegel, claiming, for instance, that 'Important, revolutionary physics, and metaphysics, has always been "literary" [= metaphorical] in the sense that it has faced the problem of introducing new jargon and nudging aside the language-games currently in place' (Rorty, *Essays*, p. 99). The fact is that Rorty is uneasily located between a Romantic hermeneutic conception, like that of Charles Taylor, which regards a strict metaphorical/literal distinction with deep suspicion, and Donald Davidson's still analytical insistence upon separating the two in the name of formal semantics, because 'seeing as'—the condition of metaphor—is not 'seeing that'—the condition of truth-determinate propositions, and thus of literal meaning. Other aspects of Davidson's conception of metaphor, though, such as his assertion that the important thing is what a metaphor 'makes us notice', already put the distinction into question, given that he thinks 'any use of language',[6] including propositional 'saying that', can make us notice a potential infinity of things. In this case it would only be if we really could definitively establish the truth conditions of utterances that the distinction

[4] Friedrich Schlegel, *Philosophische Vorlesungen* (1800–1807) (*Kritische Friedrich Schlegel Ausgabe* vol. 12) (Paderborn: Ferdinand Schoningh, 1964), pp. 316–317.

[5] Friedrich Schlegel, *Transcendentalphilosophie*, ed. Michael Elsässer (Hamburg: Meiner, 1991), p. 4.

[6] Donald Davidson, *Inquiries into Truth and Interpretation* (Oxford University Press, 1984), p. 263.

would stand in the way Davidson suggests, and this is precisely what the hermeneutic tradition to be described here thinks is impossible.

Now the desire to make the metaphorical/literal distinction is in one sense as old as the desire to separate *doxa* from *episteme*, or to eliminate the rhetorical from claims to truth, but my interest here is in a specific manifestation of what happens in the modern period when the task of philosophy comes to be seen as drawing a line between metaphor and literal truth via a theory of meaning. One now has, as usual, to go back to Kant, whose revolution in philosophy is part of what gives rise to the perceived need for a theory of meaning.

As opposed to their frequently dismissive treatment of German Idealism, or of much of phenomenology and hermeneutics, analytical philosophers have had little trouble taking Kant seriously. What Kant discusses in terms of categories and concepts can, it is assumed, easily be translated into the terms of truth-conditions and meanings. The problem analytical philosophers usually pass over, though, is what the central philosophical questions in Kant really are. These questions are generally defined within the analytical tradition via certain aspects—often those to do with transcendental arguments—of the *Critique of Pure Reason*. The first Critique is accordingly read as Kant's epistemology, which is then complemented by his ethics in the second Critique. In the hermeneutic tradition, on the other hand, the questions are more likely to be defined by Kant's broader concern, in the *Critique of Judgement*, with the ramifications of the problem of judgment, which link the epistemological, ethical and aesthetic aspects of Kant's work into an—unfulfilled, and perhaps unfulfillable—overall project. I want to contend via my story that the implications of certain questions which link the first and the third Critiques reveal the need for a revaluation of the semantic project. It is these questions which have led to the new interest in some areas of analytical philosophy in hermeneutic approaches to language and meaning.

The vital issue here is evident in a controversial part of Kantian epistemology. David Bell has pointed out that the analytical tradition has—mistakenly—rarely had much time for the so-called 'Schematism Chapter' of the first Critique, whose implications are developed in the third Critique.[7] In contrast to the analytical tradition, Heidegger claims that this chapter leads to the 'core of the whole problematic of the Critique of Pure Reason'.[8] In the light of Heidegger's claim it is hardly surprising that the vital questions in

[7] See David Bell, 'The Art of Judgement', *Mind*, vol. XCVI, April 1987.

[8] Martin Heidegger, *Kant und das Problem der Metaphysik* (Frankfurt: Klostermann, 1973), p. 109.

modern hermeneutics can be shown to emerge from the issues raised by this aspect of Kant, which is where my story really begins. The fact is that the problem to which schematism is the supposed answer has in it all the ingredients of the core problems for a 'full-blooded' theory of meaning, and Kant's attempts to overcome this problem have been repeated in various forms all over the subsequent history of philosophy, most recently being revived by John McDowell's *Mind and World*.[9]

Kant's initial aim is to explain how pure concepts of the understanding can be applied to sensuous intuitions, though the dilemma involved in doing this extends to the general problem of the application of concepts to intuitions. The problem is that the former must, as functions of thought, somehow remain independent of the vicissitudes of the empirical world for knowledge to be possible at all, whereas the latter are inherently unstable, because the patterns of sensory stimulation we receive are in all probability never exactly the same at any two moments of our lives. This is, I presume, why Quine and Rorty assume that receptivity is merely causally determined sensory stimulation and that it can therefore play no constitutive role in cognitive justifications within what McDowell calls the 'space of reasons'. For Kant, mediation between the spontaneity of the understanding and the reception of intuitions is the job of the 'imagination', whose location is—importantly—never satisfactorily established in the first Critique, moving rather furtively from the side of spontaneity, in the earlier version, to the side of receptivity in the later. Kant defines the 'schema' as follows:

> This idea of a universal procedure of imagination to provide a concept with its image I call the schema to this concept. Indeed it is not images of the objects which underlie our purely sensuous concepts, but schemata.[10]

If sensory 'images' were the sole basis of cognitive access to the world, the sheer diversity of what we receive empirically at any moment would render knowledge impossible because the already existing concept would be unable to make the always new data intelligible. What is required is an aspect of thought which can establish identities even though what it identifies are, *qua* sensory data given to receptivity, not strictly the same at all.

Kantian judgment consists, as is well known, in the subsuming

[9] See Andrew Bowie, 'John McDowell's *Mind and World*, and Early Romantic Epistemology', in *Revue internationale de philosophie* issue on Romantic Philosophy, Autumn 1996.

[10] Kant, *Critique of Pure Reason* B, pp. 179–180, A, pp. 140–141. I use the usual pagination.

of intuitions under concepts, concepts being rules for identifying what is given in intuition. Kant, though, suggests there is a major problem, to which schematism is part of his response, in any philosophical account of judgment:

> If judgment wanted to show universally how one is to subsume under these rules, i.e. distinguish whether something belongs under the rule or not, this could only happen via a further rule. But because this is a rule it requires once more an instruction by judgment, and thus it is shown to be the case that the understanding is admittedly capable of being instructed and equipped by rules, but that judgment is a particular talent which cannot be given by instruction but can only be practised (Kant, *Critique* B, p. 172, A, p. 133).

This 'talent' is required to avoid the infinite regress which results from the need for rules for the application of rules. What is at issue is the ability to grasp immediately what something is to be 'seen as', an ability which would become inexplicable if cognition were purely rule-bound. To make it clearer what is at stake here, we can put the implications of the notion of schema in terms of the question of metaphor: the lack of a firm theoretical location from which to distinguish metaphor from literal use does not obviate the need for heuristic distinctions between kinds of use of language—so that we 'see' one usage as literal and another as metaphorical—even though there may be no definitive rule-bound account of how we make the distinctions.

My main interest here is why the fear of a regress of rules of the kind suggested by Kant—which is vital to the genesis of modern hermeneutics—has again become a central topic in contemporary philosophy. In order to underline the significance of the issue and suggest the relevance of the rest of my story, let us briefly take two contemporary examples that repeat the dilemma Kant confronts, before considering some now largely forgotten historical responses to the dilemma. In computing and artificial intelligence the problem of how a computer could be programmed with 'background knowledge' in order to enable it to deal with unfamiliar situations is decisive for the increasingly discredited programme of 'strong artificial intelligence'. Hubert Dreyfus has usefully described the problem of background knowledge in his book on Heidegger's *Being and Time*:

> To compute relevance in a specific situation a computer would have to search through all its facts following rules for finding those that could possibly be relevant, then apply further rules to

determine which facts are usually relevant in this type of situation, and from all these facts deduce which facts were actually relevant in this particular situation. But in a large data-base such a search would be hopelessly difficult and *would get more difficult the more facts one added to guide the search.*[11]

The underlying problem here is, of course, exactly what leads Kant to the 'talent' which cannot be subsumed under rules, and it will turn out to vitiate many approaches to a theory of meaning. Moving even closer to the core issue, in *Making it Explicit*, a book whose very title echoes a central term—'*auslegen*', meaning 'explicate'—in hermeneutics (whilst not, incidentally, even having the word hermeneutics in its index) Robert Brandom refers, in relation to the question of interpretation, to what he calls 'Wittgenstein's Regress Argument'. The argument shows that a 'rule says how to do one thing correctly only on the assumption that one can do something else correctly, namely apply the rule'.[12] Brandom regards the argument as the 'master argument for the appropriateness of the pragmatist, rather than the regulist-intellectualist, order of explanation' in semantics (ibid. p. 23), because it prevents the regress of rules for the application of rules by grounding rules in pretheoretically constituted practices that are inherent in our 'being in the world'.

It will be evident that the structure of 'Wittgenstein's' argument, as Brandom himself acknowledges, is already clearly present in Kant's account of judgment, and we shall see a bit later that the argument should properly be called 'Schleiermacher's Regress Argument'. In both the examples just cited the role of what Kant sees in terms of 'schematism' is decisive. Only if the computer were able to short-circuit the regress of rules by ignoring all the irrelevant differences in the actual data with which it is confronted could it establish the relevant facts it requires to interpret real life situations in the manner we are inherently able to. The ability to apply rules depends, therefore, upon the active ability to 'schematize' the facts: there can be no definitive rules for this. Schleiermacher accordingly termed the schema an 'intuition which can be shifted within certain limits',[13] limits which are only accessible in the praxis of understanding and which cannot be

[11] Hubert L. Dreyfus, *Being-in-the-World* (Cambridge, MA: MIT Press, 1991), p. 118.

[12] Robert Brandom, *Making it Explicit* (Cambridge, MA: Harvard University Press, 1994), p. 21.

[13] Quoted in Manfred Frank, *Das Sagbare und das Unsagbare* (Frankfurt: Suhrkamp, 1989), p. 28.

defined *a priori*. The real question, then, is how we conceive of this practical ability, given that an account of the 'knowledge' in question is not formalizable.

Before trying to confront the question of how to conceive of this practical ability I want to continue my story by showing that the ramifications for language of this issue already came to be understood in the early modern period in ways which are, as Brandom's contentions suggest, again becoming widely accepted. In the following discussion the crucial term will be 'condition', which can easily be connected to issues in 'truth-conditional' semantics. In 1783 a major controversy, of which Kant was very much aware, broke out in German philosophy. The resonances of the controversy play a—largely hidden—role in a quite startling number of subsequent philosophical debates, including in the emergence of hermeneutics. The 'Pantheism Controversy' began when F. H. Jacobi maintained that G. E. Lessing, perhaps the central figure of the German Enlightenment, had admitted to him that he was a Spinozist. Spinozism at this time was tantamount to atheism, so the controversy had more than philosophical implications, but it is the philosophical points at issue that still have the potential to cause trouble. Jacobi's influential interpretation of Spinozism in his *On the Doctrine of Spinoza in Letters to Herr Moses Mendelssohn* of 1785, second, significantly revised edition 1789, which really set off the controversy, was concerned with the relationship between what Jacobi termed the 'unconditioned' and the 'conditioned', between God as the ground of which the laws of nature are the consequent, and the interrelated chains of the laws of nature. Cognitive explanation relies, as both Spinoza and Kant maintained, upon finding a thing's 'condition'. Jacobi asks how this can ultimately ground explanation, given that any explanation must lead to a regress in which each condition depends upon another condition, *ad infinitum*. Any philosophical system, and here the model is Spinoza, thus 'necessarily ends by having to discover *conditions* of the *unconditioned*',[14] and therefore cannot be complete in itself. For Jacobi this led to the need for a theological leap of faith, which separates God, as the unconditioned ground of being, from the chains of determined—'rule-bound'—conditions in nature. In the 1787 Introduction to the first Critique Kant, who, given the terms he employs, may very well have been thinking of Jacobi, maintains the key problem can be overcome by acknowledging that, while reason must postulate the 'uncondi-

[14] Heinrich Scholz, (ed.), *Die Hauptschriften zum Pantheismusstreit zwischen Jacobi und Mendelssohn* (Berlin: Reuther and Reichard, 1916), p. 51.

tioned ... in all things in themselves for everything conditioned, so that the series of conditions should thus become complete' (Kant, *Critique*, B, p. xx), by restricting knowledge to judgments of appearances, rather than trying to know 'things in themselves', the contradiction of seeking conditions of the unconditioned can be avoided. This does not, though, actually solve the problem of 'conditions', as the history of German Idealism and the rise of hermeneutics reveal. The structure of Jacobi's account of the problem of the unconditioned will turn out to affect any theory which tries to give an exhaustive account of the 'conditions' of any phenomenon, be it natural or linguistic. The basic issue is, for example, exactly the problem for the computer as described by Dreyfus: just adding further 'conditions' will not render something intelligible, unless that which can grasp significance in an 'unconditioned' manner is already in place.

The condition of the knowledge of appearances, of Kantian 'experience', was the 'transcendental subject', but what sort of 'condition' was the transcendental subject itself? Fichte insisted in the *Wissenschaftslehre* that for Kant's system to be grounded the I itself would have to have *unconditioned* status, thus giving the I the founding role which he thought Kant had failed adequately to explicate. He maintains this in order—in the light of Jacobi's key argument—to escape a regress of 'conditioned conditions' which would render the world's intelligibility incomprehensible. The vital aspect of the I for Fichte is the productive imagination, which, as the location of the capacity for 'schematism', is precisely what stops the regress of judgments, thereby giving rise to an intelligible world, rather than random series of 'conditions of conditions'. Whatever may be wrong with Fichte's position—and there is, as the recent philosophy of mind has begun to suggest, probably less than is often assumed—it clearly avoids the central lacuna in theories of language like those in contemporary 'semantic physicalism'. Such theories see meanings as somehow causally explicable via 'functional' states of the brain— which are precisely the sort of thing Jacobi meant by 'conditioned conditions'—without troubling to look at the ways in which the very notion of meaning is unintelligible without an account of intentionality of the kind pointed to by the idea of the schema. Despite its massive impact at the time, the deficiencies in Fichte's position did not, though, escape his contemporaries. Novalis's and Friedrich Schlegel's critiques of Fichte rely on the idea that one cannot definitively ground truth in the activity of the I. Even though it is not a 'condition' like anything in the natural world, self-consciousness cannot be said to be ground of itself, because its transient form of being is 'carried' by a being which necessarily transcends it—an argument which will, incidentally, reappear in Sartre's *Being and Nothingness*. The fact is that hermeneutics in its modern form results when questions raised by Fichte and the Romantics become connected to the new secularized conceptions of language which emerge in the work of Rousseau, Herder, Humboldt, Schelling, Schleiermacher, and the early Romantics.

Early in their careers both Schelling and Schleiermacher had extensive contact with the philosophy of Jacobi, Fichte, Novalis and Schlegel, and both initially regard the task of philosophy as being to ground the intelligibility of the world in the light of Kant's rejection of dogmatism—a task which Novalis and Schlegel soon come to regard as impossible. In the *System of Transcendental Idealism* of 1800 Schelling says of the schema: 'The schema ... is not an idea (*Vorstellung*) that is determined on all sides, but an intuition of the rule according to which a particular object can be produced.'[15] Because it is the intuition of a rule—in the sense that one must be able to apply the rule without relying on any further rule—the schema cannot itself be determined: for that, as Kant suggested, intuitions need rules of cognition. As such there can be no further grounding of this sort of 'intuition', beyond the fact of its own functioning, which is what renders the world intelligible as opposed to its consisting merely in sensory input. Schelling then startlingly concludes that: 'From this necessity of schematism we can infer that the whole mechanism of language must rest upon schematism' (ibid. p. 509). Meaning, then, depends upon a prior ground of intelligibility—the schema—and without this ground linguistic rules would only ever lead to the regress we have already observed. This ground cannot, though, be described in conceptual terms which identify its essential functions, because this would lead to another regress. In an anticipation of Heidegger's *Origin of the Work of Art*, and of the work of Gadamer, and in one of the vital moves in the constitution of modern hermeneutics, Schelling concludes the *System* by suggesting that it is only in art's meaningful transgression of existing rules that we can understand the real nature of this ground.

Talk of 'intuition' in the sense employed by Schelling therefore is nothing mysterious, it refers simply to the fact that what is in question cannot be given a grounded explanation because it must be presupposed for any explanation even to be intelligible at all. The issue raised by such a notion of intuition is actually anything but unfamiliar in contemporary philosophy. Any attempt to

[15] Friedrich Wilhelm Joseph Schelling's *Sämmtliche Werke*, K. F. A. Schelling (ed.) (Stuttgart, 1856–61), I Abteilung 3 Band, p. 508.

ground an explanation requires, as Jacobi showed, something 'unconditioned', whose status is not relative in the way that what is being explained is relative. Quine maintains, for example, in relation to the idea that 'questions of reference make sense only relative to a background language' that 'in practice we end the regress of background languages, in discussions of reference, by acquiescing in our mother tongue and taking its words at face value'.[16] Quite how we do this in Quinean physicalist terms remains, as Putnam and the position that links schematism and intentionality I have just outlined suggest, a mystery. Donald Davidson talks in a related context of an 'intuitive grasp we have of the concept' of truth (Davidson *Inquiries*, p. 267)—which is, in one sense at least, structurally analogous to how we might 'acquiesce in our mother tongue'—and assumes this 'intuitive grasp' as the basis of his theory of propositional truth. He thereby implicitly poses the question whether our grasp of the concept of the truth of a proposition is, to employ the terms we saw him using above, itself 'seeing that' or 'seeing as'. It seems clear that the grasp must be a 'seeing as', an 'intuition' in the sense at issue here, which, of course, further weakens the metaphorical/literal distinction by suggesting that a basic interpretative, schematizing capacity to 'see as' must in fact underlie the 'seeing that' which is to be explained in semantics.

It is Schleiermacher who is the first to show clearly why this is the case, in ways which are still crucial to the philosophy of language. The simple hermeneutic contention which turns out to be the basis for this whole discussion is that understanding cannot be reduced to rule-bound explanation. If one has not *already* understood, how could what one is doing in understanding be grounded by an explanation of understanding? Only if one gives priority to that which is rule-bound, as though everything about understanding is in principle like any other phenomenon to be explained in a science, could explanation, as certain versions of semantics require, take priority. Just how problematic this approach is will become apparent in a moment.

There is no time to show this here, but it is well established that Schleiermacher is thoroughly familiar with all the theoretical aspects of the Kantian and post-Kantian story I have told so far. One of the most important sources of Schleiermacher's major hermeneutic insights is his encounter with the early Romantics' new conception of '*Poesie*', of language which cannot be understood solely in terms of existing usage, whose importance

[16] Quoted in Hilary Putnam, *Words and Life* (Cambridge, MA: Harvard University Press, 1994), p. 337.

lies precisely in its capacity to reveal what cannot be revealed in any already existing way. This conception itself is explicitly seen by Friedrich Schlegel, for similar reasons to those advanced by Schelling in his *System*, as a response to the problem of grounding philosophy revealed by Jacobi. At the end of the eighteenth century in Germany such conceptions are intriguingly linked to changes in the status of wordless music, which, precisely because it is the least representational form of art, becomes the most significant form of art. The rise of 'absolute' wordless music, and the associated move of the new subject of aesthetics away from theories of *mimesis* towards theories of art as that which renders things graspable in new ways, helps open the way to conceptions of language which do not see the sole function of language as representational fixing of a world of ready-made entities, and which insist that what Heidegger will term the 'world-disclosing' aspect of language is both ontologically and logically prior to its semantically determinable aspects. The tension between the conception of language as 'world disclosure' and a conception of formal semantics is, of course, another version of the tension between metaphorical and literal language with which we began.

Now, lest this link of theories of meaning to the question of music sound too extravagantly 'Romantic', here are Wittgenstein's apparently unassuming remarks in *Philosophical Investigations* on the understanding of a sentence or proposition ('*Satz*'), which are concerned with largely the same issue:

> We talk about understanding a sentence in the sense in which it can be replaced by another sentence which says the same thing; but also in the sense in which it cannot be replaced by any other sentence. (As little as one musical theme by another.)
>
> In one case it is the thought of a sentence which is common to differing sentences, in the other something which only these words in these positions express. (Understanding of a poem.)[17]

Wittgenstein even goes so far as to say in the same context that 'Understanding a sentence in language is much more related to understanding a theme in music than one thinks' (ibid.). Although he is very concerned with the new non-representationalist Romantic conceptions of art and language of the kind much later adopted in parts of the work of Wittgenstein, Schleiermacher is also concerned—and this is very often forgotten—with what it means to talk of the 'thought of a sentence', in the manner that will

---

[17] Ludwig Wittgenstein, *Philosophische Untersuchungen* (Frankfurt: Suhrkamp, 1971), p. 227.

be characteristic of the semantic tradition which derives from Bernard Bolzano and Frege. This points to an informative constellation, which again relates to differing readings of Kant.

At much the same time as Schleiermacher develops his hermeneutics, Bolzano, as J. Alberto Coffa has shown, lays foundations for the semantic tradition. The basis of that tradition, Coffa maintains, is 'the separation of meaning from psychological processes', whereby, in Bolzano's account, 'the objective representation associated with the word "table" (i.e. the meaning of "table") should not be confused with tables, the objects of that representation',[18] or, indeed, with the subjective representations of anyone thinking about a table. 'Objective representations' were intended by Bolzano, who was essentially a Platonist, precisely to obviate the need for any recourse to 'intuition', particularly Kantian 'pure intuition' in geometry, but also intuition in the sense we have just encountered. There are as many subjective representations as there are acts of thought on the part of persons thinking about something, but Bolzano's claim is that the 'objective representation designated by any *word* is, as long as this word is not ambiguous, single'.[19] When Dummett asserts that 'words have meanings in themselves, independently of speakers',[20] and talks of the fact that 'For Frege a word simply has a sense ... he does not think that its bearing that sense in the mouth of a speaker depends upon his performing any mental act of endowing it with that sense',[21] he is therefore carrying on the tradition already established by Bolzano, in which meanings are regarded as 'objective representations'. To the extent that 'objective representations' must transcend individual acts of interpretation they must be in principle fully determinable in a rule-bound manner, otherwise it is hard to see why they should be termed objective at all. The real question is, of course, what exactly it is that constitutes an 'objective representation', or, just what is a 'sense' and how do we recognize it? Before suggesting that a central part of Dummett's own account of this issue falls prey to the argument I have been outlining, we need to dispel a few more still current myths about Schleiermacher.

Schleiermacher's essential perspective on these issues was

[18] J. Alberto Coffa, *The Semantic Tradition from Kant to Carnap* (Cambridge University Press, 1991), p. 30.

[19] Bernard Bolzano, *Grundlegung der Logik*, ed. F. Kambartel (Hamburg: Meiner 1963), p. 66.

[20] Ernest Lepore (ed.), *Truth and Interpretation* (Oxford: Blackwell, 1986), p. 473.

[21] Michael Dummett, *Frege and Other Philosophers* (Oxford University Press, 1991), p. 276.

already implicit in Kant's own account of judgment. In the *Critique of Judgement* Kant distinguishes between 'determining judgment', judgment of particulars based on a pre-existing general rule, and 'reflective' judgment, establishing a rule in relation to particulars. Reflective judgment, which is also what gives rise to the ability to apprehend things aesthetically in terms of the interrelations of their parts, cannot rely on prior rules because one of its jobs is precisely to arrive at new rules. Its function is apparent in relation to Wittgenstein's idea of understanding 'something which only these words in these positions express', which, like the significance of a new metaphor, cannot be understood by a rule. Kant's division between types of judgment is mapped by Schleiermacher onto central aspects of his theory of interpretation. He distinguishes 'grammatical' interpretation, in which 'the person ... disappears and only appears as organ of language', which largely corresponds to semantics and which relies on determining judgment, from 'technical interpretation' (which he sometimes terms 'psychological' interpretation) in which 'language with its determining power disappears and only appears as the organ of the person, in the service of their individuality'.[22] Hermeneutics requires both kinds of interpretation, but 'to carry out grammatical explication on its own is a mere fiction' (ibid. p. 164). While there is no doubt that one can identify lexical, pragmatic, syntactical and grammatical constraints in language, which can be disregarded only at the risk of wholesale unintelligibility, these aspects of language are, Schleiermacher insists, 'not positive means of explanation, but negative ones, because what contradicts them cannot be understood at all' (ibid. pp. 171–172). Despite the apparent psychologism involved in the way he describes 'technical interpretation', the rest of the remarks in this passage make it clear that completed technical interpretation, which relies upon reflective judgment, is only a regulative idea which we use to guide interpretation. We require this idea even though we have no firm grounds for thinking it can finally be attained, not least because we are, as Schleiermacher makes quite clear, not even capable of exhaustive self-knowledge, let alone exhaustive knowledge of others. Schleiermacher, despite widespread rumours to the contrary, does not, then, employ the psychologistic notion of 'empathy' in interpretation.

Most importantly, Schleiermacher also realizes that Kant's division of the kinds of judgment cannot be finally sustained, because, as was already apparent from the example of the computer, in a real interpretative situation even a determining judgment requires

[22] Friedrich Schleiermacher, *Hermeneutik und Kritik*, ed. Manfred Frank, (Frankfurt: Suhrkamp, 1977), p. 171.

interpretation in order to know what is the appropriate rule. This leads him to exactly the regress argument Brandom attributes to Wittgenstein, in which the correct way to understand the frequently misinterpreted early Romantic notion of 'art' becomes apparent:

> The complete understanding of speech or writing is an artistic achievement and demands a doctrine (*Kunstlehre*) or technique to which we give the name hermeneutics. We call art ... every compound product in which we are aware of general rules, whose application cannot in the particular case be again brought under rules.[23]

Interpretation, Schleiermacher says elsewhere, 'only bears the *character* of art because the application is not also given with the rules', and there are no 'rules ... that would carry the certainty of their application within them' (Schleiermacher, *Hermeneutik*, p. 81). Davidson, of course, thinks much the same, employing the questionable notion of a 'passing theory' for the 'art' in question, maintaining that semantics in real communication inherently relies on reflective rather than determining judgment: 'For there are no rules for arriving at passing theories, no rules in any strict sense, as opposed to rough maxims and methodological generalities' (Lepore, *Truth*, p. 446). In the following characterization of hermeneutics from the *Ethics* Schleiermacher suggests vital other reasons why determining judgment, the basis of a semantics of 'objective representations', is inadequate as a basis for interpretation:

> Looked at from the side of language the technical discipline of hermeneutics arises from the fact that every utterance can only be counted as an objective representation (*Darstellung*) [Bolzano uses the term '*Vorstellung*' when talking of 'objective representations', but it seems clear that Schleiermacher here means something very close to what Bolzano means] to the extent to which it is taken from language and is to be grasped via language, but that on the other side the utterance can only arise as the action of an individual, and, as such, even if it is analytical in terms of its content, it still, in terms of its less essential elements, bears free synthesis [in the sense of individual judgment] within itself. The reconciliation (*Ausgleichung*) of both moments makes understanding and explication into an art [again in the sense of that whose 'application is not also given with the rules'].[24]

---

[23] Schleiermacher, cited in Beate Rössler, *Die Theorie des Verstehens in Sprachanalyse und Hermeneutik* (Berlin: Dunker and Humblot, 1990), pp. 232–233 (from *Short Account of Theological Study*).

[24] Friedrich Schleiermacher, *Ethik (1812/13)*, (Hamburg: Meiner, 1990), p. 116.

In these terms there can be no understanding of an utterance solely in terms of its standing for an 'objective representation', which is independent of context, because this would ignore the fact that *all* utterances are to varying degrees context- and interpretation-dependent.

The point of the hermeneutic tradition we are considering here is, then, precisely that it does not need to rely on the assumption that a theory of 'meaning', qua definable sense attached to a word, is essential to account for the fact of understanding. Unless understanding is always already in play for actual language users there would be as little *meaning* to explain as there is when two computers are made to trade sentences with each other: it is only because the computers are in a world which is already understood by those concerned to interpret what the computers produce that the question as to their 'meanings' could arise at all. The crucial fact here is that there is an asymmetry between the production of grammatically well-formed sequences of words according to rules, and the ability to interpret such sentences in ever new situations without becoming involved in a regress of background conditions.

That the basic structure in question here remains constitutive for the hermeneutic tradition's approach to the question of 'meaning' is apparent in the following passage from Heidegger's 1928 lectures on *Metaphysical Foundations of Logic*, where Schleiermacher's regress of rules argument appears in another guise, in relation to the status of logical rules in thought:

> Thinking and the use of rules might be unavoidable for the carrying out of all thought, thus also for the foundation of metaphysics itself, but from this it does not follow that this foundation lies in the use of rules itself. On the contrary, from this it only follows that this use of rules itself requires grounding, and it further follows from this that this apparently plausible argumentation is not at all capable of carrying out a foundation.[25]

Whatever else may differ between Schleiermacher and those who follow him—and Gadamer in particular has done much to over-emphasize these differences—the basic realization that grounding meaning and truth by explanation in terms of rules is, in the strict sense, a 'non-starter' is common to the most significant hermeneutic theories.

What, then, of the analytical tradition's approaches to the issue of grounding meaning? In his most hermeneutic frame of mind, as

[25] Martin Heidegger, *Metaphysische Anfangsgründe der Logik* (Klostermann, Frankfurt, 1990), p. 130.

we have just seen, Davidson cannot be said to belong to the analytical tradition. This is evident in his famous dictum that 'there is no such thing as a language, not if a language is anything like what many philosophers and linguists have supposed' (Lepore, *Truth*, p. 446). Dummett, on the other hand, insists that 'the conviction that a philosophical explanation of thought can be achieved by a philosophical analysis of language, and ... that a complete explanation can only be achieved in this way and in no other' defines the analytical project.[26] He makes his difference from the hermeneutic tradition very clear when he claims in relation to Davidson's equation of truth and meaning that:

> if we want to maintain that what we learn, as we learn the language, is, primarily, what it is for each of the sentences that we understand to be true, then we must be able, for any given sentence, to give an account of what it is to know this which does not depend upon a presumed prior understanding of the sentence; otherwise our theory of meaning is circular and explains nothing.[27]

The account must, however, presumably rely upon understanding *some* sentences or other, or at least presuppose a pretheoretical familiarity with what it is to understand a sentence, otherwise the phenomenon to be explained does not seem to be part of the theory at all. Dummett seems to want an account of conditions of understanding minus the 'unconditioned' aspect of the subject that was implied in the notion of 'intuitive grasp'. This aspect is smuggled in via the Fregean notion of 'force', but it is clear that this will only make the problems worse, because what force is given to an utterance must be understood and interpreted via the context of the utterance by someone who already knows what it is to endow utterances with a specific 'force'.

The hermeneutic tradition can be defined by its *acceptance* of an inherent circularity in understanding, because there is in its terms no way of escaping the need to have already understood something before attempting to explain understanding: this is precisely the point of the 'hermeneutic circle' and of the arguments about regress we have already considered. As we saw at the outset, Dummett demands a theory which 'must give an explicit account, not only of what anyone must know in order to know the meaning of any given expression, but of what constitutes having such

[26] Michael Dummett, *Ursprünge der analytischen Philosophie* (Suhrkamp, Frankfurt, 1988), p. 11.

[27] Michael Dummett, *The Seas of Language* (Oxford University Press, 1993), p. 43.

knowledge' (Dummett, *Seas of Language*, p. 22). Jacobi already suggested that any such determinate knowledge leads to a regress of explanations, and the same problem will surface in Dummett. The essential divide in contemporary approaches to these issues lies, therefore, between those, like Dummett, who think that a theory of meaning must also give us an account of the notion of truth without presupposing an understanding of truth, and those like Heidegger and Davidson, who think truth must be presupposed, for the reasons we have seen.

Dummett's approach to meaning, despite the many insights it offers in other respects, seems in this respect, though, to be wholly implausible. Beate Rössler has shown that, in terms of Dummett's theory:

> even for the understanding of a relatively uncomplicated sentence one could put together an indefinite list of necessary preconditions of understanding ... on the other hand such a list, even if it could be brought to a conclusion, would lead to an infinite regress. (Rössler, *Theorie des Verstehens*, p. 140)

The regress, which relates to those we have been considering all along, results because the specification of the conditions for understanding one sentence must themselves be formulated as propositions and therefore have their own conditions of understanding, and so on. Rössler is happier with Dummett's idea that knowledge of the meaning of a sentence is also linked to the rules for verifying its truth conditions: but this just repeats another version of the same problem. How do we *decide* which rules are the right rules for the verification of a particular utterance, without again falling into a regress of judgments? The fact is anyway that, as Davidson argues in the essay cited above, one can get any word to mean anything one wants if one finds a way of getting others to understand it: there can be no generalizable verification procedure for this. Dummett's problems do not stop here: his criterion for the demonstration of the 'knowledge' required to understand a sentence is essentially behavioural, in line with the 'externalist' tendency of much of the analytical tradition. Grasping a sense is in these terms demonstrated by a performance which is intelligible to others. This presupposes that the observers of the demonstration have themselves already obtained—learned, been trained in, nay, understood?—the knowledge in which grasping the sense consists. Such a view requires either a thoroughly metaphysical assumption about the status of senses, or a final 'unconditioned' arbiter of what the sense actually is and what behaviour in fact exhibits the grasping of it. But who is this arbiter if not just another language user like the one being observed, and what shows that she really understands?

When I talk or write about x in order to articulate what I hold true of x, I generally have to presuppose that x is as I say it is for both myself and the other person, thus that something like a notion of sense or objective representation is presupposed in communication. Schleiermacher insists in this respect that 'it makes no difference whether the same thought is carried out by one individual or another individual, and every thought which is determined by its content is the same in and for every person' (Schleiermacher, *Ethik* (*1812/13*), p. 256). At the same time, though, my relationship to x cannot be definitively *shown* to be that of the recipient of my utterances concerning x: 'semantic symmetry' between the 'I' and the 's/he' perspective can only ever be a postulate because of the inherent epistemic asymmetry between two self-conscious beings. Though in most cases communication seems largely to work, my performance may well just confuse my interlocutors and continue to do so, even though our relationship to x might in fact be the same. Schleiermacher maintains in this connection that 'all communication about external objects is a constant continuation of the test as to whether all people construct identically':[28] the obligation to do this is as much an ethical as an epistemological matter. He says this not least as a way of explaining why, as Manfred Frank has suggested, we keep talking, rather than hand each other a semantic rule-book containing what we need to know and how to demonstrate it.

Schleiermacher's approach here might again seem threatened by an untenable psychologism, of the kind attacked by both Husserl and Frege, but this is not in fact the case. In a section of the *Ethics* on 'Identity of Schematism' Schleiermacher states:

> Every person is a completed/closed-off (*abgeschlossen*) unity of consciousness. As far as reason produces cognition in a person it is, qua consciousness, only produced for this person. What is produced with the character of schematism is, though, posited as valid for everyone, and therefore being in one ['*Sein in Einem*'—by which he means individualized self-consciousness] does not correspond to its character [as schematism]. (Schleiermacher, *Ethik* (*1812/13*), p. 64)

Language, then, is a 'system of movements of the organism which are simultaneously expression and sign of the acts of consciousness

[28] Friedrich Schleiermacher, *Friedrich Schleiermachers Dialektik,* ed. Rudolf Odebrecht (Darmstadt: Wissenschaftliche Buchgesellschaft, 1976), p. 373.

as the cognizing faculty, under the character of the identity of schematism' (ibid. p. 65). The 'identity of schematism' is the locus of what Frege means by 'senses' and is the condition of possibility of 'thoughts': it also plays the role of the 'knowledge' Dummett sees as the basis of semantics. The question is, though, what status one attaches to it. Dummett maintains one need not carry out his kind of analysis for a whole language, but that one can assume the kind of explanation which works for a particular expression will in principle work for all others. The problem is that he, in common with many other theorists of this kind, never actually gives us any serious examples of what he proposes as the completed realization of his kind of explanation: 'in principle' does rather a lot, not to say a potentially infinite amount of work.

From a hermeneutic point of view the reason for the lack of completed examples lies not in the heroic difficulty involved in explaining what we need to know in order to understand 'snow is white', but rather in the fact that the potential meanings of 'snow is white' are simply too diverse to be specified in terms of rules for understanding a sequence of words. This is because we live in a world which we first understand by being in it at all. The hermeneutic world does not consist just of objects or states of affairs which are then represented in language, but rather, along with interpreted objects (whose boundaries are always negotiable) to which we ascribe predicates, of practices, Heideggerian 'involvements', feelings, impulses, revelations, intuitions, relationships, moods, which may find their adequate expression in propositions, but which might just as easily be articulated in a piece of music or a poem. What we see things in the world as depends upon the kind of relationship we have to those things. This leaves open the possibility that an individual's understanding, including of 'snow is white', which is demonstrated by using it in the appropriate context, can become a revelation of new significance which was impossible without that individual's using those words in that situation. This revelation need have nothing to do with what a speaker must know 'if he is able to use the sentence correctly' (Dummett, *Seas of Language*, p. 93).

The fact is that it is far from clear what Dummett's kind of theory of meaning is really for. If we could have such 'knowledge', would we really understand our understanding of sentences we already understand any better, and would it make others' understanding of what someone says more reliable? The potential consequences of such a theory, were it to be conceivable that it could be valid, are actually rather sinister: unless one exhibits the correct behaviour, one is presumably not using language properly and does not know what one is doing. This evidently often is the case in linguistic failure, when the utterance does not do what one wants it to, either pragmatically or expressively, but it may also be the case that one is James Joyce, or that one's incorrect use is wholly adequate for achieving what is intended, even though one does not really know why. If the knowledge Dummett requires can be formulated propositionally, we are faced with the familiar regress, because the conditions of interpreting the propositions are either of the same order, and can therefore themselves be formulated as propositions, or they must have an 'unconditioned' status. This latter possibility would be a bad version of what the hermeneutic position argues is necessary anyway, namely that 'the knowledge' must be understood in a way which is not dependent on how it can be explained.

The divergence between Dummett's kind of analytical account—and it is arguable that any strictly analytical account of meaning must be defined in terms of determining judgment—and the hermeneutic account highlights a vital divergence in approaches to philosophy today. Schleiermacher's approach, rather like that of the recent Putnam, is essentially ethical and historical, rather than semantic or epistemological. Instead of assuming that the proof of 'having the knowledge' of an 'objective representation' is the prior aspect of our relationship to language and communication, Schleiermacher assumes that it is the capacity of the individual to make sense despite the rules which is fundamental:

> A simple appropriation of thoughts which have already been laid down in language is not an activity of reason, and if we assume someone whose whole thinking is nothing more than those thoughts, then that person is hardly a person at all. (Schleiermacher, *Ethik (1812/13)*, p. 264)

Such a person fails to reach the ethical level, which combines the demands for general intelligibility inherent in language with the imperative to think for oneself. On the one hand, then, he says, 'nobody can get out of language', but on the other 'the individual (*das Individuelle*) must remain within language, in the form of combination' (ibid. p. 323). The latter appears as 'style', the individual combination of the pregiven elements of language that cannot be prescribed in advance or understood in terms of rules. This means that 'there can be no concept of a style' (Schleiermacher, *Hermeneutik*, p. 172) and that due attention must be given to language as the means via which real individuals articulate their world, rather than as an entity consisting of objective representations that can be circumscribed in a theory. The ability to make sense of 'style' also means that even the questionable regulative idea of a language qua pre-existing rule-bound entity to be explained in a theory of meaning must be taken as secondary to the prior interpretative activity of individual human subjects.

One of the most telling arguments for this view is evident in Schleiermacher's attention to primary language acquisition—what Davidson terms 'the infinitely difficult problem of how a first language is learned' (Lepore, *Truth*, p. 441)—where the same threat of regress we have repeatedly observed is obviously present. If, Schleiermacher argues—and here 'gavagai' beckons—one claims that words are learned by comparison of the noise made in relation to one presumed object with that made in relation to another example of that presumed kind of object, which is supposed to result in the knowledge of an 'objective representation', one is back with the issue of schematism. If the child can only understand the word by understanding the rule for its use in relation to different cases of the object in question, one is left with the problem of how the first understanding comes about at all, given that there can be no rule for how to learn this, especially if the ability to learn rules is itself in some way supposed to be language-dependent. Schleiermacher claims the first understanding requires what he terms 'divination', which we also require in all situations where there is no immediately manifest already familiar rule for making sense of an utterance. Given this essentially contingent and individual moment in primary language acquisition, there can be no final way of establishing an intersubjective certainty that would appear in the form of 'objective representations'. Children can also, of course, produce 'false' utterances which turn out to make new sense if interpreted in the way we interpret poetic utterances and living metaphors. In the perspective proposed here, the realm of language use which was consigned to meaninglessness in the more extreme versions of analytical philosophy such as logical positivism turns out to be the real condition of possibility even of the language of verificationist science. If the very possibility of language acquisition requires the aspect of understanding which cannot be based on rules, there are no grounds for asserting that the conditions of meaning lie solely in rules or publicly communicable knowledge. What, then, does this tell us about future philosophical approaches to meaning?

It is often maintained, as we saw Rorty doing, that the analytical and the hermeneutic enterprises have essentially different aims. This is certainly the case for those theories of meaning that wish to explain what a subject understands in terms to which the subject him- or herself has no direct, 'intuitive' access whatsoever, thus in terms of what Davidson has called 'social externalism'. 'Social externalism' claims that what we mean can only be understood 'in terms of what others would mean by the same words',[29] and Davidson rightly considers it to be false: although meaning must in some way be public, it is not stable and can potentially be changed by individual innovative 'metaphorical' usage at any moment. Interestingly, similar objections to those against social externalism are in order, as Manfred Frank has shown, in relation to the later (but not always the earlier) Heidegger, who maintains that 'Language speaks. Man speaks to the extent to which he corresponds to language.'[30] An approach to philosophy which derives its dominant assumptions from the natural sciences here moves into a bizarre convergence with a philosophy famous for its conviction that the natural sciences and their application in modern technology are a manifestation of the subject's forgetfulness and 'subjectification' of being—'being', the fact that the world is intelligible at all, is, of course, what plays the role of the ground of meaning for Heidegger. What is missing in both approaches is the necessary ethical orientation towards the fact that individuals have to make sense of both the world and the languages via which they articulate the world: without an orientation which includes the epistemological implications of individual understanding, crucial dimensions of language become obscured in the name of an illusory objectivism.

So what is the end of my story? One can begin with a very brief anecdote. Before a lecture recently given by Davidson in London, it was suggested by the person introducing him that one of Davidson's great philosophical innovations was the theory of 'anomalous monism'. He also maintained in his introduction that analytical philosophy was the only serious contemporary philosophy. This seems to me symptomatic of what we need to get away from, in the name of a new dialogue between the traditions. We also, by the way, need to get away from such attitudes because both the claims made are simply false. A theory of anomalous monism was first set out by Schelling in his identity philosophy in 1804, in terms which exactly parallel those of Davidson.[31] Furthermore, it should now be clear that Davidson's most serious insights into language are not analytical at all in the sense that Dummett—who is certainly not alone in his view—proposes and that the reasons why this is so have long been available in aspects

[29] From 'Epistemology Externalized', quoted in Manfred Frank, *Stil in der Philosophie* (Stuttgart: Reclam, 1992), p. 21.
[30] Martin Heidegger, *Unterwegs zur Sprache* (Pfullingen: Neske, 1959), pp. 32–33.

of the Romantic hermeneutic tradition. These kinds of parallel are becoming increasingly frequent. John McDowell has, for example, recently proposed a new version of epistemology based in part on what is in fact Kant's account of schematism, and on its Schelling- and Schlegel-influenced revisions in Hegel's *Phenomenology*, as well as on the work of Gadamer. When Hilary Putnam calls for a renewal of philosophy which moves it away from its obsession with the method of the natural sciences he does so in terms that echo many of the concerns of the Romantic hermeneutic tradition. I am *not* suggesting here that the Romantics had already said it all before, but I am suggesting that some of their basic, largely ignored or forgotten intuitions have turned out to be very durable and that this should give serious pause for thought. Questions about the grounding of meaning and truth are most productive when they look at how Heidegger's Romantic-influenced concern with the precedence of world-disclosure before formal semantics relates to the fact that this disclosure is only possible via self-conscious sub- jects, who must be able to interpret and establish meanings, rather than just behave 'correctly' in relation to utterances. This leads in the direction of epistemology and ethics and to the need for a new look at the history of metaphysical questions about subjectivity, of the kind which formed the core of Romantic philosophy. The really interesting questions about truth and meaning are those in which the agenda is not set by the assumption that there will eventually be a scientifically grounded 'objective' answer to what truth and meaning really are—any such answer, as we saw, falls prey to a cir- cularity which results in answers dictated by the initial assumptions of the theory, or to a regress which renders understanding incom- prehensible. In this perspective it is perhaps most important to ask why so many philosophers in the modern period took and still take a path which leads to the complete repression of many of the most important Romantic intuitions about language, a path which, in its purely analytical form, is now turning out to be a dead-end. But answering that question would be another story.[32]

[31] See Andrew Bowie, *Schelling and Modern European Philosophy: An Introduction* (London: Routledge, 1993), Chapter 4; and 'Identität und Subjektivität', in Manfred Frank, *Selbstbewußtsein und Selbsterkenntnis*, (Stuttgart: Reclam, 1991).

[32] Many of the ideas set out in this essay are developed in more detail in my *Aesthetics and Subjectivity: from Kant to Nietzsche*, second edition (Manchester University Press, 1993), and *From Romanticism to Critical Theory. The Philosophy of German Literary Theory* (London: Routledge 1996).

Science and Psychology

İLHAM DİLMAN

I

I want to ask: what is knowledge of human beings and can it be acquired by experimental methods?

It is a widespread assumption in academic psychology that the methods which have been applied with great success in the physical sciences are applicable to investigations in other areas and hence to psychological investigation. The history of experimental psychology is the history of the adjustments psychologists have made to their subject to be able to apply the experimental method of the sciences to it. In the process of trimming the head to fit the cap on it they have emasculated psychology.

The knowledge they seek in this way—which is the only kind of knowledge they recognize—is impersonal, general, inductive, theoretical. It is to be applied to particular cases so as to obtain an understanding of individual people and help them to deal more efficiently with such problems as difficulties in learning at school, stress at work, problems of maladjustment, unhappiness in relationships, etc. This is the orthodox view.

Thus in a book, entitled *Psychology, The Science of Mental Life*,[1] George Miller says that advance in a science is measured in terms of theory and of practical results: 'scientific knowledge provides a foundation for technological advances, for the solution of practical problems that arise in the daily affairs of ordinary people' (p. 16). This foundation, he tells us, is to be found in the understanding it seeks of 'what people are *really* like' (p. 17). 'Like all sciences [he writes] psychology has influenced our lives at both levels. It has given us technical tricks and it has changed our conception of human nature' (p. 17). He mentions psychological testing as one example of the fruits of scientific knowledge in psychology. I quote a short passage from what he says:

They [psychological testers] began to test aptitudes, to classify interests, to evaluate achievements. Now they can pigeonhole your personality, assess your emotional stability, your masculinity, your imagination, executive potential, chances of marital bliss, conformity to an employer's stereotype, or ability to operate a

[1] Penguin Books, 1979.

turret lathe. Whatever you plan to do, there seems to be a psychological test you should take first. (p. 19)

Now the idea that a person's emotional stability or his chances at making a happy marriage can be assessed by a psychological test, in the way that his ability to operate a turret lathe can be so assessed, shows a thoughtless attitude towards life and, I believe, has done immense harm. One cannot come to know a person in this way, nor can one assess his chances at making a happy marriage by any kind of litmus test. First of all it takes time to come to know a person and, even then, one can at best only guess how he will come up in the face of a new challenge. Besides there are so many imponderables where something like a marriage is concerned that the most one can do is to make a tentative guess, adding the proviso: 'if he is lucky', 'if things go well for him'. (a) There is a place for chance in life, contingencies that are not predictable, and (b) a person, however set in his ways he may be, may always meet an old contingency in a new way.

So let me ask, what is knowledge of human beings? How does it enter into our understanding of ourselves and others as individuals? Can it be acquired by scientific observation, and does it have the kind of generality, precision and objectivity characteristic of science? Wittgenstein asks: can one learn this knowledge? Let me quote his very brief answer:

Yes [he says]; some can. Not, however, by taking a course in it, but through 'experience'. Can someone else be a man's teacher in this? Certainly. From time to time he gives him the right *tip*. This is what 'learning' and 'teaching' are like here. What one acquires here is not a technique; one learns correct judgments. There are also rules, but they do not form a system, and only experienced people can apply them right. Unlike calculating-rules.[2]

The experience which Wittgenstein has in mind is the kind one has in living one's own life. It refers to one's dealings with people in their variety in different situations, meeting with their co-operation as well as obstruction, their gratitude and their resentment, finding communion with them and at other times feeling at a loss and out of one's depth. The point is that we acquire whatever knowledge we have of mankind in *living our life*, engaging with others and suffering life's adversities. The more open we are in ourselves—that means open to hurt, grief, criticisms, as well as to the

---

[2] L. Wittgenstein, *Philosophical Investigators* (Oxford: Blackwell, 1963), p. 227.

pleasures of give and take—the more we are capable of learning from others and about life. By contrast the psychologist's laboratory is an ivory tower.

Obviously observation plays an important part here, but it belongs to our dealings with people, it is part of our participation in life's activities in the course of which we meet others. It is to be contrasted with the detached observation we have in the sciences, where observation is a skill and one trained observer is as good as another. There the observation is part of his expertise, here it comes from the individual and it is as much in his responses as it is in his eyes. What is important is that it should be first-hand—not skilled. A skill is acquired by training; being genuine in one's responses is what a person comes to in his growth.

It is in learning to be oneself, in learning to live one's own life that one comes to know people. As one comes to know people as individuals, one becomes alive to their differences and acquires an understanding of people—what Wittgenstein calls 'judgement'. This is not confined to the intellect; the understanding is an intimate part of the person. That is why psychology, in what Dr Drury in his book *The Danger of Words* characterizes as 'its original meaning', is not an *academic* subject. Drury says that in this sense 'it is the great novelists, dramatists, biographers, historians, that are the real psychologists'.[3]

So the knowledge and understanding that make a psychologist a psychologist in *this* sense are picked up in the course of living one's life and keeping one's eyes open and one's wits about. As Wittgenstein says, some can learn this knowledge; not, however by taking a course in it. For there is no general method for acquiring it and it engages the person in himself as an individual. It is not the kind of knowledge which is open to all who are intellectually qualified. It calls for personal qualities.

For this reason observation and objectivity do not mean here what they mean in the sciences. There, as I said, observation has to be dispassionate; the observer has to be detached from what he observes. There is only one point of view from which he observes it: that of the science in which he has been trained. In contrast, the human beings whom the psychologist is concerned to understand have themselves a point of view on what they are doing and on the situation in which they act. The observant person is the one who can enter into the other's point of view, appreciate how he sees things, what things mean to him, what considerations carry weight with him. Only in this way can he understand the

[3] M. O'C. Drury, *The Danger of Words* (London: Routledge, 1973), p. 41.

other's conduct—his decisions, reactions, fears and desires. He has to speak the other's language, share the life of that language with him, live in the same world. I am referring to the human world in which the identity of what forms part of it (situations, events, relations) is determined by forms of significance which have their source in the language and culture of those who live in it. There is nothing like this in the world of physics, nor in the life and behaviour of animals—in the natural sciences.

I said that the observant person in psychology is a participant in the world of the person he observes; he is not detached from it. Does that mean that there is no such thing as objectivity here? The answer is: it depends on what one means by 'objectivity'. Certainly there is a difference between biased and unbiased observation. The psychologist has to make sure that his personal likes and dislikes do not bias his appreciation. On the other hand this does not mean that he has to be indifferent to those he is trying to understand. If he were, he could not respond, enter into their point of view. So the attitude he has to develop is not one of detached interest but of concern and fellow-feeling.

In this respect he is to be contrasted with the scientific observer who is, as it were, a human instrument. What he observes constitute data for his science. His training qualifies him as such an instrument and he is objective precisely in his impersonality. The psychologist's understanding, on the other hand, does not grow from data in this sense, but from what he grasps in his responses to people 'in the traffic of human life'—to use an expression from Wittgenstein. The scientist's detachment would, therefore, disqualify him from grasping what he grasps in such responses. What is important is that he should be free in his responses from seeing things only in relation to himself. This is what constitutes bias in psychology. For it prevents the psychologist from seeing what people respond to and the considerations that weigh with them from within their point of view. It would thus stand in the way of a proper understanding of their conduct.

I contrasted scientific data which can be recorded and collected with an instrument with human conduct. Data are self-contained units abstracted from the flow of events—positions of a star, the acidity of chemical solutions, the changing voltages of an electric current. Human conduct, by contrast, is an integral part of the life of an individual person, with a particular history, participating in the life of the culture to which he belongs. It can only be identified and characterized, as I said, in the traffic of human life; not in abstraction from it. That is why the most interesting questions of psychology are not amenable to experimental investigation. For an experiment is something one can repeat. The environment in which it is repeated in the laboratory is tightly controlled. It must remain the same from one performance of an experiment to another performance of it. Otherwise it would be impossible to compare results. What is thus included in or excluded from this environment makes a causal difference to the result obtained. That is the focus of interest in the experiments: what are the factors that affect the result? But the same result must be conceivable in different circumstances; otherwise we could not say whether this or that factor in those circumstances does or does not affect the result in question.

With what psychology is interested in it is mostly otherwise. The remark that a man utters, for instance, will have a different significance in different circumstances; it will no longer be what it is—e.g. an insult, a word of praise, an encouragement. In different surroundings the same gesture, movement, or even action will manifest very different feelings, qualities of mind and character. Indeed words which are an expression of gratitude in one person's mouth may turn into an expression of irony or condescension in another person's mouth. To know what they express or mean you have to know the person who means them thus or thus. Here we have a serious logical limit to experimentation in psychology.

On the other side of the same coin, most of the states and qualities of mind and character that are relevant to what interests us in people have diverse manifestations. Consequently the words we use to refer to and describe them—'gratitude', 'arrogance', 'intelligence', etc—cover 'many manifestations of life'. As Wittgenstein puts it: the phenomena which constitute these manifestations are 'widely scattered'.[4] There is nothing to be abstracted from them all, from the diverse manifestations of love or intelligence for instance, such that we can say 'this is its essential nature'. If we abstract or construct such an 'essence' or general character in the name of science we shall leave out much that is of vital interest to us. This is one reason why there can be no unified theory e.g. of love or of learning, and why their presentation belongs to literature. It is also one reason why we should take intelligence and other psychological tests with a pinch of salt. Dr Drury tells us how, when he was in the army, a man who was found by intelligence tests to have the mental age of a boy of twelve and a half displayed much native intelligence in the job Drury appointed him to do. Manifestations of intelligence are 'widely scattered'; we can even say that intelligence is not one thing.

What the psychologist is concerned to discern and understand

[4] L. Wittgenstein, *Zettel* (Oxford: Blackwell, 1967), § 110.

in human conduct are expressions of the human soul—verbal and other—that is of individual human beings. Here it is important to remember that human beings can be themselves in what they say and do, and as such accessible to others, and they can also withdraw, put up a front, hide their feelings and intentions from others. They are capable of lying and pretence. There is nothing like this in the animal world or the world of physics, nothing like this which the physicist or the ethologist needs to take into account in his observations. For much of what the psychologist needs to understand he has to come to know people as individuals. This necessarily takes time and is not a matter of observing how they behave, as it were, through a one-way screen. He has to be receptive to others and the people he is interested in have to be open and be themselves *with him*. I emphasize the 'with him' for this is part of a two-way interaction. The scientist observes the phenomena he studies; the psychologist has to be able to talk to people and listen to what they have to say. Obviously he knows this, but the gloss that is put on this in psychology badly misrepresents what is in question. In introspective psychology what a person reveals about himself in what he tells others, including the psychologist, is treated as information provided by self-observation. The idea is that he observes in himself what no one else can observe. Thus the psychologist observes him and what he cannot observe is relayed to him by the subject of his experiments. As William James puts it: 'when psychology is treated as a natural science "states of mind" are taken for granted as data immediately given in experience'.[5] It is such data which the subject is supposed to report to the psychologist, the experimenter.

The behaviourist rightly rejects the idea of introspection as a form of observation directed to some private inner landscape. He treats what the person says about himself as part of his behaviour. In doing so, however, he misses something distinctive about human beings, namely that there are some things which we can find out about people only if they choose to disclose them to us— thoughts, feelings, wishes and memories which we may never know of unless they tell us. They have a privileged access to those not by introspection, but simply by virtue of these thoughts, memories and wishes being *theirs*. That is people have the capacity to tell others what they think, remember, intend to do, if they want to, because they can talk. It is this simple but important fact which psychologists have had great difficulty in recognizing—I mean in seeing it for what it is.

[5] W. James, *Psychology,* Abridged Edition, (The Living Library, 1948, p. 462).

I have argued that the kind of knowledge we expect to find in psychology 'in its original meaning', namely what I referred to as 'knowledge of human beings' or 'knowledge of the human soul', is not inductive knowledge. It does not have the generality of scientific laws. Wittgenstein, we have seen, speaks of what one who learns such knowledge acquires as 'judgment'—in the sense in which we may say of someone that 'he has judgment'. Its generality, therefore, lies in the way one who comes to it comes to a new perspective on life. Through it one's understanding of individuals is deepened. It is thus the generality of a perspective to which one is related personally. It is as such that it enters my dealings with and responses to people in particular situations and my judgments about their conduct.

Yet the orthodox view in academic psychology is that psychological knowledge is arrived at inductively, by generalizing what one observes in particular cases. This can then be applied to new cases. I have already quoted George Miller to this effect: 'scientific knowledge provides a foundation for technological advances, for the solution of practical problems that arise in the daily affairs of ordinary people'. There is a classical statement of this view in John Stuart Mill's 'On the Logic of the Moral [meaning 'mental'] Sciences', in *A System of Logic*, Book VI:

> Human beings do not all feel and act alike in the same circumstances; but it is possible to determine what makes one person, in a given position, feel or act in one way, another in another ... In other words, mankind has not one universal character, but there exist universal laws of the formation of character.[6]

Here is a different conception of what I learn and the way it bears on and comes into motion in each new case I meet. I quote the last paragraph of John Wisdom's 'Paradox and Discovery':

> It is, I believe, extremely difficult to breed lions. But there was at one time at the Dublin zoo a keeper by the name of Mr Flood who bred many lion cubs without losing one. Asked the secret of his success, Mr Flood replied, 'Understanding lions'. Asked in what consists the understanding of lions, he replied, 'Every lion is different'. It is not to be thought that Mr Flood, in seeking to understand an individual lion, did not bring to bear his great experience with other lions. Only he remained free to see each lion for itself.[7]

[6] J. S. Mill, *On the Logic of the Moral Sciences* (from *A System of Logic*, Bk VI) (The Library of Liberal Arts, 1965), p. 41.

[7] In J. Wisdom, *Paradox and Discovery* (Oxford: Blackwell, 1965), p. 138.

İlham Dilman

This is in stark contrast with George Miller's claim that 'psychology ... has given us technical tricks', for instance mental tests, by means of which 'now they [the psychologists who apply them] can pigeonhole your personality, assess your emotional stability, etc.' (p. 19). It is precisely such pigeonholing which, Wisdom tells us, Mr Flood avoided in his understanding of lions.

Clearly the kind of understanding Mr Flood had of his lions has greater affinity to what artists give us of what they present in their works than the one scientists give us of the phenomena they study. For the scientist is interested in general properties or common characteristics to determine common reactions. Artists, on the other hand, are interested in seeing things in their differences, to capture them in their uniqueness. Wisdom thus underlines the child-like character which Mr Flood preserved in his view of his lions however wide his experience had been in breeding many lion cubs: 'We need to be at once like someone who has seen much and forgotten nothing (he says), and also like one who is seeing everything for the first time.'[8]

This is precisely the quality of vision one finds in a good painting, biography or novel. Thus Marion Milner, a Kleinian psychoanalyst who in her youth sought to find herself and also to paint, writes of the way things revealed themselves to her when she could detach herself from her self-preoccupations:

> I was lying, weary and bored with myself, on a cliff over the Mediterranean, I had said 'I want nothing', and immediately the landscape dropped its picture-postcard garishness and shone with a gleam from the first day of creation, even the dusty weeds on the roadside.[9]

This is what Wisdom describes as 'seeing everything for the first time'. It is the opposite of what Miller tells us the scientific psychologist does: 'pigeonhole your personality.'

When someone's personality is pigeonholed one may at best come to know what is vulgarly called 'what makes him tick'. This may be useful information for someone interested in pulling his strings, in using him. But it is very far from understanding him and it is a delusion to think that this is all there is to him. In any case, the idea that everyone has strings that can be pulled is as crass a notion as that everyone has a price and can be bought. Someone who pigeonholes people does not see them with open eyes and in their depth; he makes cardboard cut-outs of them.

[8] Ibid. pp. 137–138.
[9] Marion Milner (Field, Joanna), *A Life of One's Own* (Harmondsworth: Penguin Books, 1952), p. 107.

152

Furthermore the contact he makes in his interactions with them is bound to be superficial, for he doesn't permit them to be themselves.

Let me add that human beings cannot be confined to what they are like—even where a psychologist can pull their strings. For a person—and this is where a person differs from a lion, even when seen as an individual lion—can himself be aware of what he is like and has himself a point of view on it. He is the person he is in the kind of relation he stands to it. He may be dissatisfied with himself, troubled about the way he is, consider himself to be a failure, be defiant in the way he is; he may accept it, or he may acquiesce in it. Thus, in the last case, if he is greedy for instance, he will be so in the mode of a greedy puppy. Even in such a case, though, he can take cognizance of the way he is and take responsibility for it: endorse or repudiate it. Here—we can say nothing general: this dimension of life which is distinctive of human existence necessarily eludes any scientific psychology—that is any psychology which is concerned with general or common characteristics from which to draw inferences in particular cases in the way Mill suggests.

Yet psychologists, in thinking of themselves as scientists, lose sight of this. They say, for instance, that they wish to understand the way the mind works and go on chasing after laws that govern the mind's workings. But there is no such thing as 'the way the mind works'. We may, of course, perfectly legitimately, wonder about the way a particular person's mind works. Here we are trying to figure him out as an individual: Why, for instance, is he so quick to take offence? Why does he reject people's friendly overtures so readily? Why does he like to ruffle people's feathers? What does he get out of being offensive to people? There is no general theory which will help us arrive at answers to such questions. We shall only arrive at answers here by coming to know the person in question. This involves talking to him and finding out about his past life and present circumstances, his thoughts and feelings about different things, his interests, convictions and his plans and hopes for the future. We shall make sense of all this, of course, in the light of our experience of people over a period of time.

This is precisely the kind of research that goes into writing a biography; it is the kind of thing a novelist brings before his mind imaginatively in constructing a character. What the biographer or novelist makes of this material, the way he arranges it to give us insight into the person or character presented, depends on his talent, imagination and knowledge of the human soul—in the sense I have tried to elucidate. He looks at and makes us see the person and character he presents 'from *within*', that is from within the person's or character's point of view, using his art to this effect. He makes us see the world in which the person or character moves, through his, the character's, eyes, contrasting it with the way those he interacts with see it.

Such a focus is *historical* rather than inductive. The question, 'what led up to it?', say to a bout of depression, a dispute between him and a fellow character, or a permanent feature of character he has developed from early childhood on, is not directed at formulating hypotheses about repeatable causal sequences. It seeks rather to gather an individual story which helps us to make sense of what the writer makes us see—for instance disappointments of the person with himself, contradictions within his character, failures incommensurable with his talents. I suggest that this is the only way to understand people as individuals and that is why I think that psychology in what Drury calls 'its original sense' belongs to the humanities rather than, as we are taught to think in universities, to the sciences.

Let me make it clear that I do not wish to deny that there are questions that fall within the purview of psychology, in a broad sense, that are amenable to experimental study. They concern, as Charles Taylor puts it, 'the infrastructural conditions for the exercise' of those capacities which are necessary to human conduct—such as attention, perception, memory, voluntary movements, and the functioning of the neurological systems that come into play in the exercise of these capacities.[10] They are concerned with the *constants* behind individual behaviour in its variations. As both Drury and Taylor point out, these phenomena, which are amenable to experimental, scientific study, are on the psycho-physical or psycho-neurological boundary of psychology, that is on its peripheries. I doubt that *their* study has any light to throw on individual behaviour.

If we consider the analogy of the infrastructure of a city—its sewer-system, road network, electricity, water works—this point would become plain. One takes these to be in place and in good working order when one tries to understand the life of the city—its people's occupations and preoccupations, the way its institutions run and are interconnected. If the roads were to get blocked, the sewers, electricity, telephone exchanges and water works were to stop functioning, the life of the city would grind to a halt. That is not to say, however, that one can understand that life in the way

[10] See 'Peaceful Co-existence in Psychology', in Taylor's *Philosophical Papers,* Vol I: *Human Agency and Language* (Cambridge University Press, 1985).

one understands how its telephone network or sewer system works.

The trouble with academic, experimental psychology is that, deceived by the pretensions of science, it does not recognize its own limitations. As Wittgenstein puts it at the end of *Philosophical Investigations*:

> The confusion and barrenness of psychology is not to be explained by calling it a 'young science'; its state is not comparable with that of physics, for instance, in its beginnings ... For in psychology there are experimental methods and *conceptual confusion*.
>
> The existence of the experimental methods makes us think we have the means of solving the problems which trouble us; though problem and method pass one another by.[11]

II

I have argued that insofar as psychology is a study that aims at understanding people as individuals it cannot be an experimental science. Insofar as it persists in being an experimental science it cannot contribute to an understanding of individual behaviour and motivation. I want now to give a few examples to illustrate the disaster that experimental psychology has been in this respect.

In its early stages it is understandable that in their experiments psychologists should have confused experimental and conceptual questions. I am thinking of Wundt in the 1880s and the introspective analysis he carried out of consciousness by putting experimental subjects in certain situations and asking them questions to be answered by introspection, questions about what they detect within the field of their consciousness. Wittgenstein described this as a dead-end in philosophy insofar as it was used to answer conceptual questions. We find the same procedure employed by the Würzburg School carrying out experiments on the nature of thought and the will. Of course there is such a thing as what one may call an analysis of consciousness, I mean of the moment-to-moment shifting contents of what a person experiences; but not as a means to answering conceptual questions. It would be of interest to psychology; but it is best carried out by a novelist like Virginia Woolf in her novel *To the Lighthouse*.[12] Here Wundt's 'introspective experiments' are worthless; what we need is an imaginative study, not an experimental one.

[11] *Philosophical Investigations*, Part II, Section xiv.
[12] Routledge, London, 1994.

İlham Dilman

Introspective psychology, where introspection is supposed to be what observation is to physics, not surprisingly, turned out to be barren and misguided. But behaviourism which developed in reaction to it and took its place fared no better. It was worse than confused, it was also crude. It developed a picture of human beings, of their abilities and motivation that was a grotesque caricature. I have tried to illustrate this in my discussion of B. F. Skinner's work in my book *Mind, Brain and Behaviour*[13] and I will not repeat now what I said there.

However I do not think that cognitivist psychology which replaced behaviourism fares any better. Indeed it is little more than the old wine of introspectionist psychology in new computerized bottles. I shall give you two or three examples, with my comments. They come from a book of papers given at a conference between philosophers and psychologists entitled *The Self: Psychological and Philosophical Issues*.[14] In it there is a paper by a cognitivist critic of behaviourism put forward in a paper on self-deception by Willard Day in the same volume. Day had opposed, I think rightly, the idea that an evasive response to an unwelcome suspicion about oneself, such as we find in self-deception, must be mediated by an intervening state of recognition. For knowledge or recognition is not a *state of mind*. In this way, he thought, his account escaped 'the paradox of self-deception', namely that the person who deceives himself must both recognize something about himself and, at the same time, insofar as he is deceived, not know that very same thing. With this I am not now concerned. But Day concludes, in a typically behaviouristic fashion, that since the kind of behaviour we have in self-deception cannot be understood in terms of conflicting states of mind, it is to be understood in terms of 'contingencies involving negative reinforcement'.

Secord, in turn, is critical of this. He considers the case of self-control—another instance of reflexive behaviour—and argues that we cannot hope to understand it without referring to 'cognitive processes'. He is right to criticize the ideal of operant behaviourism which puts the emphasis on external, environmental causes as the main source of human behaviour. But his idea of intermediate 'cognitive processes' simply puts the clock back and the misconceptions that go with it mar his own positive account. He replaces the behaviourist idea of 'environmental contingencies' reinforcing behaviour with what he calls 'self-intervention' and 'self-direction', and what he says in his account of the self-restraint, which he says they involve, is thoroughly muddled.

[13] İ. Dilman, *Mind, Brain and Behaviour* (London: Routledge, 1988).
[14] Theodore Mischel (ed.), *The Self: Psychological and Philosophical Issues* (Oxford: Blackwell, 1977).

The very gist of what he says is that in restraining and controlling oneself one resorts to commitment: 'Commitment [he says]helps people to carry out their intentions' in the teeth of their inclination to the contrary. The idea is that a person manages to avoid sinning by embracing a religion, he manages to keep his promise by committing himself for the future. He asks: why are promises kept. He answers: because once they are made they are costly to break.

This may be true in a particular case. But then the person in question is not really committed: he keeps his promise only because he is afraid of the consequences. The fact that he has given his word to do something carries little weight with him. This is the only kind of case where there is a *psychological answer*; and the question answered is *not* 'why do people keep their promises?' but 'why did he do what he said he would do when honouring the word he gave matters so little to him?' The general question 'why do people keep their promises?' makes no sense; it is a confused attempt to ask a conceptual question: 'what is it about a promise that makes it binding? In what sense is it binding? What is involved in committing oneself, in undertaking to do something?' These are questions best left to philosophers and insofar as a psychologist thinks he can answer them in psychological terms he can only bring in muddle and confusion. Thus in the different cases he considers Secord systematically distorts genuinely conceptual points and gives what one may call a 'corrupt' account of what it is for a person to commit himself to a course of action.

What needs to be understood is that my promise, my commitment to do what I give my word to do, is not something that *ensures* that I keep it. For the relation between the promise and the action promised is *internal*. To say that it involves a 'constraint' only means that when I give my word to do something I cannot do just anything I like. If I may be said to have 'given up certain options' that only means that if I told someone I would meet him for tea at a certain time then I cannot go to the cinema instead at that time. This is part of what it *means* to say 'I shall meet you for tea'. If I go to the cinema instead because I feel like it then I could hardly be said to have *meant* what I said. My point is that 'meaning what one says', 'committing oneself for the future': this is not a matter of what goes on in one's mind, a 'cognitive process', at the time one speaks.

I give this as an example of how little experimental psychologists know what they are talking about and how far experimental psychology remains trapped in long-standing misconceptions. It is true that psychology had, for a long time, remained under the shadow of philosophy. But when it 'liberated' itself from philosophy's arm-chair in the name of science it took the wrong turning and lost its way, and it also was left in the grip of conceptual confusions which kept it going through the same motions over and over again. Of course psychology is not an arm-chair study; but that does not make it an experimental science. There are other alternatives, and I have argued that psychology derives its insight into the individual from the psychologist's 'experience of life'. But that is very different from experimenting in a laboratory. So I am not saying that psychology should have kept in the shadow of philosophy. All the same its dissociation from philosophy in the training of psychologists has been a loss. The criticism of philosophy would have kept it from going off the rails and it would have been, on the whole, a civilizing influence.

I say this because experimental psychology has really become brash: its language is often barbaric and its view of man is shallow. It has lost its understanding of what it means to be a human being and of the kind of world in which human beings live. It thinks of the human world in terms of stimuli which human beings invariably take as reward or punishment. Human motivation is thus on the whole reduced to the carrot and the stick. Skinner quotes Hamlet who exclaimed of man: 'how like a god!' He contrasts Shakespeare with Pavlov who said of man: 'how like a dog'. He then adds that from Shakespeare to Pavlov psychology has taken a step forward by bringing man 'within range of a scientific analysis'.[15] This is precisely what I mean by psychology's wedding to science having had a decivilizing effect on psychology. In his book *Walden Two*[16] Skinner portrays his vision of the heights of human life, to be achieved by 'behavioural engineering', using 'operant conditioning' as its main tool. In my book on Skinner I compared Skinner's spokesman Frazier in *Walden Two* with Dostoyevsky's Grand Inquisitor in *The Brothers Karamazov*. The big difference between them, I said, is that the Grand Inquisitor knows the higher things he has forgone for the sake of a childlike happiness for men, knows what it means to be free and to bear responsibility for one's actions, whereas Frazier does not.[17]

In his *New Introductory Lectures on Psycho-Analysis* Freud said 'psycho-analysis was met by illuminating criticisms to the effect that man is not merely a sexual being but has nobler and higher feelings'.[18] He agreed and added: 'for us the super-ego ... is as

[15] B. F. Skinner, *Beyond Freedom and Dignity* (New York: Alfred A. Knopf, 1971), p. 196.

[16] Macmillan Publishing Co, London, 1976.

[17] *Mind, Brain and Behaviour*, p. 60.

[18] Sigmund Freud, *New Introductory Lectures on Psycho-Analysis* (New York: W. W. Norton, 1933), p. 82.

much as we have been able to apprehend psychologically of what people call the "higher" things in human life'.[19] Freud's conception of moral conscience was flawed—as I argued in my book *Freud and Human Nature*[20]—much in the way that Secord's conception of moral commitment is equally flawed. Skinner's conception of the heights of human life is flawed in much the same way. All this is inevitable when psychologists attempt to give 'psychologistic' accounts of what Freud called the higher things in human life—art, morality and religion. This does harm to their understanding of the individual as well. For it blinds them to forms of the individual's relation to these things that are not self-interested, so that the 'high' is made 'low'.

I now want to elaborate on this further by considering the following experimental research Kenneth Gergen conducted with Stanley Morse on the way other people affect a person's conception of himself, that is his identity and the worth he has in his own eyes.

I quote:

Participants in this research were students at the University of Michigan who answered an advertisement for part-time jobs in the Institute for Social Research. When each applicant arrived for the preliminary screening, he was seated in a room by himself and asked to complete a number of self-rating forms, including a battery of approximately thirty self-evaluation items fully designed by Coppersmith to tap basic levels of self-esteem. After each applicant had completed the various measures, the secretary entered the room, bringing with her another 'applicant' for the job who was, in fact, a collaborator. For some forty applicants, the collaborator was obviously very desirable as a potential employee. He wore a dark business suit and carried an attaché case which he opened to remove several sharpened pencils, at the same time revealing copies of books on statistics and philosophy. The remaining applicants were exposed to a dramatically different experience. Here the competitor entered wearing a smelly sweatshirt, torn trousers and no socks; he appeared generally dazed by the procedure and tossed onto the table a worn copy of a cheap paperback novel. After several minutes of silent exposure to the newcomer, the applicants were given additional forms to complete, including a second battery of items assessing levels of self-esteem.[21]

[19] Ibid. p. 95.
[20] İ. Dilman, *Freud and Human Nature* (Blackwell, Oxford, 1983).
[21] Mischel, *The Self*, p. 152.

The experimenters tell us that the results of this study show 'that the mere presence of the other person was sufficient to alter the manner in which the applicants conceptualized their own self-worth' and that this has 'far reaching implications'. They take it to provide experimental support for Gergen's view that there is no self over and above what others see in one, no self-esteem independent of the value which others bestow on one and of the way one measures up to others in the light of these values. This is the highly dubious conceptual claim that the self in each individual human being is a 'social construction', and it calls for philosophical criticism.

I should have thought it elementary for any real psychologist worth his salt that only a person lacking a secure sense of self or identity would thus feel undermined or reassured in his self-confidence by the presence of others who appear impressive or insignificant to them. In any case why assume that the subjects, however selected, would all react in the same way to what is presented to them by the psychologists? There is, surely, a difference between a sense of self that is genuinely secure in its own identity, that is one in which one knows and accepts who one is and feels no need to apologize for it, and one in which one's sense of inner security is in need of constant external bolstering—by other people's opinions, by favourable comparisons with others, and by artificially constructed identities, such as those that find expression in trendiness, the disporting of badges, or slavish conformity. Only in these latter cases is there some sense in talking of the self as a *construction*—'personal' when it is defensive and 'social' when it arises out of mindless conformity. When a person is real and himself there is nothing in who he is, 'his self', that is a 'construction'.

Certainly a person comes to himself, finds an identity in which he is himself, in his relations with other people, the practices, activities, interests and values he shares with them. But whether or not the self he comes to is genuine depends on the form which these relations take. It seems that Gergen and Morse are guilty of a 'psychologism' which leaves no room for the possibility of the kind of relationships with others in which a person is truly himself and has no doubt about his own identity—about where he belongs and what he wants in life.

This criticism can be developed. But this said, what particularly strikes me about this study is the triteness and juvenile character of the experimenters' conceptions of the world we live in and of the kinds of thing they think would boost people's confidence in themselves or deflate it. Human beings can, of course, be trite and shallow, as this has been portrayed in good literature. But you need depth in order to portray triteness and to contrast it with its opposite. By contrast the triteness I find in the psychological study quoted by Gergen is part of the way the psychologists who have devised this study think about human beings. They themselves seem to lack awareness of it. This I submit is an inevitable outcome of the advocacy of the experimental method of investigation for psychology. For how can you expect more than this from a world confined to scores, rewards, punishments, and 'self-administered' treats and telling-offs!

I complained about the dissociation of psychology from philosophy in universities where psychologists are educated. Let me now add that the simplistic view of the world, of which the triteness and shallowness I have mentioned are a part, is the result of the way psychology has severed itself from its literary heritage under the lure of the prestige it finds in science.

I want to finish with an example of the kind of language and concentration on trivia that you find in experimental psychology. Behaviourism is immeasurably crude, but has been superseded; so I take my example again from cognitive psychology. I take it from a survey on 'self-control and the self' by Walter and Harriet Mischel in the book from which I have been quoting. The section in question is called 'self-regulatory systems' which suggests the investigation of the mental equivalent of electronic systems. They are supposed to enable people to carry out chores, for instance, in the pursuit of certain interests and achievements. I have put this in my language. The writers in question speak in terms of 'delay of gratification', 'self-regulation', 'progress toward goal attainment', 'self-generated cognitive operations through which the person can transform the aversive "self-control" situation into one which he can master effectively', 'attentional mechanisms', etc. The examples in terms of which they think of what they seek to understand are those that can be adapted to experimental investigation—such as 'how long preschool children will actually sit still alone in a chair, waiting for a preferred but delayed outcome, before they signal with a bell to terminate the waiting period and settle for a less preferred but immediately available gratification'.[22]

After mentioning several so-called hypotheses investigated, the writers tell us:

Investigations of the role of attention during delay of gratification, however, revealed another relationship: *not* attending to the goal (potential reward) was what facilitated self-control most

[22] Mischel, *The Self*, p. 44.

161

dramatically. More detailed analysis of attentional mechanisms during delay of gratification showed that the crucial variable is not whether or not the subject attends to the goal objects while delaying, but, rather, *how* he focuses on them.[23]

This is pseudo-scientific language: it gives an air of precision and concreteness—'closer look under the bonnet while the engine was idling and a detailed analysis of the mechanisms involved revealed the cause of the drain on the charge of the battery'. But in reality what is being talked about in this high-falutin language is something which should be plain to common-sense—namely, that if you are not treating what you are doing as a means to some further end, enjoyment or the avoidance of something unpleasant, but find it interesting in itself (precisely what we found went wrong with Secord's discussion of commitment) then you will not need an external incentive to keep to it. Your interest will keep you to it and keep you from being distracted or diverted.

In any case someone who is interested in what he is doing is not interested in obtaining gratification, and the gratification he does find, when his work goes well, is simply a bonus. It does not exist apart from what he is doing—like the donkey's legendary carrot. My point is that an interest in obtaining gratification breaks up the unity of the task in hand. In contrast, if carrying it out involves doing certain things that are tedious in themselves, the interest in what one is doing and one's commitment to the task carries one on. Such interest, devotion and commitment take the task in its unity, and they are expressions of character.

Oblivious to this the writers then go on to talk of 'cognitive transformation' and come up with what is a most absurd form of experimental substantiation:

It was found that through instructions the child can cognitively transform the reward objects that face him during the delay period in ways that either permit or prevent effective delay of gratification. For example, if the child is left during the waiting period with the actual reward objects (e.g. pretzels or marshmallows) in front of him, it becomes difficult for him to wait for more than a few moments. But through instructions he can cognitively transform the reward object in ways that permit him to wait for long time periods. If he cognitively transforms the stimulus to focus on its non-arousing qualities, for example, by thinking about the pretzel sticks as little brown logs, or by thinking about the marshmallows as round white clouds or as

[23] Ibid. p. 45.

162

cotton balls, he may be able to wait for long periods ... It is what is in the children's heads [which the writers describe as 'a colour picture in your head]—not what is physically in front of them— that determines their ability to delay. Regardless of the stimulus in their visual field, if they imagine the real objects as present they cannot wait long for them.[24]

It is presumably the children's patience and self-control that are being tested or tried, and the psychologists in question show no recognition that these are qualities of character. Their idea seems to be: demean the object that tempts you and you will be able to wait, to resist the temptation. But patience is the ability to wait without doing so—just as courage is the ability to face danger without minimizing it. The education that develops such moral qualities is something very different from the kind of manipulation in our fantasy or imagination of what faces us—what is described as 'cognitive transformation'—and this can easily degenerate into fooling oneself and so into dishonesty—the sour grapes syndrome.

The latter is an instance of what George Miller calls 'technical tricks' that belong to a bogus technology which encourages a manipulative and thoughtless approach to life. Such tricks are only a palliative substitute for what can only come from the person. Thus the example by Secord of 'the individual who leaves home without cigarettes or money in his pocket so that he won't smoke'[25], and the one by Skinner of the mother who seals her lips with adhesive tape to keep herself from nagging her child, are not examples of *self-control*. Psychologists sometimes call them 'self-management'. People resort to such measures precisely because they lack self-control. It is because they have failed to come together that they use 'aids' to 'manage' their own behaviour as if it belonged to someone else—as in the case of the murderer in Secord's paper (significantly entitled 'Making Oneself Behave') 'who begs to be put into prison so that he won't commit any more murders'.

One further comment I have concerns the naivety of thought that makes what these psychologists are speaking about a discovery to them: what we respond to are not physical stimuli, as behaviourist psychologists had claimed, but the significance we attach to the things and situations that face us in our lives—and these are not 'stimuli', nor are their significances 'images in the head'. Gestalt psychologists had appreciated this nearly a century ago

[24] Ibid. pp. 45–46.
[25] Ibid. p. 267.

and had articulated it in a less naive, more sophisticated language, in their notion of our 'behavioural environment'.

What experimental psychologists are slow to appreciate is that we live in a human world, shot through with, and indeed shaped by, forms of significance which come from our culture and language. I am suggesting that the language which experimental psychologists are attempting to put in its place, in the name of science, is blind to the richness and variety of these forms. Insofar as the culture in which experimental psychology is thriving accepts that language, experimental psychology will have played some part in distancing us from our cultural heritage and impoverishing the world in which we live.

Its situation, in this respect, I would argue, is very different from that of the physical sciences. Their language is a 'suburb of our language' and draws its life from that language. Physicists themselves speak our everyday language in their civil life, and, for the most part, even in their laboratory. Experimental psychology, on the other hand, is foisting its language on us and trying to make it the language in which we think about ourselves and live our lives. If it succeeds—and it cannot do so without help from other quarters—then our life will no longer be the same, and nor shall we. Experimental psychology will thus have succeeded in moulding man to its own image of man.

To Mental Illness via a Rhyme for the Eye

T. S. CHAMPLIN

The intellectual journey on which I am about to embark, although not an unusual one in philosophy, may at first seem strange to those who are in the habit of looking to science for the answers to their big questions, including their philosophical questions. For I propose to shed light on the problematic relationship between two things, namely, mental illness and physical illness, by comparing their relationship to the relationship between two other things, namely, a rhyme for the eye—which will be explained shortly for the benefit of anyone unfamiliar with this concept—and a rhyme for the ear. Yet these two pairs of things are not related in any way by subject-matter. In philosophy, however, this sort of deliberate dislocation can be beneficial. As Wittgenstein himself once remarked, 'A philos[ophical] problem can be solved only in the right surrounding, we must give the problem a new surrounding, we must compare it to cases we are not used to compare [sic] it with.'[1]

To someone who is used to treating only scientific enquiries as serious enquiries my extended comparison between two such entirely different pairs of concepts may sound misguided, even frivolous. But a conceptual investigation is a very different sort of thing from a scientific investigation and I shall take heart from the words of a short untitled poem by Emily Dickinson which remind us of the existence of a kind of truth which is so disconcerting to its intended audience that, if it is eventually ever to do them any good, it needs to be presented to them *gradually*.

Tell all the truth but tell it slant—
Success in Circuit lies
Too bright for our infirm Delight
The Truth's superb surprise
As Lightning to the children eased
With explanation kind
The Truth must dazzle gradually
Or every man be blind.[2]

[1] L. Wittgenstein, 'Notes for the "Philosophical Lecture", in James C. Klagge and Alfred Nordmann (eds.), *Ludwig Wittgenstein: Philosophical Occasions 1912–1951* (Indianapolis and Cambridge, MA: Hacket Publishing Company, 1993), pp. 447–458 (p. 457).

[2] Poem no 1129 in Thomas H. Johnson (ed.) *The Poems of Emily Dickinson* (Cambridge, MA: The Belnap Press, 1955), 3 vols.

T. S. Champlin

Mental Illness and Physical Illness: a Puzzling Relationship

The relationship between mental and physical illness can seem puzzling, as the following questions remind us.

What has the first term in each of the following three pairs of terms, mumps and megalomania, polio and paranoia, scarlet fever and schizophrenia, got in common with the second term in each pair? Isn't the first term in each pair as different from the second as chalk is from cheese? Then why do we use the same word 'illness' to cover two such entirely different things? Why do we speak of an otherwise healthy person whose life is dominated by the irrational, patently false, belief that he is being persecuted by some of his closest friends, as suffering from an *illness*? Why drag medicine into madness? How can the mind be ill or diseased? Is it possible that one's brain and central nervous system might be functioning physically perfectly normally and yet that one might be suffering from a mental illness? Or must there always be something physically wrong with someone who is mentally ill? Is 'mental illness' nothing more than a figure of speech for a malfunctioning mind? Or might one's mind be malfunctioning and yet might one not be suffering from a mental illness of any kind? And what of cure? Does anyone, disregarding cranks with professional vested interests, know of anyone who has been cured of a mental illness? If an illness had a purely physical cause (say, a brain tumour) and a purely physical cure (say, an injection with a drug which caused the tumour cells to shrivel and die), could it still have been a mental illness? If an illness had a purely psychological cause (for example, stress brought on by overwork) and a purely psychological cure (say, participation in weekly stress-management classes), could it still be a physical illness? You can die of illnesses and diseases, and of things which are neither illnesses or diseases, such as of thirst and hunger, or of injuries caused by a blunt instrument, and, so they say, of a broken heart but has anyone ever died of a mental illness? Do any mental illnesses ever prove mortal? Depression can lead to suicide but 'He died of depression' is odd in a way in which 'He died of smallpox' or 'He died of drink' isn't. If no mental illness can be fatal, can it even be contagious? Can you catch his mental illness from close contact with a schizophrenic friend? Are mental and physical illnesses 'illnesses' in the same sense of the word?

Let us consider an actual historical case of what I believe to be an early instance of the employment of the concept of mental illness, which presents interesting problems of interpretation.

166

To Mental Illness via a Rhyme for the Eye

John Keats's Illness: Physical or Mental?

'There is no pulmonary affection, no organic defect whatsoever—the disease is on his mind, and there I hope he will soon be cured.'[3] It was in these confident tones that John Keats's doctor, Dr Robert Bree, M.D. (Oxon), delivered his diagnosis in London around 10 March 1820, less than a year before Keats's death in Rome from tuberculosis. The precise meaning of Dr Bree's words, especially of his remark, 'the disease is on his mind', was debated by Keats's friends at the time and it has been discussed more recently by one of Keats's biographers.[4]

It is perhaps just possible that all Keats's doctor, Dr Bree, meant by his words 'the disease is on his mind' was that the consumption from which Keats believed himself to be dying was imaginary. Not unsurprisingly in someone who had been an apothecary's assistant and later a dresser to a surgeon operating daily in the horrifying conditions of a London hospital in the early nineteenth century, and who had nursed his brother Tom until the latter's agonizing death from this then common and greatly feared disease, perhaps Keats had, as we today might put it, consumption on the brain. In view, however, of Keats's extremely wild and agitated state of mind at the time, another interpretation of Dr Bree's words, mentioned by Keats's biographer, is that Keats was suffering, not from a physical, but from a mental, illness. Keats, then 25 years old, was deeply depressed at the certain prospect of his imminent death. 'Professionally, I cannot be mistaken in the colour of that blood. It is arterial blood and I soon must die', Keats had told a friend upon examining flecks of blood he had coughed up. 'My death-warrant', Keats called them.[5] In view, however, of the fact that Keats was also making what his friends felt were totally unfounded allegations of unfaithfulness against his fiancee, Fanny Brawne, with whom he was desperately in love, perhaps, as we today again might put it, Keats's sickness was in the mind, not in the body. Whichever interpretation is correct, neither can save Dr Bree from having been proved spectacularly wrong about the reality of Keats's physical illness. For, when the *post-mortem* was performed in Rome where Keats died on 23 February 1821 less than a year

[3] See Hyder E. Rollins (ed.), T*he Letters of John Keats 1814–1821*, 2 vols. (Cambridge University Press, 1958), vol. II, p. 275.

[4] Robert Gittings, John Keats (London: Heinemann, 1968), p. 560.

[5] See Hyder E. Rollins (ed.), *The Keats Circle: Letters and Papers 1816–1878*, 2 vols. (Cambridge, MA: Harvard University Press, 1948), vol. II, p. 73.

after Dr Bree's diagnosis, the poet's lungs were found to have been virtually eaten away by disease.

My aim here is to propose a new way of thinking about the relationship between what, on the second of the above two interpretations, were the two broad alternatives between which Dr Bree would have been choosing when making his diagnosis, that is, between physical and mental illness. This suggestion will pave the way for the imaginative reconstruction of the emergence of the concept of mental illness from a background in which up till then only the concept of physical illness had existed. In other words, I am hoping to explain the conditions for the possibility of Dr Bree's diagnosis, on the second of the above two interpretations.

Three unusual features of my account of the relationship between physical and mental illness are worth noting: first, my account assigns little, if any, importance to the so-called 'medical model' of mental illness which figures prominently in many contemporary accounts; secondly, my account does not seek to prove that mental and physical illness are analogically related by virtue of a set of logically necessary features common to both mental and physical illness; and thirdly, I see no reason to suppose that the concept of mental illness, or, for that matter, the concept of physical illness either, owes its origin to the practice of professional medicine.

Explaining how one concept has evolved from another is not a specifically philosophical activity but it becomes one when, as with the concept of mental illness, there are philosophical puzzles surrounding the relationship between it and its putative antecedent concept of such a kind that no adequate way of accounting for the evolution of the later concept from the earlier concept seems to be possible. 'All illness is physical illness in which something goes wrong with the body', says the objector. 'In a so-called mental illness what has gone wrong is the mind. A warrant is needed for calling someone "ill" merely on account of his mental state, his madness.' What warrant could there be except that of a metaphorical extension of the use of the word 'ill' from a literal to a metaphorical case of illness? No-one would object on logical grounds to the politician who in colourful language borrows from the vocabulary of medicine and calls inflation a disease which will cripple the economy unless it is swiftly cured but they soon would object if that politician turned to the British Medical Association for economic advice and began to call economics a branch of medicine. Yet when we call madness 'mental illness' we do not treat mental illness as metaphorical physical illness. The mental illnesses studied by psychiatrists are unreflectively thought to have the same objective reality as the physical illnesses studied by the London School of Hygiene and Tropical Medicine, and the study and treatment of mental illness is accepted as being as much part of medicine as is the study of physical illness. How, if at all, are we to make sense of our behaviour? It is time to develop my comparison.

Rhymes which do not Rhyme

Someone familiar with the idea of rhyming couplets at the ends of lines of poetry may never have come across the distinction drawn by versifiers between a rhyme for the ear and a rhyme for the eye. Indeed, when such a person encounters for the first time the phrase 'a rhyme for the eye' and hears a few sample pairs of rhymes for the eye spoken aloud, such as 'bough' and 'cough', 'willow' and 'allow', he may react incredulously with, 'But these pairs of words do not rhyme! Why are these pairs of words called "rhymes" when they do not rhyme?' A rhyme is, he need hardly remind us, an audible phenomenon, detectable by the ear. The idea that there might be another kind of rhyme which, although unrecognizable by the ear, is detectable by the eyes alone, is, he tells us, a contradiction in terms. It is to him as though one had begun to speak of 'seeing sounds' or 'hearing colours' or 'smelling square roots'. Our objector realizes that one can decide to use a word with an established meaning to mean anything one likes but, as the following example will show, this is a practice of which one ought to avail oneself sparingly if a Tower of Babel is to be avoided.

Television engineers speak of seeing 'white noise' on the screen. This, to the uninitiated, mystifying turn of phrase has gained currency amongst television engineers because it is a standard feature of ordinary television sets that a pattern of dancing, snow-like, tiny white dots fills the screen when the set is switched on but is not tuned in to a signal from a transmitting station. This visual display on the television screen is accompanied by a characteristic, continuous, low-pitched, 'busy', buzzing noise from the speaker. Whence the television engineer's 'white noise', which is not, it now becomes clear, a kind of noise at all but a visual display on the screen. The one thing our objector feels sure of is that a 'rhyme for the eye', whatever it is, is no more a new kind of rhyme, in the sense in which he has been using the word 'rhyme', than the television engineer's 'white noise' is a new kind of noise in the ordinary sense of the word 'noise'.

169

When, in what follows, the question, 'How are mental and physical illness related?' arises, I want my reader to keep in mind the above objection to the idea of a rhyme for the eye, which, from the literary point of view, may be unsophisticated but is, I think, philosophically healthy and is, I hope to show, comparable to a similar objection to the idea of mental illness.

The Origin of 'Rhymes for the Eye'

It is plausible to suppose that originally in a purely oral poetic tradition in which there was no such thing as the written word, poets talked only of rhyming and rhymes and not of 'rhymes for the ear', which would have been tautological. Later, with the invention of writing, then printing, and later with the standardization of the spelling of the printed word, and especially after the arrival of silent reading, people began to introduce word endings into their poems which did not sound similar when they were read aloud and thus did not rhyme in the old sense but which looked alike on the printed page in that they were spelled in the same way. True rhymes in the old sense, such as 'laugh' and 'chaff', 'door' and 'adore', began to called 'rhymes for the ear' in order to differentiate them from mere rhymes for the eye, such as 'plough' and 'cough'. Often, of course, the two coincided and then a rhyme for the ear was also a rhyme for the eye. It is a fact that many true rhymes in the old sense were spelled in the same way and to this extent the new rhymes had this much in common with traditional rhymes. People began to talk of 'rhymes for the eye', not because they were for one moment fooled into believing that these pairs of words sounded the same and were true rhymes for the ear, but because they played the same role as true rhymes for the ear, namely, that of rounding off the ends of written or printed lines of verse in a rule-governed way and thus of producing a pleasingly regular pattern on the page.

It is not impossible to imagine poets deliberately introducing rhymes for the eye into their poetry before they had invented a special term to describe this new development. Their self-conscious practice would show that they possessed the concept of a rhyme for the eye even if their vocabulary lacked our handy label.

We can also imagine people resisting the introduction of rhymes for the eye into poetry, objecting that this made a mockery of the whole idea behind the concept of rhyming whilst others might have welcomed this development as an interestingly different, liberating approach to poetry. One side might stress the connection between poetry and public declamation, oratory and the performing arts. The other side might draw attention to the vast silent readership of poetry published in ephemeral journals who will never be called upon to open their mouths and speak aloud the poetry they silently read and inwardly learn by heart. Logic cannot decide who is right and wrong here. Taste, aesthetic sensibility and many other factors must be brought to bear in order to decide upon the acceptability of 'rhymes for the eye'.

To Mental Illness via a Rhyme for the Eye

We can come to a better understanding of the nature of mental illness and of its relationship to physical illness by thinking of the transition from the concept of physical illness to that of mental illness as coming about in a way which resembles that in which a rhyme for the eye has evolved from a rhyme for the ear. One virtue of this admittedly at first unlikely sounding analogy is that it helps to lay the ghost of both an unhelpful scepticism and also of an unprofitable realism about the concept of mental illness.

For, although a rhyme for the eye does not rhyme, that is, is not a rhyme for the ear, it is a rhyme for the eye for all that. An explanation can be given of the point behind the introduction of this curious concept and of its place in the history of versifying. We can, nevertheless, appreciate why purists may object to the introduction of the new concept and to the new more relaxed rules about what is permitted in rhyming verse. Similarly, a mental illness is not an illness, that is, is not a physical illness, and yet we have a specialized use for the phrase 'mental illness' and, on being told how totally different a mental illness is from a physical illness, we have not been given any good reason to believe that there is no such thing as mental illness. But we will now be able to see why a purist might object that the concept of mental illness pollutes the meaning of 'medicine' when medicine is thought of as a purely physiological discipline practised by those engaged in trying to understand and treat physical illnesses.

Another virtue of the analogy between mental illness and a rhyme for the eye is that it shows how concepts can be connected to each other in a way which does not depend upon the seeing of some resemblance between separate instances of them. Would-be realists about the concept of mental illness, such as Antony Flew in his *Crime or Disease?*, try to rout the sceptics, such as Thomas Szasz in his *The Myth of Mental Illness*, by claiming to have uncovered a set of relevant resemblances between mental and physical illness.[6] However, it is not because there is a resemblance between a rhyme for the eye and a rhyme for the ear that we speak of a 'rhyme for the eye'. Two words do not have to end with the same letters in order to rhyme and two word-endings spelled the same way need not rhyme. A rhyme for the eye is not a little bit like a rhyme for the ear: it is in no way like a rhyme for the ear. This comparison ought to put us on our guard against the supposition that mental and physical illness must be related in virtue of some elusive similarity between them which it is our duty to track down in order to satisfy ourselves that they both count as illnesses.

One could almost say that, in forming the idea of a rhyme for the eye, versifiers threw out the baby, that is, the actual rhyme, and kept the bath water, that is, the superficial but not universally reliable sign of the presence of a rhyme, namely, the same spelling of the word ending. We need to take seriously the possibility that something similar has happened in the formation of the concept of mental illness.

What helped the extension of the word 'rhyme' to allow it to be applied to rhymes for the eye alone was the obvious fact that both sorts of rhymes occurred at the ends of lines of poetry. There is no necessary truth here—the ideal of internal rhymes within a line of verse being not unknown—but the typical rhyme for the eye goes where a rhyme for the ear might have gone and it was position at the end of the line which kept a place warm for the word 'rhyme' in the phrase 'a rhyme for the eye'.

It is, however, possible that, after we have heard this explanation of the way in which the concept of a rhyme for the eye came to be formed—and an explanation along similar lines of the concept of mental illness—we may not think well of such concepts and may believe that they have, on balance, done more harm than good and wish that they had never existed and take care to avoid using them ourselves. In other words, scepticism about the existence of things falling under the concept may have been shown to be philosophically mistaken but such scepticism may be replaced by scepticism about the worthwhileness of the concept. Though, of course, we shall need to distinguish between something undesirable about the concept itself and an undesirable use to which a concept has been put.

It is, for example, not difficult to see why, in the field of public education policy, exception could be taken to the educationists' concept of 'mental age' as divisive in that it makes it easy to humiliate

---

[6] Antony Flew, *Crime or Disease?* (London: Macmillan, 1973); Thomas S. Szasz, *The Myth of Mental Illness: Foundations of a Theory of Personal Conduct* (New York: Hoeber-Harper, 1961)

schoolchildren whose mental age is lower than their birthday age by segregating them from their fellows whose mental age and birthday age coincide, and to endow with a false sense of their own superiority other children whose mental age exceeds their calendar age. But this is an attack on the use to which the concept of mental age has been put rather than an attack on the concept itself.

Reconstruction of the Origin of the Concept of Mental Illness

Let us assume that, at first, people talked of being ill with no idea of distinguishing between different illnesses or of giving names to the different illnesses from which they were suffering. When they began to speak of distinct illnesses and of suffering from a nameable illness, they meant a physical illness. According to our use of the concept of illness today, those who suffer from an illness and who remain fully conscious—not asleep, knocked unconscious, in a coma, drugged, anaesthetized or in a hypnotic trance, etc.,—must at some stage feel ill. This, incidentally, is what differentiates a disease from an illness. There is no conceptual connection between feeling ill and suffering from a disease, or between suffering from a disease and experiencing actual suffering, which explains why living things incapable of feelings such as trees and crops can suffer from diseases but not from illnesses. A disease affecting human beings which is typically entirely painless is not a contradiction in terms. Still, the link between suffering from an illness and feeling ill is not straightforward. One can feel ill without suffering from an illness as, for example, when one has eaten something which disagrees with one. The 'low life' journalist Jeffrey Bernard was, as those familiar with his regular column in the *Spectator* or who have seen the play based on it will recall, often unwell, but this was because he had a hangover, not because he was suffering from an illness. What converts feeling ill into suffering from an illness is the additional fact that one is on that account in a state of ill health. One is ailing. The bodies of those suffering from illnesses, such as measles, chicken pox, mumps, etc., have gone wrong in certain systematic ways which give rise to talk of the symptoms characteristic of these particular illnesses.

There was, I shall assume, already talk of the insane, crazy, deranged, mad, barmy, lunatic, nutty, cracked, of those who were off their heads, had lost their marbles, their reason, their faculties, etc. Their minds had gone wrong. But so too have the minds of the senile and the delirious and yet neither 'senility' nor 'delirium' is the name of a mental illness. Similarly, the eyes of a blind man and the legs of a lame man have gone wrong but neither 'blindness' nor 'lameness' is the name of a physical illness. Which shows that there is more to a physical illness than physical malfunctioning and hence that there is more to a mental illness than a malfunctioning mind. The 'more' in question is that one's physical or mental health has to be in some way impaired.

What the mentally ill did have in common with the physically ill, as they could now be called, was, I suggest, that by and large they were perceived not to be able to fend for themselves on their own. They were in a mess, requiring help, care, comforting, nursing, shelter, food, and sympathy, which had to be provided by others. It was not essential to their status as 'mentally ill' that they were to be treated and cured in institutions by people possessing medical qualifications and expertise. In this respect they were in the same boat as the physically ill. The concepts of physical and mental illness were both 'low tech' concepts arising amongst the broad mass of the medically unqualified populace who may well have felt little certainty or optimism about the prospect of cure in the case of either kind of illness. The best one could hope for, as in the case of many serious physical illnesses, was that the sufferer would either recover of his own accord or die without unduly prolonging his misery.

Sickness of mind is not the same sort of thing as sickness of body and was never for one moment supposed to be so. The concept of mental illness arose amongst people who did not treat the insane with indifference or as objects of derision, contempt, loathing or worship, but as deserving of their time, patience and sympathy. The mentally ill had this in common with the physically ill, in some cases the incurably ill: they were both a burden to others. Someone who possesses the concept of physical and mental illness does not need to be able to diagnose his illness to know when to say 'I am ill' or to fear that he may be becoming mentally ill. The concept of mental illness did not arise in the hospital laboratory, as other specialized medical concepts must undoubtedly have done, or in the asylum wards amongst the small talk of bullish young doctors making their morning rounds. The concept of mental illness may quite easily be imagined to have grown in obscurity in humble homes where medically unqualified relatives cared for each other in small back rooms.

In other words, the counterpart to position at the end of the line which facilitated the extension of the word 'rhyme' to cover rhymes for the eye but not the ear was that, typically, the mentally ill have in common with the physically ill the fact that they behave in ways similar to the physically ill. They often look ill and fail to carry on with their normal lives and need to be cared for by others. But do not misunderstand me. This sort of nursing and care could be provided by ordinary people and did not require attention from nurses in uniforms or from doctors with professional qualifications.

We can imagine someone resisting the concept of mental illness, as it appears that Wittgenstein once did.[7] Why, Wittgenstein asked, do we say that those who are not suffering from any form of physical illness are nonetheless ill, that is, mentally ill? Why not turn to some other analogy? Say, that of a more or less sudden change of character? Elsewhere, Wittgenstein asks us to imagine a mental illness in which the sufferer can use and understand names only in the presence of their bearers.[8] Instead of seeing the feeble-minded as degenerate, incomplete or in a state of disorder, he suggests, a far more fruitful way of looking at them would be to see in them a more primitive order.[9]

To which my reply is that a childlike mishandling of our language can, indeed, be the ominous sign of a mental illness. A mentally ill person may exhibit features which remind us of the primitive linguistic behaviour of a child. Perhaps he responds to the question 'Do you know what I did this afternoon?' with 'Yes, I went into the town,' as might a child who had not yet grasped how the pronoun 'I' is used. But the adult making this sort of blunder regularly, which is too bad to count as a mistake, would not simply on that score count as mentally ill, any more than would the child. 'Simple-minded' or 'feeble-minded' or 'mentally handicapped'—possibly. Mental illness is, however, an altogether crueller affliction. For a 'mistake' of this kind to count as evidence of mental illness it must impugn, not just your mental powers or your powers of reasoning, but your sanity. Your 'mistake' must be of the sort which could not have been made in the circumstances in which it was made and the perpetrator continue to count as sane.

The Comparison Reviewed

I wish to bring out certain parallels between the account of how the concept of a rhyme for the eye evolved from that of a rhyme

[7] L. Wittgenstein, *Culture and Value*, ed. G. H. von Wright in collaboration with H. Nyman (Oxford: Blackwell, 1980), p. 54e and p. 55e.

[8] L. Wittgenstein, *Remarks on the Philosophy of Psychology*, ed. G. E. M. Anscombe and G. H. von Wright, trans. G. E. M. Anscombe, 2 vols. (Oxford: Blackwell, 1980), vol. I, §§591 and 592, p. 110e.

[9] Ibid, §646, p. 119e.

for the ear and my story of how the concept of mental illness might have evolved from that of physical illness.

The same pair of words can be both a rhyme for the ear and a rhyme for the eye. The one does not have to exclude the other. Similarly, the same person can suffer from both a physical and a mental illness. A rhyme for the eye alone can be spoken aloud and a rhyme for the ear alone can be viewed silently on the page. Similarly, a physical illness can affect the mind and have mental symptoms, such as sudden mood swings, depression, increased irritability, etc., and a mental illness may conceivably have physical symptoms, such as loss of appetite, insomnia and permanent dryness of the skin.

We can imagine someone reading a poem aloud and insisting that if a couplet rhymes it must be pronounced in the same way and so forcing an outlandish pronunciation on a word intended as a rhyme for the eye. And we can imagine someone treating mental illness as though it was really physical illness on the grounds that if the patient is genuinely ill, then he must be suffering from a physical illness.

I said that the concept of a rhyme for the eye threw the baby out but kept the bath water in that it paid no attention to the sound of the words and concentrated instead on the superficial sign of a rhyme, the sameness of the spelling. Similarly, the concept of mental illness ignores altogether the role of bodily malfunctioning which is essential to the concept of physical illness, though this is not, I have argued, all that there is to a physical illness. We can tell that someone is mentally ill solely from his attitudes, his thoughts and beliefs and a knowledge of their context. The results of a physical examination may assist the expert in his diagnosis of a mental illness which is regularly accompanied by certain physical symptoms but the latter have no place in a description of what changes in a person count *ipso facto* as the manifestation of his mental illness. Even if it turns out that he has a brain tumour and that the tumour is the cause of his mental illness, the content of the mental illness could be given without knowledge of the tumour and the discovery of the cause has no bearing on the description of the illness.

It may be thought that Alan Bennett's play, *The Madness of George III*, gives the lie to what has just been said about the irrelevance of the cause to the description of mental illness. Bennett, who tells us that he took his cue from the work of the medical historians Richard Hunter and Ida Macalpine on the case of King George III, says that he intended his play to suggest that perhaps George III was never at any stage mentally ill but was all along a victim of an undiagnosed physical disease, porphyria, one of whose symptoms is that the sufferer displays mental confusion and talks in a wild, uncontrolled way.[10] We need therefore to distinguish between (i) a mental illness which has been caused by a physical disease, and (ii) a symptom of a physical disease which has been confused with a symptom of a mental illness. How are we to tell the difference between the former case and the latter case? In the former case, but not in the latter case, if the disease were to remit, the mental illness would still continue. The representation of George III's condition in Bennett's play is meant to illustrate the latter, rather than the former, case. In his play Bennett was not trading upon what I am alleging is the mistaken assumption that a mental illness cannot have been induced by a physical illness.

The discovery, were it ever to be made, that mental illness is always accompanied by certain changes in the blood chemistry of the brain could be compared to the discovery that whenever two words whose endings are pronounced differently are used today as a rhyme for the eye, it turns out that they were originally spelled differently, or that whenever two words appear as a rhyme for the ear but not the eye, they had once been spelled the same way several centuries earlier.

A purist might object to the concept of a rhyme for the eye as lowering the standards of poetry and as making things too easy for the cheap rhymester. Similarly, an orthopaedic surgeon might be heard objecting to having a Freudian psychiatrist in the office next door on the grounds that he does not think that psychiatry ought to be regarded as a branch of medicine. 'Unless there is something physically wrong with the patient, medicine cannot help him,' he says.

We can also imagine some poets welcoming the admissibility of rhymes for the eye as liberating them from a literary straitjacket. And we can imagine historians of medicine treating the acceptance of psychiatry as a branch of medicine as a humane, civilizing step in the history of medicine.

The word 'rhyme' in the phrase 'a rhyme for the eye' is not being used metaphorically, as 'fatigue' is used metaphorically in the phrase 'metal fatigue'. We do not treat a rhyme for the eye as a metaphorical rhyme for the ear. Similarly, the word 'illness' in our talk of 'mental illness' is not a metaphor. We do not treat mental illness as metaphorical physical illness. Whereas, when a politician says, metaphorically speaking, that the Irish Question is a minefield, he is treating it as a metaphorical minefield.

[10] Alan Bennett, *Writing Home* (London: Faber and Faber, 1994), pp. 227–240; Ida Macalpine and Richard Hunter, *George III and the Mad Business* (London: Allen Lane, 1969).

It wasn't because of a similarity between a rhyme for the ear and a rhyme for the eye that the latter are called 'rhymes'. Rather, where people saw clearly that there was no rhyme in the original sense of that word, they put their tongues in their cheeks and called a word which did not rhyme a 'rhyme for the eye' because the second word did the same job as the first, namely, that of rounding off the line of verse. Similarly, it is pointless to look for similarities between mental and physical illnesses such as paranoia and polio, or mumps and megalomania. They are, after all, as different as chalk and cheese. What allowed people to talk of 'illness' where they could see that no physical illness existed was the mentally ill had it in common with the physically ill that they were often a source of concern and were a burden to others and that both were regarded as needing to be cared for and looked after by others and so made similar demands on them.

It is possible that poets made use of rhymes for the eye and so showed by their practice that they had the concept of a rhyme for the eye before they had a neat phrase in which to refer to the phenomenon. Similarly, it is possible for people's general descriptions of the mentally ill to show that they had the concept of mental illness before the phrase 'mental illness' was in general use. In fact, my own suspicion is that the metaphor of 'mental disease', that is, of the mind's being diseased, was often used in the nineteenth century by those who had the concept of mental illness.

The fact that spelling was standardized through the influence of printing and the possibility of silent reading no doubt greatly assisted the introduction of the idea of a rhyme for the eye alone. Such rhymes occupied the same role as genuine rhymes in the old sense, namely, that of being placed at the ends of printed lines of verse. Similarly, the standardization of the names of physical and mental illnesses and the standardization of their treatment will have assisted the formation of the concept of mental illness. Similarly, the fact that the mentally ill were treated as people, who, like the physically ill, needed care, nursing and comfort will have helped to establish the concept of mental illness. Furthermore, because those who were not thought to be ill in the old sense were not turned away by those in positions of authority who were already responsible for caring for the physically ill, the mentally ill came to be accorded the status of patients by professionally qualified doctors.

I am not suggesting that the public concern displayed for the mentally ill was always in their best interests. The institutional care which began to be provided for the mentally ill in the nineteenth century, especially for the insane paupers, seems to me to have often been cruel and in many ways worse than the more casual, haphazard system of public care provided in earlier centuries. Just as the sort of debtors' jail occupied by Dickens's Mr Pickwick in fiction and by the novelist Robert Fielding in real life seems to have been less horrible than the later model penitential reformatory run by earnest Victorian prison reformers in which the inmates were kept in solitary confinement in order the better to repent of their sins and were forced to wear a hood when taken outside their cells except during their once weekly attendance at chapel. My point is simply that, for the concept of mental illness to arise, we need to imagine how it was that people who were not thought to be physically ill, but who nevertheless needed looking after, were responded to as in need of care in the same way in which one might respond to someone suffering from a physical illness. Whether the care was all that it was cracked up to be is another matter.

A Problematic Relationship Revisited

The challenge I set myself was to explain how we came to acquire the concept of mental illness. For the purposes of the challenge, I assumed without proof that the concept of mental illness came into widespread use some time during the nineteenth century. I also assumed that before the emergence of the concept of mental illness people talked of 'illness', 'disease' (but not of 'physical illness' or of 'physical disease', for this way of speaking presupposes, and hence postdates, the distinction between mental and physical illness), 'complaint', 'sickness', 'malady', 'infirmity', 'ailment', etc. I also assumed that people already talked of madness, insanity, lunacy, derangement, of people troubled in their minds, who had lost their wits, their reason, their minds, etc.

Why did I think this was a challenge suitable for a philosopher rather than a historian of ideas? A historian of ideas could, after all, explain how it was that we acquired the concept of mental age without any assistance from a philosopher. He could explain that in the early years of this century the French psychologist, Alfred Binet, gave paper and pencil tests to large numbers of schoolchildren, obtained average scores for his tests graded for different age-groups, and so found it possible to say that a child of ten years of age who got the average score obtained by seven year olds on the same test had a 'mental age' of seven. But 'mental illness' seems more recalcitrant.

The concept of mental illness causes offence in a way that the concept of mental age does not. This is because we can see that the talk of 'mental age' evolved out of a comparison between a person's own calendar age and the calendar age of the average person achieving the same score in graded tests of his mental powers. But by 'mental illness' we seem to refer to an old familiar thing, namely, insanity, by the name of something quite different, namely, illness—unaccountably until what Emily Dickinson would have called an 'explanation kind', preferably of the sort that 'dazzles gradually', is provided.

The challenge I have set myself is demanding because a mental illness and a physical illness appear to be two such dissimilar things belonging to two quite different categories and yet our talk of mental illness does not seem to be a matter of metaphorical extension as does our readiness to talk, say, of the 'loudness' of a colour or of 'white noise' to mean a visual pattern on the television screen. But even this difference, big as it is, does not get to the heart of the matter. It would hardly be a challenge at all to explain why we talk of mental as well as of physical handicaps and yet, what greater difference could there be between Down's syndrome and a limp? This is because there is no desire to say in the latter example that the word 'handicap' has two senses in spite of the huge difference between the two sorts of handicaps. But there is a temptation to say that there cannot be another sort of illness apart from physical illness and that 'mental illness' is at best a metaphor or, at worst, a misnomer.

There is also another aspect. The questions I asked earlier are interesting questions in their own right which test our understanding of the concept of mental illness, and of physical illness too, for that matter, but they can also be treated as real life examples of the ancient, myth-eaten, philosophical problem of the relationship between the body and the mind, between the mental and the physical. For it is part of this ancient problem that philosophers, because of their preconceptions about how the mind and the body are related, generate and perpetuate the problem by their use of the words 'mental' and 'physical' in queer, off-colour, ways. A pain in the thumb from the prick of a needle, for example, is said according to the time-honoured tradition to be something 'mental' whilst the needle which causes the pain and the thumb in which the pain is felt are both said to be 'physical' things. Our modern questions about the relationship between mental and physical illness help us to return these ordinary, everyday words, 'mental' and 'physical', to their normal posts. The fascinating thing is that these posts are not to be found in the places where one is first inclined to go looking for them, as the history of philosophers' attempts to chart the borders separating the mental from the physical confirms.

Commonly Asked Questions

Finally, in the light of the foregoing extended comparison, I shall try to answer a number of questions about mental illness which might be asked by a thoughtful person familiar with the literature on the topic.

(1) Is 'mental illness' a metaphor?
I have argued that the answer is 'No'. What cannot be ruled out, however, is the possibility that metaphors may have been used for mental illness, even though 'mental illness' itself is not a metaphor. I suspect that 'mental disease' and Dr Bree's use of 'disease on the mind' in his diagnosis, quoted earlier, of John Keats may be such metaphors. In other words, someone who was mentally ill was said, metaphorically, to have a diseased mind or to have a sickness in his mind. Literally speaking, the mind cannot be sick or diseased but it is worth noting that when we say today that someone is mentally ill we are not saying that his mind is ill. In fact, to say of someone 'His mind is ill' would suggest that the speaker has not grasped our concept of mental illness. It is the person, not his mind, that we call ill when we invoke the concept of mental illness.

Interpretation is complicated by the fact that 'mental disease' can also be used as a metaphor for physical disease. Indeed, General Paralysis of the Insane was once widely referred to as a mental disease on account of the fact that this physical disease resulted in insanity. But that does not make GPI a mental illness.

The 'mental/physical illness' contrast is like the 'mental/physical pain' contrast. We talk of 'mental pain', in contrast to 'physical pain', because we have seen people react to suddenly hearing bad news as though they had received a physical blow to the body. They gasp, double up, clutch at themselves, reel, and gesture as though they had been physically hurt. Bad news can come as a blow. But this gives us no reason to speak of the mental pain felt by someone in such circumstances as pain only in a metaphorical, not a literal, sense. 'Mental illness' is not a metaphor in the way that 'mental disease', 'love-sick' and 'having a sick mind' (when said of someone who is accused of serious moral depravity) are all metaphors.

(2) Did Plato invent the concept of mental illness?
It has been suggested that Plato invented the concept of mental illness.[11] However, an examination of the relevant passage in the
Republic (*Republic* 444) reveals Plato condemning injustice as spiritual disease in which there is disharmony between three elements
in the soul of the unjust man, much as physical disease was once
explained to be an imbalance between the four humours making
up the body. Plato is using the medical metaphors beloved of
clergymen who fulminate against pride as a disease of the soul.
The outlandishness and falsity of an observation are, I realize, no
impediment to a philosopher's having said it but it would, surely,
have strained the credulity even of Plato's more uncritical followers, had he told them that to act unjustly was to be mentally ill.

(3) Isn't the word 'illness' used in two different senses in the
phrases 'mental illness and 'physical illness'?
The word 'rhyme' does not require two entries in the dictionary
describing two senses of the word 'rhyme' just because we speak of
both rhymes for the eye and rhymes for the ear. For the same reason the existence of mental and physical illness does not give us two
senses of the word 'illness' as does our use of the word 'concerned'
to mean either *worried* or *involved*, when, for example, one is concerned *in* some escapade or concerned *at* the rise in crime. Does the
word 'handicap' bear two senses which ought to be recorded separately in the dictionary because there are physical as well as mental
handicaps? Surely not. Yet a lisp is a very different sort of thing
from educational subnormality. The following differences in what
it makes sense to say about mental and physical illness really do
exist but they do not provide the evidence for multiple senses of the
word 'illness' which it is at first so tempting to read into them.

Some physical illnesses are infectious whereas no mental illnesses are or could be. No one can die of a mental illness as they can
of a physical illness—not even the depressive suicide who dies as a
direct result of his depression. No mental illnesses are trivial
affairs of brief duration of a few days, as are some minor physical
illnesses. In the absence of an ulterior motive, sufferers might be
expected to complain of their physical illnesses but in the case of
some mental illnesses, such as hypomania, the symptoms are ela-
tion, enthusiasm and booming self-confidence. 'Better than well' is
how the manic in the grip of his mania says he feels at the height of
his 'high'.

[11] By Anthony Kenny in his 'Mental Health in Plato's *Republic*' in the
Proceedings of the British Academy for 1969, pp. 229–253.

(4) Has the concept of mental illness been formed by analogy with physical illness on the so-called 'medical model' of insanity?

What is meant here by those who talk of 'the medical model' of insanity? It cannot be that the advance of medical science has shown that all illness has only physical causes, and that therefore, in calling the insane 'mentally ill', the medical experts are saying that all mental illness has a physical cause too. For our concept of physical illness allows us to distinguish between the physical and the non-physical, that is, psychological, causes of physical illnesses such as asthma and eczema. It is not a contradiction in terms to speak of a mental illness brought on by a purely physical cause, such as the ingestion of a drug which has damaged the brain resulting in the victim forming bizarre and insane delusions and in his being diagnosed as suffering from schizophrenia.

Rather, the so-called medical model of insanity must be that, just as there must be something which has gone wrong with the body of someone who is suffering from a physical illness, so there must always be something which has gone wrong with the body of someone who is suffering from a mental illness. The brain, of course, is today the preferred bit of the body which is supposed to be malfunctioning whenever there is mental illness whereas in earlier times it was the spleen or the bowels. This sounds like an empirical hypothesis about the causation of mental illness, insisting that there will never be a case of someone who is both mentally ill and at the same time physically perfectly normal with a normally functioning brain. If this is correct, it is hard to see how this empirical hypothesis can have shaped the concept of mental illness. It is rather that the concept of mental illness has made this hypothesis possible because the concept does not require that, as a matter of logic, mental illness must always have a non-physical, psychological, cause.

Has the concept of mental illness been framed by analogy with physical illness in the manner suggested by Antony Flew in his *Crime or Disease?*[12] Flew searches for things which are true of physical illness as a matter of logical necessity and then claims that some of them apply equally to mental illness. Thus, according to Flew, all physical illness incapacitates and so, he maintains, does all mental illness. What differentiates physical from mental illness is, he alleges, that the causation of mental illness is psychological rather than physical. The other analogies Flew appeals to are discomfort and distress, and the sufferer's complaining to others and wishing to be free of his painful, incapacitating, condition.

[12] Anthony Flew, *Crime or Disease?* (London: Macmillan, 1973), ch. II, 'Disease and Mental Disease'.

In assessing Flew's claim, we need to keep in mind the difference between feeling ill without suffering from an illness (after having been poisoned, say, or after eating something which disagrees with one) and suffering from an illness without necessarily feeling ill (as might, say, a plague victim in a coma). More awkwardly, Flew's allegedly logically necessary common features do not fit the bill. It is infirmities, not illnesses—some of which can be quite trivial—that incapacitate as a matter of logical necessity. And contrary to what Flew says, a mental illness might lack a psychological cause and have instead a purely physical cause. It is possible to suffer from an illness without experiencing suffering, as in the case of the unconscious plague victim. As he lapses into a coma, the person suffering from the illness is freed from pain but not from his illness. If Flew's account of illness were correct, effective painkillers would cure us of our illnesses. When Flew finally gets round to considering psychopaths who, when interviewed in psychiatric prison hospitals, are hale and hearty and do not complain of their mental condition at all, he finds that the concept of an illness has been stretched too far and condemns as woolly-minded the liberals who would protect such criminals from the rigours of the ordinary criminal law by diagnosing them as suffering from a mental illness. Which is why he pronounces such so-called psychopaths to be bad, not mad.[13] I think Flew's inability to accommodate the psychopath in his account of mental illness reveals a defect in his analogizing method of making sense of the concept of mental illness.

(5) Is mental illness culturally relative in any important way in which physical illness is not?

Different cultures will for all sorts of reasons influence the distribution of both physical and mental illness amongst their members. But when the philosopher speaks of cultural relativity he has something more specific in mind. The law is culturally relative in the sense that the self-same activity can be legal in one country and illegal in another. A hard-headed scientist will tell you that, unlike the law, medicine is not in this sense culturally relative. The self-same symptoms cannot be symptoms of influenza in France but not in England. English and French doctors can differ over what they regard as an illness but a correctly diagnosed case of influenza in France would be influenza if the sufferer lived in England, whether his condition is recognized here or not. One cannot ever get rid of one's illness merely by crossing a state border as one sometimes can of the criminal status of one's behaviour. If, however, as has been alleged, mental illness is culturally relative like

---

[13] Ibid., pp. 75–78.

the law, this will provide a reason for not placing the study of mental illness on a par with that of physical illness within the discipline of objective medicine.

Some philosophers, starting out from the position that mental illness is the absence of mental health, have equated loss of mental health with the loss of mental healthiness, and have gone on to identify being mentally ill with having an unhealthy mind. From this there is but a short step to the relativistic observation that what is deemed healthy by one person or in one culture may be deemed unhealthy by another elsewhere.

But mental health is not the same thing as mental healthiness, any more than suffering from a physical illness, and thus being in ill health, is the same as being unhealthy. It may be unhealthy to be obese but obesity is not an illness. Someone who is worried about his mental healthiness keeps his mind agile by training it with logical puzzles testing his mental powers as an athlete might train his body with weight lifting in order to increase his physical prowess. But however sluggish the mind of the couch potato, he can take comfort from the thought that this does not entitle anyone to count him purely on that score as mentally ill. 'A healthy/ unhealthy mind' can be used as a metaphor in ways that are undoubtedly culture-relative and value-laden, for example, in matters connected with sexual immorality and political extremism. Middle-class parents may talk anxiously of the unhealthy appetites and interests of their teenage offspring on discovering that he or she has become a member of the National Front Party. However, none of this shows that one of the main symptoms of schizophrenia, hearing voices saying unpleasant things about you, for example, is a symptom of mental illness in one culture but not in another.

(6) Do we owe our concept of mental illness to Freud?
Freud's early studies of hysterics, that is, of patients who display something similar to the classical symptoms of an illness or disease in the absence of the appropriate physical causation, have been taken to show how the concept of mental illness first arose, with 'hysteria' being counted as the name of the first mental illness to be officially designated as such.

Curiously, in view of their other differences, both Flew and Szasz subscribe to this theory.[14] If a patient towards the end of the nineteenth century presented with what to his doctor looked like

[14] See Szasz, *The Myth of Mental Illness*, Book I; and Antony Flew, 'Mental health, mental disease, mental illness: "the medical model"', ch. 6 in Philip Bean (ed.), *Mental Illness: Changes and Trends* (Chichester: John Wiley & Sons Ltd., 1983), p. 131.

the symptoms of some physical disorder or disease but without the underlying physical causation, he was described as a hysteric, who might be suffering from such things as hysterical blindness, hysterical appendicitis, hysterical paralysis, etc. The warrant, according to this theory, which still has its supporters today, for introducing the epithet 'mental' in the description of hysteria as a mental illness was that, in the absence of any discernible organic lesion, there were supposed to be psychological causes present, for example, unconscious motives.

But this account will not bear close examination and is, anyhow, a travesty of Freud's own theories. Suppose the driver of a car is tried in court and found guilty of reckless driving resulting in the death of a child pedestrian. A few months after the accident the driver complains to his doctor that his lower right leg, including the ankle and the foot, feels numb and is paralysed and that he finds driving difficult. Specialists, however, find nothing organically wrong with him. His leg and his brain are in normal working order. But it is noted that it is with his right foot that he applies the brake when driving his car and that he accepts that in the fatal accident he was at fault in not braking sooner. If that was all that was wrong with the driver, would we have any reason purely on this account to say that the driver was mentally ill? I submit that we would not. Little wonder that Szasz finds the concept of mental illness elusive, since this is how he pictures its origins. But, as we can see, such circumstances cannot have provided the appropriate setting for the emergence of the concept. The above case might be called 'hysterical paralysis' or 'hysterical numbness' but it is not, as it stands, one of mental illness. For the label 'mental illness, to be warranted, the story needs to make reference to the life of the mind, to the sufferer's mental—that is, his psychological—state so that it can be seen in what way his sanity has been impaired.

(7) Do we owe our concept of mental illness to a misnomer foisted upon us by a political power struggle involving the law and the medical profession in eighteenth- and nineteenth-century Europe? This suggestion has been made by some writers who have made a special study of the sociology of psychiatry.[15] I think, however, that there is a problem with the coherence of this account.

There is no doubt that misnomers do arise from the

[15] For example, by Michel Foucault in his *Madness and Civilization: A History of Insanity in the Age of Reason*, trans. Richard Howard (London: Tavistock Publications, 1967).

machinations of the politicians who make our laws. Consider the case of 'noise pollution' in our own times. If dogs are allowed to urinate in public swimming pools, the water in the pools will be polluted. But if a noisy dog barks all night long in a densely residential area, the dog is not polluting that neighbourhood. Twenty dogs all barking at once will be noisier, and more of a nuisance to the neighbours, but they will not, by their barking, at least, pollute anything. However, as a result of a poorly attended late night sitting in the House of Commons, what had been thought to be an uncontroversial bill was ambushed in its final stages and an amendment was added to a clause giving powers to Local Authorities' Environmental Health Officers to control various forms of pollution. Noise was smuggled into the bill under the heading 'Control of pollution' and thus the phrase 'noise pollution' was born. Local Authority Environmental Health Officers have thus acquired statutory powers under the Act to control noise if it constitutes a public nuisance. This development has, however, had so far no effect whatsoever on the concept of pollution but it does influence the vocabulary we use to describe noise that is a public nuisance. Of course, it is conceivable that this misnomer might eventually affect the concept of pollution, in which case the word 'pollution' might become watered down to mean no more than *public nuisance*. As things are, all that can be said is that the Act has given rise to the use of the misnomer of 'pollution' to describe a noise which is also a public nuisance.

Let us accept that as a result of legislation in Europe in the eighteenth and nineteenth centuries the insane were placed within the power of the medical profession. Since these doctors were already dealing with people who were suffering from physical illnesses and diseases, the new group were said to be suffering from illnesses too. But, so the story goes, since the new group was not suffering from physical illness and was abnormal in respect only of its mental, not its physical characteristics, its members were said by the medical profession to be 'mentally ill'.

We are supposed to have fallen into the trap of taking literally a misnomer used as a metaphor and of supposing that 'mental illness' was real illness. The example of 'noise pollution' shows, however, that it is harder than one might imagine for a misnomer to produce conceptual change and that if it were to do so, the result would be relatively innocuous.

What, after all, is this trap into which we are all supposed to have fallen? Does our readiness to talk in terms of mental illness lead us to think of mental illness as physical illness? By no means. We draw sharp logical boundaries between the two and can laugh

187

at an academic textbook on psychiatry when it tells us that in a common complication of childhood fevers 'what is called by the lay person an episode of *delirium* ... counts as a psychosis'.[16] It is clear from the context that the authors have been tempted into this absurdity by the plausible but—I have argued—mistaken idea that mental illness is to be equated with mental malfunctioning. Is it that our mistake is simply to think that a mental illness is an illness? But what sort of a mistake is this? Was it a mistake to call a rhyme which was only a rhyme for the eye a rhyme?

Conclusion

It is not as though the concept of physical illness, which predates the concept of mental illness, was bound to accommodate the concept of mental illness, any more than the concept of a rhyme for ear was always ripe for the emergence of the concept of a rhyme for eye. In each case an imaginative initiative of a 'tongue in the cheek' kind was required in which there was a willingness to use a word where it had, by the standards of the then prevailing usage, no business to be. The recognition of psychiatry as a branch of medicine alongside, say, orthopaedics, so as to enable us to countenance the curious possibility of a kind of illness which is never minor yet which, although it can result in the sufferer's death, can never prove fatal, namely, a mental illness, is a pioneering, mouldbreaking, step which can, I have been suggesting, be profitably compared to the impact upon poetry of the step taken by those versifiers who first tolerated non-rhyming rhymes for the eye among their rhyming couplets. Once these new concepts had taken root, and instances falling under them had gained acceptance, neither medicine not poetry would ever be quite the same again.

This development is not like the extension of the concept of a number in mathematics to include signed and unsigned, cardinal and ordinal, real and imaginary, rational and irrational, simple and complex, etc., numbers. Our talk of mental illness no more extends the original concept of illness than our talk of a rhyme for the eye extends our original concept of a rhyme. Nor is it to be compared with our description of, say, the performance of an opera as a delight for both the ear and the eye, or with our readiness to speak of both mental and physical handicaps or disadvantages. Sceptical opposition to the concept of mental illness is often,

[16] R. G. Priest and J. Steinert, *Insanity: A Study of Major Psychiatric Disorders* (Plymouth: Macdonald and Evans, 1977), p. 22.

I believe, an out-of-focus version of the correct view that the emergence of the concept of mental illness is not to be assimilated to either of these more conventional linguistic developments.

This relatively recent kink in our speech and thought produced by the concept of mental illness has, in its own way been quite as revolutionary in its implications for medicine as have the more celebrated decisions of earlier generations to include first geometry, then algebra and, later, mechanics, trigonometry and set-theory alongside arithmetic in the ever expanding, conceptually similarly hospitable, subject of mathematics.

Can There be an Epistemology of Moods?

STEPHEN MULHALL

By entitling her recent collection of essays on philosophy and literature *Love's Knowledge*,[1] Martha Nussbaum signals her commitment to giving a positive answer to the question posed by the title of this paper. If love can deliver or lay claim to knowledge, then moods (the variety of affective states to which human nature is subject) must be thought of as having a cognitive significance, and so must not only permit but require the attentions of the epistemologist. As Nussbaum points out, such a conclusion runs counter to a central strand of thinking in both ancient and modern philosophy. The rational or cognitive side of human nature is often defined in contrast to its affective or emotional side, the latter being understood as having no role to play in the revelation of reality. On the contrary, where reason and the senses can combine to disclose the way things are, moods typically cloud that cognitive access by projecting a purely subjective colouration onto the world and leading us to attribute properties or qualities to it which have at best a purely personal and internal reality.

Nussbaum contests this understanding of the passions through her reading of Aristotle's moral philosophy. According to that reading, emotions are composites of belief and feeling, shaped by developing thought and highly discriminating in their reactions; they can lead or guide an agent, picking out objects to be pursued or avoided, working in responsive interaction with perception and imagination. Anger, for example, requires and rests upon a belief that one has been wronged or damaged in some significant way by the person towards whom the anger is directed; the discovery that this belief is false can be expected to remove the anger. Furthermore, the acceptance of certain beliefs is not just a necessary condition for emotion but a constituent part of it—even a sufficient condition for it; if one really accepts or takes in a certain belief, one will experience the emotion—experiencing the emotion is necessary for full belief. If a person believes that X is the most important person in her life and that X has just died, she will feel grief; and if she does not, this must be because in some sense she doesn't fully comprehend or has not taken in or is repressing these

[1] Oxford University Press, 1990.

191

facts. This cognitive dimension to the structure of emotions leads Nussbaum to conclude that the passions are intelligent parts of our ethical agency, responsive to the workings of deliberation and essential to its completion. There are certain contexts in which the pursuit of intellectual reasoning apart from emotion will actually prevent a full rational judgment—by, for example, preventing access to one's grief or love, without which a full understanding of what has taken place is not possible.

Since, however, Nussbaum's main concern is with moral philosophy and literature, she does not develop her general claim about the cognitive dimension of emotions in any detail, and she manages to suggest (however unwittingly) that the knowledge love can provide primarily concerns the person whose passion it is rather than the world that person inhabits, and that it is a primarily ethical species of knowledge. In the essay which gives her collection its title, for example, the knowledge that Proust's Marcel acquires by his love—the knowledge that that love constitutes—is the knowledge that he loves Albertine; it is, in other words, a species of self-knowledge that reveals his capacity for self-deception. In this lecture, I want to explore the question of whether the passions might be considered to have a cognitive function which goes beyond the realm of the ethical, and which is more than reflexive in its focus. My primary guide in this exploration will be the Heidegger of *Being and Time* (BT).[2] In that early, unfinished work, Heidegger argues that moods are one aspect of the way in which human mode of being (what Heidegger refers to as 'Dasein' or 'there-being') discloses or uncovers the world we inhabit; and, perhaps most notoriously, he rests fundamental claims about the nature of both human beings and their world on a highly detailed epistemological analysis of the specific moods of fear and anxiety. I intend to argue that these claims and arguments prefigure and underpin more recent work in the Anglo-American philosophical tradition, reveal important weaknesses in the still highly influential Kantian conception of epistemology, and imply that a radical revision of our conception of the role and nature of philosophical thinking is called for. In so doing, I will deploy and elaborate ideas and arguments developed by Stanley Cavell in his work on Wittgenstein and Emerson.

I. Fear: Subjectivity and Self-Interpretation

Heidegger's analysis of moods in *Being and Time* is embedded in a broader analysis of the ways in which Dasein's relation to its world

[2] Trans. J. Macquarrie and E. Robinson (Blackwell, Oxford, 1962).

is a comprehending one. He underlines this by claiming that, insofar as we think of our commerce with the world as a relation between subject and objects, then Dasein is the Being of this 'between'. In other words, Dasein is not trapped within a mind or body from which it then attempts to reach out to objects, but is rather always already outside itself, dwelling amidst objects in all their variety. Dasein's thoughts, feelings and actions have entities themselves (not mental representations of them) as their objects, and those entities can appear not merely as environmental obstacles or as objects of desire and aversion, but in the full specificity of their nature, their mode of existence (e.g. as handy, unready-to-hand, occurrent, and so on), and their reality as existent things. This capacity to encounter and disclose entities *as* the entities they are is what Heidegger invokes when he talks of Dasein as the clearing, the being to whom and for whom entities appear as they are. This disclosedness is seen as having two aspects or elements, 'Befindlichkeit' and 'Verstehen' (standardly translated as 'state-of-mind' and 'understanding' respectively); and the former picks out what Heidegger thinks of as the ontological foundation for—that which makes it possible for human beings to experience—moods.

What Heidegger labels 'Befindlichkeit' is an essentially passive or necessitarian aspect of Dasein's disclosure of itself and its world. The standard translation of 'Befindlichkeit' as 'state-of-mind' is seriously misleading, since the latter term has a technical significance in the philosophy of mind which fails to match the range of reference of the German term. Virtually any response to the question 'How are you?' or 'How's it going?' could be denoted by 'Befindlichkeit' but not by 'state-of-mind'; the latter also implies that the relevant phenomena are purely subjective states, thus repressing Heidegger's constant emphasis upon Dasein as Being-in-the-world, as an essentially worldly or environed being. 'Frame of mind' is less inaccurate, but still retains some connotation of the mental as an inner realm; so it seems best to interpret 'Befindlichkeit' as referring to Dasein's capacity to be affected by the world, to find that the entities and situations it faces *matter* to it, and in ways over which it has less than complete control.

The most familiar manifestation of this underlying ontological or existential structure is what Heidegger calls the phenomenon of 'Stimmung' (standardly translated as 'mood'). Depression, boredom and cheerfulness, joy and fear, are affective inflections of Dasein's temperament that are typically experienced as 'given', as states into which one has been thrown—something underlined in the etymology of our language in this region. We talk, for example, of moods and emotions as 'passions', as something passive rather than active, something that we suffer rather than something we inflict—where 'suffering' signifies not pain but submission, as it does when we talk of Christ's Passion or of His suffering little children to come unto Him. More generally, our affections do not just affect others but mark our having been affected by others; we cannot, for example, love and hate where and when we will, but rather think of our affections as captured by their objects, or as making us vulnerable to others, open to suffering.

For human beings, such affections are unavoidable and their impact pervasive; they constitute a fundamental condition of human existence. We can, of course, sometimes overcome or alter our prevailing mood, but only if that mood allows, and only by establishing ourselves in a new one (tranquillity and determination are no less moods than depression or ecstasy); and once in their grip, moods can colour every aspect of our existence. In so doing, according to Heidegger, they determine our grasp upon the world: they inflect Dasein's relation to the objects and possibilities amongst which it finds itself—one and all being grasped in relation to the particular, actualized existential possibility that Dasein presently *is*. In this sense, moods are disclosive: a particular mood discloses something (sometimes everything) in the world as mattering to Dasein in a particular way—as fearful, boring, cheering or hateful; and this reveals in turn that, ontologically speaking, Dasein is open to the world as something that can affect it.

As we have seen, however, it is easier to accept the idea that moods disclose something about Dasein than that they reveal something about the world. Since human beings undergo moods, the claim that someone is bored or fearful might be said to record a simple fact about her; but her mood does not—it might be thought—pick out a simple fact about the world (namely, that it is, or some things within it are, boring or fearsome), for moods do not register objective features of reality but rather subjective responses to a world that is in itself essentially devoid of significance. In short, there can be no such thing as an epistemology of moods. Heidegger wholeheartedly rejects any such conclusion. Since moods are an aspect of Dasein's existence, they must be an aspect of Being-in-the-world—and so must be as revelatory of the world as they are of Dasein. As he puts it:

A mood is not related to the psychical... and is not itself an *inner condition* which then reaches forth in an enigmatical way and puts its mark on things and persons... It comes neither from 'outside' nor from 'inside', but arises out of Being-in-the-world, as a way of such Being. (BT, 29: 176)

194

Heidegger reinforces this claim with a more detailed analysis of fear as having three basic elements: that in the face of which we fear, fearing itself and that about which we fear. That in the face of which we fear is the fearful or the fearsome—something in the world which we encounter as detrimental to our well-being or safety; fearing itself is our response to something fearsome; and that about which we fear is of course our well-being or safety—in short, ourselves. Thus, fear has both a subjective and an objective face. On the one hand it is a human response, and one which has the existence of the person who fears as its main concern. This is because Dasein's Being is, as Heidegger puts it, an issue for it—for human beings, the nature and form (and so the continuation) of their existence is a question for them rather than something determined by their biological nature; living is a matter of taking a stand on how to live and of being defined by that stand. The disclosive self-attunement that such moods exemplify confirms Heidegger's earlier claim that Dasein's capacity to encounter objects typically involves grasping them in relation to its own existential possibilities. On the other hand, however, Dasein's Being is put at issue here by something in the world that is genuinely fearsome, that poses a threat to the person who fears; and this reveals not only that the world Dasein inhabits can affect it in the most fundamental ways, that Dasein is open and vulnerable to the world, but also that things in the world are really capable of affecting Dasein. The threat posed by a rabid dog, the sort of threat to which Dasein's capacity to respond to things as fearful is attuned, is not illusory.

Even the relation of moods to those undergoing them—what I have been calling the subjective side of the question of moods—should not be understood in an unduly subjective way. For Heidegger, Dasein's Being is Being-with—its relations with others are internally related to its own individual existence; accordingly, its individual states not only affect but are affected by its relations to others. This has two very important consequences. First, it implies that moods can be social: a given Dasein's membership of a group might, for example, lead to her being thrown into the mood that grips that group, finding herself immersed in its melancholy or hysteria. This point is reinforced by the fact that Dasein's everyday mode of selfhood or individuality is what Heidegger calls the they-self—a mode of existence in which the thoughts and opinions of others determine our sense of who we are, in which our individual answerability for our own existence has been displaced upon or swallowed up by whatever we deem to be the common or agreed-upon way of living one's life. 'Publicness, as the kind of Being that belongs to the "they", not only has in general its own way of having a mood, but needs moods and "makes" them for itself' (BT, 29: 178). A politician determining judicial policy on the back of a wave of moral panic is precisely responding to the public mood.

The socialness of moods also implies that an individual's social world fixes the range of moods into which she can be thrown. Of course, an individual is capable of transcending or resisting the dominant social mood—her own mood need not merely reflect that of the public; but even if it does not, the range of possible moods open to her is itself socially determined. This is because Dasein's moods arise out of Being-in-the-world, and Heidegger understands that world as underpinned by a set of socially-defined roles, categories and concepts; but it means that the underlying structure even of Dasein's seemingly most intimate and personal feelings and responses is socially conditioned.

This Heideggerian idea underpins Charles Taylor's notion of human beings as self-interpreting animals.[3] Taylor follows Heidegger's tripartite analysis of moods, arguing that an emotion such as shame is related in its essence to a certain sort of situation (a 'shameful' or 'humiliating' one), and to a particular self-protective response to it (e.g. hiding or covering up): such feelings thus cannot even be identified independently of the type of situations which give rise to them, and so can be evaluated on any particular occasion in terms of their appropriateness to their context. But the significance of the term we employ to characterize the feeling and its appropriate context is partly determined by the wider field of terms for such emotions and situations of which it forms a part; each such term derives its meaning from the contrasts that exist between it and other terms in that semantic field. For example, describing a situation as 'fearful' will mean something different according to whether or not the available contrasts include such terms as 'terrifying', 'worrying', 'disconcerting', 'threatening', 'disgusting'; the wider the field, the finer the discriminations that can be made by the choice of one term as opposed to another, and the more specific the significance of each term. Thus, the significance of the situations in which an individual finds herself, and the import and nature of her emotions, is determined by the range and structure of the vocabulary available to her for their characterization. She cannot feel shame if she lacks a vocabulary in which the circle of situation, feeling and goal characteristic of shame is available; and the precise significance of that feeling will alter according to the semantic field in which that vocabulary is embedded.

[3] See *Philosophical Papers* (Cambridge University Press, 1985).

It is not that the relationship between feeling and available vocabulary is a simple one. In particular, thinking or saying does not make it so: not any definition of our feelings can be forced upon us, and some we gladly take up are inauthentic or deluded. But neither do vocabularies simply match or fail to match a pre-existing array of feelings in the individual; for we often experience how access to a more sophisticated vocabulary makes our emotional life more sophisticated. And the term 'vocabulary' here is misleading: it denotes not just an array of signs, but also the complex of concepts and practices within which alone those signs have meaning. When one claims that, for example, no-one in late twentieth-century Britain can experience the pride of a Samurai warrior because the relevant vocabulary is unavailable, 'vocabulary' refers not just to a set of Japanese terms but to their role in a complex web of customs, assumptions and institutions. And because our affective life is conditioned by the culture in which we find ourself, our being immersed in a particular mood or feeling is revelatory of something about our world—is cognitively significant—in a further way. For our feeling horrified (for example) then not only registers the presence of something horrifying in our environment; it also shows that our world is one in which we can encounter the specific complex of feeling, situation and response that constitutes horror—a world in which horror has a place.

This is why both Taylor and Heidegger claim that the relationship between a person's inner life and the vocabulary available to her is an intimate one; and since that vocabulary is itself something the individual inherits from the society and culture within which she happens to find herself, the range of specific feelings or moods into which she may be thrown is itself something into which she is thrown. How things might conceivably matter to her, just as much as how they in fact matter to her at a given moment, is something determined by her society and culture rather than by her own psychic make-up or will-power. It is this double sense of thrownness that is invoked when Heidegger says: 'Existentially, a state-of-mind implies a disclosive submission to the world, out of which we can encounter something that matters to us' (BT, 29: 177).

If we return to the objective side of the question of moods, Heidegger's analysis of fear as potentially revelatory of the way things are in reality—his argument against what might be called a projectivist account of moods—is strongly reminiscent of one developed by John McDowell.[4] In essence, the projectivist is

---

[4] See J. McDowell, 'Values and Secondary Qualities', in T. Honderich (ed.), *Morality and Objectivity: Essays in Honour of J. L. Mackie* (London: Routledge, 1985).

struck by the fact that when we characterize something as boring or fearful, we do so on the basis of a certain response to it, and concludes that such attributions are simply projections of those responses; but in so doing, she overlooks the fact that those responses are to things and situations in the world, and any adequate explanation of their essential nature must take account of that. So, for example, any adequate account of the fearfulness of certain objects must invoke certain subjective states, certain facts about human beings and their responses. However, it must also invoke the object of fear—some feature of it that prompts our fear-response: in the case of a rabid dog, for example, the dangerous properties of its saliva. Now, of course, that saliva is dangerous only because it interacts in certain ways with human physiology, so invoking the human subject is again essential in spelling out what it is about the dog that makes it fearful: but that does not make its fearfulness any less real—as we would confirm if it bit us.

The point is that there are two senses in which something might be called subjective: it might mean 'illusory' (in contrast with veridical), or 'not comprehensible except by making reference to subjective states, properties or responses' (in contrast with phenomena whose explanation requires no such reference). Primary qualities like length are not subjective in either sense; hallucinations are subjective in both senses; and fearfulness (like secondary qualities and moral qualities, in McDowell's view) is subjective only in the second sense. In other words, whether something is really fearful is in an important sense an objective question—the fact that we can find some things fearful when they do not merit that response (eg house spiders) shows this; and insofar as our capacity to fear things permits us to discriminate the genuinely fearful from the non-fearful, then that affective response reveals something about the world.

II. Heidegger and Kant: Objectivity and Externality

It might be thought that the case so far marshalled against the projectivist has been given more plausibility than it deserves by our exclusive focus on the example of fear. Like love and anger, fear is a response to specific situations or objects, and so can be more easily characterized as responsive to aspects of those situations or objects; but if we shifted our focus from emotions to phenomena that might be more naturally characterized as moods—depression, boredom, despair, cheerfulness, tranquillity—their links to specific circumstances are acknowledged to be far more tenuous and indirect (if indeed they have any such links at all) and so make it more difficult to characterize their colorations of our world as revelatory of reality.

A key point about such moods is, of course, the passive or necessitarian mode of their advent which we mentioned earlier; we experience them as something into which we can be thrown or thrust without warning or control, neither their onset nor their dissolution necessarily triggered by any particular event in either our minds or our world. It seems natural, therefore, to regard them as entirely subjective phenomena—as psychological or affective filters temporarily and arbitrarily imposed on our experience, and to which we must submit without allowing them to deceive us into thinking that they reveal anything other than our own mental state. This same sense of submissiveness is, however, precisely what leads Heidegger to *reject* the projectivist idea that they are purely subjective or inner phenomena. As he puts it: 'A mood assails us. It comes neither from "outside" nor from "inside", but arises out of Being-in-the-world, as a way of such Being' (BT, 29: 176). In other words, insofar as moods do assail us, then they can as legitimately be thought of as coming from outside us as from inside us. This suggests not only that they cannot be regarded as wholly subjective; it also, and more fundamentally, implies that moods put the very distinction between inside and outside, subjectivity and objectivity, in question.

We can best explore the implications of this suggestion by relating Heidegger's conception of moods to Kant's famous and highly influential attempt to explicate and anchor the distinction between subjectivity and objectivity in human experience in the Second Analogy of the *Critique of Pure Reason*.[5] Kant begins by noting that we distinguish in our experience between the order in which our senses represent different states of an object (the subjective temporal order) and the order of those successive states in the object itself (the objective temporal order). For example, when I successively perceive the various parts of a house, I do not judge that my perception of its basement must either succeed or precede my perception of its roof; but when I perceive a ship sailing downriver, I do judge that my perception of it upstream must precede my perception of it further downstream. Since, however, according to transcendental idealism, I never apprehend objects in themselves but only successive representations of objects, I can judge that certain sequences of representations represent changes of state in the object (that is, I can experience an event) only if I can regard their order as irreversible—only, that is, if I subject them to

[5] Trans N. Kemp-Smith (London: MacMillan, 1929).

199

an *a priori* temporal rule (the schema of causality). As a condition of the possibility of the experience of an objective succession, this schema is also a condition of the succession itself (as an object of possible experience). In short, the schema has 'objective reality'; its application alone makes possible both the experience of an objective temporal order and (of course) the experience of a merely subjective temporal order. In its absence, the very distinction between inner and outer orders of experience would have no ground.

This line of argument has famously been criticized by Strawson as depending upon a *'non sequitur* of numbing grossness'.[6] On his account, Kant begins from the conceptual truth that in the perception of causal sequence of states A–B, the observer's perceptions must follow the order: perception of A–perception of B; but he then illicitly presumes that this conceptual necessity in the order of perceptions of an event establishes the causal necessity of the relevant event. In other words, Kant can only reach his conclusion about the objectivity of the causal order by distorting both the location and the kind of necessity invoked in his premise. I trust that it is by now equally well-known that Strawson's criticism itself depends upon a profound misunderstanding of Kant's argument. As Allison has demonstrated,[7] Kant is not assuming that the subjective order of our perceptions is a datum or given piece of evidence, from which we must attempt to draw inferences about a putative objective order of events. To do so would be to occupy the position of a transcendental realist, someone who treats objects as things in themselves which exist independently of, although constituting the causal origin of, our experience; but Kant explicitly argues that such a person could not account for the possibility of an objective temporal order, since any such order would by definition be entirely independent of the subjective order of representations to which the transcendental realist thinks we are restricted. Neither is Kant an empirical or dogmatic idealist, someone who thinks that objects are nothing more than constructions from subjective representations or sense data—that only subjective representations are real.

When Kant talks of 'the subjective order' to which the schema of causality is applied, he is rather speaking as a transcendental idealist, and so must be considering it not as something introspected or actually represented, but as the indeterminate preconceptualized material for sensible representation; it is what would remain if

[6] In *The Bounds of Sense* (London: Routledge, 1966), p. 137.

[7] H. Allison, *Kant's Transcendental Idealism* (New Haven: Yale University Press, 1983).

(*per impossibile*) we could remove the determinate structure imposed on the sensibly given (the manifold of inner sense) by the understanding. His claim is that if all we had were this indeterminate subjective order, we would not be able to represent any temporal order at all (whether subjective or objective); since however, we can do so, that manifold must be conceptually ordered by the understanding by subsuming it under a rule. As Kant puts it, 'I render my subjective synthesis of apprehension objective only by reference to a rule in accordance with which the appearances in their succession, that is, as they happen, are determined by the preceding state' (A 195/B 240).

In other words, this subjection of perceptions to a rule is not the means for making the perceptions themselves into objects, but rather the basis for conceiving of a distinct, objective temporal order in and through these perceptions. Kant does not claim that the subjective order of perceptions is itself causally necessary, and that this property is the basis for our inferring that these perceptions reflect a causal necessity in the successive states of the object they represent. Any such property could only be recognized if the order of perceptions is already conceptualized and thereby made into an object for introspection, which in turn presupposes that it is distinguishable from an objective temporal order; but the recognition of this property is supposed to be the condition for the possibility of making such a distinction. The irreversibility to which Kant refers is thus not that of a given perceptual order, which we can inspect and then infer that it is somehow determined by the object; it is the conceptual ordering of the understanding through which the understanding determines the thought of an objective succession. Prior to this conceptual determination there is no thought of an object at all, and so no experience.

Given that Kant's transcendental perspective is not touched by Strawson's criticisms, might the conception of experience which grounds its explication of subjectivity and objectivity be otherwise put in question? We can return to the main thread of my discussion by noting that Heidegger's interpretation of moods as assailing us entails that those aspects of our experience are not tractable by the distinction between the subjective succession of apprehension and the objective succession of appearances that Kant proposes. As Stanley Cavell has put it, discussing a passage of Emerson:[8]

> The fact that we are taken over by this succession, this onwardness, means that you can think of it as at once a succession of

[8] Attributed to Emerson by Cavell; cf. 'Thinking of Emerson', in *The Senses of Walden* (SW) (San Francisco: North Point Press, 1981).

> moods (inner matters) and a succession of objects (outer matters). This very evanescence of the world proves its existence to me; it is what vanishes from me. (SW, p. 127)

Kant claims that the possibility of distinguishing an objective from a merely subjective order of experience is anchored in an irreversibility or necessity of succession imposed on the manifold of inner sense by its subsumption under a rule; to judge that we have perceived an event—a change of state in an object of experience—we must judge the order of our perceptions of those states as necessary. But when we experience an alteration of mood—our present cheerfulness assailed by the onset of depression, or fearfulness resolving into boredom—we experience that alteration as something to which we are irreversibly or necessarily subjected; according to Kant's argument, we must therefore regard it as both a subjective succession (something to which we are subjected) and an objective one (something imposed upon us from without). On these terms, we must conclude that the successions of our moods track transformations in the world as well as transformations in our orientation within it. When, for example, our apprehension of the world as a cheerful place is annihilated by a sudden apprehension of it as dreadful, we find ourselves inhabiting a new world as well as a new stance towards that world; as Wittgenstein once put it, the world of the unhappy man is not that of the happy man. The evanescence of our mood—our inability to credit our lost sense of good cheer—is matched by the evanescence of the cheerful or cheering world it revealed; and this mutual exclusion of moods and of worlds itself reveals something about both—that the world and our moods are mutually attuned, and that both can slip from our grasp.

One way of expressing this attunement would be to say that moods must be taken as having at least as sound a role in advising us of reality as sense-experience has—that judging the world to be dreadful or boring may be no less objective (and of course, no less subjective) than judging an apple to be red or green. As Cavell puts it: 'sense-experience is to objects what moods are to the world' (SW, p. 125). The problem with the Kantian attempt to ground the distinction between subjective and objective orders of experience is that it is exclusively geared to sensory experience of objects and not to such experiences as moods; and by relying upon an impoverished conception of experience, it is fated to generate a correspondingly impoverished conception of the reality which that experience reveals. In particular, it accommodates the fact that our experience is of objects whilst failing properly to accommodate the fact that those objects are met with in a world.

The basic principle of Kant's transcendental idealism is that 'the conditions of the *possibility of experience* in general are likewise conditions of the *possibility of the objects of experience*' (A 158/B 197); and the twelve categories of the understanding give us those conditions. But the implication of Heidegger's and Cavell's accounts of moods is that these categories—functioning as they do to relate our representations of objects to one another—articulate our notion of 'an object (of nature)' without articulating our sense of externality; more precisely, they articulate my sense of each object's externality to every other (making nature a whole, showing it to be spatial), but not my sense of their externality to me (making nature a world, showing it to be habitable). Instead, that idea of objects as being in a world apart from me is registered in Kant's concept of the thing-in-itself; and the problem is that that concept (or the concepts which go into it—the concepts of externality or world) do not receive a transcendental deduction. Kant fails to recognize that these concepts should be seen as internal to the categories of the understanding, as part of our concept of an object in general; and by dropping those concepts into the concept of the thing-in-itself, he makes it impossible to resist the conclusion that he is claiming that there are things, somethings or other, that we cannot know—that our knowledge of reality has limitations rather than limits.

What Heidegger undertakes to provide in *Being and Time* is, of course, something that looks very like a transcendental deduction of the concept of a world, understood as that in which objects are met; he thereby attempts to show that there are more ways of making a habitable world—more layers or aspects to it—than Kant's twelve categories allow. In the next part of this paper, I shall attempt to show how his analysis of moods contributes to this enterprise—how the epistemology of moods casts light on the worldliness of human experience.

III. Anxiety: The Finitude of Self and World

Perhaps the most famous of Heidegger's analyses of mood is his discussion of 'Angst' (anxiety or dread)—a discussion heavily indebted to Kierkegaard. It begins by distinguishing anxiety from fear. Both are responses to the world as unnerving, hostile or threatening, but whereas fear is a response to something specific in the world (a gun, an animal, a gesture) anxiety is in this sense objectless. The distinctive oppressiveness of anxiety lies precisely in its not being elicited by anything specific, or at least in its being entirely disproportionate to the specific circumstances which appear to have triggered it; either way, it cannot be accommodated by responding to those specific circumstances in any concrete way (e.g. by running away). According to Heidegger, what oppresses us is not any specific totality of objects but rather the *possibility* of such a totality: we are oppressed by the world as such—or more precisely, by the worldliness of our existence, our Being-in-the-world. Anxiety confronts Dasein with the knowledge that it is thrown into the world—always already delivered over to situations of choice and action which matter to it but which it does not itself fully choose or determine; it confronts Dasein with the determining and yet sheerly contingent fact of its own worldly existence.

But Being-in-the-world is not just that in the face of which the anxious person is anxious; it is also that *for* which she is anxious. In anxiety, Dasein is anxious about itself—not about some concrete existential possibility, but about the fact that possibilities are the medium of its existence, that its life is necessarily a matter of realizing one or other existential possibility. In effect, then, anxiety plunges Dasein into an anxiety about itself in the face of itself; and since in this state particular objects and persons within the world fade into insignificance and the world as such occupies the foreground, then the specific structures of the they-world must also fade away. Thus, anxiety can rescue Dasein from its fallen state, its lostness in the 'they'; it throws Dasein back upon the fact that it is a being for whom its own Being is an issue, and so a creature capable of individuality.

> [I]n anxiety, there lies the possibility of a disclosure that is quite distinctive; for anxiety individualizes. This individualization brings Dasein back from its falling, and makes manifest to it that authenticity and inauthenticity are possibilities of its Being. These basic possibilities of Dasein ... show themselves in anxiety as they are in themselves—undisguised by entities within the world, to which, proximally and for the most part, Dasein clings. (BT, 40: 235)

What Heidegger claims to identify here is an experience of uncanniness. Anxiety makes unavoidable the realization that human life is always conducted in the midst of objects and events, and that typically we bury ourselves in them—in flight from acknowledging that our existence is always capable of being more or other than its present realizations, and so that we are never fully at home in any particular world. This uncanniness highlights the finitude of Dasein's freedom; Dasein is responsible for choosing its mode of life, but must do so without ever fully controlling the circumstances in which that choice must be exercised, and without ever being able entirely to identify itself with the outcome of any particular choice that it makes. It is always haunted by the choices it didn't make, the choices it couldn't make, and its inability to choose to live without the capacity to choose—the conditions of freedom for a finite creature, a creature that must inhabit a spatio-temporal world.

In other words, the uncanniness of anxiety reveals the world as one component of Dasein's finitude. More precisely, by revealing the conditionedness of human freedom, it demonstrates the externality of the world to its human denizens; for those conditions reflect the fact that human existence is essentially worldly or environed, that the natural world of objects and events is one which we inhabit, and so that the world must be thought of as both intimately related to us and yet separate from us. Furthermore, anxiety elucidates the relative autonomy of the world as a function of its being at once evanescent and permanent. The uncanniness anxiety induces shows that each particular arrangement of objects and events will be succeeded by others, so no such arrangement can be thought of as exhaustive of the significance of the world as such, which exists rather as the horizon of possibilities within which actuality is encountered; and yet, insofar as Dasein is capable of being entirely absorbed in the present arrangements of its world to the point at which it loses its sense of itself as free to live otherwise than it does, anxiety teaches us that the world answers to our conceptions of it—that its successions can be fixed or frozen, and so that the world is such that it constantly and obediently becomes what we make of it. In short, according to Heidegger's epistemology of anxiety, the world's externality must be understood as its inexhaustible capacity to be all the ways our moods tell us it can be—its capacity to be apart from us and yet be a part of us.

IV. Moods and Criteria: The Mutual Attunement of Heidegger and Wittgenstein

Heidegger's claim that moods are revelatory of the world forms part of his more general claim that the passive or necessitarian aspect of human existence—our thrownness, our openness to 'states-of-mind'—forms part of the human capacity to comprehend the world we inhabit. Earlier in *Being and Time*, he argued that the fundamental basis of this comprehension is something he calls 'Rede' (literally 'talk', but standardly translated as 'discourse')—an ontological structure that both is and is not essentially linguistic. According to his analysis, Dasein's encounters with objects are all implicitly structured in terms of 'seeing as': we see a given entity as a table, a door, a carriage, and so on, and thus locate it in a certain field or horizon of significance—one which links the object to other objects and raw materials, to certain goals or outcomes, to other people (customers, fellow-workers) and to a particular existential possibility of our own (a project for which the object might or might not be useful). This socially constituted field of intelligibility is what Heidegger thinks of as the worldhood of the world—that which conditions the possibility of any and all of our encounters with the objects of the world; and the structure of this field of intelligibility—the articulations of this widely ramifying cultural web of concepts, roles, and functional inter-relations—he terms 'Rede'. As this term suggests, Heidegger sees a close relation between this field of significance and language. Since any language itself has a worldly existence, our capacity to grasp symbols and sentences must itself be understood in terms of the articulations of the field of significance; but precisely because language is the way in which discourse is expressed, its structure must be seen as internally related to the basic articulations of language—the categories or concepts in terms of which we grasp an entity as a particular kind of thing. Accordingly, insofar as the worldhood of the world is grounded in discourse, it must be understood in terms appropriate to the distinctively human capacity for language; in Heidegger's vocabulary, the ontological structure of the world must be understood in existential terms.

How might such an understanding preserve the world's autonomy from human beings—however relative that autonomy turns out to be? How in other words, can such an account of the world respect its separateness from us as well as our intimacy with it? This difficulty is parallel to one that emerges in Wittgenstein's later philosophy, and I want to suggest that the solution to that difficulty can provide us with a way of seeing how Heidegger might sustain his own balancing-act. I have in mind Wittgenstein's conception of criteria or grammar, and the conception of language that goes with it. For Wittgenstein, criteria govern the use of words; they articulate its grammar, the ways in which it can be combined with other words to formulate propositions that might or might not be true of reality. Assume, for example, that our criterion for a liquid's being water is that it have chemical composition H_2O. That is not itself a claim about reality, something that might be true or false; it doesn't claim that any particular liquid does have that chemical composition, or that any such liquid is to be found anywhere in the world, and so it cannot be falsified if such eventualities occur. It simply licenses us to substitute one form of words ('water') for another form of words ('liquid with chemical composition H_2O)'); it determines that whenever the latter is illicitly applied, so is the former. Such articulations of grammar are therefore akin to definitions, and definitions are not descriptions; they are, however, an essential precondition for constructing descriptions since they confer meaning on the terms used in the description.

I suggest that we think of criteria as akin to Heidegger's discourse; the grammatical structures they constitute are articulations of intelligibility, that which makes it possible for us to encounter objects as objects of a particular kind, and so ground the comprehensibility of worldly phenomena—that is, the human capacity to disclose the world. Since any such grammatical structures will individuate phenomena in ways that express human interests and human nature—since the ways in which criteria tell one object from another will reflect the distinctions that matter to their users, their shared sense of what is natural and what outrageous, what useful and what pointless—the worldhood of the world will in this sense be internally related to human culture and forms of life. Since, however, grammatical structures are not in the business of representing reality (since, like rules, criteria cannot coherently be assessed in terms of truth and falsity), then their rootedness in human practices and human nature cannot be said to undercut the world's independence from its human denizens. On the contrary: the world's autonomy finds expression, amongst other things, in reality's capacity to falsify putative descriptions of it; and given that such descriptions could not be constructed without criteria to give meaning to their constituent terms, it could be argued that the disclosedness of the world by grammar is precisely what makes possible the world's independence from human representations of it.

As we saw earlier, however, Heidegger implies that the world's relative autonomy or externality should be understood as a function of its evanescence and permanence—its capacity to answer to and yet transcend our conceptions of it. Does Wittgenstein's idea of the autonomy of grammar help to illuminate that further implication? To see that it does, we need to appreciate the consequences of the autonomy of grammar or discourse for our understanding of scepticism—surely the key point at which modern philosophy has studied the externality of the world. From a Wittgensteinian perspective, scepticism—like any other philosophical dogma—is rooted in confusion concerning the grammar of the terms it employs to give expression to its doubts. In claiming, for example, that although we typically believe that the world exists, we should rather regard it as a highly doubtful hypothesis, the sceptic fails to appreciate that the world's existence—unlike the existence of a given object in the world—is not something in which we 'believe', not an 'opinion' that we hold on the basis of evidence. By the same token, however, it is equally wrong to contradict the sceptic by arguing that we can be certain of the world's existence; if the concepts of belief, doubt and evidence do not apply here, then neither does the concept of certainty. There is, accordingly, a truth in scepticism: the sceptic rightly renders untenable the common-sense view that we can claim to know of the world's existence. Moreover, insofar as the sceptic's scepticism results from a refusal to employ such concepts as 'belief' and 'world' in accordance with our usual criteria—insofar as her scepticism amounts to an attempt to speak outside language games—then it must be acknowledged that our ordinary agreement in the criteria we employ is precisely something that is, and must remain, open to repudiation; anything whose existence requires the continued investment of consent is vulnerable to the withdrawal of that consent.

Of course, on Wittgenstein's view, criteria establish the connection between words and world; so the consequences of their repudiation are grave—the loss of the human capacity to word the world, the fate of finding oneself saying something other than one meant, or unable to say anything meaningful at all. In other words, since criteria disclose the world, their repudiation amounts to making the world vanish from our grasp; in this sense, scepticism makes manifest the evanescence of the world, its capacity to answer to our conceptions—including the conception that it is beyond our grasp. Since, however, a repudiated agreement can always be resuscitated (since it is possible to restore the link between words and world by recalling the sceptic to her criteria) then Wittgenstein's attempts to overcome scepticism amount to an attempted demonstration of the permanence of the world—of its being beyond our capacity for annihilation.

What, however, has this talk of criteria and discourse to do with moods? The connection can be seen at several levels. Most obviously, the sceptical impulse is itself characteristically associated with a specific mood. Insofar as its doubts about the reality of the external world are seriously held or generated (and not viewed as merely a dramatic device for introducing epistemological problems), scepticism is pervaded with anxiety of a kind that precisely matches Heidegger's analysis of it. The sceptic feels an abyss to open up between herself and the world, a sense of its insignificance and nothingness; she experiences a hollow at the heart of reality, and an essential uncanniness in her own existence—a sense of herself as not at home in the world. And of course, given that sceptical anxiety embodies a truth—given that it rightly perceives the inadequacy of cognitive models of our basic relation to reality, and shows that criteria are subject to the withdrawal of consent—then its onset can properly be thought to reveal something fundamental about the world and our inhabitation of it: namely, that our relation to the world is not one of knowing—that the world is not knowable.

However, the connections between criteria and moods run deeper even than this—something that is happily (fortuitously?) registered in the fact that, when Wittgenstein describes the mode of our ordinary agreement in criteria, he uses the term 'Ubereinstimmung'—a word which contains Heidegger's term for moods ('Stimmung') and which invokes exactly the same notion of attunement to the world. For the idea of agreement Wittgenstein wishes to invoke is not that of coming to an agreement on a given occasion (for example, agreeing to a contract), but that of being in agreement throughout (like being in harmony); human beings who agree in the language they use are mutually voiced with respect to it, mutually attuned from top to bottom. This idea of attunement is further specified in the way criteria register the distinctions that matter to their users; if (with Cavell) we think of criteria as in this respect telling what counts or matters to human beings, the multiple connections with Heidegger's understanding of moods should be clear. As we have seen, for Heidegger, moods manifest the human capacity to be affected by the world (to find that we are attuned to it and it to us), they have a social as well as an individual aspect, and they are ultimately grounded in the discourse-based human capacity to disclose or reveal reality. Since criteria make manifest a culture's sense of what matters in the world as well as making knowledge of that world possible, Wittgenstein's sense of our mutual attunement in grammar precisely parallels Heidegger's invocation of our mutual attunement in discourse.

Perhaps most fundamentally, however, both philosophers draw a critical lesson for philosophical method that is itself attuned to a further aspect of moods—their passivity or givenness. Both regard the structures of grammar or discourse as the proper domain of philosophical analysis or description, as the last word in understanding the nature of worldly things and the nature of the being who is alone capable of understanding worldly things; as Wittgenstein puts it, what must be accepted—the given—is the form of human life with language, the ramifying grid of mutual attunements that govern our access to the world. The method of treating philosophical confusions that he advocates is therefore one of recalling us to our criteria, of bringing us to accept them as the fundamental condition of our existence—as a structure that we always already occupy and that we cannot simply choose to reject (on pain of unintelligibility). A final comparison with Kant's philosophical vision may help here. For Kant, experience is a function of combining concepts and intuitions, where concepts are based on the spontaneity of thought, and sensible intuitions on the receptivity of impressions. Thinking is therefore understood as a matter of synthesizing impressions, of the understanding taking up the given manifold of experience and imposing an organization upon it; the intellectual hemisphere is active and the intuitive hemisphere passive. In short, for Kant, there is no intellectual intuition. For Wittgenstein and Heidegger, by contrast, true thinking is passive or receptive; just as one can only overcome scepticism by recognizing that the world is not to be known or grasped in cognition but accepted or acknowledged as the condition for the possibility of knowledge claims, so more generally one can make philosophical progress only by recalling and accepting criteria or the structures of discourse. In short, there is only intellectual intuition; and this receptivity of genuine thinking reflects the fact that human beings are creatures who lead their lives in a world which matters to them, a world which is at once evanescent and permanent, and revealed as such by the mutual attunement of moods and world.

Feeling and Cognition

BARRIE FALK

There is a common view that as well as being conscious of the world in virtue of having thoughts about it, forming representations of its various states and processes, we are also conscious of it in virtue of feeling it. What I have in mind is not the fact that we have feelings *about* the world—indignation at this, pleasure at that—but that we sensorily feel its colours, sounds, textures and so on. And this feeling form of consciousness, it's often thought, constitutes a peculiarly intimate and intense focus upon things. The feel of the first drops of rain on one's face and the sounds of the gull's cry will quickly be recognized for what they are; and the fact that events of this sort are occurring will thereafter hold one's attention just insofar as they are relevant to some current business. But what can also happen is that such experiences cut through any current concerns and cause a state in which, for a time, one does nothing *except* feel the soft coolness of the rain and the particular quality of the bird's cry. We can become absorbed, it seems, in the mere presence of these phenomena and this is an experience to which we attach great value.

But common as these thoughts are, they would be regarded by most contemporary philosophers as exhibiting serious confusions about the nature of sensing, knowledge and consciousness. I agree that they do and I will say something about this. I will argue however that, despite the confusions, there are significant and important truths to be found along these lines.

I

A style of philosophy that endorsed and relied heavily on the thought that feeling is a mode of cognition independent of representing was classical empiricism in its various forms. The picture, roughly delineated, was as follows. The world acts on the sense organs and, to use Hume's vocabulary, produces 'impressions'. These constitute our sensory, feeling knowledge of the world. Copies of the impressions, called 'ideas', will then form in the mind and persist there in various structures, independently of the current perceptible scene. For Hume, it was evidently just a matter of common sense and not something requiring further elucidation to say that impressions are ways of feeling the world, not thinking of it, for he excuses himself from giving an account of the difference between impressions and ideas on the ground that 'everyone will readily perceive the difference betwixt feeling and thinking'.[1] Thinking, he takes it, is a matter of *operating* on the impressions. One classifies them or their ideas in various ways, associates one with another according to various principles and thus, on the basis of some current impression, comes to form beliefs about how things are beyond the immediately perceptible scene. Thus construed, thinking constitutes an obviously crucial but none the less mediated form of contact with the world. One can think, of some unperceived thing, that it's blue or smooth, but such thoughts are only possible because one has previously had direct contact with blueness and smoothness in the form of impressions. Having these impressions constitutes one's real grip on what blueness and smoothness *are*.

The most pervasive modern criticism of this picture concerns its account of the relation between the impression and the higher level operations of classification and inference. Under the influence of Wittgenstein, most philosophers have rejected the idea that these classificatory activities can be guided by and are subordinate to an awareness of one's sensory states which is antecedent to the higher level activity. I will say something about this later. What concerns me immediately however is the relation between the impression and the world. Recall that, on the classical picture, impressions are not just states of which we are conscious. They are states of consciousness of the world, direct registerings of bits of the current perceptible environment. That is to say, bits of the current environment are the *contents* of the impression states, what they are *about*. But the impressions do not acquire their content in the way that thoughts do, by being rule-governed deployments and arrangements of the signs of which they are composed. That would destroy their status as *direct* registerings of the world. They have their content rather just in virtue of being *caused* by the states of affairs that constitute the content.

And this is just the trouble. How can state x, thought of as something like a mere reflection of state y, have state y as its *conscious* content? There's no problem about x containing the 'information' that y in the modern sense, of its being an indication of y's presence. And for this reason the occurrence of x might very well cause the creature in which it occurs to behave in a way that is appropriate to the presence of y, or, in a thinking creature, cause the thought that y. But unless we simply help ourselves to the idea that there is a feeling medium which, without further explanation,

[1] Hume, *Treatise of Human Nature*, Book 1, Part 1, Sect. 1.

can be taken as a consciousness of what affects it, the purely causal relation between feeling and the object that is felt which the classical theory needs is precisely inadequate to produce a state with conscious content.

It is worth noting that the difficulty in reconciling the requirements of a feeling cognition's being a feeling and its being a cognition occurs also in the case of emotional feelings. These are caused, not, like sensory feeling, by the direct impact of the world upon the sense organs, but by knowledge-informed perception of the world and by further thoughts and beliefs about it. For this reason, a creature's emotionally aroused state essentially involves awareness of the world. The emotion, in current jargon, has an 'object'. But this intentional, content-bearing nature of the state seems wholly accountable for in terms of its thought component, which could of course occur in a non-emotional structure. How the feelings of bodily arousal and behavioural dispositions which constitute the emotional component can do anything other than *accompany* the thought component is quite opaque. Certainly the mere talk of 'objects' will not explain it.

II

It might seem then that my opening question, whether feeling can itself be a mode of cognition, has been answered in the negative. How we feel the world and how we feel about it is of course of great importance to us—it is perhaps even a tautology to say so. But feeling is always something that confronts cognition, as an object for it, and has no cognizing contribution of its own to make. The field is thus left open for the ideal of a completed objective description of the world, which will say everything that is true of it. Such a description will of course need to include a set of statements about how, as a matter of fact, creatures like us happen to feel the world and why. But the feelings themselves will not be understood as having, as it were, any independent cognitive bite.

However, things are not so simple. It may be true that feeling cannot provide a cognitive contact with the world that is independent of representing it; but it also seems to be the case that representation cannot do its job *without* the cooperation of feeling. To see what I have in mind, let us return to the classical empiricist picture and, in particular, to its account of the relation between the impression and the higher level cognitive activities of classification, inference and so on. The empiricist's idea is that the impression constitutes the causal interface between world and mind: on the one hand, it is a direct, feeling consciousness of the world; on the other hand, it is accessible to higher level thinking. Now I have argued that it cannot be a direct contact with the world and yet retain its status as a content-bearing, conscious state. But if, acknowledging this, we therefore abandon the idea that the impression has content and think of it as the immediate, *non*-content-bearing impact of the world upon us, it ceases to be accessible to higher level thought. For how can thought make contact with what is not thought? It is only if I think of my current sensory state as a perceiving *of* red or smoothness that I can take it as a ground for making appropriate comparisons and inferences to how things are in the rest of the world. And what sort of contact can thought have with things *except* that which consists in lodging them appropriately within the general body of the thinker's beliefs about the world? To suppose that thought can be anchored in a prelinguistic or preconceptual grasp of the impression is to lapse once more into the idea of a medium—this time a thought one—which is automatically conscious of what affects it.

It seems then that the impression must either fail to be a consciousness of the world or it must fail to be accessible to thought. In either case, the empiricist account of the relation between mind and the world fails.

But this is not just a problem for classical empiricism. The moves I've spoken of were an attempt to find, within experience, the subject matter of our thinking, the world our thinking is *about*. And this seems to be a requirement for any account of our cognitive nature which, with Kant, takes thinking to be the activity of relating components of our experience. We need some account of *what* is related. In his recent, influential book, *Mind and World*, John McDowell insists that, if knowledge is just a matter of thinking or conceptualization, 'the world goes missing'—what we call knowledge will spin 'frictionlessly' in the void.[2] McDowell himself, insisting as he does that the empiricist notion of what is felt—what he calls 'the given'—is a delusion, argues for there being a level of experience constituted by what he calls 'passive conceptualization'. Experiences of colours, sounds etc. must be thinkings, since they are capturable by thought; their passivity as thinkings however allows them to figure as that which is other than our own activity. I don't find this metaphor illuminating. I don't see that we have any grip on the notion of experiencing what is passively conceptualized which is independent of the notion of what is *presented* to us in experience. And this is just the notion that we need to make sense of.

[2] J. McDowell, *Mind and World* (London: Harvard University Press, 1994)

III

I want to suggest a different approach. Classical empiricists and all who have focused on this issue have concentrated on the secondary properties—colours, sounds, etc.—as the locus of our felt contact with the world. But these are not the only plausible or, I think, the most basic candidates for that role.

Consider a well-known example (slightly adapted) from Wittgenstein.[3] Look at a row of meaningless marks and next to it that row reversed. And now compare this with a meaningful array—say a cursive inscription of the word 'pleasure'—and its reverse. Each figure will differ perceptually from its reverse in an analogous way but, Wittgenstein argues, in the case of 'pleasure' there is a further and different difference. Here, the first inscription will look neat, tidy; its reverse will appear untidy, scrappy. What sort of property is this untidiness?

One feature of the situation, clearly relevant to the fact that the property occurs in the one pair of cases and not the other, is that the cursive inscription 'pleasure' is composed of parts that are familiar to us and which we have learned to operate with in various ways. Seeing a mark we recognize as the letter p arouses expectations about what can and cannot follow. The letter l, which our scrutiny next encounters, conforms to these expectations and the two together establish further ones, and so on. One's glance thus proceeds smoothly across the array—'smoothly' but, as Wittgenstein beautifully puts it, without 'skidding'. In contrast, the reversed inscription, adjacent to and obscurely like the ordinary array, resists our scrutinizing habits. And of course none of this is the case with the pair of arbitrary sets of marks.

But if it's right to suppose that the properties of tidiness and untidiness make their appearance because of this relation to the perceiver's scrutinizing habits, it's clear that they are not perceptible properties in any strict sense. The perceiver's skills and memory could be manipulated in such a way as to cause the tidiness to go, without changing what is presented to the eye. On the other hand, they are not non-perceptible properties, attributed to the objects in a non-perceptual context. The perceiver could have thoughts about the fact that the inscriptions conform to or frustrate his expectations and, on this basis, ascribe them the property of doing so. But the phenomenon we are concerned with is the fact that the object *looks* tidy.

[3] L. Wittgenstein, *Philosophical Investigations*, trans. G. E. M. Anscombe, (Oxford: Blackwell, 1958), Part II, § xi. p. 198.

IV

To make sense of this, we need to adduce two further phenomena. Notice first that the scrutinizing response to the various arrays causes them to acquire a further set of properties, which have to do, roughly speaking, with the relation of their parts. I'll give a couple of examples. The inscription 'pleasure', perceived as a set of English letters, is a figure that clearly *advances* from left to right. This is not because the eye passes over it in that direction— obviously that could be and is likely to be what happens when one looks at the other arrays. It is because the eye-movement is *demanded* by the figure and thus, so to speak, adheres to it. This is brought about by a two-stage process. The first mark is recognized as a p, which we are familiar with as characteristically combining with what follows to the right. And so on. The whole array thus *makes sense* when scanned in this way and it is, I claim, *as* what makes sense that it demands the left–right scrutinizing move- ment—as what *has* made sense and as what continues to suggest that sense. The point emerges especially clearly in the way we talk about paintings. The path in the foreground, we say, leads the eye to the middle distance—but it only does so because it is already recognized as depicting a path and not some vertical structure standing parallel to the picture plane.

Here then is one of the sources of that difference between the inscription 'pleasure' and its reverse which is additional to the dif- ference between the arbitrary sequence and its reverse. In the first pair, there is a clear sense contrasted with a resistance to our sense-making; in the second, there is no sense to be made in either case.

A second example of the organizational properties that scrutiny induces is this. Familiarity with English letters gives our recogni- tional grasp of them a fair degree of flexibility, allowing for differ- ent writing styles and minor imperfections of production. A mildly deviant instance of some letter, with, say, lots of gaps in it, will therefore still be recognized as a clear unit. So, when we see a char- acteristic 'pleasure' inscription, the regular spacing of what are already taken as units will be a salient feature of the experience. (Think of how sensitive we are to failures of this on the printed page.) In contrast, the regularity will be only tentatively present in the 'pleasure' reverse case, since, although the units are in fact reg- ularly spaced, they will not stand out so clearly as the obvious units in terms of which the figure has to be organized. And in the other pair, regularity will be absent in both original and reverse. Here, the scanning queries about which gaps mark a unit's boundaries and which are mere imperfections of production will receive an unstable answer in both cases.

These examples will suffice, I think. The phenomenon we're dealing with, generally understood, is what Wittgenstein calls the 'visual impression'.[4] And the point I'm making is that although having a particular visual impression relies on one's having deployed conceptual capacities, the impression is what *results* from this, and doesn't just consist of the deployment itself. What happens is that the high-level responses a visual object stimulates can in some cases adhere to the object and thus determine its look.

I turn now to the second phenomenon we must adduce to explain such properties as tidiness, which is that the responses the various arrays elicit have certain affective properties. The objects we're presented with can lend themselves easily or only with difficulty to our letter-deciphering skills, or they can frustrate them altogether. They can contain more or less redundant material, making the comprehending scrutiny more or less hesitant or decisive. In some cases—the well-known ambiguous figures—different and incompatible decipherings are possible and perceivers find that their perceptual grip on the object is unstable and shifting. The claim is not, notice, that the mode of interaction between the object and one's processing or conceptual response to it is, in general, present to one as a feeling state. There must be many such interactive states, appropriately determining a creature's behaviour, that are below the level of conscious access. And even when they're not in principle below the level of consciousness, they don't have to be felt. Wittgenstein points out that although we may be struck on occasion by the familiarity or the strangeness of some scene—a phenomenon related to, but not the same, as the one I'm discussing—we are not in general struck by the inconspicuousness of inconspicuous things.[5] The point is just that we *can* be 'struck' by some such scenes; and given that we can, the general structure of our perceptual relation to things must be understood in such a way as to provide conceptual space for that possibility.

V

Bearing these two points in mind—the adherence of one's scrutinizing response to the object and the possibility of affective awareness of that response—let me now return to my main business of understanding such properties as neatness and untidiness.

[4] See Wittgenstein, *Philosophical Investigations*, Part 2, § xi, passim.
[5] *Philosophical Investigations*, p. 595.

217

I insisted earlier on the fact that feeling states have no content other than that of the representational state they accompany. And there seems to be no reason to alter that judgment in the face of those feelings I have just adduced. The feelings of being unimpeded in one's activity, of frustration or instability are, like all feelings, modes of awareness of oneself, whose wider causal context one may or may not know of. But suppose we try to teach someone the conditions of application for the term 'untidy', where this is to be used as the name of a visual quality. We must choose as teaching paradigms those objects which we are confident will *affect* the learner in a particular way. They must be those with indistinct visual units, having parts that are not assimilable into the most natural overall pattern or which set up countervailing patterning tendencies. Learning to apply this concept, therefore, makes essential use of a feeling the object induces. Now there is nothing especially remarkable about this. Presumably one learns the concept of the fearsome, say, by noting the connection between certain objects and the feelings they induce. But the case of the untidy is different. We learn it not by observing and registering a pairing of object and feeling, but wholly by looking at the object—that is, the appearance. And this is because the feeling of untidiness is not separable from the appearance, as trembling and the desire to flee are separable from seeing the tiger. Feeling the untidiness is how *the scrutinizing activity which constitutes the appearance* feels.

This, I claim, is why we say that we feel the untidiness, rather than merely having feelings *about* it and this is the *interesting* truth in the thought that, as Hume put, '[the mind has a] great propensity to spread itself on external objects'.[6] Like all conscious feeling, the consciousness is of a state of oneself. However, the state of oneself consists in the fact that the conceptual processing elicited by the object before one is unstable, contradictory etc. And since this processing, for reasons I have explained, adheres to the object, it carries the feeling with it, out into the world. When we learn to represent an object as having the property of untidiness, we therefore find ourselves simultaneously feeling the represented property. This is not because feeling is a parallel mode of representation; it is because what is represented—the untidy look—is something to which feeling already adheres.

VI

I turn now to some of the implications of this argument. The first is this. At the start of the paper, I set out the problem which follows

[6] *Treatise of Human Nature*, Book 1, Part 3, §XIV.

from the failure of the classical empiricist programme. The empiricists' idea was that the causal interface between perceiver and world is graspable in the form of the sense impression. Anxiety about whether our conceptualizing activity has a world, has what is other than itself, to act on is thus assuaged. But if we reject the sense impression, as we must, the anxiety returns with full force, for we seem to reject with it any way of bringing the causal interface back within the scope of our experience.

My argument, I tentatively claim, offers such a way. The conceptual moves I have described, allowing us to represent the world as neat, untidy, etc., operate *within* and not from *outside* the causal interface. What permits this is the complexity of the case of causal interaction I have adduced. The world acquires certain properties as a result of how we respond to its initial effects. If, therefore, we learn to represent the world as having the properties constituted by the feel of these respondings and, along with this, become aware of feeling the property we represent, we thereby become aware of the world as the recipient of our representing activity, accepting it, accepting it only tentatively or rejecting it. It is not a matter of *representing* it as being the recipient—that would be just another thought about the world. Rather, when a visual impression of an object decisively forms, or oscillates or can be kept in place only by willed inattention to other features of the thing, we feel the operation of our representing capacities on material that is outside it.

VII

I turn now to a second area where, I think, my argument has useful application. This concerns the claim, mentioned at the start of the paper, that feeling the world, as opposed to representing it, provides a peculiarly direct contact with it, a contact, furthermore, where our true understanding of its perceptible properties is located. The idea is that when, as I put it, some perception cuts through my current business, I return to a level of awareness that is undiluted by the classificatory activity and long term interests that that business involves. This idea is not rescuable. It depends, for one thing, on the assumption, criticized above, that there is a feeling medium, automatically conscious of what affects it. It also, relatedly, assumes that understanding the nature of some object is achievable by bare contemplation. And one must ask how knowledge of a thing can be anything other than relating it to others in a systematic way, lodging it within one's overall understanding. What *is* there for bare contemplation to discover?

But against all this, we need to set the fact that there *do* exist states in which one's attention is held by the pure appearance of things. No thinking—assigning the object to its kind, working out the implications of its presence—is going on, and yet the mind on such occasions is certainly not empty. We need some understanding of this state—a way of understanding our relation to the world which will provide a place for this possibility.

I offer the following suggestion. First, I need to make the following point. I have presented my main argument in terms of one rather narrow example, and a full justification of the implications I draw from it requires a richer account of the general phenomenon the example illustrates. One generalizing route one could take would be to recognize that the felt properties of things are not confined to those produced by the responses they elicit from our conceptualizing powers. There is, for instance, our interaction with things with respect to the spatial orientation we perceive them to have and the range of possible movements we attribute to them on this basis. This, I have argued elsewhere,[7] leads to our perceiving such (felt) properties as being squat, top-heavy, poised. And obviously the point generalizes to other sense modalities. Our patterning response to auditory phenomena is especially apparent—think of the structuredness of musical experience. I will not however go into these matters here. What follows is based on the assumption that this generalization is possible.

Suppose then that I walk alone into a wood. It gets quieter and more dense; I come suddenly to a small clearing and there, behind a tangle of undergrowth, on a slope facing the sun, I find a cluster of primroses. This can be an agreeable experience and the flowers and the whole setting hold my attention. Many things are going on here. What I want to consider in particular is the nature of this attention. On the one hand, I don't blankly stare. I will think perhaps about the seclusion of the place the primroses have found to grow in and my mind move to Kantian thoughts about the autonomy of natural beauty—an orderedness which is *for* nothing, which exists independently of my or anyone else's purposes, and so on. But on the other hand, these are just thoughts; and it's not clear how having them can be, as it seems to be, a *part* of the contemplation of the scene, rather than something that brings it to an end.

The argument I've presented can be applied to this case. I have, we can assume, the normal awareness of what I'm doing and

---

[7] See my 'Consciousness, Cognition and the Phenomenal' in, *Supplementary Proceedings of the Aristotelian Society*, Vol. LXVII (1993) pp. 55–73..

where I am. But notice that that there will also be a strong feeling component. There will be the time I've been walking (the awareness of duration—a major and too little discussed component of our affective lives), the increasing quietness and shade, the sudden brightness of the flowers and the sunlight. There will also be a sense of the contingency of my encountering the flowers, given, again, not just the awareness, but the feeling, of nothing having determined the particular path I followed through the wood. This is not the feel of a highly specific skill-based response to the presented material, as in my earlier discussion; it is the feel of a prolonged period of complex perceptual and bodily interaction with one's surroundings. But even so, the feel, as in the earlier case, is constitutive of properties I ascribe to what I see. I mentioned the secludedness of the flowers. What is that if not the property of their being in a place far from my normal activity, which I have stumbled upon by chance and could so easily have missed—the latter being, remember, properties of the walk which I feel and don't merely know of? But seclusion is only one aspect of what one finds. The contingency of the encounter with the flowers, their brightness and structuredness, which makes them so much self-standing units in an otherwise amorphous scene, are constitutive of their presenting themselves as, for instance, wholly self-sustaining and other than the observer.

These words are imprecise. But that, I think, is how it has to be, and is something that reflects an important difference between this sort of case and the earlier one. There, I argued, the complex relation one has to familiar signs has been channelled into conceptual skills—the ability to use the words 'neat', 'scrappy' and so on. The result, in accordance with the usual effect of engaging in a conceptualizing response to the world, is that one is distanced from this relationship. When an instance of it occurs, it will straightforwardly-—without deliberation—elicit the concepts from one who possesses them and put such a person in a position to simply observe the presence of the neat, the scrappy and so on. Now the felt 'otherness' of the flowers is not a look they present; nor is feeling it something clearly located in our conscious lives by a stable concept. It emerges from a complex of fluid relations we have with the world and with sophisticated thoughts about the place in it that our nature bestows on us. Words such as 'otherness' can be no more than gestures in its direction.

The result is that, unlike the neat and the untidy (and the poised and top-heavy), the otherness of the flowers is not something one just occasionally feels *in addition* to noticing the fact that it obtains. The cluster of thoughts and feelings one has—the secrecy of the place, awareness of one's solitude, the clarity of the flowers' form and colour—is the only vehicle there is for being conscious of it. That is why one contemplates the scene, why 'staring' here has a point: it is only by consciously gathering all the experiences it offers and holding them together that one can keep a grip on its property of otherness. And it is at least part of the reason why such an experience has, as I put it earlier, a peculiar intimacy and intensity. Awareness of the flowers' otherness is not constituted by its eliciting a concept, whose effect is then to distance the reflective consciousness from the scene, making it *de trop*, in Sartre's sense. Since the awareness is constituted purely by feeling, the experience is one in which one *feels* one's cognitive powers successfully engaging with the world.

Believing in order to Understand

CYRIL BARRETT

The theme of this season of lectures is hermeneutics, *Verstehen* and humane understanding. It is my contention in this paper that long before Droysen or Dilthey, Windelband or Rickert came up with the notion of cultural science (*Geisteswissenschafte*), it had been flourishing in the scholastic tradition of theology and philosophy of religion, though I am not sure that its practitioners would thank me for saying so.

The Christian Church was forced into philosophy from an early date in face of criticism of its doctrines. A solid reasoned defence was put up by Tertullian, Clement of Alexandria, Origen, Basil, Gregory of Nazianzus, Gregory of Nyssa, and, above all, by Augustine. At first the Fathers of the Church were mainly on the defensive, attempting to show that, even if the faith is not a product of reason, it is not contrary to reason. From this they moved to the more ambitious project of making faith intelligible as far that is possible in view of the fact that it cannot be arrived at by reason alone but is revealed through a prophet. The leading proponents of this view were Saints Augustine, Anselm and Thomas Aquinas.

Initially, at least, they were hermeneutic. They had no intention of attempting to explain or prove (*erklären*). Their aim was to make as intelligible *as possible* the mysteries of faith (*Verstehen*). Later they thought, in a curious way, they could prove the validity of Christian doctrine in a deductive and scientific manner, an absurdity that I shall not consider.

There were two principles upon which they relied. The first was that you must believe in order to understand the faith. The second was that, having believed, you can and should try to understand— you believe in order to understand.

The origin of this notion is curious. It crops up in several places in Augustine's writings: in *De Trinitate* (5.2.2), *De Doctrina Christiana* (2.12.17) and *De Libro Arbitrio* (2.3.7). It is based on an Old Latin translation of Isaiah 7:9. Later translations have: 'Unless you believe, you will not remain permanently (continue be fully established)'.[1] But it suited Augustine to use the old translation, and his most refined expression of it was:

[1] The Hebrew is beyond me but the Greek is 'éan piseús éte oúde suñéte' (if you do not believe you will not understand). This is the Septuagint, what Augustine would have read in North Africa. But

Cyril Barrett

'Understand, so that you may believe what I say; believe, that you may understand the word of God' (*Intellige, ut credas verbum meum; crede, ut intellegas verbum Dei*) (Sermo 43.7.9, Pl. 38, 258). Anselm puts it like this in the first chapter of the *Proslogion*, his address to his monks (as distinct from his *Monologion*, his personal reflections), he says:

> O Lord ... I yearn to understand some measure of your truth, which my heart believes and loves. For I do not seek to understand in order to believe but I believe in order to understand. For I believe even this: that I shall not understand unless I believe.[2]

That is all very well, and sounds well, but what does it mean? How can you believe what you do not understand? Obviously one cannot either believe or disbelieve without understanding the words, especially the key words in which some idea is couched. You can't either believe in or not believe in apocatastasis, if you do not know what the word means. This is what Augustine meant when he exhorted his listeners to understand what he is saying in order to believe him. But that is not enough. Understanding the words and sentences, though necessary, is not sufficient to induce belief. As Wittgenstein says:

> In one sense, I understand all he says—the English words 'God', 'separated', etc. I understand. I could say: 'I don't believe in this', and this would be true, meaning I haven't got these thoughts or anything that hangs together with them.[3]

This last phrase 'anything that hangs together with them' is rather important and gives a clue as to how one can believe something without understanding anything more than the meaning of the words in which it is expressed.

John Henry Cardinal Newman (the mysterious H. Newman referred to at the beginning of Wittgenstein's *On Certainty*) in his *Grammar of Assent* points to the vastness of our beliefs that are

[2] *Proslogion*, ed. and tr. J. Hopkins and H. Richardson (London, 1974), in *Anselm of Canterbury*, vol. 1, p. 93.
[3] *Lectures and Conversations on Aesthetics, Psychology and Religious Belief*, ed. D. C. Barrett (Oxford, 1966), p. 35 (hereafter *LC*).

Jerome's Vulgate has: 'Si nor credideritis non permanebitis' which has been translated in the King James version as 'If you will not believe, surely you shall not be established' (whatever that means). The New Revised Standard version has 'If you do not stand firm in faith, you shall not stand at all.' This has the virtue of neatness. But for the purpose of this paper all this is idle erudition.

224

based on nothing more than the understanding of the words in which they are expressed. His favourite example was that the belief that Great Britain is an island (strictly speaking, a group of islands) was held in 1870, before superterrestrial photography, without any convincing evidence that this was so.[4] There were maps, but anyone can draw a fraudulent map; and many did with no malicious intent. More convincingly, we can cite our belief that if we press a switch, we will get light or heat; if we turn a key, a motor will start; if we dial a number a bell of sorts will ring in someone's house and we can speak to them: if we press a button we can watch a football match; and—for me the most miraculous of all—if I shove a sheet of typescript into a machine and dial a number someone in Norway or Finland gets a replica of it. We believe all this but few of us understand how it happens.

This belief without understanding is rational for two reasons which, perhaps, merge into one. They are (1) the authority of someone you trust, be it a parent, relative, friend or prophet; and (2) experience.

If what you are told turns out to be nearly always true, even though you do not know why, do not understand, that is a good reason to believe it is true. The light goes on; the iron ring heats up; the motor starts; the phone is answered; the match appears on the screen; the fax goes through. All these beliefs are based on the authority of someone we can trust, even though they may not understand any more than we do what it is they are telling us. Their testimony is based on experience, not on understanding, just as ours is. As Wittgenstein put it in *On Certainty*:

> I am told, for example, that someone climbed this mountain many years ago. Do I always enquire into the reliability of the teller of this story, and whether the mountain did exist years ago? A child learns there are reliable and unreliable informants much later than it learns facts which are told it. It doesn't learn *at all* that that mountain has existed for a long time: that is, the question whether it is so does not arise at all. It swallows this consequence down, so to speak, together with *what* it learns.[5]

And how can things be otherwise? How could a child cope with the world and living in it if it had to wait until it understood all it was told? And to live it has to be told a lot.

As Wittgenstein says the child learns to discriminate between reliable and unreliable informants, those who give it false information either deliberately, out of malice or jokingly, or out of

[4] *An Essay in Aid of a Grammar of Assent* (London, 1930), pp. 188–209.
[5] *On Certainty*, (Oxford, 1979), §143, p. 21 (hereafter *OC*).

225

ignorance. This comes about because a child learns a whole network of facts some of which do not square with others or with experience.

To quote Wittgenstein again:

> When we first begin to *believe* anything, what we believe is not a single proposition, but a whole system of propositions. (Light dawns bit by bit over the whole.) (*OC*, §141, p. 21)

I would differ from Wittgenstein here on the point of calling it a 'system' (*System*) of propositions. A system is, or, at least, aims to be coherent, but there need be no coherence in what a child learns. Its discrimination consists in sorting out the contradictions and inconsistencies. That is why I prefer to speak of a 'network' of beliefs—a term not alien to Wittgenstein's thought. But on the main point we are in agreement. Belief begins with an accumulation of propositions, not single propositions; and light dawns bit by bit. This dawning of light may involve understanding that one proposition is not compatible with another. However, the main point is that *belief proceeds understanding*.

Though that is a point, it does not advance us much further where Augustine and Anselm are concerned. Their concern is not with believing that lights will go on, rings heat, phones are answered or faxes go through, but with mysteries. Electricity and telecommunication are to some extent, intelligible to experts, but mysteries are, by definition, not comprehensible to humans, at least not in this life. So what is there to understand if one believes?

Neither Augustine nor Anselm discuss this in their works, though the answer is implicit in what they wrote. What we can understand is not the mystery but its implications, particularly its implications for our way of living. Let's take a few examples.

Let us start with Anselm's so-called ontological arguments for the existence of God. What we can learn from them—whatever Anselm thought we could learn—is that, if God is the being greater than which none other can be conceived, he must have the following properties: (1) He must have the greatest positive attributes conceivable; (2) He must be a being who cannot not exist, whose non-existence is inconceivable, or, in philosophical jargon, he must be a necessary being; (3) he must be unchanging, that is, eternal, atemporal, the same for ever. Whether this proves, as Anselm thought, that he must exist is another matter, which does not concern us here. The point I want to make here is that, though we do not learn to understand who or what God is—far from it— we learn something about what it is to believe in a monotheistic God.

A more practical understanding of a mystery would be to understand the consequences of a belief that all human beings were created in God's image and likeness. A poor image and likeness, perhaps, but sufficient to make it intolerable to discriminate between people on the basis of sex, wealth, class, education, social status, to say nothing of colour and race. They are all 'God's children'—Sentimental,? I don't know. At any rate, healthy, sentiment.

These examples are common to the three great Western religions: Judaism, Christianity and Islam. Within these faiths there is room for another kind of understanding and misunderstanding, otherwise known as heresy, depending on your point of view. This is a matter of interpretation of the sacred texts. I am fairly certain that this is not what Augustine and Anselm had in mind but it is relevant to the notion of understanding beliefs. I shall deal with it briefly.

Within the three great faiths there are numerous, one might say, multitudinous, interpretations of the sacred books. In Christianity alone one has only to name three major doctrines—the Trinity, the Divinity of Jesus Christ and the Eucharist. On the Trinity, on the one hand, we have the Councils of Nicea and Constantinople I, on the other, the Arians, Sabellians and Macedoninans. On the divinity of Christ, we have the Councils of Nicea, Constantinople I, on the other the Arians, Sabellians and Macedonians. On the divinity of Christ, we have the Councils of Nicea, Constantinople I, Ephesus and Chalcedon, on the one hand, and the Monophysites, Monothelists, Nestorians and many others, on the other. On the Eucharist we have Zwingli's belief that it is only a symbolic ritual and there was no change in the substance of bread and wine, Luther's Consubstantiation, Calvin's Virtualism, and the Fourth Lateran Council's definition of Transubstantiation. Since the Second Vatican Council Roman Catholic theologians have come up with Transignification and Transfinalization.

This, as I have said, is not what Augustine and Anselm meant by believing in order to understand, and, in most cases, quite the opposite. I think that for that reason it should be pursued a little further, to explain the correct by the deviant. In each case the Councils stood for mystery and the condemned doctrines were attempts to make the doctrines intelligible. This is perhaps best demonstrated in relation to the doctrine of the Trinity which most non-believers consider more outrageous than the doctrines of the Incarnation, Resurrection or Transubstantiation.

Many people balk at the notion of a Triune God, three persons sharing one nature. One must admit that to the human mind in its present state it is incomprehensible, though Graham Greene once

227

said that he was prepared to believe in as many persons as you want: why stop at three? Well, obviously, the theologians have an answer to that. At least two Christian denominations have nothing to do with the doctrine of a Triune God on the grounds of its unintelligibility. One is the very rationalist faith which some people might not regard as Christian at all, Deisim, favoured by Herbert of Cherbury, Wollaston, Toland and Voltaire. It treats Christianity as a natural, not a revealed, religion. Unitarianism, on the other hand, accepts Christian doctrine purged of the supernatural and the mystery. A good example of it is Tolstoy's The *Gospel in Brief* which excludes all references to the Trinity, miracles, the Transfiguration and the Resurrection.[6] It ends with the death of Jesus. But unitarianism accepts the moral stature of Jesus and his teaching, not solely on rational grounds, but on his testimony and authority. Though the Councils of the Church would have severely disapproved of Unitarianism, they have this in common: their beliefs are not wholly based on reason, but also on witness and authority. They of course differ on intelligibility for those Christian denominations that include mystery and the supernatural among their beliefs. This brings us back to question of how mysteries can be understood if they are, by definition, beyond comprehension.

Here it might be appropriate to point out that not all theologians have shared the views of Augustine and Anselm on the matter of understanding the Christian faith. On the contrary, because of the incomprehensibility of its mysteries and the supernatural nature of the beliefs that the Christian faith commends—and the same might be said of all great religious faiths they are to be believed. The most notorious expression of this view is Tertullian's: 'It is certain because it is impossible' (*Certum quia impossibile est*) (*De Carne Christi* 5); sometimes rendered as 'It is certain because it is absurd.' There are echoes here of St Paul in the first three chapters of I Corinthians where he compares the wisdom of men with the foolishness of God. Unlike most other Fathers of the Church who tried to show that their faith did not contradict reason, Tertullian welcomed the contradiction of a God who could die and a Man who could rise from the dead. I think Kierkegaard would have approved. But it is not within the scope of this paper to discuss this issue, only to draw attention to it, and so to speak, circumscribe the position of Augustine and Anselm between the extremes of Deism and Unitarianism, on the one hand, and Tertullian, on the other.

[6] Count Lev Nikolayevich Tolstoy *The Gospel in Brief* (New York, 1896).

To return to the question of believing in order to understand I should first suggest something that might be a helpful, if not ambitious, approach. It is often said that, unless you embrace a set of beliefs and commit yourself to them, you can never understand them properly. There is a trivial sense in which this is true, the sense in which one can never properly understand what it is to be a woman or a man, a pygmy or an Africaner, a slum dweller or an aristocrat unless you are or have been one. In a less trivial sense, you cannot understand what it is to be married or a monk, a Marxist, extreme nationalist or a fundamentalist, of whatever persuasion, unless you have been one. There are indefinitely more examples. Newman in his *Grammar of Assent* expresses this admirably in his distinction between notional and real assent in terms of commitment. If you give a notional assent you commit yourself to nothing more than the understanding of concepts and propositions (notions).[7] Thus a Jewish art historian might have a better understanding of Catholic iconography and the theology that lies behind it—e.g. the doctrines of the Immaculate Conception and Assumption—than most Catholics, but this does not commit him to behaving as a Catholic. Likewise, a Jesuit might have such a knowledge and understanding of Marxism that he is called on—or was—to settle differences of interpretation in the Academy of Science in Moscow. But his understanding is totally uncommitted.

Real assent, on the contrary, commits the assentor to accepting the reality or ideology to which he assents, whether it be a Catholicism, Marxism, National Socialism, fundamentalism, anarchism, extreme nationalism, agnosticism or atheism. But the commitments need not be as extreme as that. One can give a real, as opposed to a notional, assent to the propositions as unsensational as equality before the law; a fair wage for a fair day's work; equal opportunities of work for both sexes, every race, religion and political persuasion; the need for care of the hungry, homeless, disabled, the aged and the mentally ill. But you can also have just a notional assent—agree with the idea without any commitment to do a blind bit about it.

When it comes to belief in religious mysteries a real assent is manifest in one's outlook and behaviour, in the part which the mystery plays in one's life.

That part may be, as I say, no more than an outlook on the world and on life. Someone who sees the world and its inhabitants as God's creation will view it differently from someone who

---

[7] *Grammar of Assent*, pp. 36–97.

regards it as a phenomenon of chance. But it is usually the effect on behaviour that makes the difference between notional and real assent. There is a remarkable story in the life of the seventeenth-century missionary in Cartagena, Columbia, who met and cared for slaves arriving from Africa. On one occasion he cried out to a woman helper who ran away at the sight and stench of a slave just arrived off a ship: 'Martha! Martha! Come back. She has been redeemed by the blood of Our Lord Jesus Christ.' If you consider that a bit extreme perhaps a less dramatic and more philosophically correct example would be Wittgenstein's example of a person who believes in the Day of Judgment:

> Suppose somebody made this guidance for life: believing in the Last Judgment. Whenever he does anything, this is before his mind ... It will show, not by reasoning or by appeal to ordinary grounds for belief, but rather by in regulating for all his life. (*LC*, pp. 53–4)

Here is surely understanding based on belief—regulating all your life on a belief in a mystery, the Last Judgment. Someone who does not regulate his life by a belief that he will be judged in an afterlife by what he does in this and that he has to forgo certain pleasures, does not fully understand what this belief entails.

That is all very well and true, but I still don't think it measures up to what Augustine and Anselm meant by believing in order to understand. It takes 'understanding' in the sense of experience. Someone who has never galloped a horse, skied down a steep slope, flown in a balloon or made love does not really understand these experiences, though their imaginative and descriptive experiences may surpass reality. Even though commitment is tougher and more real than either notional or imaginative understanding, it does not necessarily involve what can be truly called understanding. So we must try again.

Once more I turn to Newman. This time it is to his notion of the development of doctrine. One of Newman's reasons for leaving the Anglican Church for Rome was his discovery that the so-called accretions to Christian doctrine by Rome were developments of doctrine and not accretions at all. Moreover, many if not most of these so-called accretions had been accepted by the Anglican Church itself. It is traditionally held that Christian doctrine, as revealed by Christ and recorded by the Apostles and St Paul, was fixed in the first century AD and cannot be changed or develop. Of course, doctrines were defined by Councils of the Church, but this, in spite of accusation of accretion, does not constitute the addition of new doctrine. It is designed to preserve the purity of doctrine which it is the duty of the Church to do,

This is known as the repository of the faith as preached by the Apostles. How then can doctrine develop? This is possible by gradual growing awareness of its implications.

As Newman says:

> from the nature of the human mind, time is necessary for the full comprehension and perfection of great ideas; and that the highest and most wonderful truths, though communicated to the world once and for all by inspired teachers, could not be comprehended all at once by the recipients, but, as being received and transmitted by minds not inspired and through media which were human, have required only the longer time and deeper thought for their full elucidation.[8]

In other words, the doctrine remains intact, but the understanding of it develops over time. Indeed, according to Newman, the original recipients of the Christian message had comparatively little understanding of it, any more than illiterate believers have today. But they had, and have, what he calls an 'impression' or 'implicit reason' or 'inward idea' of divine truth. These impressions, reasons and ideas pass into explicit form by the activity of our reflective powers. It is not necessary for them to be explicit. As Newman says: 'a peasant may have a true impression, yet be unable to give a true account of "it".' Indeed, he—and the Church in general at some time for that matter—may not be aware even that he has this impression. This is a commonplace in epistemology. No one is, or can be, aware of everything he knows. The development of doctrine is, thus, nothing more than the bringing to consciousness and fuller understanding what one has implicitly believed all along.

Would this account meet with the approval of Augustine and Anselm? I can't see why not. Nor can I see what else would, given that mysteries cannot be *explained*, which rules out one sense of 'understand'. They might balk at the peasants being left off the task of trying to understand. But at least they believe, and, if their reflective powers are not quite up to it, does that matter? This, however, raises the question of the audience Augustine and Anselm are addressing: are they believers or unbelievers, the converted or unconverted? In the case of Anselm we know he was addressing his monks whom we can assume to be believers, but he slightly queered the pitch

[8] *An Essay on the Development of Christian Doctrine* (London. 1909), pp. 3–121.

231

by addressing the fool, who says in his heart there is no God, as well.

Augustine was more polemical. However he went out of his way to elucidate the implications of Christian belief. Whether this was done to attract converts or to defend the faith or simply to elucidate Christian doctrine perhaps even Augustine was not quite sure. Nor does it matter. Like Newman he was a convert and like him he describes in great detail the steps that led to his conversion. But it is not obvious that either aimed at making converts by their *Confessions* and *Apologia*. For the most part, by their sermons and treatises, they set out to expound and make explicit what the faithful believe, but here I must say a word about Aquinas.

Aquinas undoubtedly belonged to the 'believe in order to understand' tradition of Augustine and Anselm. But he may give the impression at times he went further than they into rational, deductive proof of certain beliefs. Perhaps he did. His *Summa Contra Gentiles* was intended as a summary of Christian doctrine for the help of his Dominican brethren going on missions of conversion. In that work, and in his great, unfinished textbook, the *Summa Theologica*, he seems to offer proofs for, say, the existence of God and the indestructability, if not the immortality, of the soul. This is true. But he does not do anything of the kind where Christian mysteries are concerned. He clearly distinguishes between natural and revealed beliefs, between what can be arrived by reason alone and what cannot. Where mysteries are concerned, he differs not one whit from Augustine and Anselm. Indeed, as often as not, he quotes Augustine at the beginning of his answers to theological questions.

To return to error. It is curious, but not altogether surprising, that doctrine develops best, if not exclusively, in face of error, or what comes to be called heresy. The early Church was content to baptize in the name of the Father, Son and Holy Ghost (Matt. 28.19): to believe that Jesus Christ was entirely human and had literally walked on earth; and to practise a ritual known in the Acts of the Apostles (2.42) as the 'breaking of bread', now called the Eucharist. But, by the second century AD, questions about the Trinity arose, soon followed by questions about the humanity of Christ and his divinity in relationship to the other persons of the Trinity. In the eleventh century one Berenger challenged the doctrine of the Eucharist. These challenges have produced endless debates through the ages which have led to endless declarations in Councils, from Nicaea (325) to Lateran IV (1215). What these declarations amount to is not so much saying what the mysteries mean but what they cannot mean.

And now let me sum up.

We began with Augustine's elegant: 'Understand, so that you may believe what I say; believe, that you may understand the word of God.' That raised two questions. The more general philosophical question: how can we believe what we do not understand? And the more specifically philosophico-theological question: how can we understand a mystery even if we do believe it, since mysteries are, by definition, beyond comprehension, beyond the reach of human reason and understanding? The answer to the first question was that we can at least understand the words and sentences in which the mystery is expressed; and secondly, we can accept and believe it on the authority of a witness whom we trust. This procedure is not confined to religious belief. As Newman, G. E. Moore and Wittgenstein have pointed out, most of our beliefs are based on authority and have to be so if we are to survive.

Even scientists, much less the ordinary adult, cannot check everything. And as for children they would not know how to go about it until they had some experience of the world. In the case of religious belief, where the stakes are higher, parents. teachers, books and 'reliable informants' are not enough. We need prophets, that is, people who, by the way they live and what they say, convince us that they are inspired teachers, revealers or interpreters of the will of God. (That, incidentally, is the definition in *The Concise Oxford Dictionary*, and you will have noted that there is no mention of foretelling the future.) Such prophets were, of course, Abraham, Moses, Jesus and Mohammed in the West. About the East I do not feel competent to speak. If someone wishes to add to the list, well and good.

The second question—namely, how can we understand what is, by definition beyond, understanding?—is certainly more difficult to answer and, some would say, an absurd question, no question at all. Yet there are many senses of 'understand', and I have played around with them. There is the sense in which commitment to a belief gives an insight or, at least an experience of it, that a mere notional understanding of it could not give. But this would hardly satisfy Augustine or Anselm, and certainly not Aquinas. However, there is another sense of 'understand' that can be applied to mysteries, and that is, understanding their implications and consequences, not only the intellectual but also the practical, moral ones. It is, in my view, this kind of understanding that they and Newman had in mind, and which they tried to impart in their sermons and treatises.

Data and Theory in Aesthetics: Philosophical Understanding and Misunderstanding

RONALD HEPBURN

This paper has a twofold structure: both parts concern philosophy's understanding (or misunderstanding) of its data—in the area of aesthetics. The first part (I) considers aesthetics as philosophy of art: the second part (II) considers aesthetics as concerned also with the appreciation of nature.

I

(a) Philosophers who write aesthetic theories have tended to see the key concepts of their account of the aesthetic as grounded in their distinctive philosophical understanding of basic features of human nature and the human situation. If we ask, what are the 'data' on which their aesthetic theories are founded, we have to include their general philosophical vision as well as more specific and concrete components—works of art themselves, critical interpretations, and the aesthetic experiences to which works of art give rise. The philosophical contribution, on such a (traditional) view, remains a highly significant one: we are invited to see aesthetic theory not only as a detached, specialized, abstract self-contained study that aims only at philosophical insight—but as having a normative relevance to, and potential impact upon, criticism and appreciation of the arts themselves at any time. The foundational key concept or cluster of concepts, that comprises the core of such a theory, such as Mimesis, Expression, Formal Unity, can be employed to commend, to deplore, to correct, trends in art.

Others, however, see that view of aesthetics as thoroughly wrongheaded.

(b) Philosophers of art—they say—need to show a much greater modesty before creative artists and actual works of art. They must defer to those who have *authority* in the production of art, an authority a philosopher does not have: not try to dominate, or domineer, from a metaphysical height. Grand philosophical theories are bound to distort and misrepresent the arts, to inhibit their development. They manifest hybris.

'Both theory and appreciation,' writes Arnold Berleant, 'must rest on what happens in art.'[1] Changes in the arts must be matched by changed aesthetics. Richard Kuhns makes a contrast between seeing painting in terms of 'the needs of a philosopher whose imperialism would overwhelm the arts and integrate them into a way of thinking about the ultimate nature of things'; and seeing it in terms of 'the needs and actions of a painter whose tasks are immediate in both painterly and perceptual terms'.[2]

On this contrasted view, then, what is vital is that the arts develop according to an inner logic which is theirs alone. Problems and challenges arise in any period and require highly specific insight and expertise on the part of artists to deal with them: once dealt with, new challenges will arise. On the same side of this opposition, also against tyrannical philosophical theorizing, other defenders of particularity in aesthetics can appeal to the anti-generalization side of Wittgenstein's aesthetic thought: let us focus our thoughts on the bass that moves too much, the door or wall-picture—or indeed *ceiling*—that is now too high, now too low, and at last—Thank God!—just right.

Philosophers need to accept a very circumscribed role. They must above all accept the actual on-goings in the arts (procession of movements, styles, fashions, revolts and counter-revolts), and refrain from trying to excogitate what artists *ought* to be doing, in conformity with some would-be philosophical understanding of the aesthetic enterprise.

We may be reminded of a parallel view of *moral* philosophy, where the work of the philosopher is limited essentially to an overhearing and analysing of the current language and concepts of morals, rather than sharpening or deepening moral understanding.

No doubt it is good for the philosopher of art to be humble; but this (I think) is carrying it too far. More wisely, Flint Schier saw the value of art as 'emerging out of a particular structure consisting of other values, perfectionist and aesthetic values that exist independently of the art world'. 'If the value of art is ... radically incommensurate with, or unconnected to, our other values', he

---

[1] *Art and Engagement* (Philadelphia: Temple University Press, 1991), p. 32. It is not unfair to quote Berleant as urging respect for current trends and critical appraisals of the arts, though his overall position in that book is much too complex to be summed up in that way.

[2] *Mind*, **104** (July 1995), 653–654. He is paraphrasing and favourably commenting upon an essay by Flint Schier.

wrote, it becomes a mystery how 'we ever come to be sensitive to the value of art'.[3]

It is surely possible that a practising artist may be moved *both* by pressures highly specific to the state of his particular art *and* by his feeling for certain more pervasive, deep-running, non-relativistic sources of aesthetic satisfaction and fulfilment— maybe never articulated or analysed. Likewise his reader or spectator or listener. If a philosopher reminds us of these sources, he is not necessarily 'bullying' the arts; not all theory-proposing philosophers seek to 'overwhelm' them. Neither (it remains arguable) need they take up a purely receptive posture, feeling obliged to welcome whatever goes on under the title of 'art' and to trim their theorizing to accommodate it. Our task here may be to find a point of reflective equilibrium. Failures, mistakes and distortions in past philosophies of art do not entitle us to infer that the whole endeavour to ground aesthetic concepts in a general axiology or metaphysic is misguided: it may just be highly complex and full of pitfalls.

(c) With some philosophers of art tending to be over-deferential to the art-institutionalists and relativists in aesthetics, there may be point in reaffirming some aesthetic values that do seem to have a claim to be grounded in an understanding of the broadest human situation, affirmed non-relativistically, and which are not seen as replaceable by norms emerging from the ever-changing practice of the arts themselves.

We can make most sense of them if we see some of these values as concerned with partial mitigations of basic human deficiencies, with necessary needs arising from our nature and situation in the world: others with no less intelligible aspirations. None of them by itself will generate a single-concept aesthetic theory but they may well furnish a cluster of key concepts, principles, ideals—some intriguingly interlinked. In particular, certain of them form pairs of what I shall call seeming-contraries in 'paradoxical co-presence'. One of the remarkable facts about the arts is their capacity to satisfy several of these values simultaneously. We move between the transcendentally necessary, or something very close to it, and (in the field of the arts themselves) serendipitous contingency—what we find can be done with pigments, strings, reeds, the complex meanings and sounds of words.

[3] Dudley Knowles and John Skorupski (eds.), *Virtue and Taste: Essays on Politics, Ethics, and Aesthetics in Memory of Flint Schier*, Philosophical Quarterly Supplementary Series, Volume 2 (Oxford: Blackwell, 1993), p. 191.

At the value end, here are some reminders of these concepts, selectively and very briefly listed. They are of course as familiar as Kant's categories.

(i) *Unity*. In J. N. Findlay's words, aesthetic experience celebrates ever the *same* triumph, the 'triumph of concentration over random dispersion'.[4] Unity is a necessary feature of all perception and reflection as such, but again it is peculiarly intensified in aesthetic experience. One has to add: what is *accepted*, what *counts*, as unity is constantly under negotiation between artist and appreciator.

(ii) *Form*. The synthesizing and grasping of a complex manifold as one object-of-experience take us close to concern with perceptual *form*, pattern, structure: more than usually effective deliverance from the inchoate, the confused—which are oppression and defeat to perception. Again, what is *acceptable* form in art is continually open to persuasion and rethinking.

(iii) *Plenitude*. I shall use the word 'plenitude' for art's ability to intensify conscious awareness through such means as the 'all-in' use of language-resources in poetry, of sound-resources in music, of spatial relationships in visual art. Such heightened, compressed, dense meaningfulness can lead us to speak of *multum in parvo*, a phrase with powerful theological resonance.

(iv) *Communication/Expression*. In very many contexts, success in achieving plenitude (as density of meaning) is startling success also in *communication*. It is utterly familiar, but true, that one main value of art is its power to enhance intersubjective communication: communication of otherwise unattainably specific, individual, emotional qualities, visions of humanity, visions of the world.

(v) *Truth*. A serious work of art may be valued as a reinterpretation or 'criticism' of human life, or of some limited significant area of it—one that aims to illuminate, i.e. to express or reveal truth, by non-discursive, imaginative means.

(vi) *Disengagement and Vitality*. 'Disengagement', for long unchallenged as a main feature, maybe *the* principal feature, of the aesthetic, has its current critics. Developments in the arts—it is eloquently argued today—make clear that the appreciator of the arts has to *participate*, to be involved, engaged, not passively to spectate. The appreciator's task can even sometimes involve actively completing the artistic process.[5] Here, it will be said, is a

[4] Quoted in my essay 'Findlay's Aesthetic Thought', in Cohen, Martin and Westphal, *Studies in the Philosophy of J. N. Findlay* (Albany, NY: State University of New York Press, 1985), p. 194; see *The Transcendence of the Cave* (London: Allen and Unwin, 1967), p. 217. I owe a substantial debt to Findlay's writing.

[5] Berleant, *Art and Engagement*, p. 26.

vivid example of a concept shaped by philosophy (eighteenth-century philosophy) that needs to be ousted in the light of current practice in the arts. Nevertheless, although I too want to deny that the appreciation of art is an inert and passive affair, I think that a broad, but not empty, conception of the disinterested and contemplative can be defended as still relevant to a well-founded aesthetic theory. It can be illuminating to deploy it in explicit conjunction with a companion-concept, one at first sight contrary to it, namely vitality or life-enhancement. How can these contraries work together?

There can be disengagement from practical, acquisitive, manipulatory, utilitarian concerns of life: but with an experiential quality far from torpid or vapid: a disengagement closely akin to, and often directly involving, wonder. Such a coupling is hardly a novelty. Kant, for instance, combined his version of disengagement with recurrent acknowledgement of the 'enlivening', 'quickening', proper to the play of imagination and understanding. Such quickening is facilitated by all manner of artistic devices, devices as basic as metaphor with its enabling, its *requiring*, of creative leaps of the mind in search of new meanings—since old meaning is blocked by the context. Far from being an 'academic anachronism',[6] both contemplativeness, stillness as well as vivid life can be held essential components in human fulfilment. A fine work of art can maximize both values at once.

Schiller too gave seminal expression to those deeply rooted values. He describes mankind as moving from passively *suffering* to actively *mastering* both outer and inner turmoils. It is a movement from immediacy to grasp, synthesis, equilibrium and inner freedom. 'What is man, before beauty cajoles from him a delight in things for their own sake or the serenity of form tempers the savagery of life? [*die ruhige Form das wilde Leben besänftigt?*] Either he hurls himself upon objects to devour them: or the objects press in upon him to destroy him, and he thrusts them away in horror. In either case his relation to the world of sense is that of immediate *contact* ... he finds rest [*Ruhe*] nowhere but in exhaustion ... '[7] Schiller conceives of a stage where aesthetic taste itself looks only to the exciting, the 'bizarre, the violent and the savage', and shuns 'tranquil simplicity' [... *vor der Einfacht und Ruhe*]. But more developed forms of aesthetic experience have disinterestedness, tranquillity and vitality. At its apex (in Schiller's rapturous account of the Juno Ludovisi), it offers at once a 'state of utter

[6] Berleant, *Art and Engagement*, p. 32.

[7] F. Schiller, *On the Aesthetic Education of Man*, ed. E. M. Wilkinson and L. A. Willoughby (Oxford: Clarendon Press, 1985), pp. 170–173.

repose and supreme agitation' [*der höchsten Ruhe und der höchsten Bewegung*].[8]

It cannot be taken for granted that the arts make a genuine advance (one that aesthetics should endorse), should they discard the stillness side of this duality and give way to the violent thrills, 'immediate contact', of that earlier stage of development.

(vii) '*Paradoxical co-presence*' can be identified in several other forms. It is true of some works of art that they are essentially extended in time, and yet our experience of them is also, in an important sense, time-transcending. Individual notes of music are transcended in a melody, melodies in a movement; syllables in words, phrases, lines, a whole poem, yet these pass no less in temporal flow. Freedom and inevitability make yet another pair. For instance, on aesthetic excellence in mathematics, Bertrand Russell once wrote that it displays 'in absolute perfection that combination, characteristic of great art, of godlike freedom, with the sense of inevitable destiny'.[9]

What sort of *understanding*, then, lies behind the affirming of such principles and goals of art-experience as I have been listing? On what grounds can we urge the arts to respect and promote them? I suggested that the values of art connect with the obverse of several basic deficiencies—forms of finitude—which are integral to the human condition. We delight in the vivacity and self-transparency of conscious awareness, the *pour-soi*, as we are depressed by its flaggings and flickerings, its fallings away towards torpor. Engagement with practical tasks and demands disperses and dissipates our striven-for unity of being; so art-experience is a highly prized heightening of consciousness, through the integration of complexly-connected components of art-works. Likewise the tight integration of spatial relationships in a painting, of temporal materials in music, facilitates release from practical anxieties and a self-sustaining, intensified vitality.

Why should those paradoxically co-present 'opposites' be especially valued? Because in these the *either–ors* of finitude are overcome by something closer to the *both–ands* of metaphysical-religious ideals. It is precisely on that account that theology has often described its metaphysically perfect being in terms of coincidence of opposites. I am not saying (though it may begin to sound like it) that in art man plays at being God; just that there is an intelligible and significant continuity between some of the values

[8] Ibid. pp. 210f, 108f.

[9] Bertrand Russell, *The Autobiography of Bertrand Russell, 1872–1914* (London: Allen and Unwin, 1967), p. 158: quoted from Yi-Fu Tuan, *Passing Strange and Wonderful* (1995), p. 16.

of the aesthetic and the metaphysical–religious domains. To an important extent, then, the values of art are not *sui generis*, not isolated from the values relevant to other areas of life.

On this reading, the philosopher of art may be able legitimately to point to values that some current trends in the arts are neglecting, or to permanently important tasks they are not fulfilling. To say this is not to say, absurdly, that a philosopher can legitimately propose specific practical tasks for art. Nevertheless, the principles I am concerned with are deep—closer, one might say—to the categoreal and *a priori* than to the empirical.

The clearly *normative* nature of the metaphysically-grounded principles prevents the philosopher from being merely a recorder and analyst. One implication is that philosophical aesthetics should differentiate itself from *sociological* enquiry into the arts. Sociologically-centred aesthetics flattens out the task of a philosopher of art and attempts to present him with already-processed, already-evaluated data, concerning what has been (and continues to be) produced in the sphere of art by social forces, understood in historicist and determinist (that is, would-be scientific) style. Here as elsewhere, the philosopher cannot rest simply in the role of evaluatively neutral, quasi-scientific commentator—whether on art or on morality, but he always legitimately reworks and in some measure remakes, his material, as he selects, sifts through, organizes it—i.e. seeks ('non-scientifically') to *understand* it. There is a relevant parallel in moral philosophy: for some moral philosophers' analogous commitment to 'scientific understanding' has been likewise uneasy and fitful: their avowed aim may initially be a 'science of man' but (like Hume) they may well end up by alternating between something deserving that title, and the commendation of particular acts and attitudes and the deprecating of others. (The humane, undogmatic, critical, are commended: the 'monkish' deprecated.)

(d) The acknowledging of 'deep' values, rooted in a philosophical understanding of the human situation as such, is not at all incompatible with our *also* acknowledging other, less abstract, values which do come and go, or are now emphasized and now softpedalled. The philosopher of art's *understanding of his data* has to be thought of as many-levelled, incorporating a hierarchy of values and aims. Some are linked to technical change, or to developing genres, traditions, movements. Below them lie the deep, categoreal ones.

Critics of the arts may implicitly or explicitly rely, in their interpretations and appraisals, on principles of different levels. In particular cases, it may be disputable to *what* level a principle or value belongs:—whether it is historically transient, or deeply-rooted. I have been arguing, for instance, that 'disinterestedness' or 'disengagement' is more deeply entrenched in the hierarchy than its current detractors believe.

That my 'deep' principles are neither archaic nor solely the subject of philosophers' theorizing, may be readily shown. Here, for instance, is a critic of contemporary art drawing upon some of the 'deepest'. In *The Times* of 27 May 1995, Richard Cork commented on paintings by Leon Kossoff. In particular, he wrote about

> a splendid picture called *Here Comes the Diesel, Early Summer.* [The arrival of the train is enough to set] the whole picture into ecstatic agitation. Energy surges through the scene ... A quotidian stretch of industrial north London is transformed through Kossoff's avid vision into a place of wonder. The moment will soon pass, and the restless mobility of his mark-making implies a keen awareness of transience. But flux is arrested here, in all its turbulence, and endowed with the redemptive power of art.

We note 'ecstatic agitation' ... 'energy' ... 'wonder'. Then while there is 'keen awareness of transience', yet 'flux is arrested'. (A splendid case of the paradoxical co-presence of contrary notions!) Also art's 'redemptive power': 'redemptive' with its obvious religious resonance illustrates also that 'continuity' I mentioned between religious and aesthetic. We see too how recognition of even the most abstract metaphysical, and metaphysical–religious, values can make an impact directly on the quality of an individual's aesthetic experience, and (through critical communication) help to determine the experience of others.

It is not only philosophers who are moved to philosophize in the presence of art; others tend to be far less inhibited than they! Many artists themselves have been powerfully influenced by a philosophical style or set of doctrines, or a philosophy of man— albeit often in a popularized and simplified version. This being so, it would be strangely ironical if the aesthetic theorist alone had to occupy the place of a pure spectator of the arts, and venture no philosophical comment or criticism that stems from his own understanding of his data.

II

A second set of problems about understanding arises over the aesthetic appreciation of nature, where the objects of appreciation range from small-scale natural items, snowflakes, spiders' webs, shells, to landscapes, skyscapes, the immensities of space and time. We need to distinguish two areas of enquiry in this Section.

(a) There is the question of *'understanding-how'* to manage, balance, orchestrate the various possible components of such experience of nature. And

(b) since understanding can feature also as one of the *components*, we have to ask: How far does it matter that we *understand* what is before us and constitutes the object of our aesthetic attention? Could some kinds of understanding possibly *fight* with other components, or even in some circumstances *undermine* rather than enhance the total experience?

(a) First, then, consider 'understanding' as it appears in the phrase, 'understanding how to approach nature aesthetically'. In art-appreciation we have various bodies of criticism to guide our responses, often with authority; we have knowledge of developing genres and evolving forms. Not so with nature. What we engage in with nature is a kind of responsive-creative aesthetic activity, both receptive and formative. It is improvisatory and in important measure *free*, an activity of regulating and structuring our emerging episodic experience. We deliberate where to let our attention settle. We decide whether to admit *this*, to soft-pedal or exclude *that*: perhaps how widely to extend the initial context—for instance, from shell, to beach, whole coastline ... planet. No doubt, these decisions tend to go on at a pre-verbal, pre-conceptual level. In this paper, we are most concerned with the *cognitive* components, which can be of many kinds, historical, scientific, ecological. But in actual experience these will be fused with purely sensuous components, expressive qualities, formal qualities. And the cognitive factors themselves may generate new, distinctive emergent emotional qualities. In all this we are neither exclusively tracing nature as it is in itself; nor are we engaged in a wholly self-generated fantasy.

To develop this account a little further, we need to spell out more explicitly some of those components and the factors we seek to synthesize.

Suppose I am contemplating the movement of deer across a hillside under snow. They emerge from the edge of a forest on to open country. In order to attend to these not as objects of *scientific* understanding, but as objects of *aesthetic* experience, how much more (and less) is required than sheer perception of events? For a start, once again there needs to be a wondering *disengagement*—disengagement from utility-programmed concern with forestry as commerce and animals as food: disengagement even from the network of cause-effect explanations.

243

But not, I think, disengagement from concern with *objectivity* or with *truth*. We do want to be sure that it is *nature's* resources that we are experiencing and celebrating. In the aesthetic case, truth is incorporated not through the devising of illuminating theory, but in memorable episodic experience, 'epiphany'. Or at least we hope it will. Failure here can result from such factors as sentimental falsification or self-protective selectivity.

We wish, also, to enjoy a sense that the natural aesthetic object of experience is not only nature as it is, somewhere, some of the time, but nature as it is *presently actualized and apprehended*. 'Only here and now is this, precisely this, to be experienced!' Whatever layers of thought, whatever understanding of nature contribute to the experience, we want to retain a strong sense of the present actuality of, say, this river-bank at dawn, or—before one's very eyes—that skein of migrating geese in flight, or these towering cumulo-nimbus clouds around which one's aircraft is manoeuvring its way.

If a scientific understanding of natural objects were our sole aim, no doubt we should feel obliged to damp the *emotional–expressive* components of our experience. Not, however, if the aim is aesthetic appreciation. For there we are free to encourage and foster emotional responses to items or scenes of nature, whether understood scientifically or non-scientifically or in both ways, responses in terms of human wantings and fearings, exultations and shrinkings of spirit. (On this topic, more shortly.)

In aesthetic appreciation of nature, we may even meet versions of those *paradoxically co-present* features (such as the vital and the still), for which I have been claiming high importance in appreciation of the arts. There may be, for instance, a convergence of understanding of past and the perception of present states. As nature exists only in time, and in constant change, we cannot dismiss realizations of earlier states of the object of experience— imaginative extensions of awareness back in time, whether recent or 'deep' time; and these components can part-determine how we see nature now. Compare Simon Schama:—'*Landscape and Memory* is built round ... moments of recognition ... when a place suddenly exposes its connections to an ancient and peculiar vision of the forest, mountain, river ... '[10]

That theme of paradoxical co-presence should not be judged arcane or precious:[11] it can be a feature of childhood experience.

[10] *Landscape and Memory* (London: Harper Collins, 1995), p. 16.

[11] For other examples, see my 'Landscape and the Metaphysical Imagination', *Environmental Values,* 5 (1996), 191–204.

For example, in his recent book, *Passing Strange and Wonderful, Aesthetics, Nature and Culture*, Yi-Fu Tuan sensitively describes children's love of what he calls 'nooks': a tree-top house, a hollow in bushes, or the like offer both a 'womblike hollow' and an 'open space', and can capture 'for the child the basic polarities of life', 'darkness and light, safety and adventure, indolence and excitation, multisensual ease and visual alertness ... past and future cease to exist, displaced by a transcendent present.[12]

What is it like to *synthesize* such diverse constituents as I have been listing into a unified episodic experience (for unity can be a key concept to us in nature—as in art-appreciation)? Consider some examples, in each of which a cluster of natural components makes an aesthetic unity-to-perception.

I perceive a landscape as *louring* or *threatening*: another has a *forbidding* or an *alien* look. I perceive a hushed landscape as *expectant*: a busy, variegated, brilliant landscape as *vibrant*, Kokoschka-like—in this case drawing one man's art into my synthesis. I see the cliffs and mountains of an island rising above a misty sea as *dreamlike* or *visionary*, or even '*unreal*'.

I look up at the full moon, and a sense comes to me of its *sphericality* and its *floating in space*. I look back to land or sea, and there comes to me now a sense of the earth also as a sphere floating in space. With that change, the *emotional* quality of my experience changes too. Now I feel the earth's isolation in space, chilling and thrilling at the same time. Formally also, there is a sense of the two spheres over against each other, in a silent opposition.

Examples by themselves hardly take us into the epistemology; but farther we cannot go here. Certainly, though, we are in the territory of Wittgenstein's *Philosophical Investigations*, the sections on the dawning of aspects and related phenomena. What is it (Wittgenstein asks there) 'to *see* an object according to an *interpretation?*' 'Was it *seeing* or was it a thought?'[13] A little earlier, he asked: 'What does it mean to say that I "*see the sphere floating in the air*", in a picture?' '"The sphere seems to float". "You see it floating", or again, in a special tone of voice, "It floats!".'[14]

What is our *goal* in integrating such components into a single experience? I suspect that the goal is internally related to those components themselves, and cannot be separately expressed. We might ask ourselves whether the goal is to *maximize emotional impact*? But that might be attainable only by suppressing factors

[12] New York, Tokyo, London, Kodancha International, 1995, p. 22.

[13] L. Wittgenstein, *Philosophical Investigations*, trans. G. E. M. Anscombe (Oxford: Blackwell, 1958), pp. 200, 204.

[14] Ibid. p. 201.

which we judge ought not to be suppressed—a strong element of illusion might do it! I could maximize my awe and amazement by elaborating a fantasy that the sunset clouds are brilliantly lit golden palaces in the sky ... But: why not admit such illusion? Well, because I am already also working with that conflicting criterion for desirable aesthetic experience—that it remain faithful to understanding how things really are ... That checks my fantasy.

And yet: emotional intensity and specificity are indisputably important features of aesthetic experience. A legitimate concern with them must check, for instance, a tendency to let conceptualizing, theorizing or reverie weaken or obliterate them. The perceived sights and sounds of nature must count for far more than a trigger for reflection.

Perhaps it would do more justice to the phenomenological complexity to introduce a concept of *aesthetic mode*, or *aesthetic concern*, rather than to talk simply and solely of particular, unified aesthetic experiences. *Now* aesthetic concern tightens, concentrates into attentive, intense, sensorily centred and engaged episodes, and *now* it loosens into meditation or reverie. All of these will have components ranging from the sensuous to thought and theory, but in very differing proportions and prominence.

'Understanding how' to use such criteria in practice is a matter of making very rapid multiple practical judgments: to judge when one movement of the mind, if intensified further, will begin to encroach upon the deployment of another: when, e.g., particularity or poignancy is about to be lost, if the context, the catchment of thought, or memory, or anticipation is further broadened.

Often enough we will not even attempt to involve every factor or kind of component. But the most fully developed aesthetic approaches to nature may well be mindful of most of the factors I have mentioned—aiming to maximize the operating of each, consistently with the fullest acknowledgment of all the others.

(b) Consider, next, a sample of the questions that arise over understanding as *one of the components* of aesthetic experience of nature. The importance of understanding as a component is in fact one of the most debated current issues in this area.

In the *British Journal of Aesthetics* (October 1995), for instance, Holmes Rolston III reflects thoughtfully on the claim that, 'we cannot appropriately appreciate what we do not understand'. Another writer on environmental aesthetics, Yuriko Saito, argues that nature's 'story', which will certainly include an ecological narrative, must be allowed into a full aesthetic experience of nature. She notes that not every aesthetic theory will accommodate this:

for instance, a Zen aesthetic will not allow immediacy to be diluted by conceptual thought.[15]

How far are we properly concerned here with scientific understanding, and how far with non-scientific? Obviously, as we look out upon a landscape, we can appropriate aesthetically the thought of the ancient volcano that produced the plug or sill that dominates the landscape's forms: or the thought that this mountain-range resulted from the collision of massive tectonic plates, which are still exerting unseen their enormous pressures.

Clearly, though, no single determinate scientific view of a landscape can constitute *the* proper object of aesthetic appreciation. There is not only the macroscopic geological perspective, but also that of, say, crystallography, and a possible account in terms of fundamental physical theory. With the latter in mind, it would surely exaggerate to claim that any and every mode of scientific understanding can become ingredient in occurrent aesthetic experience. What can be so assimilated has to be limited to what is imaginable by man—the surface-geological, certainly, where we imaginatively superimpose our understanding of earlier states of the landscape before us (while the valley was still under the ice, let us say). Or we may import in imagination some of the evolutionary past of the living organisms now before us. But clearly there must be stopping-places in our importing of scientific understanding, and these will depend essentially on the limitations of imagination (and knowledge) to bring data of more than a certain complexity to bear on the scene at a given time—out of innumerable earlier states and stages, from the Big Bang onwards.

If we move from individual natural items to nature as a whole, our sense of its part-chaotic, part-lawful complexity plus (on the margins) the mystery of its origins or of its always-being-there, may well prompt a respect, or 'intellectual love of God', as a constant component in serious aesthetic experience. It will modify, and be modified by, the features of particular items, particular forests, seacoasts, moors and marshes.

In a word: scientific understanding, as we incorporate it into an aesthetic experience, loses its evaluatively neutral character—and so is transformed into a *scientifically grounded non-scientific understanding*. It takes on emotional qualities that are dependent on needs, anxieties, hopes, satisfactions. We delight also in other aspects such as formal arrangement, which are themselves dependent upon contingencies of observer's location, perspective and scale. Indeed, the realization of our humanly unique mode of

[15] Paper read at the First International Conference on Environmental Aesthetics in Koli, Finland, in the summer of 1994.

enjoying the landscape—its relativity to our perceptual capacity—can itself enter as a cognitive element in the experience. There can surely be no argument against the counterpointing of a scientific understanding of, say, a thunderstorm and a thoroughly 'life-world' mode of experiencing it, as *drama*—approach, climax, restoration of tranquillity...

There remains a much more specific, and certainly a very familiar theme to be acknowledged. It is true that on some occasions, before some landscapes, we may well say: 'Never mind understanding: let us just open ourselves to the beauty, the loveliness of it!' Why indeed not? Yet we may be unable to exclude from our experience a wistfulness on account of the fragility of the natural objects before us, and maybe a *frisson* of anxiety about their future. In fact, a mindfulness of that kind is sometimes held to be even morally required. I am of course thinking of the imperative expressed powerfully in so much current writing—the imperative of ecological concern.

Some writers do indeed see our ecological responsibilities as demanding to be taken into account in any and every aesthetic approach to nature. We must respond to the predictions of scientists about nature's future states, seeing nature as threatened in a variety of, what are to us, grim and depressing ways. If we judge the near-extinction, say, of some animal species to be sad, deplorable, because it is better to have maximal diversification of life-forms rather than their constant depletion, then (on this view) sadness has to be ingredient in our aesthetic appreciation of animals of that kind. (In what I go on to say, I do not in any way imply that, at the level of practical reasoning and intervention, the issues of environmental damage and its remedying are other than critically important.)

Consider, then, the claim that we are required, in any aesthetic experience of bird, beast, lake or meadow, to ensure that we build in some reference to threat of extinction or of coming damage. Perhaps the threat is from acid rain, or from climatic change that will ultimately remove that item from the landscape. Now this is a disturbing proposal: if taken literally, would it not amount to a self-sabotaging of aesthetic enjoyment as such? For a constant enveloping doom-laden expressive quality would be likely to predominate and would obliterate discriminations of quality. A generalized, morally urgent environmental concern would be claiming its right to *displace* the luxury of fine tuning. Worthy priority is here being given to environmental understanding and its moral implications, but with very unhappy effects on the aesthetic.

If we see the aesthetic dimension of experience as indeed concerned with the heightening, enhancing of discriminatory power, and therefore precisely with the diversifying of human experience, it would be supremely ironic—perhaps irrational?—to permit or even require it to be dominated by a generalized sense of environmental doom. This element of understanding would surely have become wildly, usurpingly over-emphatic.

Anxieties and forebodings arise, however, not only over ecological (in part at least preventable) damage, but also over wholly inescapable future transformations of our environment.

We realize that *all* of the planet's presently contemplated features will eventually, in the more distant future, be drastically altered and finally destroyed. But always to insert the thought of that future in the cluster of components which make up my aesthetic experience *now* is, once more, to modify radically, and with irreversible thoroughness!, its overall emotive quality—certainly to overwhelm any delight in fine perceptual discriminations. Hence, again the strong suggestion of self-undermining, self-sabotaging. We certainly do not *want* incessantly to go down the track that sets out from nature's rewarding, enjoyable forms and textures, dutifully adds the realization of how things stand with that same nature, in the longer term, 'ultimately'—until the global experience comes to be bleakly dominated by the thought of the transience of those loved objects.

To resist that movement of mind would need some sort of regulator, some imperative. But how articulate its nature and principle?

No doubt we could again appeal to the practical stratagem of checking the deployment of one aesthetic component before the point at which it threatens to overwhelm others. But to invoke that stratagem on its own, in such a serious context and without further thought or preparation, might seem *ad hoc* and facile.

We do, however, learn to handle an analogous situation in our perception of human beings, through a kind of discipline of the attention: perhaps we can apply something of the same to our problem with aesthetic appreciation of nature. Think of a painting of an old man or woman, where the imminence of death and dissolution is signalled by an emphatic rendering of skull (just) beneath the skin. Though that, more generally, symbolizes the *universal* human lot, we do not judge it incumbent to read-in that same final state whenever we look at *any* human being, so cancelling any appreciation of present human flourishing, animation and health. No; because that would amount to bringing forward the obliteration of quality and discrimination, to advance that gratuitously, and thus prevent the actualizing of valuable states of awareness.

Can we add: so (in all essentials) with the problem of knowledge of nature's ephemerality, as a component of aesthetic appreciation of nature? I think we can. We can see that problem as setting yet a parallel challenge to 'understanding-how', to the management of attention so as neither to evade, nor to be overwhelmed by, the depressive and destructive.

Yet another analogy can be invoked between aesthetic objects and persons—in this case with the relation between friends. In a close friendship, different levels of knowledge and concern are visited on different occasions. Some encounters will be light-hearted, skimming the surface only: others reach to the depths, in intimate awareness of the complexity of the other. Both levels are valued components of the friendship, though they are not of *equal* value. The relationship is not, and cannot be, conducted perpetually on the deepest level. There is an important element of *freedom* whereby the friends can blamelessly meet on the casual levels, provided that they are available to each other on the deeper levels as well. That freedom, I suggest, is a valuable feature of the *aesthetic* mode of experience also, too valuable a feature to be jettisoned.

We can find a helpfully close parallel in the sphere of the arts. In recent years, artists who have sought to realize beauty in their work have often been accused of evading their duty of bearing witness to the sombre and the unlovely aspects of the age, even of collusion in its evils. It can, however, be argued that artists bear witness to these evils most powerfully and poignantly, if indirectly, when in addition they can point to certain canvases, poems and works of music, and say, 'There is also *this*, and *this!*'—in the midst of ugliness and corruption, the love-evoking, the beautiful.[16]

We have yet to note a third, still more comprehensive, challenge to the objective of responding aesthetically to nature, with understanding. That comes in any claim, whether from science or metaphysics, that nature understood as it ultimately is, nature as it is in itself, does not possess attributes to which we *can* aesthetically respond: that the farther one goes towards understanding the world, the less scope remains for aesthetic experience. It is argued that if one thinks-in the scientific background, consistently and in a thoroughgoing way, that would work towards weakening or dissolving the aesthetic perception, not enriching it. The aesthetically appreciable qualities (secondary qualities, and emergent tertiary

---

[16] Compare A. Savile, 'Beauty and Truth: the Apotheosis of an Idea', in *Analytical Aesthetics*, ed. R. Shusterman (Oxford: Blackwell, 1989), Chapter 7.

qualities) do not appear in the scientist's inventory of what is really or basically in nature. Moreover, the scientist's own understanding is itself expressed in terms—like wave and particle, (black) hole, string—terms known to be metaphorical. They are drawn from the life-world repertoire of perceptible events and the macroscopic entities involved in them, although scientists know well enough that these do not simply map on to the features of nature itself. And surely the same is true of much speculative metaphysics: metaphor abounds there also.

In a lively article in the *Journal of Applied Philosophy* (1994)[17] Stan Godlovitch asks how, within the context of an environmentalist concern for nature, we might develop an aesthetic of nature which is 'acentric', free of the anthropocentric and so able to 'appreciate nature on its own terms' (p. 18). For Godlovitch, this does not mean merely that we build-in our scientific understanding to the aesthetic appreciation of nature. 'Science', he claims, 'is directed to forge a certain kind of intelligibility'; it 'de-mystifies nature by categorizing, quantifying and patterning it' (p. 23). If this is cognition, it is a 'human-centred cognition'. A more resolute intent to understand drives us—drives Godlovitch—to recognize nature as 'categorically other'. Only a 'sense of mystery', of 'aloofness' (more distant than the disinterested) and a 'sense of insignificance' are aesthetically appropriate and sustainable (p. 26). Godlovitch allows us neither a sense of awe, nor of wonder: only 'a sense of being outside, of not belonging' (pp. 27ff).

If doing justice to the role of understanding in aesthetic experience means being ruthlessly 'acentric' in the sense just described, then we have serious reason to doubt whether such an aesthetic is in fact possible.

If we wish to go on seeing the aesthetic as above all anchored in the ideal of maximally vivid, intensified and discriminating consciousness, then the focal realisation of nature's ultimate unknowability will certainly not bring us nearer to that ideal: quite the contrary! Here, emptiness is all. We have a progressive cancelling of sensory, perspectival and scientific components—like the work of an over-zealous negative theologian, who strikes out all our concepts in turn as inapplicable to deity. We started with ' plenitude': we risk ending with attenuation to nothingness. Is not this outcome a *reductio ad absurdum* of the initial project to think our way towards a more adequate aesthetic of nature? It may signal that we cannot give the cognitive component *total precedence*

[17] Stan Godlovitch, 'Ice-Breakers: Environmentalism and Natural Aesthetics', *The Journal of Applied Philosophy* (1994), pp. 13–30. The following page-numbers in the text refer.

over the other components of aesthetic experience, if we also want to go on seeing such experience in the way I have described it.

Of course, it is true that our understanding of nature is selective and partial, taking in what we can assimilate, and leaving out the vastnesses and minutenesses beyond that meagre zone of our receptivity. But surely acknowledgment of that circumambient mystery can coexist with, can be an enduring backcloth or frame to, our benign exploitation of the sensory, scaled and humanly selective, the factors that constitute aesthetic experience as we know it, and can be integrated with these factors, rather than allowed to obliterate them. What prompts that acknowledgment may be items on the margins of experience—new life, new death, the disclosure (perhaps with the help of the Hubble telescope) of a multitude of distant constellations.

Integrated (I suggest) with the elements of aesthetic experience, rather than obliterating, ousting these ... That directly contradicts Godlovitch where he describes nature as 'categorically other than us, a nature of which we were never part', and claims that the aesthetic attitude should be 'a sense of being outside, of not belonging'. Surely he is wrong to characterize our situation in these terms. Why should we describe what we do not know of nature as 'belonging' to nature any more than we ourselves belong to it, and any more than what we do know of nature belongs to it? Why should we rule ourselves out from belonging—as if we had grounds for believing that we and our life-world had only a dubious claim to reality, compared with the unknowable nature beyond even the grasp of science?

Whatever the *causal* relations between unobservable physical entities and the perceptible, phenomenal world, and between unknown and known, those dependencies surely do not entitle us to judge the phenomenal *unreal*, or to place it low in a scale of degrees of reality. All we perceive from our own perceptual standpoint is *actual*, is *nature*. Nature as it is in itself cannot exclude, has to *in*clude, the phenomenal. So understood, it remains a proper object of aesthetic concern.

Anti-Meaning as Ideology: The Case of Deconstruction

ROBERT GRANT

Don't look for the meaning; look for the use. (Wittgenstein)

A few years back the Yale deconstructionist Paul de Man was posthumously discovered to have written repeatedly for a Belgian collaborationist journal during the Nazi occupation. So far as I am aware, de Man in his American period espoused no particular politics.[1] Indeed, the Left frequently regarded this as a cause for complaint, since most of them (to some extent rightly, as we shall see) thought of de Man and deconstruction as being their natural allies.

These revelations caused something like an academic equivalent of the Wall Street Crash, at any rate on the Left. Lesser luminary after lesser luminary joined a full-scale stampede out of deconstruction, post-structuralism and the rest, all anxiously protesting that they had never really believed it, that it was all old hat, even that they had always known that it was politically suspect. Had they been more honest, they might have seen that deconstruction for the most part had always been irrelevant to any straightforwardly activist politics, since those, being premised on the translatability of theory into practice, must depend on the assumption of a fairly close fit between words and the world. That is a relation, of course, which deconstruction and post-structuralism generally have been at pains to deny.

There is no precise definition or description of deconstruction. I should incline merely to call it a minor, localized swirl or vortex in the broader current of the *Zeitgeist*, since in its various usages it may mean any or all of the following: a semantic (or rather antisemantic) theory; an interpretative method; a generalized cultural outlook; or, at its widest, the entire order of things. Seen in this last perspective, deconstruction is a disintegration to which every human artefact and conception is not only subject, but is also constantly, and unknowingly, subjecting itself.

Oddly enough, deconstruction still enjoys some official protection, of a kind to which I shall advert later. The reason, I suppose, is that it has nowadays become a metonym for the whole current of

---

[1] There was, however, a 'shock-horror' rumour circulating in the early 1980s, to the effect that de Man's sympathies were Republican.

253

Franco-American post-New Critical ideology. (I originally wrote 'thought' there, but no, what I mean is ideology, which stands to thought in much the same relation as a prayer-wheel stands to prayer.)

Why that particular bundle of theories and assumptions should receive, or stand in need of, institutional endorsement is a difficult question. Perhaps one reason lies in the apparent eagerness of liberal institutions (and universities are that or nothing) to prove their good faith by bending over backwards to appease or accommodate whatever most threatens them.[2] (It is curious that the universities have never extended this same indulgence to National Socialism, except, notoriously, in pre-Hitler Germany, when they were still free not to.)

Never the positive creed of more than a small academic minority, deconstruction nonetheless enjoyed something like a fifteen-year ascendancy, a long time for an intellectual fashion. This cannot be explained by its intellectual merits, which are few. Suppose that, unlike the typically impetuous deconstructionist, we were to try to be fair. We might, then, just number among them deconstruction's ability to suggest, in its account of play, disseminated meaning and the like, one source of the peculiarly teasing aesthetic satisfactions to be found in certain similarly *recherché* works of art (by M. C. Escher, say, or Vladimir Nabokov). Furthermore, the idea (to be examined later) that 'writing' and 'textuality' are in some sense independent of an authorial presence might be thought to throw some light upon so-called poetic or fictional 'impersonality'. At least to this reader, however, the resulting illumination represents a wretchedly poor return on an enormous outlay of time, effort and (above all) intellectual forbearance.

Deconstruction, I shall maintain, cannot be true even in its own terms, not least because one of its central claims is to have abolished the very notion of truth. So the final explanation of the attraction it exerted upon its subscribers can only be sociological or ideological. There is a pleasing irony here. For in one sense of

---

[2] In the case of universities, this seems to be true only when the surrounding political order is also liberal. In the apartheid era the South African universities (at least, the English-speaking ones) put up a splendid resistance to the Nationalist government's attempts to limit academic freedom, control admissions, etc. Their reward was to be ostracized by British and American universities. Not one of the latter, so far as I know, has subsequently raised even a peep of protest about the current (nongovernmental) political attempts forcibly to 'Africanise' the University of the Witwatersrand (i.e. to limit academic freedom, control admissions, etc.).

the word, deconstruction is an ideology, being a more or less ready-made, self-conscious, all-explanatory theoretical belief-system dedicated to the unmasking of less self-conscious beliefs. Such beliefs are what it would itself call 'ideological'. But it too is ideological in precisely that same, second sense, being a set of (to my mind plainly) false beliefs which have nevertheless survived and even flourished on account of the unacknowledged interests they serve. (Indeed, most 'unmasking' theories are deeply vulnerable to their own central inquisition, viz. *cui bono?*)

Deconstruction 'did something' for its subscribers, made them feel good or important in some way, performed some vital function in their mental economy or social life that was wholly independent of what, given deconstruction's panoptic intellectual pretensions, was the only thing that mattered, its objective plausibility. (It also did their careers no harm, to say the least, but I shall pass over that.) But we should first examine deconstruction's substantive content, such as it is (for it vehemently denies having any, or at least any of a kind which might expose it to refutation).[3] To understand that, an excursion is required into deconstruction's immediate precursor, structuralism.

As everybody knows, structuralism originated in the linguistics of Ferdinand de Saussure, expounded in his lectures at the University of Geneva between 1906 and 1911.[4] Saussure's most

[3] 'On veut rendre l'écriture imprenable, bien sûr' (Jacques Derrida, *Glas*, Fr. edn., p. 76; quoted in Jonathan Culler, *On Deconstruction: Theory and Criticism After Structuralism* [London: Routledge and Kegan Paul 1983], p. 136). The deconstructionist aspiration to lofty unfalsifiability (akin, one might say, to some kind of 'will to power') has often been noted. It bears, moreover, a curious inverted resemblance to the confident foundationalism it purports to reject. On the first of these points see e.g. Stuart Sim, *Beyond Aesthetics: Confrontations with Poststructuralism and Postmodernism* (Hemel Hempstead: Harvester Wheatsheaf 1992), p. 59; Roger Scruton, *Upon Nothing* (Swansea: University College of Swansea, 1993), pp. 14–16.

On the second (to which I shall return), see J. G. Merquior, *From Prague to Paris: a Critique of Structuralist and Post-Structuralist Thought* (London and New York: Verso 1986), p. 233: 'Far from rejecting the foundationalist outlook, Derrida offers a mirror-image of it ... in the end Derrida shares the belief that for determinate meanings to obtain, language must have an absolute foundation.' Some of this diagnosis is credited by Merquior to M. H. Abrams, 'How to do things with texts', *Partisan Review* (1979) pp. 566–588.

[4] These constitute his posthumously-compiled *Course in General Linguistics*. All references to Saussure in the main text above are to this work, tr. Wade Baskin, intro. Jonathan Culler (London: Fontana 1974).

important features for our purposes are these: the division of the sign into signifier and signified; the arbitrariness of the connection between them; the principle of difference; and the distinctions between *langue* and *parole*, synchrony and diachrony, and syntagmatic and associative relations.

First, signifier and signified. According to Saussure, this distinction is purely theoretical, since in practice signifier and signified are inseparably united in the sign. In spoken language, the signifier is the *sound* which a word makes, the signified is the *concept* or mental image associated with that sound. Saussure is wholly unconcerned with the world of extra-linguistic *things* or *objects*, of referents in short, and how those relate to the world of signs.[5] Many commentators, including C. K. Ogden and I. A. Richards in *The Meaning of Meaning* (1923), have thought this a grave omission.

Second, the arbitrariness of the sign.[6] All this means is that there is no natural or 'given' reason why, for example, the sound 'cat' should signify the concept *cat*. It is sufficient merely that it does so and is generally understood to do so. (The point is readily confirmed by the fact that other languages have different words for 'cat'.)

Pace various post-structuralists, including Derrida, it is important to note what the arbitrariness of the sign does *not* mean. It does not mean that the individual, like Lewis Carroll's Humpty Dumpty, can mean anything he likes by a particular sign, either in using or in interpreting it. He is not, of course, actually prevented from doing so, but if he does, the penalty he pays is that of unintelligibility, i.e. of not meaning anything *to anyone else*. 'By himself', says Saussure, 'the individual is incapable of fixing a single value.'[7] (The term 'value' here means, as in mathematics, any determinate signification.)

[5] Common sense and everyday usage (both generally anathema to post-structuralists) suggest that where there is a sign, it must be a sign *of* something, and that that something, whatever its true metaphysical status, is the referent, or thing referred to. For deconstruction and post-structuralism generally, however, signs refer only to other signs (whatever that is supposed to mean), and so on into infinity. I can see that the sign 'cat' signifies the furry quadruped of that name; but what the animal itself may be a 'sign' of (barring mere *folklorique* associations such as luck, witches, nine lives, walking by itself etc.) is anyone's guess. Underlying the whole preposterous notion there is almost certainly a confusion (possibly deliberate, but in any case not worth unravelling here) between natural and non-natural signs, i.e. between symptoms and signals, and also one between reference proper (which is after all held to be impossible) and other forms of relation.

[6] Saussure, *Course*, p. 67ff.

[7] Ibid., p. 113.

In short, though the *choice* of signifier is arbitrary, the sign's subsequent *use* is not, for if it were, the sign would simply fail to signify. Its ability to signify, its immediate stability, depends wholly on the unthinking agreement of the existing community of language-users, a consensus which the individual alone is power-less to change. This fact seems to be an underlying object of resentment in left-wing post-structuralist thought such as Foucault's or Barthes's. The idea appears to be that although the lexicon is arbitrarily constituted, and therefore in principle changeable, its relative fixity is not due simply to the straightfor-ward exigencies of communication, but is somehow engineered by dominant groups (or indeed by the dominant majority) within the socio-linguistic community. These, through their supposed 'con-trol' of language, impose their own equally 'arbitrary' moral values upon 'deviant' individuals or groups. 'Language', Barthes announced in a characteristic hyperbolical flourish, 'is fascist.'[8]

Now, values may conceivably be arbitrary (in the sense of being culture-relative), they are undeniably embodied in language (which is not, however, to say that they are *imposed* by it), and some people clearly find them oppressive or wish to substitute other values for them. But those are not problems for linguistics, let alone for Saussure's, which are rootedly anti-semantic. By that I mean that Saussure (so to speak) puts the world in brackets, and with it morals and politics. He is simply not concerned with the meanings of words, and their immanent socio-political implica-tions. Saussure's austere psychologism has something in common with Husserl's 'phenomenological reduction', in that both regard the objects respectively of language and consciousness, not as non-existent, but simply as irrelevant, indeed as obstacles, to a proper study of the processes involved.[9]

Saussure's principle of difference is admirably characterized by Roy Harris as 'the idea that every semiological fact is constituted by an imaginative juxtaposition of other unrealized possibilities'.[10]

[8] From Barthes' inaugural lecture at the Collège de France, quoted in Merquior, *From Prague to Paris*, p. 158. Presumably, therefore, if Barthes thought, through the use of language, to compel his audience's assent, he must have been fascist too, while they (if he succeeded) were both victims of and collaborators with fascism.

[9] I was irritated to discover, after writing that sentence, that Terry Eagleton has also made the comparison in his *Literary Theory* (Oxford: Blackwell 1983). Worse, he even uses the word 'cat', as I have done, to illustrate the arbitrariness of the sign. (Though I suppose that is merely one of the many familiar uses of a cat.)

[10] Roy Harris, *Reading Saussure: a Critical Commentary on the Cours de Linguistique Générale* (London: Duckworth 1987), p. xv.

Words acquire their identity purely through their differences from other words. The signifier *bat* is what it is, not because of anything intrinsic to bats (be they propulsive implements or nocturnal winged mammals), but simply because *bat* is not *pat* or *bet* or *bag*, and so on. This difference is purely phonic and graphic, in other words formal. It has nothing to do, in itself, with meaning or reference.

Following Saussure, some structuralists extended the principle of difference from the signifier to the signified, so that, for instance, the distinction between the concepts *father* and *mother* appeared only as a formal, not as a substantive, difference. This rather questionable example is Saussure's own, and points to what seems to me structuralism's most disabling weakness. 'In language', runs Saussure's most famous formulation,

> there are only differences *without positive terms*. Whether we take the signified or the signifier, language has neither ideas nor sounds that existed before the linguistic system, but only conceptual and phonic differences that have issued from the system.[11]

The problem here is whether one can so separate the concept from its referent as to treat it (the concept) as a product of pure, formal difference (from other concepts). It seems to me that one cannot. For, just as the signifier is inseparable from the signified, so the concept (the signified) is inseparable from the thing that it is a concept *of*. (That, in part, is simply what it is to *be* a concept. Concepts are transitive.)

By that, of course, I do not mean that the referent has somehow to be physically present, available or existent. It might be something, such as a unicorn, whose lack of any concrete instances is actually part of its description. Or it might be the reference of an entire sentence, but of one with a negative truth-value. Or it might be a concept in the everyday sense of the word, an abstraction such as 'redness' or 'arrogance', to which we can refer independently of any accompanying instance. What I do mean is that the Saussurean concept or signified (if we think there is such a thing) acquires its identity either from its various instances (as experienced or credibly reported) or, if its object is non-existent, by being modelled upon some plausible combination of analogues. (Thus, though no unicorn has ever existed, the *idea* of a unicorn, i.e. of a horse with a single, central horn, and endowed

[11] *Course*, p. 120.

with certain morally symbolic attributes, is perfectly intelligible.)[12]

However all that may be, it is implausible to see the difference between the concepts *father* and *mother* as purely formal (though it may well *also* be formal). The contrast is clearly substantive in origin, being retrospectively derived from the real-life distinction between fathers and mothers, and finding its appropriate registration in the lexis. Saussure does, however, say two things which suggest that his universe is after all not wholly language-generated (i.e. Sapir–Whorfian). First, he says, 'the statement that everything in language is negative is true only if the signified and the signifier are considered separately; when we consider the sign in its totality we have something that is positive in its own class'.[13] In other words, the sign taken as a whole does appear to engage with the world ('the world', whatever its precise metaphysical status, being construed simply as the locus of possible reference). Secondly, although signs proper are distinguished by what Saussure calls 'opposition' rather than by difference, these oppositions are said to 'imply' 'phonic and conceptual differences'.[14]

[12] Some would argue that the whole (originally) Lockean notion of there being a 'concept' or 'idea' intermediary between the signifier and the referent (yet which is also somehow still part of the 'sign') is otiose and misleading. For them the true 'signified' is simply the referent, whatever its status (tangible, abstract or wholly imaginary). See, e.g., Merquior, *From Prague to Paris*, pp. 231–232:

> Saussure himself ... stresses that the 'same signified' exists both for French '*boeuf*' and for German '*Ochs*'. If indeed the same concept works both sides of the Rhine, could it be by dint of a translinguistic reference to the same animal, which insists on grazing outside the world made of Whorf's ... signifieds?

Again, consider the following:

> Nothing is gained ... by introducing the idea of concepts into the theory of the sign ... the sign signifies the thing (table, mountain, God, idea of civil obedience, whatever), not the concept of the thing. Otherwise, we should be involved in an infinite regress, with signs standing for concepts standing for concepts standing for concepts and so on.
>
> The signified cannot be *in* the sign, or part of it, in the way that the signifier *is* the sign. The reality of the signified is not part of the sign, but a condition of application of the sign. (Geoffrey Thurley, *Counter-Modernism in Current Critical Theory* [London and Basingstoke: Macmillan 1983], p. 172)

[13] *Course*, p. 120.

[14] Ibid., p. 121.

Taken together, those statements might suggest that although the world (at least in part) is structured by language, language is also structured by the world. (One could go further, and substitute 'conceptual schemes' for 'language' in that last sentence.) The case of sentences, which are complex, syntactically ordered signifying units, appears to show this. Just as no sentence can be constructed without syntax, so the fact that there is such a thing as syntax at all seems to depend upon the prior possibility of semantics; for we cannot ascertain the syntactical status of a sign (identify it as a part of speech), and thus understand the sentence in which it figures, unless we have some previous idea, which structure or 'difference' alone cannot supply, of what it refers to.[15]

This can be seen, perhaps unexpectedly, from a nonsense sentence such as Chomsky's *colourless green ideas sleep furiously*. It is only because we know the reference of each word individually that we can understand the ensemble as simultaneously (i) syntactically viable (or rather, viable-*looking*, a sentence of sorts) and (ii) nonsense. The incompatibility of each word with its neighbours is not linguistic (i.e. determined by some grammatical rule) but practical; it is a fact, not about language, but about the world. The situation is much the same with Saussure's 'oppositions'. Unless we already know what 'black' and 'white' mean (that is, what black and white *are*), we cannot perceive them as an opposition or see why they are supposed to be one.[16] If all the foregoing is true, then, the whole structuralist project collapses, since, despite what seem to be Saussure's concessions to the contrary (just illustrated), it rests almost entirely on the premise that formal entities such as syntax and difference are sufficient to generate meaning.[17] So far as post-structuralism relies on a similar exclusion (or indeed denial) of reference, so far must it share the same fate.

[15] Of course, I am not saying that the logical properties of linguistic systems cannot be studied independently of what sentences obeying the rules of such systems might actually mean in any specific case. What I am saying is that syntax in general depends upon the possibility of reference in general.

[16] While preparing this lecture for publication, I have discovered some apparent echoes in this and the previous paragraph of Raymond Tallis's excellent *Not Saussure: a Critique of Post-Saussurean Literary Theory* (London: Macmillan 1988), pp. 72–74. Having consulted his book some months earlier, in haste, and without taking notes, I was not conscious of any borrowings while writing; but if borrowings they were, I happily acknowledge them now.

[17] It seems as though Merquior would wish generally to dissociate Saussure from this assumption (see note 12 above), in other words to orphan the movement he (Saussure) fathered.

The English word 'language' is best avoided in this context, since it covers both the abstract linguistic system, *langue*, and language in use, *parole*, the set of all actual and possible sentences and sentence-parts. *Langue*, Saussure's chief concern, is roughly speaking *parole* formally or systematically considered, which means (as I have already suggested) with all notion of reference (that is, of actual language-use) bracketed out.

Saussure perhaps forgot that, so far from being 'natural', *langue*'s apparent all-determining, Platonic authority was no more than the consequence of his having abstracted it from actual language-use in the first place. *Langue* is 'without positive terms' simply *by definition*. It follows that difference, as a feature of *langue*, must also be (as I have already said it is) purely formal, a vacancy waiting to be filled. Yet, as we shall see, it is this hypothetical abstraction, this absolute non-entity, which, while it is perfectly suitable for Saussure's purposes, the leading deconstructionist Jacques Derrida solemnly hypostatizes into what he calls *différance*, the foundation of his supposedly anti-foundational (non-)system.

Two further Saussurean distinctions deserve notice. The first is that between synchronic and diachronic relations. Synchronic relations are those, such as difference, which obtain between linguistic items in immediate use. Diachronic relations, such as etymological derivation, are irrelevant *as such* to immediate meaning. For an example (mine), suppose I tell my children not to be silly. I know, as they do not, that the word 'silly' is historically related to the German *selig*, meaning happy or blessed, and that this derivation throws an interesting light on our moral conceptions.[18] Nevertheless none of this information plays the slightest part in my utterance, which my children can understand completely, without remainder. The meaning of my utterance is constrained and determined, wholly circumscribed, by its occasion of use (which is solely and precisely what makes it usable).[19]

Finally, syntagmatic and associative relations. Syntagmatic relations are those which hold between the terms of a syntagm, that is, of a linear, sense-making series (the parts of a word, phrase or sentence). Associative relations (later called paradigmatic relations)

---

[18] As should be obvious to anyone who reflects upon the heroes of *The Idiot* and *Parsifal*, both 'holy fools'.

[19] Compare H. P. Grice, in his seminal article 'Meaning' (1957), on the importance of context in the interpretation of utterances: 'A man who calls for a "pump" at a fire would not want a bicycle pump' (Paul Grice, *Studies in the Way of Words* [Cambridge, MA: Harvard University Press 1989], p. 222).

are those obtaining between the linguistic items actually selected for use and others which, though absent, they call to mind, by way of either similarity or contrast, and through both form and content. These *de facto* unemployed or excluded terms compose a potentially infinite set, and resurface later in Derrida's so-called 'traces' (though those, as far as I can see, are also not wholly distinct from Saussurean differences).

We can now skip the entire history of post-Saussurean structuralism (Jakobson, Lévi-Strauss and the rest) because nearly everything significant in deconstruction can be traced back to Saussure, whether deconstruction embraces, modifies or breaks with him. One may as well go straight to Derrida.

I had better say straight away that reading Derrida produces an effect on me varying between an immense weariness and total allergy syndrome. And so it does, I imagine, on most people accustomed to educated discourse, who expect to see something like a perceptible line of argument, a manifest point and the same adhered to, neither the reader's intelligence nor his patience insulted, contradictions and paradoxisms eschewed rather than flaunted, proper evidence produced for whatever is being asserted, objections anticipated and honestly dealt with, and so on. Like many, I first came across Derrida in the late 1960s, in the Parisian journal *Tel Quel*, but dipped into him again in the late 1970s, when he was first becoming big business in English-speaking academia. In the few weeks before I delivered the first version of this paper,[20] and with a reluctance overcome only by the most grinding self-discipline, my eyes traversed or re-traversed some hundreds among Derrida's thousands upon thousands of pages. Since then I have subjected myself to a good deal more of the same, but without, I am afraid, undergoing any miraculous conversion.

I am aware that not everyone would call this reading him. I would say three things in reply: first, that to all intents and purposes Derrida, at least in his own estimation, and certainly in his own practice, has destroyed the whole notion of meaningful,

[20] A paper given at Boston University in November 1994, as part of the Andrew Mellon Seminar series, under the general rubric of 'Theory and Description'. The text given here is substantially that delivered a year later at the Royal Institute of Philosophy. For publication I have added a certain amount of extra material, some of it new, but most being restored from cuts enforced by the lecture medium. This note is as convenient a place as any to record my gratitude to Bob Hale, John Leake, Gregory McCulloch, Anthony O'Hear, Christopher Ricks, Roger Scruton, Jon Westling and David Womersley, for their various comments and suggestions.

Anti-Meaning as Ideology: The Case of Deconstruction

evidentially-based reading. Secondly, apart from his increasing recourse, over the years, to a would-be 'playful' obscurity, apart also from a few novelties (such as printing two separate discourses side by side, to be read simultaneously), Derrida's characteristic manner and subject-matter are so obsessionally repetitive that a hundred pages chosen at random would probably yield much the same content as his entire *oeuvre*. (A parallel: how much pulp fiction, or indeed Shakespeare, do I have to read before I can form a just opinion of it?). Thirdly, I am engaged to say something about deconstruction generally. It may be that there are professional expositors of deconstruction, such as Jonathan Culler and Christopher Norris, who actually represent it better than Derrida, de Man and the rest of the pantheon, even though they (Culler and Norris) write with a fair degree of clarity and cannily hedge their bets as to its validity. At any rate, I make no apology for relying on them at least as heavily as on the original. If they, who have a *prima facie* interest in making it seem, if not necessarily persuasive, then at least serious and coherent, cannot do so, we may reasonably suppose that it is not.

Derrida's thinking is so to speak disorderly on principle, since any pretensions to rationality would be what he calls 'logocentric'.[21] Nevertheless, one has to start somewhere, so I shall begin with his notion of 'presence'. This can be approached through his views on writing (*écriture*). Derrida is struck by the priority which (as he would have it) philosophers and linguists have always accorded to speech. One is, as it were, incarnate in one's spoken words, since one is physically present, speaking them and hearing oneself do so (what Derrida calls *s'entendre parler*).[22] One is not, however, 'present' in the same way in one's writing, which enjoys a certain quasi-independence. (This seems plausible enough. For example, I can dissociate myself from something I have written, as from something I have said, not in the sense of denying that I ever wrote or meant it, but in the sense of not now intending it or not now wanting to stick by it. But I cannot as a rule plausibly dissociate

[21] This mysterious term, though central to deconstructionist discourse, is never clearly defined, either by Derrida or by his expositors. (Presumably to do so would be to succumb to what it condemns.) See Jacques Derrida, *Of Grammatology*, tr. G. Spivak (Baltimore and London: Johns Hopkins University Press 1976), p. 43; John M. Ellis, *Against Deconstruction* (Princeton: Princeton University Press 1989), p. 30ff. Culler's attempt to reduce it to some kind of intelligibility is probably the best that can be hoped for (*On Deconstruction*, pp. 89–110). See also Merquior, *From Prague to Paris*, p. 214.

[22] See Culler, *On Deconstruction*, pp. 107–110; Derrida, *Of Grammatology*, pp. 7–8, 20, 166.

myself from something I am actually engaged in uttering,[23] any more than an adulterer caught *in flagrante delicto* can intelligibly dissociate himself from the act he is engaged in performing.) What Derrida deduces from this supposed 'privileging' of speech over writing (and indeed from philosophy generally, though that exists almost entirely in written form)[24] is the idea that our culture is built on a delusory 'metaphysics of presence',[25] whether that 'presence' be of the subject or of the object.

The idea is not new, and can be traced back to Nietzsche, and, beyond him, to the Sophists of ancient Greece (whom he admired).[26] All it really amounts to is a kind of extreme idealism, scepticism or anti-realism, which aims to expunge from discourse all reference to an objective world in which things are 'present'

[23] Something like this holds, I believe, even in the case of fictional utterance or story-telling, which, contrary to what most of the literature alleges, conforms fairly uncontroversially to a standard speech-act pattern, which is simply this: 'I invite you to imagine that *S*.' What I can and do dissociate myself from, and am understood as author to be dissociating myself from, is the intention of actually uttering *S*, the body or content of the fiction, *in propria persona*. I put *S* mentally in inverted commas, as though it were reported speech, even though it is I who have devised it. (No wonder Plato wanted the poets banished.) From this perspective there is no substantive difference between spoken and written fictions, since in neither of them is the author immediately 'present'.

[24] There is an important sense, as I have just conceded, in which speech might seem to be 'prior', and of course speech existed before writing; but the idea that philosophers generally have ever accorded anything other than purely temporal priority to spoken language is preposterous. So is Derrida's whimsical attempt to reverse what he sees as the speech/writing 'hierarchy'. On these matters Derrida's critics are pretty well unanimous (and his defenders strangely silent). See e.g. Ellis, *Against Deconstruction*, Ch. 2; John Searle, 'The word turned upside down' (review of Culler's *On Deconstruction*), *New York Review of Books*, 27 October 1983 (quoted Merquior, *From Prague to Paris*, p. 216); Scruton, *Upon Nothing*, pp. 18–21. For a more charitable view (M. H. Abrams's) see note 31 below.

[25] A vague notion of what this might mean can be gathered from Derrida, *Writing and Difference*, tr. Alan Bass (London: Routledge and Kegan Paul 1978), pp. 279–280, 292, and *Of Grammatology*, p. 12. For a clearer account, see Culler, *On Deconstruction*, p. 92ff.

[26] 'The first work of throughgoing deconstruction ... to come down to us, so striking in its wholesale anticipation of the contemporary project as to demand reconsideration of the cultural and philosophical context that could have conditioned it, is the fifth-century BC treatise *On Not Being, or On Nature* by Gorgias, the argument of which was summarized by Sextus Empiricus: "Firstly ... nothing exists; secondly ... even if anything

just as persons are 'present' in their speech. (Forget about whether things and persons really exemplify the same kind of 'presence'.) As a metaphysical doctrine, Derrida's is vulnerable to the usual anti-sceptical arguments. If there is no objective world, or if the so-called objective world is in fact wholly language-determined (as in the so-called Sapir–Whorf hypothesis, alluded to earlier), the only criterion of 'truth' or 'reality', if we admit them as meaningful categories at all, will be consensus.

But what can it mean, to say that the so-called objective world is 'in fact' language-determined? What does 'in fact' mean? How can we make truth-claims about language or anything else without reference to some independent state of affairs? By that, of course, and with Kant and Wittgenstein in mind, I do not mean something transcending language's capacity to express it. (Derrida's 'transcendental signified' is a straw man.)[27] I mean merely whatever the following example illustrates: that, although we have both a word and a concept 'cat', the animal to which they refer exists independently of both (as it does also of such words as *Katze, chat, gatto,* etc., and their related concepts, which of course, since what is here

[27] It is essentially what realists, in Derrida's caricature of realism, are supposed to believe in, viz. the 'thing in itself' or 'metaphysical presence' (see e.g. *Of Grammatology*, pp. 49-50). I shall return to this question.

---

exists, it is inapprehensible by man; thirdly ... even if anything is apprehensible, yet of a surety it is inexpressible and incommunicable to one's neighbour." "Against the Logicians", I. 65.' (Howard Felperin, *Beyond Deconstruction: the Uses and Abuses of Literary Theory* [Oxford: Clarendon Press 1985], p. 104n.)

See also Stanley Fish: 'modern anti-foundationalism is old sophism writ analytic' (quoted Sim, *Beyond Aesthetics*, p. 97); Christopher Norris, *Deconstruction: Theory and Practice* (London: Methuen 1982), pp. 60–61 (on Nietzsche's view of Socrates' victory, in the *Gorgias*, over the sophist Callicles): 'Truth is simply the honorific title assumed by an argument which has got the upper hand—and kept it—in this war of competing persuasions.' Norris seems not to consider the converse possibility, that truth, just because it is the truth, is dialectical trumps (i.e. maximally persuasive), and therefore that an argument which exemplified it might deservedly 'get the upper hand'.

Norris's is like the view that history is written by the victor, or the opinion of Thrasymachus (who celebrated the alleged fact) or of Marx (who deplored it) that 'justice is the interest of the stronger'. In later writings such as *Deconstruction and the Interests of Theory* (London: Pinter 1988) and *What's Wrong with Postmodernism* (Hemel Hempstead: Harvester Wheatsheaf 1990) Norris tends more towards a humanist quasi-realism (aligning himself with, e.g., Karl-Otto Apel and the later Habermas). However, this could simply be a tactical self-distancing from the de Man *débâcle*, of the kind that I began by noting.

in question is a 'natural kind', are identical with our concept 'cat'). I can no more stroke the word 'cat', than the concept 'cat' can catch mice; and the truth of what I say about the cat will depend, not on my saying it, or on your agreement with me, but on what the cat actually is and does (for example, sit on the mat).

If you agree with me, it will not be because consensus is the criterion of truth or identical with it, but because in ordinary empirical matters agreement, where it obtains, is the consequence of standard verificatory procedures (looking, checking, etc.). And yes, 'standard verificatory procedures' effectively means 'agreed-upon verificatory procedures'; but to agree on such procedures is not to forestall or guarantee the outcomes, nor to deliver an advance consensus as to what they will be. The procedures for establishing truth or falsehood are the object of consensus simply because they have, in fact, proved effective in establishing those things.

In short, things are not true or false because we agree that they are; we agree that they are true or false because on inspection they have turned out to be so. And if, as Derrida says, nothing is objectively true,[28] it follows that nothing he says can be objectively true, including the statement that nothing is true. So, since he gives us

[28] Derrida nowhere commits himself to so plain and unequivocal a statement. (His habit is never to commit himself to anything, which in part accounts for his stylistic oddities: see Scruton, *Upon Nothing*, pp. 2–6, which centres on Derrida's simultaneous 'taking back' of anything that he might seem to be asserting.) But it is the underlying principle of his entire discourse. The ensuing paradox—that deconstruction cannot be true either—is fleetingly noted (in relation to de Man) by Culler (*On Deconstruction*, pp. 278–279; cf. also p. 149), who seems blithely unruffled by it.

It should nevertheless be observed that when it suits him Derrida is perfectly capable of claiming that 'in no case is it a question of a *discourse against truth* or against science. ... I repeat, then ...: *we must have* [*il faut*] truth. ... Paraphrasing Freud, ... we must recognize in truth "the normal prototype of the fetish". How can we do without it?' (*Positions*, tr. Alan Bass [London: Athlone Press 1981], p. 105). But even there, in that reference to 'the fetish' there is something like a 'taking back'. A more spectacular, full-blooded example can be found in Christopher Norris's account of Derrida's recent quasi-realist (sc. anti-postmodernist) backslidings. The following extract is surely walking on water (and *à deux* too, by the look of it):

Derrida's aim ... is not to argue that the humanistic disciplines lack any critical force; that they are products, one and all, of a self-deluding enterprise blind to its own real motives. Rather, he is defending the principle of reason, the enlightenment desire for clarity and truth, *in so far as that project can be 'deconstructed' to reveal what it harbours of a hidden agenda all the more powerful for its rhetoric of Kantian disinterest.* (*Deconstruction and the Interests of Theory*, pp. 195–196: italics mine)

no objective reason to believe him (there being, according to him, no objective reason to believe anything), there seems to be no reason why we should bother to read him, unless it be as a kind of surrealist poetry.[29] There might, I suppose, be some who wish to share his evident masochistic enjoyment at the spectacle of his self-impalement on the spikes of a very old paradox, one so rusty, indeed, that it most obligingly deconstructs itself.

Now, in a sense, to abolish 'presence' is what Saussure does by suspending reference. *Langue* is and means nothing in itself. It is not an utterance, nor a stock of potential utterances. It is merely an underlying principle of utterance, consisting of a multiplicity of rules, differences, and the rest, all total blanks until filled out by real-life discourse or *parole* (the thing from which they were abstracted in the first place). This brings me to Derrida's notions of *archiécriture* and *différance* (one of his English titles is *Writing and Difference*).

Archiécriture is variously translated as *arché*-writing, protowriting or *Urschrift*. It contains a quibble on the French prefixes (from a single Greek original) *arché-*, meaning primitive or primordial, as in *archéologie*, and *archi-*, meaning supreme, as in *archiévêque* (archbishop). And, if anyone cares, it probably also contains a hidden pun on the word *architecture*. Although some impressionable people find it witty, Derrida's punning, like his creation of neologisms, circles around its central underlying obsessions in so apparently random and uncontrolled a manner as frequently to be indistinguishable from free association, glossolalia or schizophrenic babble. I must confess to finding it, and Derrida's style generally, perfectly excruciating.[30] As Dr Johnson said of Macpherson's Ossian, any man might write like that, if he would only abandon his mind to it.

Archiécriture first appears in Derrida's treatise *Of Grammatology*

[29] This observation, or something like it, has frequently been made. See, e.g., Felperin, *Beyond Deconstruction*, pp. 132–133; Eagleton, *Literary Theory*, p. 139; Culler, *On Deconstruction*, p. 147; Art Berman, *From the New Criticism to Deconstruction* (Urbana: University of Illinois Press 1988), pp. 217, 257 (citing Geoffrey Hartman's view of Derrida's *Glas*), 279; M. H. Abrams, 'Construing and Deconstructing' in Rajnath, (ed.), *Deconstruction: a Critique* (Basingstoke: Macmillan 1989), p. 32; P. D. Juhl, 'Playing With Texts', in J. Hawthorn (ed.), *Criticism and Critical Theory* (London: Edward Arnold 1984), p. 71; etc.

[30] 'The whole text [sc. *Glas*] bristles with "witty" puns whose quality the reader may assess by knowing that on page 7 Hegel is assimilated to an eagle because the French pronunciation (egl'/aigle) uncannily captures something of the magisterial coldness of the philosopher, "an eagle caught in the ice". This goes on for almost three hundred pages' (Merquior, *From Prague to Paris*, p. 211).

(1967). What he means by it is a notional discursive medium underlying, and logically prior to, both speech and writing.[31] Roughly, it is discourse divested even of such attenuated vestiges of 'presence' as everyday writing contains. It contains no subjects and no objects. I shall say nothing about Derrida's obscurantism in continuing to call it *écriture* when it is not actually writing (he has a word for this trick, 'palaeonymy', which means deliberately altering the meaning of a concept, whilst perversely retaining its original name).[32] It is hard not to conclude that, at least in one of its aspects, *archiécriture* is nothing more or less than our old friend *langue* given a Left Bank face-lift. For it too, like *langue*, is an empty infinity of differences, a *silence éternel des espaces infinis*, but one whose very emptiness amounts to a kind of substantiality, an object of implicit assertion about the world and its non-existence.

This brings us to Derrida's most famous invention, *différance*. On the one hand, as I said earlier, *différance* is simply the ensemble of Saussurean differences hypostatized into a single, almost agent-like entity; on the other, it is semantic indeterminability. Any given term, like the utterance in which it figures, is held to be indeterminable, that is, subject to semantic slippage. This is in consequence, first, of the supposedly implicit co-presence in it of all the other terms from which, by virtue of Saussure's principle of difference, it is distinguished. In other words, there is a sense in which every designation and every proposition owes its identity to whatever it is not. So much is perhaps uncontroversial, even trivial. But it is something more to say that everything which a given thing is not (to wit, every last thing else) is somehow part of it, or enters into its constitution, or is made conspicuous in that thing by its apparent absence.

Secondly, any utterance or part-utterance is destabilized by the

[31] *Of Grammatology*, pp. 8–9, 40–41, 44, 158–159, etc. See also Culler, *On Deconstruction*, pp. 101–102; Tallis, *Not Saussure*, pp. 220–223. A very fair-minded account is given by Abrams in Rajnath, *Deconstruction*, p. 36:

> Derrida is not claiming that the invention of writing preceded speech in history; he is deploying a device designed to get us to substitute for the philosophical idiom of speaking the alternative idiom of writing, in which we are less prone to the illusion, as he conceives it, that a speaker in the presence of a listener knows what he means independently of the words in which he expresses it, or that he establishes the meaning of what he says to the listener by communicating his unmediated intention in uttering it.

[32] Derrida sometimes calls it 'palaeonomy': 'the "strategic" necessity that requires the occasional maintenance of an *old name* in order to launch a new concept' (*Positions*, p. 71). See also Culler, *On Deconstruction*, p. 140.

Anti-Meaning as Ideology: The Case of Deconstruction

infinite number of concentric contexts in which, since nothing can be understood out of context, it must be considered if its total meaning is to be grasped. In Derrida's words, 'no context permits saturation'—that is, no context is final or definitive.[33] For these two reasons ultimate meaning is endlessly deferred or *différé*. Not only can a meaning never be clearly separated from everything it does not mean, but the wider the context in which it is situated the more, so far from being enriched or completed, it is actually eroded.

These various components of *différance* are not only unrelated, they are also incompatible, not least because they start from opposite ends of the signification process, one from *langue* and the other from *parole*. The first, Saussurean difference, is abstract, and prior to any meaning whatever. It is a systematic precondition, indeed a guarantee, of meaning. The second, deferral, begins from actual utterances. It postulates a world of immediate, more or less graspable meanings which, by recalling the absent possibilities from which they are distinguished, or by being continuously thrust into ever-expanding contexts, are eventually dispersed or dissipated either in an endless regress, or in an all-embracing ubiquity of non-meaning, a discursive outer space littered with the empty shells of past utterance, like spent rocket cases.

As far as the contextual argument goes, Derrida has evidently allowed himself to be mesmerized by the so-called hermeneutic circle, which his fevered imagination has exaggerated into a high-speed centrifuge. The hermeneutic circle consists of the following paradox, first noted by the theologian Schleiermacher: on the one hand, an object of interpretation is intelligible only in relation to the whole of which it forms part, that is, to its context (and similarly to its own parts, if it is itself a whole); on the other, the whole, being made up of such objects, can be understood only through them, its parts. Derrida's typically absolutist, all-or-nothing claim comes down in the end to this, that because nothing can be described exhaustively, pinpointed to the last atomic detail of its contextual location in every possible world, nothing can even begin to be understood.[34]

The simplest solution to this feeble teaser, I submit, is empirical.

[33] 'This is my starting point: no meaning can be determined out of context, but no context permits saturation' (Derrida, 'Living On: *Border Lines*', in Harold Bloom *et al.*, *Deconstruction and Criticism* [London: Routledge and Kegan Paul, 1979], p. 81).
[34] Cf. Thurley, *Counter-Modernism*, p. 189: 'We can "know" something, as Russell pointed out, without having to claim that we know everything about it, nor do we have to make the definition of the nature of a thing synonymous with everything that is relevant to its "absolute" nature—its *Ding-an-sich*-ness.'

269

It is an everyday fact that we both learn and come to understand things (including the hermeneutic circle); and we do so precisely because, with a little knowledge, limited but sound enough as far as it goes, we can board the circle of understanding at the circumference, and gradually, as our experience deepens and grows, work our way to the centre. As Hegel long ago explained, an understanding may be widened, even superseded, without thereby being invalidated. *Aufhebung*, the means by which mind's self-understanding advances, is a process of resolution, not of cancellation.

Derrida's *différance* is a quite literal chimera, a grotesque hybrid, a walking category mistake. On the one hand it signifies a formal absence of meaning, prior to its appearance (or, if you like, as in Saussure, the mere mechanism by which meaning is generated); on the other, it is the process by which, according to Derrida, meaning falls subject to change and decay. Derrida, of course, would not acknowledge even the conception of a category mistake. For his whole drift is towards intellectual entropy, towards the undermining and eventual abolition of all categories, distinctions, genres, hierarchies, singularities, indeed of identities generally. His project is, quite literally, the undoing of thought, and with it everything that depends on it. (And that, whether or not it forms part of Derrida's intention that it should, includes cultural and social constructs, 'forms of life', as Wittgenstein would call them, and the values on which they are built.)

It is not hard to detect here a certain inverted resemblance to both Spinoza and the idealist tradition stemming from Hegel. By exposing them as illusory or logically incoherent, these thinkers dissolve the relations between particulars, fusing them into ever larger and larger particulars, until, in a final holistic convulsion, everything resolves itself into a vast, single, all-embracing particular, be it God, Nature, or the Absolute. Derrida presents a catabolic mirror-image of the same process. His universe terminates, not in a single All, but in a single Nothing; not in the One behind the Many, but in a giant, all-cancelling, absolute Zero.

As I have already noted, another Derridan concept, the 'trace', derives from Saussure's 'associative relations'. 'Traces' are, in effect, equivalent to the non-selected or excluded terms in those relations.[35] They are distant kin, perhaps, to what a literary critic would call associations. Potentially infinite in number, they are seen, especially by other post-structuralists such as Foucault, as a

---

[35] On the other hand, as also already noted, 'traces' seem not wholly to be distinct from 'differences', or from whatever is thought (invisibly or otherwise) to mediate them:

Anti-Meaning as Ideology: The Case of Deconstruction

kind of ghostly, marginal remainder, a banished collective Other, which (like the forest and the Red Indians in *The Scarlet Letter*) nevertheless hangs about, always threatening to disrupt the explicit meaning of a text, utterance, discourse or even culture. (It is noteworthy, by the way, that those last-mentioned things are seen as being categorically of a piece. Both discourses and cultures are treated as kinds of collective utterance, though their subject-matter, it seems, is nothing but themselves.) The notion of 'trace' has, and is perhaps designed to have, socio-political overtones.[36]

The least that needs to be said here is that a false analogy is at work. Saussure's excluded terms are excluded simply because they are not, at any given moment of utterance, those required to

[36] One might remark, for what little it may be worth, that Derrida was brought up in French Algeria, the son of a rabbi. That is, he belonged to a not wholly assimilated minority within a dominant colonial culture. He may well have learned both how to exclude, and what it is like to be excluded. And his reckless readings could well be kin to the wilder allegorical flights and creative 'readings-into' characteristic of *midrash* (Jewish scriptural exegetics): 'So many things are omitted and taken for granted [in the Torah], that an open invitation was given ... to fill in the tantalizing lacunae of the text. The result [was] a vast playground of rabbinic fancy' (S.M. Lehrman, *The World of the Midrash* [London and New York: Thomas Yoseloff 1961], p. 11). Another analogy might be those writers who allege, on the evidence of ciphers 'discovered' in the text, that Bacon wrote Shakespeare. The difference, however, is that both midrashists and Baconians offer to uncover the hypothetical author's (God's or Bacon's) intended meaning, whereas Derrida, and deconstructionists generally, have freed themselves from any obligation to recognize what George Eliot called an 'equivalent centre of self', and thus in effect usurp the (usually known) authorship. Some commentators have suggested that Derrida owes something to the cabbalistic tradition.

The principle of difference compels us ... to consider every process of signification as a formal play of differences. That is, of traces.
    ... Whether in the order of spoken or written discourse, no element can function as a sign without referring to another element which itself is not simply present. This interweaving results in each 'element' ... being constituted on the basis of the trace within it of other elements of the chain or system. This interweaving, this textile, is the *text* ... Nothing, neither among the elements nor within the system, is anywhere ever simply present or absent. There are only, everywhere, differences and traces of traces. (*Positions*, p. 26)

Positions, being a series of interviews, makes Derrida's eponymous 'positions' clearer than they would otherwise be. The book is also, in Merquior's phrase, 'mercifully short'.

convey the intended meaning. Things are otherwise in poetry,[37] but in ordinary discourse communication demands that signification be narrowed to serve the immediate end, and that, by tacit consensus, wider associations (as we have seen with the etymology and original meaning of the word 'silly') be excluded. But in the Foucaultian view, and in Derrida's also, when ideas are reduced to the condition of mere vestiges or traces, it is not because they are not needed, but because they have been 'repressed', more or less *à la* Freud. Derrida speaks unashamedly of the 'suppression' of *différance* (*différance* being effectively the irreducible cosmic given, the rich, pullulating welter of indeterminacy) by the imperious fiction of 'presence' (i.e. the idea that signs, or as he would say, signifiers, are translucent, and can actually signify, that is mean something).[38] One can then go on, with such critics as Edward Said, effectively to identify them as the suppressed discourse of oppressed people.[39]

No one denies, I suppose, that people can be oppressed, or ideas repressed (that is, driven out of consciousness to a point where they are not readily retrievable). It is not impossible, either, that repression can be used as an instrument of oppression (consider brainwashing, or the various non-coercive means of reducing slave populations to docility). But it is not clear that this has anything very much to do with the original concept of the 'trace'. Somewhere an independent dynamic or political meaning, at all events a substantive meaning, has been smuggled in.

This leads to another category-problem. There seems to be agreement that 'traces', whether repressed or merely latent, form part of *archiécriture*, or the universal substrate.[40] But if this is so, how come they are the only substantive signifying forces remaining

[37] In poetry a meaning may regularly be foregrounded, even (so to speak) endorsed, despite (and by) being explicitly ruled out. When Marvell's mower calls the glow-worms 'country comets', saying that they foretell, not the death of princes, but only the fall of the grass, he implicitly sees the death of princes as part of the natural cycle, like the mowing. Yet he does so whilst positively denying any connection between the two orders of phenomena. (See 'The Mower to the Glo-Worms'.)

[38] *Of Grammatology*, p. 166. See also Culler, *On Deconstruction*, pp. 108–109. To put the point more brutally, and thus make its triviality obvious, meaninglessness is dispelled (or, if you must, 'repressed') by meaning. (And a good thing too, especially where practical considerations are at stake, as they must sometimes be even for Derrida. See note 28 above.)

[39] See Said, 'The Text, the World, the Critic' in J. V. Harari (ed.), *Textual Strategies: Perspectives in Post-Structuralist Criticism* (London: Methuen 1979), esp. p. 181ff.

[40] See Tallis, *Not Saussure*, p. 223; Culler, *On Deconstruction*, p. 99.

at that level? Every other meaning has either evaporated (by being endlessly deferred), or exists merely *in posse*, in the sense of having a syntactical berth ready prepared for it, whenever it should choose to present itself. Why, where every other meaning is effectively absent, does repressed or latent meaning survive? Or have we here merely another of those mechanical hierarchy-reversals so central to deconstruction, whereby the last shall be first and the first last?

I do not know, and neither (I suspect) does Derrida. But the deep-seated confusions and contradictions of Derrida's thought do help to explain his apparent breadth of appeal (amongst those who find him appealing). His formalist, Saussurean side, loftily dedicated to the systematic elimination of meaning, entrances the aesthete, the dilettante, and the post-modernist. I am thinking of a tendency which might conceivably be extrapolated from the writings of people such as Geoffrey Hartman and Richard Rorty. (Rorty, by the way, and so far as I know, is the only philosopher of repute who has ever taken Derrida even half-seriously. Hartman at least deserves credit for the coinage 'Derridadaism',[41] which shows that he has seen something of Derrida's point.) Such people find Derrida 'amusing' simply because he overturns, or makes to overturn, the apple cart of commonsense or 'bourgeois' realism (which they also associate with realism in art and literature).

Derrida's radical political implications, on the other hand, give encouragement to those who, having first tipped its bourgeois contents into the gutter, would now set about re-stocking the apple cart with all manner of exotic and forbidden fruit, not to mention windfalls and rejects.[42] Such people are realists, but of a revolutionary rather than commonsense kind. For them, public discourse is the product of power, and the sole reality apart from power itself. What they seek is not the destruction of order, but the

[41] Geoffrey Hartman, *Saving the Text: Literature/Derrida/Philosophy* (Baltimore: Johns Hopkins University Press 1981), p. 33. See also, for comment, Merquior, *From Prague to Paris*, p. 238 and n; Culler, *On Deconstruction*, p. 137n.

[42] According to Richard Rorty, 'deconstruction stands ... in the same relation to "normal" criticism and philosophy as "abnormal" sexuality or science do to their "normal' counterparts—"each lives the other's death and dies the other's life"' (Felperin, *Beyond Deconstruction*, p. 139, quoting Rorty, 'Philosophy as a Kind of Writing', in *Consequences of Pragmatism* [Minneapolis: University of Minnesota Press 1982], p. 107). One may take Rorty's point, whilst denying that there is or could be any such thing as 'abnormal' science. 'Abnormal' science is simply pseudo-science, viz. magic.

'return of the repressed', the bringing to birth of a hidden, previously marginalized order which, with Derrida's help, they suppose themselves to have detected, secreted almost invisibly in the interstices of official culture.

Though there is some warrant for it, this aspect of Derrida seems to me more an invention of his followers than actually there in his writings. Nevertheless, it has constituted a very considerable part of his appeal, and only the more alert radicals, such as Terry Eagleton and (lately) Christopher Norris, have seen that Derrida's central, sweeping relativism and anti-realism (or, to speak more accurately, those of deconstruction generally) must disable the radical's agenda quite as thoroughly as they ever undermined the citadels of bourgeois culture.[43] (Not that the bourgeois seemed greatly bothered.)

Whether *archiécriture*, *différance* and the domain of the trace are ultimately three things, or two things, or one is as undecidable as all meaning is according to Derrida. It is impossible to make consistent sense of his terminology, and likewise of the world to which his writings would refer if reference were possible. The whole is really a congeries of slippery metaphors which melt and flow into each other only to separate again, but which occasionally seem to congeal, like the metaphysical vision they embody (and which has, in truth, no substance apart from them), into a single, ill-defined entity. That, depending on our perspective, is first one thing, then another, then the next, and finally (if there ever is an end to it all) an all-encompassing, quasi-literary, Barthesian mega-text into which everything else, the entire collection of subordinate metaphorical 'texts' of which experience is composed, can be resolved.[44]

I shall return to 'textuality' shortly. For the moment, let us take one final look at the related matter of reference and its near-antithesis, metaphor. (Metaphor in large part underlies fictional utterance, which in turn serves as a metaphor for the world-as-text). One key source of post-structuralism's intellectual confusion is an early fragment of Nietzsche's, 'On Truth and Lie in an Extra-Moral Sense'. In this overwrought, excitable, ultra-nominalist excursion, deferred to by both Derrida and Foucault,

[43] See e.g. Eagleton, *Literary Theory*, pp. 141ff; also (more generally) Norris, *Deconstruction and the Interests of Theory* (London: Pinter 1988) and *What's Wrong with Postmodernism: Critical Theory and the Ends of Philosophy* (Hemel Hempstead: Harvester Wheatsheaf, 1990).

[44] See Roland Barthes, 'From Work to Text', in Harari, *Textual Strategies*; Culler (on Derrida's idea of a 'general text'), *On Deconstruction*, p. 130.

Nietzsche doubts whether language can ever express reality adequately and whether designations and things can ever coincide.[45]

First (he says), language is conventional. It begins 'in regularly valid and obligatory designations'. These (it seems) falsify experience, by subsuming its uniqueness and multiplicity under would-be stable taxonomies. Worse, by extending themselves through successive well-concealed metaphors, they come to colonize the entire experiential field. (Although one might say that in a sense all designation, apart from proper names, is quasi-metaphorical, in assimilating, under some unifying concept, otherwise disparate, or at least separate, events.) Like Hobbes's covenant, they serve only human convenience. In short, language captures 'only the relations of things to man', not the 'thing in itself'.

This points us towards two cardinal post-structuralist errors, both of which result from pitching the semantic and epistemological stakes too high. One is to suppose that conventional designations cannot genuinely refer. They can and do (indeed, there are no others), so long as we agree on what it is that they refer to. That agreement, indeed, is already implicit in the act, or fact,[46] of designation. Moreover, certainly in the case of physical objects, and indeed with other things (as we have seen in the case of the word 'silly'), the original referent may endure however much its original designation may slip out of alignment with it. When the gap becomes too wide, a new name is found for the old referent, the old name often having attached itself spontaneously to a new referent. (On the other hand some names, such as 'phlogiston', simply fall out of indicative or practical use altogether when their supposed referents are found not to exist, or when the phenomena they were invoked to explain turn out to be differently constituted and thus require a new name, e.g. 'oxygen', for the agent involved.)

There is nothing regrettable about any of this, except (some might say) that, as earlier observed, we as individuals are powerless to control it. But if we could, communication, as also noted

[45] See Walter Kaufmann (ed. and tr.), *The Portable Nietzsche* (New York: Viking Press, 1967), pp. 42ff.

[46] That distinction (between 'act' and 'fact') is meant merely to note that some designations (e.g. 'nylon', 'penicillin', 'quark') are proposed and adopted deliberately, while most are inherited, accepted and used unselfconsciously, without question. But each kind is founded on consensus, and the consensus in each case on convenience. The distinction lies merely in the type of consensus. It has an obvious political parallel in the distinction between a legitimacy based on contract (Locke and liberalism) and one presupposed in 'tacit consent' (Hume and conservatism).

earlier concerning Humpty Dumpty, would come to a stop, just as it has whenever any other single, non-consensual agency (such as the totalitarian state) has attempted to control it. And that would be infinitely more regrettable than our inability to impose our private meanings on the world, even supposing (*pace* Wittgenstein) that there were such things.

The other, closely related, error is to suppose that the only 'real' reference could be to a thing-in-itself, that is, to 'ultimate' reality. But the whole point of Kant, as of the later Wittgenstein, was to dispense with 'things-in-themselves'. The only reference we either have or need is to 'things in their relation to man'. This category, however, excludes neither 'natural kinds' nor scientific objects. Doubtless those exist independently, and in that sense are indeed 'things-in-themselves', but they also enter into and form part of our world, where it is still possible for us to perceive (or imagine) them as they are, undistorted by our practical interests. The reason is that practical interests are not our only ones. We also have (and take) an interest in objective knowledge, which is just what makes such knowledge possible. It does not matter that we cannot step outside our own perspective or our various language-worlds, that is, outside the world of designatable things, of phenomena, of the knowable. There is, indeed, a kind of confusion involved in lamenting, from within those worlds, and in their language, our inability totally to transcend them, and in regarding as 'true' or 'real' only whatever is imagined to do so.

As I have already said of Derrida, deconstruction is typically all-or-nothingist.[47] (No doubt some future Spengler will identify it as a cultural epiphenomenon of digital electronics, where, switch-fashion, everything is either 'off' or 'on'.) There is more than a whiff of existentialist brinkmanship in its make-up. Everything is played out in the glare of some garish ontological melodrama. It is supposed that because 'ultimate' reality is beyond our grasp, ordinary human, language-bound reality, and language itself, must be a snare and a delusion, a malign Cartesian demon. They are not. Generally speaking, language refers to what we want it to refer to. And for the most part that too exists, in its own right, whether or not it is a so-called 'product' of language, or has been picked out in accordance with our needs, abilities and interests. (Tables are a functional kind, and have been so picked out; cats are a natural kind, and therefore have not. But once we have decided what we mean by 'table' and 'cat' it is simply true or false that there is or is not a table or a cat before us. We know, moreover, that in the case

[47] See Abrams in Rajnath, *Deconstruction*, p. 42.

of the cat something is in question that is in no way determined or qualified by our interests or 'forms of life'.) It might be said, in fact, and nothwithstanding their radical nominalism, that deconstructionists are at heart disillusioned rationalists or transcendental realists, who, hoping for immediate personal access to an ultimate, extra-human reality, had subsequently discovered, to their great annoyance, that the only reality on offer is one they are compelled to share with others.[48]

Here the political, Foucaultian side of the theory, already adverted to, comes in: those others, therefore, perhaps without meaning to do so, are actually constraining and manipulating me. Or maybe someone or something is manipulating them. This is the logic of paranoia. Indeed, deconstruction has been characterized by Paul Ricoeur as one among several typically modernist 'hermeneutics of suspicion', the others being those of Marx, Freud and Nietzsche.[49] It seems the perfect exemplification of Sartre's

[48] See note 3 above, esp. the quotation from Merquior. Here is as good a place as any to note that the deconstructionist account of, and assault on, language and meaning are closely analogous to the Left's view of, and characteristic hostility to, free markets. For both language and the market are spontaneous, consensual systems of exchange, whose values (meanings and prices) are the outcome of innumerable single transactions. Both (like another such system, culture) naturally defy the attempts of individuals to force them to conform to their own preferred overall patterns. Individuals can only do so, in either case, by recourse to the organs of government, and even then not without unforeseen, undesired and in general hugely counter-productive consequences. There seems to be agreement among commentators, irrespective of their sympathies, that, though structuralist by descent, deconstruction grew out of *les évènements de mai 1968* and (as I began this paper by observing) is a broadly left-wing phenomenon. (See, e.g., Berman, *From the New Criticism*, p. 102; Eagleton, *Literary Theory*, pp. 142ff.; Felperin, *Beyond Deconstruction*, p. 213; Scruton, *Upon Nothing*, pp. 7–19, 31. See also note 60 below.)

Later, however, the movement split not once but twice, one wing of it (what I go on in the main text to call its aesthetic or ludic tendency) either retreating into an ironic, postmodernist quietism (Lyotard *et al.*), or plunging defiantly into a brash, near-nihilistic celebration of junk culture. (The latter, to the Left, is the natural outcome of the rule of the market, and perhaps plausibly enough. But one can support the market without thinking it ought to *rule*. Indeed, if it is truly to be free and we are to benefit from it, it must itself be subject to regulation. See the present writer's 'The Politics of Equilibrium', *Inquiry*, 35 [1992], esp. pp. 430–431.)

[49] *The Rule of Metaphor*, tr. R. Czerny (London: Routledge and Kegan Paul 1978), p. 285. The relevant passage is cited in the course of Christopher Butler's sensible discussion of Nietzsche's and Derrida's view

insight to the effect that, in the words of one of his characters, Hell is other people.

To return, however: why does the literary or fictional analogy, together with the idea (if distinct from the latter) that everything in the end is 'text', underlie so much of the deconstructive enterprise? First, because literature (I am using the word interchangeably with fiction) is *écriture*. In writing, as we have seen, the subject (that is, the writer) need not be actively 'present'. Secondly, literature does not refer, at least not in the ordinary sense. Its objects are not 'present', being imagined rather than independently real. (It may perhaps be permissible to regard them instead as abstract types of real-life objects, and thus to see literature as a kind of generalizing imaginative discourse, but we cannot go into all that now.) Being thus non-referential, from a post-structuralist or deconstructionist viewpoint literature can serve as the paradigm of all discourse.[50]

[50] 'The statement about language, that sign and meaning can never coincide, is what is precisely taken for granted in the kind of language we call literary ... A work of fiction asserts, by its very existence, its separation from empirical reality, its divergence, as a sign, from a meaning that depends for its existence on the constitutive activity of this sign ... It is always against the explicit assertion of the writer that readers degrade the fiction by confusing it with a reality from which it has forever taken leave' (Paul de Man, *Blindness and Insight: Essays in the Rhetoric of Contemporary Criticism* [New York: Oxford University Press 1971], p. 17).

(in 'On Truth and Lie' and 'White Mythology' respectively) that metaphysics is the ghost of (officially) dead metaphor (Butler, *Interpretation, Deconstruction and Ideology* [Oxford: Clarendon Press 1984], p. 20ff. For another summary of Derrida's 'metaphorics' see Abrams in Rajnath, *Deconstruction*, p. 59. 'White Mythology' is to be found in *Margins of Philosophy*, tr. Alan Bass [Brighton: Harvester Press 1982]).

My own view of this etymologistic (and thus very un-Saussurean) notion may be deduced from my comments above concerning the disjunction between the history and the current use of the word 'silly'. I deny that previous meanings (or indeed any other meanings irrelevant to the matter in hand) have any power automatically to influence or determine the sense in which, or intention with which, an expression is being employed. Cf. Ricoeur again: 'It is use in discourse that specifies the difference between the literal and the metaphorical, and not some sort of prestige attributed to the primitive or the original' (*Rule of Metaphor*, p. 291, quoted Butler, p. 139). To be fair, however, Derrida does admit that 'to read within a concept the hidden history of a metaphor is to privilege *diachrony* at the expense of system', i.e. is un-Saussurean (*Margins of Philosophy*, p. 215). On the all-decisive importance of relevance, see Dan Sperber and Deirdre Wilson, *Relevance: Communication and Cognition* (Oxford: Blackwell 1986).

Anti-Meaning as Ideology: The Case of Deconstruction

Thirdly, at least in theory, literature can be read any way one chooses, in the sense that, especially in the contemporary academy, there are no practical or immediate sanctions (such as ridicule) against absurd, stupid or perverse readings (indeed, there are plenty of rewards for them). To a certain sort of mind a text, unlike an author, is gratifyingly docile. (An analogy with various sexual perversions suggests itself.) It can admit a plurality of contradictory readings yet hold the reader actively responsible for none. If society or public discourse are anything like that, we can all enjoy manipulating them in our imaginations. A text cannot fight back, or take its revenge on wilfulness or incompetence, in the way that reality can. In this light, the fictional or textual view of the social cosmos cannot but appeal to the political fantasists found everywhere in humanities departments. Being allegedly stitched together out of unacknowledged rhetorical tropes, the world can be 'undone' and its hidden dynamic 'unmasked' by armchair revolutionaries, mere literary critics, who have never in their lives engaged in serious political reflection. This is the 'subversive' face of textuality.

Its other face is the aesthetic, or ludic. The world is a post-modernist fiction, to be 'read' as such. Perhaps after all this view is the most plausible, not in itself, but as accounting for the appeal of the literary analogy. Here the world appears as a boundless Text, signifying everything and nothing, rich in possibility, but with nothing actualized which might disrupt the elegance of the scene with its uncouth reminders of 'presence'. The Text, the *arché*-writing, the endless play of traces and differences, all these figurative conceits and many more combine to form a vast, shimmering Valhalla or Crystal Palace, glimpsed across a crevasse of non-reference and anti-meaning.

Mocking the realist's stupidity, yet secure against his envious criticisms, this splendid edifice waits only for the gods of deconstruction and their acolytes to cross the rainbow bridge and enjoy immediate vacant possession.[51] For the palace is empty, its emptiness being designed to ensure that the inhabitants shall disport themselves unchallenged by squatters or other unbidden riff-raff from the world of reference, with its boring materiality and its importunate claims to attention.

In fact, when you think about it, nothing could actually be more bourgeois, in the bad sense, than deconstruction. It is the brand-new, post-modernist housing estate (with guard dogs and high wire fence), the spiritual home, in short the ideology, of the

[51] I hope I may be forgiven for here making explicit the allusion to *Das Rheingold*. For some reason, as I write, the creations of Sir Richard Rogers spring to mind.

upwardly mobile thinker, the intellectual *parvenu* or *arriviste*. Deconstruction's manner is suffocatingly pretentious, and its characteristic tone one of insufferable conceit, as can be seen from Derrida's clownish (and if I may say so, deplorably ill-bred) encounter with Searle.[52]

In that exchange Derrida shows himself either unable or unwilling to understand what a speech-act is. As Searle rightly observes, Derrida signally fails to distinguish between use and mention (a distinction, note, which fictional discourse obliterates, since there all is mention, or something analogous to it).[53] For this reason Derrida thinks that a speech-act is 'iterable', that is, remains the same speech-act in whatever context it is uttered or repeated (note the conflict with what he says elsewhere about the contextual erosion of meaning). But of course a speech-act is not 'iterable', any more than my hammering a nail into the wall on 25th July last is 'iterable', or than Heraclitus could step into the same river twice. All of those, like utterances or performances of any kind, demand the presence (or 'presence') of the *agent*, simply because they are actions and not just reported actions.

Two things, though, really are 'iterable', and really do persist throughout changes of context. Neither is a speech-act, though each is mistaken by Derrida for one. The first is the actual sequence of words, the sentence, used in the original speech-act, which, since the context as well as the words can be reported (that is, mentioned), remains identifiable as having once constituted a speech-act of a certain kind, and that one in particular.

The other is the *formula* of certain speech-acts, such as the words used at a swearing-in ceremony, which stands to them much as *langue* stands to *parole*. In other words, they become a speech-act only when somebody appropriately qualified actually pronounces them on cue and *in situ*. It is tedious to have to remark these distinctions, but it is also quite funny to watch Jonathan Culler, who ought to know better, trying to flannel his way out of them in defence of his hero's assumed intellectual virtuosity.[54]

[52] The exchange is summarized and illustrated at some length in Culler, *On Deconstruction*, pp. 110–134. See also Norris, *Deconstruction: Theory and Practice*, pp. 110ff.

[53] I have no space here to argue out this point about fictional discourse, but a hint as to the direction such an argument might take may be gathered from note 23 above.

[54] Much the same is true of Norris (*Deconstruction and the Interests of Theory*, pp. 79–80). He, like Derrida, confuses a sentence (which *is* 'iterable') with a speech-act (which, being an event, is not). As it happens, a passage he cites from Donald Davidson, and uses (erroneously) as a stick

Speaking of competence, let me make some very brief observations on deconstruction in practice.[55] The most I can do here is draw attention to a piece by Paul de Man in what was once *the* graduate post-structuralist's primer. This is a collection from the late 1970s, entitled (with characteristic militarism) *Textual Strategies*, and stuffed to the gunwales with top brass, many of them, including Barthes, Derrida and Foucault, already on the Valhalla housing list.

De Man's essay, 'Semiology and Rhetoric', discloses that a well-known passage in Proust, which to the untutored eye concerns the young Marcel reading in a darkened room on a hot summer day, really 'acts out and asserts the priority of metaphor over metonymy'.[56] No sooner have we recovered from this blinding revelation than, still rubbing our eyes, we learn a couple of pages later that 'after the deconstructive reading ... we can no longer believe the assertion made ... about the intrinsic, metaphysical superiority of metaphor over metonymy'.[57]

[55] At the original time of writing I had not seen Abrams's admirable dissection of J. Hillis Miller's so-called 'double' reading (i.e. first 'straight' and then 'deconstructive') of Wordsworth's 'A slumber did my spirit seal' (see Abrams in Rajnath, *Deconstruction*, pp. 47–60). The analysis, like Miller's piece, raises profound questions about how, and at what precise point, a reading ceases to be plausible and becomes fantastic (i.e. ceases to be a *reading* and becomes something else, say a 'reading-into').

[56] Twenty-something years ago, at a fairly grand academic dinner, I was placed next to a lady whose critical opinions now command worldwide celebrity and respect. I mentioned *To the Lighthouse*, a work I still hold in some esteem. 'Oh,' she said, 'well, really, it's all about presence and absence, isn't it?' Since then, oft when on my couch I lie in vacant or in pensive mood, those words come unbidden to mind, and everything just seems to fall into place (particularly so much as pertains to the nature and requisites of academic success).

[57] Though clearly overawed by de Man's brilliance, the ever-scrupulous Culler nevertheless confesses that he cannot actually discover which metaphor de Man is referring to (the nearest candidate appears

to beat Searle with, makes the distinction plain: 'the same declarative sentence may have the same meaning when used to make an assertion, to tell a joke, to annoy a bore, to complete a rhyme, or to ask a question' (Davidson, *Inquiries*, p. 269). The very fact that a sentence can be thus *used* in different speech-acts makes it clear that it is not, of itself, the same thing as a speech-act; and that the 'meaning' of which Davidson is speaking is not illocutionary but abstract and inert, the sentence's so to speak 'dictionary meaning' (as of a single word), which is mobilized (and further determined) only in actual utterance (rather as a word is in a sentence).

But such fiddle-faddle apart, consider what de Man says about the rhetorical question at the end of Yeats's great and profoundly moving poem, 'Among School Children'. Whilst acknowledging its noblest products, Greek philosophy and the Christian religion, Yeats nevertheless deplores the human propensity to separate spirit from flesh and body from soul, in short to reduce everything to murderous rationalist dichotomies. 'How can we know the dancer from the dance?', he asks. And the question answers itself: we can't. That is what the question means.

For some lunatic reason, however, de Man proposes to take the question literally, despite the fact that nothing in the poem supports such a reading, even at the deepest imaginable levels of irony. (Indeed, why stop there? Why not take the dance and the dancer literally too?) I should have been more impressed had de Man queried the last couplet of Marvell's 'The Garden', which really does seem ambivalent as between a literal and a rhetorical question, a reading for which I think the rest of the poem gives pretty convincing warrant.[58]

Rational, which is to say relevant and appropriate, interpretation is hardly to be expected from those who impugn the very idea of rationality, and for whom anything or anybody may be taken as a text, any text as fair game, and every season as open. I am not persuaded, either, that the underlying theory is much more than a conjuring trick designed to impress, first, the conjuror himself, and secondly, the vulgar. Certainly I have seen little to suggest that deconstructionists, however ingenious and even (on occasion) erudite, possess much intellectual competence in the normal

---

[58] The final couplet is this: 'How could such sweet and wholesome hours / Be reckoned but with herbs and flowers?' Taken rhetorically, the question implies that the hours spent in the garden were indeed innocent (as the speaker has constantly been at pains to stress), and could not be better emblematized than by the said floral clock. When, however, it is taken literally (to mean something like 'How could anyone possibly think that such sweet and wholesome hours ... etc.?'), invisible ironic quotation marks appear round *sweet and wholesome*, and *but* changes its meaning from 'except' to 'merely'. The irony spreads to the speaker's protestations concerning the harmlessness of his retreat, and proves justified by the powerful intimations of sensual temptation and moral peril (as of Eden just before the Fall) underlying the idyllic surface descriptions. Contrary to the immediate closing suggestion, there is another, weightier 'reckoning' to be made.

---

rather to be a synecdoche: Culler, *On Deconstruction* pp. 244–245 and n). The metaphor which springs to my mind is that of the Emperor's New Clothes.

sense.[59] (But then, says the deconstructionist, the whole point is to put the 'normal' in question. And for him, of course, to 'question' something is automatically to refute it.)

I may be wrong, of course. It may be not intellectual competence, but intellectual scruple, which deconstruction lacks. The end result, however, is the same. So the question returns with which I began: why did anyone want to believe in deconstruction, and why did it survive for so long?

I have given two answers already, explaining deconstruction's appeal by its content, or rather its drift. In its ambiguous way, deconstruction offered something to both the aesthete and the radical, though they fell out over de Man. But there is a further possibility. Deconstruction's strongest recruitment incentive might conceivably have been altogether unrelated to its actual content, and have lain rather in what was something like a totemic function. Perhaps what really mattered was the movement's own Saussurean 'difference', the fact that it was 'alternative'.[60] It served as a counter-cultural rallying-point, not as a rule for students, but for the numerous tribe of half-educated, not-quite-good-enough academics whom the enormous expansion of tertiary education in the

[59] I am certainly not convinced by Norris's repetitious, mantra-like insistence, in reply to Ellis (*Against Deconstruction*), on Derrida's 'rigorous critique', 'analytical work of the highest order', 'sustained analytical grasp', 'high level of sustained argumentative force', 'logical rigour, consistency and truth', 'highly disciplined process of argument', 'sheer critical acumen and intellectual grasp', 'stylistic brilliance', 'rigorously consequential logic', 'extreme analytical precision', 'meticulous analytical close reading', 'maximum degree of analytical clarity and rigour'.

All but one of those phrases occur in thirteen consecutive pages (pp. 145–157) of Norris's *What's Wrong with Postmodernism*. Barring a couple of short, drab and (given the exorbitance of the claims) wholly unpersuasive quotations, not one is accompanied by a scrap of evidence, nor, I believe, could any easily be found among the reams upon reams of Derrida's vague, inflated, inconsequential ramblings. I do not doubt Norris's sincerity (at least as perceived by himself), but the cumulative effect of his assertions is largely one of bluster, as of one whose bluff has been called. Derrida's critics, he says on p. 160, will have to show precisely where his arguments go wrong. Derrida's disciples, it seems to me, will have to show, not so much where his arguments go right, as where there are any to be found at all.

[60] Since it featured in both my lecture and the original seminar paper I have, on revision, let this quasi-structuralist explanation stand, despite its implausibility (which the sentence immediately following in the main text merely underscores). The ballyhoo concerning de Man's Nazi past is surely sufficient testimony to the importance of deconstruction's ideological content. Nor can one imagine that absolutely *any* 'alternative' literary

last twenty or thirty years had sucked into existence. Anyone who has attended an academic literary conference in the last decade and a half will know what I mean.

To join this 'alternative academy' it was necessary, not to understand deconstruction, but merely to sign up for it. Deconstruction has approached nearest to orthodoxy in literary or para-literary disciplines, in the sense that it is still fairly imprudent even now for an academic hoping for tenure or promotion to express open hostility to it. (One who did would almost certainly never get a job in a 'new' university, i.e. former polytechnic. Politics apart, there are two reasons for this. The first is that those disciplines are the least well equipped to resist intellectual fads, being the least constrained by facts or hard evidence (and consequently enjoying the greatest interpretative freedom). The second is that to interpret and evaluate a fictional utterance properly is about the most difficult thing in the world. It requires not only knowledge and intelligence, but also skill, taste and flair, which are even harder to come by. Here theory avails nothing; but if one already has nothing, and is being paid to say something, one can have no other recourse than to theory, or something got up to look like it.

A Brazilian anthropologist, the late J. G. Merquior, identified a modern tendency, to which the cult of deconstruction clearly belongs. He called it Theorrhoea.[61]

Let me leave you with some further reflections, on which I have no space to elaborate. Deconstruction possessed many features of a

[61] Merquior, *From Prague to Paris*, pp. 247, 253ff.

---

theory (e.g. one that ascribed all authorship to extra-terrestrials) might have served the same turn.

Though nearly everywhere mixed up indiscriminately with Marxism, feminism, psychoanalysis and the 'hermeneutics of suspicion' generally, in France and the US deconstruction was very largely an élite phenomenon. In Britain, by contrast, its chief stronghold was the humanities departments of polytechnics (all of them 'new' universities since 1992), where it observably fed on academic and social *ressentiment*. Deconstruction is not, I think, fully understood unless it is seen, at least in one of its aspects, as part of a Gramscian 'counter-hegemonic' project, in which 'great' or canonical literature is treated as somehow reinforcing the politico-cultural status quo, and as thus to be 'deconstructed', 'read against itself', put on a level with junk culture, and so on. (And the Gramscian project is fully compatible with the 'upward mobility' already noted, since it involves the so-called 'long march through the institutions'.) At the same time, however, and with all that said, I still think the elementary point (main text, following) about the appeal of, and need for, theory simply *qua* theory is valid.

religion.[62] It had prophets and oracles (Derrida, de Man, and the rest), charismatic figures whose utterances seemed to be not wholly meaningless, yet were still tantalizingly obscure, and therefore required exposition. For this purpose a priesthood (Culler, Norris, Hawkes, Belsey[63] and others) sprang up to mediate the message to those who were ready for, or who needed, something in which to believe.

A good many of the congregation believed, not in the message as such (for its obscurity remained largely unabated), but simply in the importance of belonging to something which offered them solidarity and support. A liturgy was devised, full of riddling terms. Most were barely comprehensible, but that did not matter. For their real function was to act as a shibboleth to exclude the enemy, as a medium of phatic communion amongst friends, as a curse on infidels, and as a kind of white noise to fill the spaces between thought, indeed to suppress thought altogether if it threatened belief.

If you were to ask who profited most from this religion, I should say it was the priests. No one can doubt, however, that they, and deconstruction generally, ministered to a genuine need. But then, I suppose, so equally does another analogue of the deconstructive movement, indeed of the entire literary theory racket. I mean the pop music industry, with its stars, promoters, groupies and fans. And indeed, the likeness of contemporary French intellectual life (where the whole thing began) to show business generally has frequently been remarked.

[62] According to Roger Scruton (*Upon Nothing*, pp. 2, 28-36), its actual significance is theological. See also the same author's *Modern Philosophy: an Introduction and Survey* (London: Sinclair-Stevenson 1994), Ch. 30 ('The Devil').

[63] Terence Hawkes, *Structuralism and Semiotics* (London: Methuen 1977); Catherine Belsey, *Critical Practice* (London: Methuen 1981).

Perictione in Colophon

EDITED BY ROGER SCRUTON

The following extract comes from a recently discovered Xanthippic dialogue, which tells the story of Archeanassa's return to her native Colophon. Archeanassa travelled, it appears, as the emissary of Plato, who had instructed her to recover the manuscripts of the poet Antimachus, ostensibly for the library of the Academy, but in all probability to take revenge on the poet by burning his literary remains. (See Phryne's Symposium, 1176a, *for an account of the distressing relationship between these three people.) The dialogue exists only in fragments: some concern Archeanassa's adventures on the journey, others describe the city of Colophon, now a Persian administrative centre, its Greek culture extinguished, its temples in ruins, and its streets darkened by high-rise buildings. The inhabitants visit the town either for work, or for the girls who dance in the night-clubs. One such girl is Perictione, grand-daughter of the great Perictione, whose talent as a dancer would have been famous throughout Hellas, had not her son Plato done his utmost to conceal it. How Perictione the younger came to Colophon the dialogue does not tell, although it seems that she lived well and independently, was a leading member of the Greek community, and retained the interest in philosophy which had been awakened at Phryne's symposium.*

In her efforts to find the manuscripts of Antimachus (including an early version of the famous Lyde *which she too wished to destroy) Archeanassa is led to Perictione, with whom she discusses many topics besides their circle of Athenian friends. Very few of the conversations between the two women are complete, although some fragments on music and architecture could perhaps be edited into a readable form. In the following passage Perictione recalls an encounter with the great Xanthippe.*

Although my grandmother taught me the art of dancing, Perictione said, it was Xanthippe who explained its meaning to me. I happened to be walking with her one afternoon beneath the Acropolis, when we were overtaken by a gang of young men hurrying in a state of excitement. Stopping one of them, Xanthippe enquired into the cause of their haste, and was told that Xylophantes and his Screaming Corybants were about to perform at the Odeion.

And why is that so interesting? She asked.

287

The young man looked confused.

Why, he replied, the music is wonderful. We listen and jig about. Sometimes we throw up our arms, and there are those who scream.

And what is the point of doing that?

It's not something you *do*, the young man said, after a moment's hesitation; it's something that happens to you.

But still, there must be a point to it, she persisted.

Yes. It's therapeutic. Gets it out of your system.

Being impatient to join his companions, he cut the conversation short and hurried after them. Xanthippe pondered the young man's words for a while, and then turned to me.

Have you ever noticed, she asked, that when people wish to deny responsibility for their actions, they will describe them in medical terms?

I asked her to explain.

I mean, when asked the point of doing something, they refer to its effect on the organism. Just as this young man believes that the purpose of listening to Xylophantes is to rid his system of some poison, in the same way, you notice, people justify obscene pictures, and lewdness in the theatre. It rids us of our base desires, they say, and so makes for a healthier community. Without it, people would put into practice what otherwise they are content to see merely represented on the stage. Have you not heard this defence?

Indeed I had, and I begged Xanthippe to explain what is wrong with it.

Had our young man stayed awhile, I should have asked him what he meant, when he told us that his jigging and screaming 'gets it out of the system'. Maybe this frenzy puts it *into* the system. For have you not noticed how those who poison themselves with wine, like my poor Socrates, will always tell you that by drinking they rid themselves of something worse?

Yes, I said, and they assume the right to say things and do things which decency forbids, on the assumption that they thereby rescue us all from the threat that they might say or do these things when sober.

I see that you understand my point, she replied. It is with wine as with other drugs that we take when our bodies have no need of them. It fills the soul with emotions that seem of the greatest importance, as though our very essence were distilled in them, and yet which, once released into the air of rational discourse, vanish at once, insubstantial as dreams. And while these feelings live in us, we remain convinced that we are fulfilling a long-delayed duty to our psyche, and that our more sober companions are repressing their nature in a dangerous way.

But surely, Xanthippe, there are forces in the psyche which we barely understand, which operate, as it were, without our consent, and which we must strive to release if we are not to succumb to them.

Do you think so? she replied, and fell silent.

As you know, the philosopher had the habit of dawdling, and would sometimes come to a complete standstill, oblivious to her companions, awaking with a start after several minutes as though surprised by her surroundings. Witnessing the admiration that this conduct excited, Socrates tried to copy it, but with patchy success. I was not surprised, therefore, when Xanthippe drifted to one side of the road and, without so much as a sign that the conversation had ended, began to stare into the horse-pond by the temple of Demeter.

I came to her side, and for several minutes stood to watch two ducks, male and female, which had settled in the middle of the pond and were circling each other with bright and expectant eyes. A kind of rhythmic dance began, the female weaving in a double loop and the male imitating her, so as to remain alongside. It was a charming sight, and I became so absorbed by it as almost to forget that the greatest philosopher in Hellas, the teacher of Socrates and Aristotle, was standing dumbstruck next to me. The female duck took sudden fright, and rose in the air with a rush of wings and water, her mate in hot pursuit. Xanthippe, jolted from her stupor, seized me by the arm and resumed her speech.

Often you hear tell, do you not, of courtship among the animals. How many poets have delighted us with their descriptions of the birds, who seem to approach each other with such shame-clad interest, who dance as those two did, fleeing to another place only to dance and delay again. And this behaviour, so like that of human lovers, invites us to describe it as we should our own. These birds, we say, are driven by love and desire, they pay court to each other, dance in anticipation, and finally join in a bond of love, as though the vow of marriage awaited at the end of all their agitation. Do you not see an error in this?

A charming error, Xanthippe.

Precisely. And you know that there are two kinds of charm: the charm of enchantment, and its opposite, the charm of disenchantment, the charm which compels us to take all charm away.

I asked her to explain this paradox.

Just as a man can be delighted by the behaviour of a dog, when he sees it as he would the conduct of his human friend, so can he be delighted by the conduct of a human being, when he sees it as he would the behaviour of a dog. There, he tells himself, is the truth of our condition! And like as not he laughs. I think you know this state of mind?

Surely I do, Xanthippe.

Alone among the works of nature, she went on, the rational being is subject to illusions. Only the rational being has an interest in falsehood. His world is not given but created, and he himself draws up the plan. It is a world made in his own image, and in making it he makes himself. When we observe the natural order, we do not confront impersonal forces or a blind machine. We look into a mirror, and our own face returns our gaze. For us, the wind does not make a sound only: it howls, moans and sings to us. The sun smiles on us, and when we walk along the shore on a summer night, the sea sleeps for us beneath the moon. Truly 'all things are full of gods',[1] and all happenings are doings—though we don't know whose. We coax nature from her mute detachment with our prayers, and bring her into the human community. We dress her as a person, make her a partner in our dialogue, and endow her with will, freedom and an immortal soul. When we describe the mating of birds as though it were the courtship of man and woman, we merely continue the story, seeing all that lives and moves in human terms.

Illusions are necessary. But they are never secure. And this, my dear Perictione, is our modern destiny. We knew the world of our ancestors, and we knew how full and beautiful it was. But we saw that its beauty depended on a false idea. The cynics and sceptics expelled the poets and priests. We had given nature a face, they told us, but the face was ours and moved only with our own emotions—like the mask of the actor which lives and changes with the spectator's mood. Unmasked at last, nature is mute, impassive, governed not by will or reason but by the iron laws of physics. The gods, we have discovered, are no more lasting than the temples built to worship them, and if the world endures for us, it endures without a soul.

I could not help remarking, as Xanthippe spoke these words, that she glanced towards the temple of Demeter and saluted, as though to ask that the goddess forgive her.

But this is only one half of our predicament, she went on. The disenchanted world is one in which our projects and desires find no endorsement. All around us we encounter cold, unyielding and metallic things. Our methods of enquiry, the philosophers tell us, show the world as it really is, and it is a godless world—a world in which every change is explained by causes and in which nothing has a goal, not even those things like the mating of ducks, which seem so full of purpose. And we ourselves are part of this world,

[1] Thales.

offspring of the natural order, animals like any other, who differ from the rest of creation only in our need to tell ourselves consoling stories—including the story of creation itself.

Our efforts to live in such a world, while safeguarding all that has been most dear to us, are attended by grief of a kind which only a rational being can know. And thence arises the charm of disenchantment. Knowing that we cannot stand against the force of science, we decide instead to join it. We pull down our dear illusions, hurry impatiently onwards, to the point where nature will be stripped of her moral clothing, and stand before us as she really is—not a she but an it. In this way we take revenge on the hopes which disappointed us.

And then we invent for ourselves another story, the story to end all stories. The old illusions, we tell ourselves, were the enemies of happiness. It was they which set us against our fellow men, which bound us in chains, and which cheated us of love, life and freedom. We have nothing to fear from science; on the contrary, only when the cloud of illusion has been dispelled, will we know what it is to be free. And we begin to hunt the world for illusions, in order to expose the imposture by which the mind of man was governed. Every attempt to clothe the world in will and personality is derided, and bit by bit the face is scratched from the world's cold surface, until nothing of our image remains.

Nor does the process end when the gods have been driven from their sanctuaries and dispelled into air. For amid the ruined temples unhappy faces linger, uncertain of their destiny, forsaken and forsworn. These, we persuade ourselves, are the victims, who suffer, not from the loss of their convictions, but from the fact of having once possessed them. Better to be born with no illusions, than to see our world destroyed.

Naturally, I answered the great philosopher, this state of mind is familiar to me, for I was brought up in the midst of it. No other joy has been offered to my generation, than the joy of pulling things down. Nevertheless, the charm of disenchantment seems but a thin reward. The cynics tell us to distrust the old illusions as the enemies of freedom. But they also tell us that greatest among our illusions, is that of freedom itself. In which case we shall emerge from our illusions, only to know the full extent of our bondage. We will know ourselves as parts of the great machine, our life no more significant than the life of the animals, and blameless as theirs. Indeed, this is now happening, and even explains the feelings of that young man, as he joined in the stampede to hear the songs of Xylophantes. For such young people there are no gods, but only human idols.

Xanthippe stood for a while in thought.

But are these idols not illusions too?

I think not, I replied, and I shall tell you why, O most revered Xanthippe. When Xylophantes gets up on stage it is for two purposes—first to sing a tuneless song, the words of which are full of a cynical distaste. The second is to shake and writhe and squawk—to become animal, or lower still than animal, a part of the machine. And in this way his followers, led by the charm of disenchantment, find their idol converted, in the very act of worship, into something spiritless and strange. Here before them is the very truth of their condition—the world as it is in itself, free from all enchantment, free even from freedom itself. And in worshipping this thing, the followers of Xylophantes throw in their lot with emptiness, acknowledge that nothing matters, since mattering is a mere illusion, and glory in the nothingness of human hopes.

Well, said Xanthippe, this is grim indeed. But you do not imply, I hope, that you share the feelings which you describe? Or am I to infer that no-one in your generation can escape them?

I found it hard to answer her. For you know that Granny had given me the most elevated education, compelling me to read the classics, teaching me the old dances, bringing me up in the old religion, even initiating me into the mysteries. Not a day would pass without a speech from her on the Homeric virtues, on the sacred liturgies, on the noble characters of tragedy, on the imperatives of taste and the fine points of style in art and music. I was to carry the light of civilization into the cave of the future—so she envisaged it, and all her instruction was devoted to this end. At the same time, however, I sensed that she inwardly withdrew from the things that she taught me, that her elenctic irony, as she called it, was a veil for inner doubts, and that her very sophistication had lifted her above the facts it fed on, so that her spirit floated free of them and judged them from afar. She was the highest point that our civilization could reach, the point of supreme self-consciousness. And consciousness breeds doubt. Such self-knowledge could endure thereafter only for a generation, in the works of Uncle Plato and the rest of Phryne's circle. But to my generation it was already something theatrical—a set of costumes which lifted you for a moment onto the stage, but which were ridiculous if worn by the audience.

Of course, Perictione went on, Granny deeply influenced me. Thanks to her, I looked on Athens, in those days when still I thought of living there, with an ironical detachment. I saw the emptiness and vulgarity of popular art and music, the steady loss of knowledge, the decline in piety and virtue, the irreparable disorder that was spreading through the roots of society. I took pride in the good taste which led me to understand and scorn these things, and to set before myself those high examples which Granny had taught me to admire. At the same time I could not quite believe in the old gods. I knew the liturgies by heart, but to me they were more poetry than religion, and when I performed the act of worship, it was as a dancer—representing myself, but not being myself. And secretly I was tempted by that other and lower world which Granny had taught me to despise. I sought out young people for whom Aeschylus and Stesichorus meant nothing, who sneered at the gods and heroes while having only the vaguest acquaintance with their names, and whose idols were the likes of Xylophantes. I learned some of their songs, in Phrygian mode, and—while inwardly scoffing at their clumsy words and melodies—would sing along with the crowd of my cronies, sometimes wiggling obscenely as they did, and feeling my body within its crust of high culture like a moth striving to break from its chrysallis into light and air.

Not that I had the remotest desire to live in that lower world. Far from it; my ambition was to be a lyric poet, and a dancer in the high tradition to which Granny belonged. Still, I was young, and needed to share what others of my age were feeling. Hence I had come to experience this 'charm of disenchantment' from inside. And I held the feeling as it were suspended within me, turning it over and over in the withering light of consciousness, knowing that it belonged to the lowest part of me and was, in truth, a rank betrayal of my inheritance.

Because of this, my only reply was to shrug my shoulders, as though to shake off Xanthippe's question. She suggested that we sit for a while, since her bones were weary, and finding a hospitable table by the sanctuary of Delphic Apollo, I called out for fruit and water to refresh us. After we had eaten, and gossipped about matters of no philosophical importance, Xanthippe returned to her theme.

Tell me, she inquired, do they really dance to the music of Xylophantes—if music it is?

Well, as the young man said, they sway and jig about.

Would you call it dancing? She asked.

What's in a word?

Nothing, she answered, short of everything. Words rightly used and to good effect show the truth of things. And here I see an answer to our great dilemma.

What great dilemma?

Well, we did not express it quite so drastically. But our problem, you recall, was this. If we follow the philosophers, and look for the truth of things, then one by one the gods and heroes vanish, religion, morality, beauty and freedom follow them in disarray,

293

and nothing remains save the meaningless machinery of nature. If, on the other hand, we follow the priests and the poets, and try to live in an enchanted world, we are haunted by the knowledge that this world is our creation. What can be made can also be unmade, and bears no authority greater than our own desire. Moreover, whatever I make is a lesser being than I. Hence the gods lose their power over me. I cease to stand in awe of them and piety, far from being restored to us, receives a mortal blow. The dilemma is that we seem to have no path before us save these two, and the end of each is disillusion.

So what is your answer?

Let us take one of those retreating steps which your grandmother delighted in. I asked you whether you would describe those movements, prompted by the noise of Xylophantes, as dancing.

Yes. And I still wonder why we should avoid the word.

You remember the ducks on the horse-pond? Well, were they dancing?

Their movements were like a dance, certainly.

But not really a dance.

I agree with you, Xanthippe, but for the life of me I cannot say why.

Then you have forgotten your grandmother's lessons. Few things were more important to her, as I recall, than rules—the rules of etiquette and morality, as well as those of harmony and style. And dancing is governed by rules.

The ducks too appeared to follow a rule, as they swam in loops together.

Appeared to follow a rule, yes. But we must distinguish rule from regularity. The heart which beats in steady rhythm obeys no rule in doing so. Rules exist only where there is the possibility of disobedience, and only where we can distinguish the right way from the wrong way to proceed.

Perhaps, then, it is only rational beings who can obey a rule.

And are ducks rational?

I suppose not, I said, though for the life of me I could not prove the point.

Let's delay the proof, for we do not need it. Imagine Calliope, a nervous woman who claps her hands involuntarily whenever she enters a room. And imagine Pasariste, a bold egoist who has formed the policy of entering any room with a clap of the hands, as though to announce herself. To outward appearances these women behave in the same way, do they not?

I suppose so.

Yet they are doing different things. Their movements are identical, but their actions distinct. Calliope's clap is a habit, Pasariste's a policy. The first is a regularity, the second a rule.

So far I accept your argument, I said.

Could we make such a distinction in the case of a duck? Could we distinguish a duck which regularly quacked on taking flight, from a duck which quacked as a matter of policy?

What conceivable grounds could there be, for making such a distinction?

I think we could generalize the point, could we not? Animals are creatures of habit, as we are. But their habits are not chosen. When a bird meets a female and struts before her, we do not think of this as a custom—as though the bird had learned these manners and now took pleasure in displaying them. Such movements come into being as the heart-beat comes into being: they belong to the repertoire of instinct. If they look like a dance, it is only in the way that regularities sometimes look like rules. But where we cannot distinguish rule from regularity, we cannot speak of rule.

And therefore, I put in, we cannot speak of dancing.

I assume not, she said.

But perhaps there are dances that have no rules.

No rules, she added, save this one: that there should be no rules.

Which permits me to say, I replied, that the followers of Xylophantes are, in their own way, dancing.

Let me make another distinction, she said, ignoring me. Many of our actions have a purpose, have they not?

Indeed they have.

For instance, my purpose on going out today was to set up shop by the tomb of old Socks and sell my tapestries. And this I should now be doing, had I not fallen in with my friend Perictione and, for the sake of philosophy, cancelled my resolve.

You are too kind, I said.

But do all our actions have a purpose?

Surely they do—for purpose is the mark of a rational being, who does nothing without a reason, and is answerable before god and man for all that she does.

To act without purpose, Xanthippe said, is not to act without reason. Consider this conversation: does it have a purpose?

No single purpose, I conceded.

Surely, she insisted, no purpose at all. Else why should we find it so agreeable?

But do we not aim at the truth?

Speak for yourself, she said. Even if truth is my long-term hope, it is not my aim in speaking now. So far as I can see, I am enjoying myself. And it is the conversation that I enjoy, wherever it may lead, and even if it turns in some quite frivolous direction, or takes the form of my chats with your grandmother, in which only irony and paradox were welcome.

Are you saying that conversation is purposeless? I asked.

Not purposeless, but not purposeful either. Or rather say that it is purposeful without purpose. And the same is true of much that we most esteem.

I seemed to recall this idea from another context. Maybe it was one of Granny's sayings, though she had so many, since, for her at any rate, conversation did have a purpose, which was to lift the mask of common sense—not in order to expose the bare reality, but so as to replace the mask with a more amusing one of her own. But I digress.

And since we are in a mood for distinctions, Xanthippe went on, let me make another: that between purpose and function. When we enquire into the nature of dancing, we ought surely to consider the broader category to which it belongs—the category of play. It is obvious, is it not, that play has a function: it is the safest way to explore the world, and to prepare the child for action. But this function is not the purpose. The child plays because he wants to play: play is its own purpose. Indeed, if you make the function into a purpose—playing for the sake of learning, say—then you cease to play. You are now merely in earnest, as some barbarian philosopher once expressed it.

Let me take another example. Friendship has a function: it binds people together, making communities strong and durable; it brings advantages to those who are joined by it, and fortifies them in all their endeavours. But make those advantages into your purpose, and the friendship vanishes—for the motive of friendship has been undermined. Friendship is a means to advantage, but only when not treated as a means. The same is true of everything worthwhile—education, for instance, sport, hunting, oh yes, and dancing. You might say that all time that is not spent in such pursuits is wasted time. I think it was Xenophon who said as much, in his book on hunting.[2]

But surely people often dance for a purpose, I protested. For example, they dance at the festivals so as to honour the gods. I have heard of people who dance in order to summon the rain, and when I dance it is with a view to shaming those who imagine they could dance as well as a grand-daughter of the great Perictione.

[2] Xenophon, *Kunergetika*. Although Xenophon implies this, he never explicitly says it. A much later, post-Xanthippic, philosopher tells us that 'all time wot is not spent in 'unting is wasted time' (Jorrocks, as reported by R. S. Surtees in *Handley Cross*).

Xanthippe thought for a while, and then answered:

Consider the game of draughts. This too may be played 'for a purpose'. There are those who play draughts with their neighbours, for the purpose of friendship. There are those who play in order to relax, or to demonstrate their skills. But all these purposes must be set aside, the moment we begin to play. The player has one purpose only—which is to play as best he can, and according to the rules. If his purpose were to make friends, who knows whether this might not be more effectively achieved by disobeying the rules, by fooling about, by deliberately losing or by exchanging draughts for some other game? When playing we are purposeful: but there is no purpose which animates our actions, beyond the aim of playing draughts.

And you say the same of dancing?

Not exactly. For I admit that dancing is complex, and I am describing only a part of it—although a central part, I think, and the one which explains the high esteem in which this art is held.

And do you distinguish the purpose of dancing—which for you is dancing itself—from its function?

I do, she replied. But I should say that dancing has many functions. It teaches us to make graceful gestures, to move in a pleasing way. Through dancing we learn charm and cheerfulness, and come to know the life within us and its inexhaustible flowing. None of these are *why* we dance: think of these things while dancing and you will quickly tie yourself in knots. But there is also a deeper function to dancing, and one of which we Athenians know less, I think, than our Aeolian cousins.[3]

You mean the erotic? I said, recalling the experience with Parmenides which Granny was so fond of relating.[4]

If you insist. But the erotic is only part of it; and let us be under no illusions—the erotic exists in many forms and is shaped by its expression. And this too is a function of the dance—not to release our erotic feelings, but to give them discipline and form. Rather than describe this function as erotic, I should prefer the word 'conjugal'. For it captures the strange phenomenon I have in mind.

And what is that?

Let us return to the ducks. What tempted us to describe them as

[3] Xanthippe may be referring to the choirs of young girls, for whom Saphho wrote many songs, and which formed little domestic clubs suffused by a quasi-erotic tenderness. See Claude Calame, *Les Choeurs de jeunes filles en Grèce archaïque*, two vols. (Rome, 1977).

[4] The experience is recounted by the elder Perictione in *Perictione's Parmenides*, contained in *Xanthippic Dialogues*, ed. Roger Scruton (London, 1993).

dancing was not the rhythm of their movements so much as their moving together in time: they were fitting their motion to a common pattern. Now it seems to me that there are two forms of dancing. There is that of which you are so skilled a practitioner, which you can dance alone as much as in company, and which is in some way addressed to the spectator. And this I should number among the theatrical arts, since it is not so much an action performed as an action represented. In this kind of dancing you become a mask, and that is why your grandmother was so good at it. But there is also the dancing which is available to the rest of us, and this kind of dancing is a human action, performed in company, and addressed to the others with whom we dance.

And here is the deep reason, as it seems to me, why animals cannot dance. For consider what it means when we 'dance with' another—how much is captured in the little word 'with'! It is as though the music became an intermediary between you and me, giving to my feet not only a cause of movement, but a just reason, a reason that lies in you. The 'why' of my step lies in that step of yours, and over my feet and yours there lies the charm of music, so that we move not only with each other, but with that purely spiritual thing, the music, whose motion is not of the body at all. Thus rightly does Pindar say 'the footstep hears, as the dance begins'.[5] The footstep of a person who dances is no longer the step of an animal—for no animal is so completely without purpose as this, and at the same time so fully guided by reason.

And yet, I put in, is this not the music's doing?

Music, she replied, lives in the one who listens. Music is not sound, any more than sculpture is bronze. It is the living order that we hear in sound, when we hear it as music. To hear this order is to move with the music, which becomes a voice for us, the voice of the other with whom we dance.

I sensed in Xanthippe's words so vast a weight of theory, that I refrained from asking her to explain them, lest we should lose the thread of our conversation. So I gently reminded her that she had promised to describe the deeper function of the dance.

Yes, she said, I was coming to that. For it is this little word 'with' that leads us to our goal. It is a word upon which I have often meditated, since it describes my own condition. I am with old Socks, and have been with him, moving with him, talking with him, singing with him, in all the long years since he died. 'Being with' is a state of the soul, a direction outwards to the other. Even if the other is dead or unborn, even if he is merely imaginary, the 'withness', if I may invent a word, remains, and gives form and

[5] *Pythian Odes*, no. 1.

direction to our feelings. If you ask me what we really learn from dance, then withness would be my reply. Indeed, were it not for dancing I fear that we should never learn this precious thing. I even sense in this an explanation of our modern sadness.

Not caring for explanations of our 'modern sadness', I asked Xanthippe to be a little more precise about this withness business. You do not solve a philosophical problem, I said, merely by inventing a word—a word, moreover, that is gramatically impossible. It is as though a philosopher were to answer the problem of contingent existence by saying that things have 'thrown-ness'. Not, I hastened to add, that a civilized thinker could be quite so self-indulgent.

You are right, Perictione, and I owe you an explanation of this peculiar word which, however much I push it from my consciousness, obstinately returns to pester me. Suppose, then, that the city fathers were to announce a public holiday, and declare that wine would be distributed free of charge in the Prytaneum. And suppose that Clerophon, or some other thug, in his impatience to receive yet another dose of public charity, runs to the place, not stopping to talk to those who address him, pushing aside those who obstruct him, thrusting to the front of the queue, and seizing the largest share on offer. Such a man is not *with* the others whom he meets, but decidedly against them, as I am sure you will concede. And something similar should be said of anyone whose purposes are so urgent that others do not count for him. Nowhere is this lack of withness more troubling than in love and desire. For are we not repelled by the one who makes his purpose too plain, who cannot hesitate, who brushes aside our protests and regards decency, shame and courtship as a waste of time?

We are indeed, I replied, and my sigh made clear to her that, in this matter at least, I needed no instruction.

More, she added: do we not require of a lover that he hesitate even to acknowledge love as his purpose, that he approach us as though all purposes were still to be acquired?

I nodded.

And is this not the meaning of courtship, she went on, that it is not so much a postponement of a purpose, as a period in which purpose is set aside, so that man and woman can be truly free in each other's presence? That is how it seems to me, at least. And anything else, to my way of thinking, is shameful. The period of courtship is like an extended dance—lasting for months or even years—as the partners move with each other, sometimes conversing, sometimes in silence, purposeful but without purpose, and all the while shaping their desires through the idea of union. This is not a preparation for

299

love, but a creation of love. For love is the child of hesitation, and courtship the godparent who bestows its name.

The withness of courtship survives and grows through marriage, lives on beyond death, and changes the very features of those who are schooled in it. So now let us define this thing more generally. Withness is the state of being which leads us to hesitate before others, to jettison our purposes, to rest for a while in conversation, courtesy or ceremonial gestures. It is something more than respect, something more than obedience to the moral law, something more than good manners or good will. And it extends to all who have an interest in our being—to the dead and the unborn as much as the living. And that is why we should value dancing—and no dancing more than that which permits us to dance with strangers, to change partners as we move in formation, and to step with those whom we shall never love or desire.

I fear you are describing a vanished world, Xanthippe. If that is what you mean by dancing, then young people of my generation have ceased to dance, and would pour scorn on those who offered to teach them.

True enough, said the philosopher. Hence we must bear witness to this thing which will shortly disappear. Dreadful would the future be, were the stories no longer told of what it might have been, had the gods looked on us more kindly.

After giving voice to this strange remark, Xanthippe sat for a while humming a tune beneath her breath. The day was drawing to a close, and I had nothing much to do until later in the evening, when Xylophantes would have left the stage, the crowd of his admirers would be released onto the streets, and a particular young man, who I am ashamed to say was always one of their number, would be waiting for me in the precinct of Aphrodite Pandemos. I suggested to Xanthippe that we order wine from the nearby tavern, and when I produced the necessary obols and explained how well provisioned I had been since Granny's journey across the Styx, she readily assented to the idea. I suggested we pour a libation to Granny, and she, concurring, insisted that we drink to Socrates too.

A few bowls later, when the shadows lay like drunken guests across the table, the philosopher started tapping her fingers on her thigh. To my enquiry she replied that all her life there was a matter she had failed to understand, and which words seemed unable to encompass.

And what is that? I asked.

I mean rhythm, she said, on which melody hangs like the fruit on a bough.

She swallowed from her bowl, lent back on her stool, and uttered a loud laugh.

I am reminded, she said, of my last dance with old Socks. It was the evening before his trial; we had just read the indictment and were in fits of laughter at the pompous language of this Meletus, 'good man and patriot' as he called himself, trying to put into legal language the accusation that I myself had made against old Socks and which all of Athens knew already—that he was a corrupter of the youth. We had no idea that such a charge could hold up in court, or that Socks would be condemned and executed. It all seemed too wondrously absurd and such anxieties as we felt we happily drowned in wine. I had prepared a few speeches, in case he needed them, and they did, in the event, turn out rather handy. It was great fun to rehearse them in the kitchen, myself trying to keep a straight face in the role of Meletus, and Socks standing on the table, booming on about the honour of the city and how he will not stoop to defend himself as craven cowards do, dragging his wife and children into the court-room to beg in tears for their protector's life.

And then, after a bowl or two, he started to sing, a number by Stesichorus with a catchy iambic rhythm, and invited me to join him on the kitchen table. Now, despite his clumsy build and somewhat pudgy legs, old Socks was an agile dancer, and could stay on his toes for hours at a time, dancing to his own song, clapping his hands above his head and often releasing whoops of joy as he turned and leapt in time to the music. And such a prodigy of energy was he, that he could interrupt his singing with dialogue and still maintain the rhythm in his feet, which seemed to dance to a soundless music of their own. And it is those bare feet of Socrates that I recall, dancing among crumbs and peelings on our kitchen table, when I wish to remind myself of joy. For those feet had been lifted from their animal nature. They were no longer flesh and bone, no longer a mere adjunct to the mind that governed them, an instrument of motion. They were Socrates himself, and moved in dialogue with my feet, for all the world as though our words and smiles were theirs. And as I watched them—rough, horny and encrusted with dirt—I had a vision of something that I can only describe as immortality. In some way those feet, having lifted themselves and all their earthy essence into the realm of spirit, broke free of earth entirely and danced on forever, leaving infinite footprints, so to speak, in some other dimension of being.

Now I don't say that there is any literal truth in that. But the metaphor forced itself upon me. No other words could quite capture my experience on that happy evening. And it was Socks himself who explained the matter.

You see, Xanthippe, he said between snatches of song, puffing a little and his face aglow, we do not live only here and now. Eternal shadows are cast by our movements, and eternal echoes follow our words.

And yet, I replied, it is very much here and now that we are dancing.

Socks whooped and spun round in a most fetching way.

That is exactly what I mean. For what animal lives in the present?

Do not all animals live in the present? Indeed, should we not say that, lacking reason, they have no vision of anything except the present?

Precisely, he replied; they are so full of the present that they have no concept of it. Here and now make sense only by contrast with then and there. Unlike the animals, we experience the present as the tip of hidden time, and for us the present is 'always'. It contains the meaning of those hidden times—not past times only, but possible times, times that might have been. What has been and what might have been point to one end, you might say, which is always present.

And here he resumed his song, changing to anapests so that at first I had difficulty in keeping time. But again those feet of his, which smiled and sang across to mine, led me into their orbit and we danced in harmony. Watching him, I began to understand what Socks had said. Only sometimes, and only in certain frames of mind, do we live in the present moment. This happens by an act of will, which is also a renunciation of purpose. The here and the now come before us only when the veil of purpose has been drawn aside, and we confront the present moment, a lone wave on the sea of possibilities. The moment then resounds in us, and this resounding is what we mean by eternity.

I was inclined, therefore, to agree with my husband, that animals know nothing of this, that just as it is only a rational being who can visit the past or dream of possibilities, so is it only a rational being who can live in the present. And I saw that this existence in the present moment is not an ordinary or easy thing, but a rare achievement. Just as I thought I had worked out for myself what kind of achievement it is, old Socks again interrupted my thoughts with a whoop and a clapping of hands, and began to punctuate his song with dialogue.

So you see, my dear Xanthippe, that we should study how to enter the present, which is not, as the vulgar think, a house of ill-fame whose door stands ever open, but the holiest of temples, into the precinct of which only the initiated can find their way. And here is the strangest part—do please attend to my feet, your cross-rhythms are distracting me—yes, the strangest part: that we encounter the here and now only when our purposes are cancelled.

I told him I had already figured this out.

Of course you had, by the dog. But do you see what light this casts on human conduct?

I confessed that I had not thought this far. After a few more bars of his song, and having danced off the table to swallow a bowl of wine and danced back again, Socks continued his breathless instructions.

A man driven by a purpose, he said, eats up time. Each moment is thrown like a sacrificial offering into the machinery of his desire, and expires without a trace. There are those who say that life has a meaning only for the man with a purpose. I say rather the opposite, that meaning comes to us when purpose is set aside. But not any renunciation of purpose will produce this effect: for purpose is rightly overcome only in company and only through the encounter with another soul, in conversation, music or some other thing that approximates to dance.

But do we not set our purpose aside when we contemplate a picture or a sculpture or when we read a work of poetry? And are such arts not also passages to meaning?

All art, he shouted, has its origin in dance. Those who read or sing or watch alone are not really alone: another soul speaks to them through the words, the forms or the music. They are like the solitary dancer, who dances not alone, but with himself. All dancing, as I remember you saying the other day, is dancing with ...

With that he reapplied himself to the dance so vigorously that I stumbled from the table and fell in a heap against the wall. For half an hour more he danced and sang, until his feet were glowing through their veil of dirt, and his tunic was soaked in sweat. And I smiled as I watched him, my soul dancing along with him, and a calm joy filling my senses.

Xanthippe sighed, and turned to me with a smile.

So there, my dear Perictione, she said, we have a kind of answer to our dilemma, and I can only wonder at my stupidity for not having thought of it before.

I confessed that I did not follow her.

Our dilemma was this: either we embrace the way of disenchantment which the cynics recommended, in which case we believe ourselves to be no better than parts of the great machine. Or else we succumb once again to enchantment, but in full knowledge that the gods and nymphs are our own invention, with no more power than a dream. But do you not see in this a grave simplification?

Many, I said, for it is true that words always seem simpler to me that the things they describe.

I mean, said Xanthippe, our dilemma leaves out the most important fact, which is that human beings create themselves, and they do so, not alone, but through dialogue and dancing. And although that which I create is of necessity a lesser being than I, that which I create in company with others may be greater—perhaps indefinitely greater. And here, in dancing, we have the proof.

When two people dance together they are doing something which is its own motive: dance and dancer are one, and the reason for placing your foot just here, your hand just there, is given only in and through the dance. There is no purpose governing these movements, nothing that enables us to say that this or this is the most efficient way to the goal. Each movement is a response to another, which is its sole and sufficient reason. What I do, when I dance, I do only because this purposeless practice exists. But it is a practice that transforms the world. It releases me from the tyranny of purpose and allows me to enter the present moment and to be wholly at one with it—so much at one that I can hear in these footfalls the echo that spreads before and behind through infinite time.

Now it is true that when people cease to dance something goes from the world, something man-made, yet irreplaceable. But we should no more question the reality or power of this thing than we should question the reality and power of a temple, just because it was built by human hands. In bringing this purposeless thing into being we propagate neither myths nor stories; we tell no lies about the gods, and invent no concepts beyond the one which describes this very action—the concept of dance. Yet we also change the world and give it meaning.

Return for a moment to our ducks. Ask yourself now why they were, and why they were not, dancing. They were dancing because their behaviour so closely resembled ours when we dance. But they were not dancing, because they were not acting with the *reason* that inspires the dancer. Only those creatures dance who possess the concept of dancing. Only they can lift themselves free from the world of purpose, to converse with another in a dialogue of movement.

So far as that goes, I remarked, the followers of Xylophantes might as well be dancing. For they too have the concept, and they too respond to the rhythm that they hear, and which comes to them from the lyres and tambours of the screaming Corybants.

But there you have it, she said. The rhythm comes to them from elsewhere, but is not *theirs*. Why else should Xylophantes require so much noise, such a crude and emphatic beat, which compels even the stones of the theatre to vibrate in time? Often, when Socks danced after dinner, there was no sound save the squeak of his leathery feet on the table and the occasional stanza of a song. Yet rhythm was in those feet, and magnetized the air surrounding them. Say, if you like, that the followers of Xylophantes dance; but be aware of all that is missing here from the old way of dancing. Be aware that to move in time to a beat is not yet to dance with another, nor even to dance with oneself. Indeed, I suspect that if we were to inquire into the matter, we should find ourselves obliged to make a distinction between rhythm and beat, and to question much that now passes for music.

Although I am in deep water here, and find myself at a loss to say what rhythm is, or why rational beings alone respond to it, I will venture nevertheless a criticism of Xylophantes and his followers. For between them they have devised a substitute for dance which more thoroughly destroys the art than any legal prohibition. Let us take a parallel example. Just as animals are unable to dance, so are they unable to fall in love, to plight their troth, or to do any other of the things which humans do, on the long troubled journey from virginity to marriage. But we could imagine Diogenes, or some other cynic, saying: take away the myths, look with a dispassionate eye on our acts and feelings, strip everything bare of the vain ornaments with which we disguise it, and we find that humans are prompted by the very same force as compels the animals. Deep down we are the same as them: in essence love and courtship are but sex.

But this again, I said, is the charm of disenchantment.

Indeed it is, she replied; but the charm is a deception. For when a philosopher say that the deep-down source of love is sex, and sex a thing that we share with the animals; and when he adds in the peculiar tone of voice which the expression demands, that therefore sex is the *essence* of love, and all those 'higher' things like courtship mere accretions: not only does he confuse the nature of a thing with its explanation; he puts before us an entirely false idea of essence. He has fallen victim to the greatest of modern illusions, a myth, as Socks used to describe it, of the half-educated. He has imagined that the essence of a thing is the part which is hidden from us, the part which we discover only by delving deep beneath the surface until a chance similarity with some other and simpler thing so vividly strikes us, that we believe we have at last struck truth. Love and desire are reduced to unconscious forces, which work in us we know not how, and we ourselves are conceived as passive victims in those very enterprises into which we put all our highest motives and desires.

Now you are speaking like Granny, I said, and such a vivid image came before me of my relative, that I laughed aloud, and sipped from my bowl with the same flourish of high-born contempt that she affected.

Yes, Xanthippe concurred, I am indeed speaking like my dear dead friend. For did she not famously say, that it is only a shallow person who does not judge by appearances? And here, I believe, is what she meant. We imagine that we discover the essence of things only by tearing down what we have contributed—showing the world as it might have been, had we done nothing to alter it. Human labour, the cynics say, builds paper castles in the world of seeming; the world of being remains always remote from us and unchanged. But there is a hole in their argument. For that which we create is created for our uses, for our senses, and for our thoughts. Such a thing can *only* be appearance: not *mere* appearance, but appearance in its final flowering, when essence and appearance are one. You no more reach the essence of the human world by delving beneath appearances, than you reach the essence of a picture by scraping away the paint.

And when the cynic tells us that love is nothing but sex, and sex nothing but the clamorous instinct that we share with the animals, he does not describe reality. He alters it. To the extent that we believe him, we set about to transform the human world, to build in the garden of courtship a realm of lust. This realm is not less real than the one it destroys; but it is not more real either. It is built to another and uglier design, and we live in it as they live in the Babylonian towers of Persia, estranged and uncomforted, preying on each other, and deprived of the precious gift of withness.

But why should we wish to do so terrible a thing? I asked.

There lies the appeal of the cynical philosophy, she answered. It is the philosophy of those who have lost the art of setting their purposes aside, who are hurrying onwards like leaves on the wind of desire, and who recognize no hesitations. The charm of disenchantment lies in the infinite permission that it bestows. Desire erupts unhindered into the disenchanted mind, fills every corner with its liquid urgency, and presses on to its satisfaction, unimpeded by courtesy or shame. The cynical philosophy is one with the new style of dancing—if dancing it must be called. Xylophantes shows his followers the way of purpose: there is, in their movements, neither withness nor shame. The noise from the stage endorses their desires, and holds desire aloft as sovereign. The new kind of dancing is therefore no longer a dancing with—not even with oneself. It is lonely, with the loneliness of a purpose that will not suffer its own extinction.

And now you see why the cynical philosophy is so widely believed—not because it is true, but because it so perfectly describes the world of the human being who is now striving to create himself. By believing it, we help to realize that world, just as, by moving to the sound of Xylophantes, we destroy the old world which wars against it.

But is there any hope for that old world? I asked her.

Oh, she replied with a yawn; there is always hope, provided we do not make the supreme mistake.

And what is that?

The mistake of hoping for the impossible.

So what is possible? I asked. And truly I wished to discover. For what rational being, who knows what it is to be with her fellows, to set her purposes aside, and to enter the eternity of a present moment, could live with the belief that never again will this experience be hers or anyone's? Alas, Xanthippe, who had finished the amphora, lay slumped across the table, in a sleep from which I tried in vain to wake her. Shaking the last drops into the dust, and with a hasty prayer to the muses, I hurried off to my date.

Index of Names

Index of Names